LECTURES ON MICROECONOMICS

LECTURES ON MICROECONOMICS

THE BIG QUESTIONS APPROACH

ROMANS PANCS

THE MIT PRESS

CAMBRIDGE, MASSACHUSETTS

LONDON, ENGLAND

This book was set in Melior by Westchester Publishing Services.

Library of Congress Cataloging-in-Publication Data

Names: Pancs, Romans, author.
Title: Lectures on microeconomics : the big questions approach/Romans Pancs.
Description: Cambridge, MA : MIT Press, [2018] | Includes bibliographical references and index.
Identifiers: LCCN 2017051235 | ISBN 9780262038188 (hardcover : alk. paper)
ISBN 9780262552899 (paperback)
Subjects: LCSH: Microeconomics—Examinations, questions, etc.
Classification: LCC HB172 .P215 2018 | DDC 338.5—dc23 LC record available at
    https://lccn.loc.gov/2017051235

CONTENTS

NOTATION

MATHEMATICAL NOTATION

$\lim_{x \downarrow a} f(a)$ the ("right") limit of function f as x decreases as it approaches a.

$\lim_{x \to a} f(x)$ the limit of function f as x approaches a.

$\lim_{x \uparrow a} f(a)$ the ("left") limit of function f as x increases as it approaches a.

$\mathbf{1}_{\{a \in A\}}$ an indicator function, whose value is 1 if $a \in A$ and is 0 otherwise.

$|A|$ the number of elements in the set A.

$\mathbb{R}$ the set of real numbers.

$\mathbb{R}^n$ the n-dimensional Euclidean space.

$\mathbb{R}_{++}$ the set of positive real numbers.

$\mathbb{R}_+$ the set of nonnegative real numbers.

$\varnothing$ an empty set.

$a \cdot b$ the dot product $\sum_{i=1}^{n} a_i b_i$.

$a > b$ if a and b are scalars, then a exceeds b; if a and b are vectors, then $a_i \geq b_i$ for all i, and $a_i > b_i$ for some i.

$a \geq b$ for all i, $a_i \geq b_i$.

$a \gg b$ for all i, $a_i > b_i$.

$A \subset B$ A is a subset of B, meaning that every element in A is also in B.

$A \supset B$ A is a superset of B, meaning that every element in B is also in A.

$A \times B$ the Cartesian product of sets A and B.

a_{-i} vector a without its ith component; $a_{-i} = (a_1, a_2, \dots, a_{i-1}, a_{i+1}, \dots, a_n)$.

f' the derivative of a function f of a single variable (i.e., $f'(x) \equiv df(x)/dx$).

f_{ij} the cross derivative of a function f with respect to its ith and j^{th} arguments (i.e., $f_{ij}(x) \equiv \partial^2 f(x)/(\partial x_i \partial x_j)$).

f_i the partial derivative of a function f with respect to its ith argument (i.e., $f_i(x) \equiv \partial f(x)/\partial x_i$).

ECONOMICS NOTATION

$\bar{e}$ the vector of aggregate endowments of all goods.

e_l the aggregate endowment of good l.

$\succ^i$ agent i's strict binary preference relation.

$\rhd$ a strict binary power relation.

e_l^i agent i's endowment of good l.

u^i agent i's utility function.

x an allocation or an effort profile.

x^i agent i's consumption bundle or his effort.

x_l^i agent i's consumption of good l.

$\mathcal{I}$ the set of agents, with cardinality I and a typical element i.

$\mathcal{L}$ the set of goods, with cardinality L and a typical element l.

ABBREVIATIONS

c.d.f.   cumulative density function.

DA   deferred acceptance (aka Gale-Shapley) algorithm.

FWT   the First Welfare Theorem.

p.d.f.   probability density function.

RSD   random serial dictatorship algorithm.

SD   serial dictatorship algorithm.

SWT   the Second Welfare Theorem.

TTC   top trading cycles algorithm.

SPECIAL SYMBOL

Full appreciation of a problem marked by this symbol requires creative use of software (such as Wolfram's *Mathematica*) to visualise the results.

Preface

The Big Idea

You are fortunate to be holding this book—or any book. You are alive. What are the chances? If the world were poorer or less populous today, you might not have been born. Or, if born elsewhere or in an earlier epoch, you might have been already dead by violence, disease, or starvation. But here you are, in this relatively prosperous time and place. Something must have gone right! But what? This book is about the few basic principles that enable individuals to do better collectively than they would have done individually. These principles fall under the rubric of economics.

You may object that you do not feel lucky or that the misery of your fellow travelers could have been alleviated if the society had been organized more cleverly. This book is about that, too. Each glimpse of understanding that you gain, you will be encouraged to channel toward a quest for a better design of policy or institutions, at home, at work, and beyond.

The book's content and organization are based on the premise that one masters economic concepts and techniques best by attempting to tackle the fundamental economic and philosophical questions that one cares about most. To this end, the book's material is organized around the big, substantive questions:

- When do markets help translate individuals' uncoordinated, selfish actions into outcomes that are best for all? (Adam Smith posed this question and, in response, conjured up the "invisible hand," which we will formalize.)

- Do markets change people and, if so, for worse or for better? That is, are markets moral?

- How should exchange be organized when markets fail or are impractical to set up?

- What lessons does the dog-eat-dog environment of the jungle hold for the modern society?

- Translated into the language of modern economics, do Karl Marx's ideas have merit?

- Why is there so much income inequality? Or is there too little?

- Will the proliferation of superhuman robots immiserate humans?

- What might a socialist society look like? Are we there yet?

- Can Immanuel Kant's categorical imperative (aka the Golden Rule) possibly work when everyone has his own idiosyncratic idea for how he would like to be treated?

- How can the society that demands fast highways, new markets, and easy ways to communicate become worse off if you give it some of what it demands?

- Is there a logical impossibility inherent in the United States Declaration of Independence when it calls for liberty and the pursuit of happiness?

This book offers answers. I hope you find yourself occasionally disagreeing with these answers. The book's goal is not to persuade but to show how to reason toward one's own conclusions. In fact, I hope you disagree even with the way some of the questions are posed, for the goal is not to indoctrinate you to view the world through a particular lens. Instead, the goal is to display a kit of lenses—economic models—that you would be able to combine in order to build a magnifying device to your own specifications.

Here is what you should expect:

1. You will learn how to pose a question rigorously and how to follow through with an answer. That is, you will develop a habit of sitting down and thinking about a formal model. Especially productive in working toward this goal will be the time you spend alone with the end-of-chapter problems.

2. You will appreciate that even the broadest and most ambitious questions—in fact, particularly such questions—beg for a model, however narrow and naive. You will end up debating the relative merits of different economic systems and ways of life anyway, and unless you commit yourself to a model, you will end up debating loosely, stumble over an inconsistency in your argument, and will be defeated, whether or not your argument has merit.

3. You will learn to interpret models. A good test for a deep understanding is to try to explain as much as possible in plain English, without invoking jargon of any kind. This skill will enable you to reach audiences beyond classmates and professional economists.

4. You will learn to think as both a moral philosopher and an engineer. The moral philosopher seeks efficiency and fairness and, perhaps, also seeks to satisfy some of the ethical fads prevailing in the society. The engineer is an economics expert, who knows how to do best subject to constraints. One must juggle both roles when designing institutions and even some products, such as self-driving cars.[1]

5. You will learn to see the natures of economic and philosophical inquiries as not incommensurable. This vision will encourage you to carry over questions and techniques from one discipline to another.

6. You will develop an appreciation of economics as a nonsectarian discipline and, along the way, may discover the pleasures of being nonsectarian more broadly. Because of the common language of mathematics and the commitment to rigor, it is impossible for economists to persistently talk past each other. The book's ideas range from libertarian to socialist. One model argues for egalitarianism, while another advocates inequality. It is up to you to decide which model suits the context and reflects your values (or, perhaps, prompts you to revise your values). The book will inoculate you against ideologies by training you in the language of modern economic theory, enabling you to reason about a wide range of economic and social issues on your own terms.

7. Perhaps most importantly, the acquired knowledge will make you a better citizen and a more enlightened—and, hence, happier—individual. In the words of Landsburg (1993): "Economics in the narrowest sense is a science free of values. But economics is also a way of thinking, with an influence on its practitioners that transcends the demands of formal logic. With the diversity of human interests as its subject matter, the discipline of economics is fertile ground for the growth of values like tolerance and pluralism."

THE LANGUAGE OF MATHEMATICS

The arguments in this book are in the theorem–proof format, known as mathematics. This format helps distinguish the results derived in the context of fully specified

---

1. To see the importance of morals in the design of products, ask yourself whether you would rather buy a self-driving car that would swerve off a bridge to save the lives of forty kids in an oncoming school bus driven by a negligent driver, or would you prefer a car that, for an additional monthly fee, puts your life first? And, in the case of an inevitable collision, would you like your car to save your life or your passenger's?

models from educated speculations. Besides, an argument typeset as a proof is more transparent than one scattered all over the chapter.

Mainstream economics has been mathematical since the early 1950s, when John Nash proved equilibrium existence in games, and Kenneth Arrow, Gérard Debreu, and Lionel McKenzie proved equilibrium existence in competitive economies, thereby demonstrating once and for all the value of mathematics in economics. Today, mathematical modeling is the indisputable framework for facilitating and organizing economic discovery. Mathematics renders deep economic insights broadly accessible and verifiable to a keen, but not necessarily prodigious, mind at the moderate cost of mastering a limited number of mathematical concepts. The disputes of first-rate minds can be adjudicated not on the basis of their charisma but on the basis of rigorous mathematical arguments submitted to the scrutiny of peers. Mathematics is an ideology-free language shared by economists of every persuasion, who are eager—because able—to engage in a single Conversation.

By not shying away from mathematics, the book aims to engage the reader in this Conversation. There is no other way to engage: "[A]ny argument which is carried out with sufficient precision is mathematical [...]" remark Gale and Shapley (1962) in a Nobel-prize recognized paper, which proves a seminal theorem without a single equation or a piece of notation. Precisely in this inevitable sense is this book mathematical.

THE INTENDED AUDIENCES

The book is aimed at multiple audiences:

1. an undergraduate student looking for a sophisticated yet introductory text in microeconomic theory, or

2. a graduate student or a researcher in political philosophy, law, government, or public administration looking for an introduction to how economists think as they build their models.

Whichever audience you belong to, you should possess a certain mathematical sophistication, which stands for the appreciation of theorem–proof-type arguments (e.g., by contradiction, by contraposition, and by induction), univariate calculus and optimization, and some probability. If you are unsure whether that is you, consult part I and appendix A5 of Simon and Blume (1994) before reading this book and, as you read the book, delve into part III of Simon and Blume (1994) when and if the need arises.

The book and end-of-chapter problems are replete with multivariate constrained optimization problems. All of these problems but problem 3.5 can be solved by substituting the constraint into the objective function and then invoking univariate optimization. References and guidance will be provided for any additional mathematical results that will crop up in the book.

How to Use This Book

Chapter 1, on the Walrasian model of general equilibrium, is the only prerequisite for the chapters that follow. The Walrasian model epitomizes the essence of economic reasoning: a cause may affect the consequence in a way that is complex, indirect, and counterintuitive. In the subsequent chapters, the Walrasian model is invoked and extended and serves as a benchmark and an inspiration for alternative models. So, read it. (But if stuck in the middle of chapter 1, skip on; you may just be able to get away with it.)

The remaining chapters can be read in any order. Each chapter cross-references its predecessors, to bring out the common themes. But these cross-references are not indispensable.

Each chapter's narrative continues in the end-of-chapter problems. Most of these are challenging, designed to elaborate on the insights presented in the main text rather than to merely test comprehension. I hope you find gratification in tackling such challenges.[2] Try as many problems as you can and then compare your thinking to the suggested solutions, available for odd-numbered problems at the book's home at the MIT Press: http://mitpress.mit.edu/lectures-microeconomics. Do not be discouraged if you periodically need to peek at the solutions for hints; you will still be learning that way.

The book cites the research articles on which it draws. The reader may wish to check out these articles (all available online, at jstor.org or in working-paper versions), if only to read the introductions and see how the authors' interpretations differ from the book's. To illustrate ideas, the book points the reader to a myriad of nonacademic sources: works of fiction as well as *Vanity Fair*, *The Atlantic*, *The New Yorker*, the *New York Times*, and the *BBC News*, among others.

Prior Art

The book is not a monograph on my research but an exposition of ideas that range from sixty-year-old theories with proven pedagogical value to the cutting-edge research by leading contemporary economists. Classical topics are covered in chapters 1 and 3 and in sections 4.3, 6.3, and 9.4. The choice of topics, unusual for an introductory textbook, has been informed by the market-design revolution of the last thirty years, marked by the 2012 Nobel award to Alvin E. Roth and Lloyd Shapley for the theory and practice of market design.

Chapter 1, the core chapter, builds on the lecture notes on general equilibrium assembled by Jonathan Levin and subsequently revised by Ilya Segal and used

---

2. This hope is grounded in the research summarized by Linden (2011): "[I]deas are like addictive drugs. [...] [C]ertain psychoactive drugs co-opt the pleasure circuit to engage pleasurable feelings normally triggered by food, sex, and so on. In our recent evolutionary lineage (including primates and probably cetaceans), abstract mental constructs have become able to engage the pleasure circuitry as well, a phenomenon that has reached its fullest expression in our own species."

in the first-year PhD program at Stanford University. Their notes draw heavily on Mas-Colell, Whinston, and Green (1995, part four). The general equilibrium theory of competitive markets is sixty years old and is at the core of every economics curriculum.

Chapter 2 focuses on the experimental work (Falk and Szech, 2013a; Henrich et al., eds, 2004) concerned with the morality of markets.

Chapter 3 covers foundational ideas in matching theory, which go back to the seminal papers of Gale and Shapley (1962) and Shapley and Scarf (1974) and are surveyed by Roth and Sotomayor (1990) and Abdulkadiroğlu and Sönmez (2013). The model of Piccione and Rubinstein (2007) is central to the interpretations in this chapter. The chapter's nearly notation-free, verbal style of exposition was influenced by the course Paul Milgrom taught at Stanford and goes back to the seminal paper of Gale and Shapley (1962).

Chapter 4 covers the textbook exposition (e.g., Kreps, 2012, section 15.4) of the core convergence in general equilibrium theory, as well as John E. Roemer's work on analytical Marxism (Roemer, 1988) and, with Hervé Moulin, on socialism (Moulin and Roemer, 1989). The model of socialism is a product of the axiomatic resource allocation theory, which adopts the rights approach of moral philosophy to formally derive just allocation rules.

Chapter 5 presents the model of Garicano and Rossi-Hansberg (2004), who build on the superstars theory of Rosen (1981) to explain how competitive markets can amplify the inequality in ability to deliver an even greater inequality in income. The chapter discusses arguments against and in favor of inequality, with the argument in favor being due to Becker, Murphy, and Werning (2005).

Chapter 6 sketches a menagerie of models that comprise an economics vocabulary that can be co-opted to discuss the moral limits of markets. The chapter then zooms in on Spence's (1973b) seminal model of signaling, a counterpoint to the Walrasian model.

Chapter 7 is based on Roemer's (2010) formalization of Kant's categorical imperative. This formalization is compared to the reigning paradigm of Nash equilibrium.

Chapter 8 draws on the ideas at the intersection of economics and computer science—algorithmic game theory (Nisan, Roughgarden, Tardos, and Vazirani, eds, 2007) and the theory of networks (Jackson, 2008)—in order to illustrate that optimal policy design can be subtle. While the first-best policy may be well known and simple, moving partway toward it may be detrimental to welfare; this insight is the classic sixty-year-old theory of the second best (Lipsey and Lancaster, 1956).

Chapter 9 runs through the occasionally uncomfortable implications of three approaches to justice: utilitarianism (due to Jeremy Bentham and John Stuart Mill), John Rawls's maxmin criterion (Rawls, 1971), and the theory of just deserts (an essentially free-market idea advocated by Nozick, 1974). The chapter concludes with a glimpse into social choice theory by discussing Sen's (1970) impossibility of a Paretian liberal.

FOR THE INSTRUCTOR

The book was developed and used to teach a semester-long Intermediate Microeconomics Honors course at the University of Rochester in 2014 and 2015. Even if with little experience in economics, students come to class with their own life experiences and philosophies, which help them engage with the book's material. The book can serve in at least three roles:

1. As the main textbook in an upper-level undergraduate or a master's course dealing with matters of economic policy and design. The ideal student would be a double major in economics and mathematics.

2. As a supplementary textbook in an intermediate microeconomic theory course.

3. As a resource for students at the master's or doctoral level in the disciplines that draw on normative economics: law, social and political philosophy, and public policy and administration. Such students would require some prior acquaintance with microeconomics and the formulation and proof of general propositions.

Should the instructor adopt the book for an intermediate microeconomics course, he should be aware that, with the exception of general equilibrium and signaling, the choice of the book's topics is unusual. Consumer and producer theory are skipped; their elements are introduced only as needed.

Should the book be used in teaching a semester-long course (fifteen weeks, three hours a week), a possible allocation of hours across the nine chapters is

$$9 + 3 + 9 + 6 + 6 + 3 + 3 + 3 + 3 = 45.$$

ACKNOWLEDGEMENTS

This book was conceived in 2013, when, on sabbatical, I enjoyed the hospitality of the Economics Department at UCLA. The book was completed in 2017 at ITAM. I thank the University of Rochester (and, in particular, Mark Bils and Hari Govindan, the consecutive chairs of the Economics Department) and ITAM (and, in particular, Diego Dominguez, the chair of the Economics Department) for fostering academic environments of extraordinary freedom and for making it possible for me to teach courses based on this book's manuscript. I am grateful for the vocal participation to the University of Rochester students who took my ECO 207H class in 2014 (especially Alice Gindin and Moritz Weidner) and 2015 (especially Max Eber, Jake Jares, and Joseph Linden).

Three anonymous MIT Press reviewers of the early draft have provided invaluable guidance.

I thank Patrick Harless for numerous conversations over the years about the ideas within and without these covers. Lina Lukyantseva has commented on the entire manuscript and has checked all end-of-chapter solutions. Many colleagues have read and commented on individual chapters of this book: Andrei Gomberg, Piotr Evdokimov, Matthew Kovach, Eun Jeong Heo, Arina Nikandrova, Patrick Harless, Ed Green, Bertan Turhan, and Matthew Knowles. Several students have read through and commented on substantial portions of the manuscript and have assisted me with the work on the manuscript in other ways: Yuki Tamura, Vyacheslav Arbuzov, Michelle Avataneo, Mario Vazquez, Alice Gindin, Emilio Coya, Ricardo Miranda, and Zach Taylor. For incisive remarks, I thank Ben Golub.

The book's recurrent characters, Alice and Bob (and, occasionally, Carol and Dave), are the products of my imagination. Any resemblance to actual persons, living or dead, is purely coincidental.

CHAPTER 1

GENERAL EQUILIBRIUM IN COMPETITIVE MARKETS

1.1   INTRODUCTION

The world populated by self-interested individuals has a remarkable amount of order that no one individual in particular is responsible for. There are no reserves of surplus shoelaces and flash drives waiting to be claimed, nor is there any shortage thereof. In 2011, the Cheesecake Factory®'s target was to never run out of food ingredients while wasting at most 2.5% of ingredients—an astonishing target, given the randomness of customer arrivals and their orders.[1] The puzzlement at the degree of congruence between what is supplied and what is demanded is summarized well by Arrow (1973):

> From the time of Adam Smith's *Wealth of Nations* in 1776, one recurrent theme of economic analysis has been the remarkable degree of coherence among the vast numbers of individual and seemingly separate decisions about the buying and selling of commodities. In everyday, normal experience, there is something of a balance between the amounts of goods and services that some individuals want to supply and the amounts that other, different individuals want to sell [sic]. Would-be buyers ordinarily count correctly on being able to carry out their intentions, and would-be sellers do not ordinarily find themselves producing great amounts of goods that they cannot sell. This experience of balance is indeed

---

1. See Gawande, Atul. "Big Med." *The New Yorker*, August 13, 2012.

so widespread that it raises no intellectual disquiet among laymen; they take it so much for granted that they are not disposed to understand the mechanism by which it occurs.

Any adequate model of an economy must be consistent with the congruence between what individuals wish to sell and what others wish to buy. This chapter is devoted to such a model.

The observed congruence of the goods supplied and the goods demanded is imperfect, however. There is unemployment, which is surplus labor. Does the existence of the unemployed mean that demand and supply cannot cohere in all markets at the same time? Must at least one market—say, the labor market—remain imbalanced? The model we study has the answer: the balance of supply and demand in all markets is logically possible.

The economies with the observed congruence of supply and demand tend to be rich. Economies with shortages of some goods and overproduction of others (the Soviet Union in 1980s, Venezuela in 2000s and 2010s) tend to be poor. Is there a connection? Adam Smith surmised a connection when he observed (Smith, 1776): "It is not from the benevolence of the butcher, the brewer, or the baker that we expect our dinner, but from their regard to their own interest." The markets' tendency to translate self-interest into nonwasteful—so-called efficient—outcomes can be established formally and is a nonobvious result: the First Welfare Theorem. By contrast to the congruence of supply and demand, which laymen tend to take for granted, the First Welfare Theorem mostly goes unrecognized by the layman.

This chapter's model is general equilibrium. In the **partial equilibrium**[2] framework, which is concerned with a single good, one seeks a price to equate the values of two functions: demand for, and supply of, the good. Partial equilibrium framework is limiting because, in practice, supply and demand in one market typically depend on prices in other markets, directly or through the consumption of goods in those other markets. (For instance, a butcher's demand for bread depends on his wealth, which depends on the price of meat, which the butcher sells.) A coherent theory of prices and of the coordination of economic activity in the entire economy must consider the simultaneous equilibrium, or **general equilibrium**, in all markets.

This chapter describes some of the main ideas of general equilibrium. It asks the questions that are good practice in the analysis of any equilibrium concept; these questions will be revisited repeatedly in subsequent chapters in the context of different models. Is equilibrium efficient? Does it exist under sufficiently permissive conditions? Is it unique? Are there theoretical reasons to believe that, when it exists, an equilibrium would prevail? (As we shall see, even asking this question

---

2. Bold type is used throughout to highlight definitions.

is controversial.) How do changes in the economic environment affect equilibrium outcomes?

This chapter is abstract. It focuses on the basic tenets and insights of the general equilibrium theory, while relegating specific applications and extensions to the end-of-chapter problems and the subsequent chapters. Sections 1.2–1.7 are indispensable for appreciating the subsequent chapters. Sections 1.8–1.11 delve deeper into the strengths and weaknesses of the general equilibrium paradigm and invite you to recognize more phenomena (e.g., market socialism, financial and insurance markets) as potentially within the scope of this paradigm. Section 1.12 describes how the theory fares against empirical evidence.

1.2   AN EXCHANGE ECONOMY

We focus on a pure exchange economy; there is no production. Finitely many agents exchange finitely many goods. Each agent is endowed with a bundle of goods. The model is static (or so it will appear for most of this chapter); agents have a one-off opportunity to engage in unfettered exchange of their endowments, after which they consume the bundles obtained as a result of this exchange.

Formally, an exchange *economy* comprises I agents, indexed by $i \in \mathcal{I} \equiv \{1, ..., I\}$, and L goods, indexed by $l \in \mathcal{L} \equiv \{1, ..., L\}$. Each agent i has a **private endowment** $e^i \in \mathbb{R}_+^L$, an element in the positive orthant of L-dimensional Euclidean space. His consumption bundle, typically denoted by x^i, $\hat{x}^i$, or y^i, is a vector in the **consumption set** $\mathbb{R}_+^L$. The agent ranks consumption bundles according to a utility function $u^i : \mathbb{R}_+^L \to \mathbb{R}$, which encodes his preferences; a more preferred good is assigned a higher value of the function. The **exchange economy** is denoted by $\mathcal{E} \equiv (u^i, e^i)_{i \in \mathcal{I}}$.

Denote the **aggregate endowment** of good l by $\bar{e}_l \equiv \sum_{i \in \mathcal{I}} e^i_l$, the vector of aggregate endowments by $\bar{e} \equiv (\bar{e}_1, \bar{e}_2, ..., \bar{e}_L)$, and the matrix of individual endowments by $e \equiv (e^i)_{i \in \mathcal{I}}$. Without loss of generality, let $\bar{e} \gg 0$; the good whose aggregate endowment is zero may as well be omitted from the model. The matrix of individual consumption bundles is called **allocation** and is denoted by $x \equiv (x^i)_{i \in \mathcal{I}}$. Allocation x is **feasible** if $\sum_{i \in \mathcal{I}} x^i \leq \bar{e}$.

1.3   PREDICTION: THE CONTRACT SET

We would like to predict an outcome of unfettered exchange of endowments in an exchange economy. For instance, we can conduct an experiment by inviting a couple dozen individuals into a room, endowing each of them with goods, and then encouraging them to freely exchange their endowments. What should we expect to see when we revisit the agents in an hour or so? What will the agents' final bundles look like?

At the first glance, the question seems ill-specified; we need more information. What is the protocol according to which the endowments are exchanged? Is it an auction or decentralized bargaining? Instead of specifying a detailed protocol for unfettered exchange, we can adopt a reduced-form—so-called **axiomatic**—approach summarized in the hypothesis: any protocol that successfully operationalizes the concept of unfettered exchange is likely to lead to an outcome that satisfies certain assumptions, or axioms. In the present context, in addition to the plausible assumption that exchange does not last ad nauseam (i.e., traders eventually arrive at some allocation and stay there), we assume that

1. No trader is worse off as a result of the exchange than he would have been by simply consuming his endowment. That is, there is no coercion; nor does anyone err by trading against his interest. Formally, allocation x is **voluntary**: $u^i(x^i) \geq u^i(e^i)$ for all $i \in \mathcal{I}$.

2. All gains from trade have been exhausted; no money has been left of the table, as it were. That is, no agent can be made better off without another agent becoming worse off. Formally, allocation x is **Pareto efficient** (or, simply, **efficient**): there is no other feasible allocation $\hat{x}$ such that $u^i(\hat{x}^i) \geq u^i(x^i)$ for all $i \in \mathcal{I}$, with a strict inequality for some $i \in \mathcal{I}$.[3]

The allocations that satisfy the two properties listed above comprise the **contract set**. It is a subset of the **Pareto set**, which is defined to be the set of all Pareto efficient allocations.[4]

The prediction that the outcome of unfettered exchange will lie in the contract set, even though normatively appealing, makes strong demands on the agents' cognitive abilities.[5] For instance, an agent who plans an intricate chain of ultimately beneficial trades may see his plan go astray for reasons he did not anticipate. Then, he may end up with a bundle that is inferior to his endowment; the final allocation would not be voluntary (in our formal sense of the term). Alternatively, agents may fail to see that gains from trade remain at a particular allocation, especially if a complex multilateral exchange is required to realize these gains. In this case, the final allocation may not be Pareto efficient. (Whether and when it is easy for agents to

---

3. An allocation that is not Pareto efficient is said to be **inefficient**.

4. While some texts (e.g., Varian, 2010) take "contract set" (or, more commonly, "contract curve") to be synonymous with "Pareto set," we distinguish the two (as do Mas-Colell et al., 1995). We also distinguish the contract set from the core (definition 4.1).

5. Terms "positive" and "normative" will occur often. The **positive** is concerned with facts: what is, was, or will be. The **normative** is concerned with what ought to be and depends on one's morals and values.

realize that the allocation they have arrived at fails to be Pareto efficient is explored in problem 3.5.)

1.4 A REFINED PREDICTION: WALRASIAN EQUILIBRIUM

Still, the contract set is a rather large set and, so, may not be particularly useful for prediction. The set is large in the sense that it does not specify how exactly the gains from trade are allocated among agents. This agnosticism may be warranted. Economics may have nothing more to say. The allocation of the gains from trade may depend on agents' charm and persuasion skills, which are outside the model and outside the purview of economics.

An alternative, which we pursue, is to tease out economic restrictions on the allocation of the gains from trade by considering situations in which agents are numerous. A typical situation is at a gas station. One of many, an individual customer has no say in the price that he pays. Nor does the gas station, disciplined by its numerous competitors, have much latitude in setting its prices. Furthermore, the amount that the customer pays is linear in the amount of gas that he buys; the price per gallon is constant.

Formally, we refine the contract set by assuming that the outcome of unfettered exchange is as if each agent (i) cannot affect how much he pays for any given bundle and (ii) pays an amount that is linear in the quantity of each good that he trades. The refinement remains agnostic about the exact trading protocol; it only assumes that the allocation of the gains from trade is as if the agents have been trading all goods at a constant prices. (That we are indeed dealing with a refinement of the contract set will become clear in due course, in corollary 1.1.)

Assumption (i) above is the price-taking, or **competitive**, assumption. For it to hold, each agent must (rightly or wrongly) believe himself to be so insignificant relative to the rest of the market as to be unable to affect the prices, for instance, by haggling. The competitive assumption is most appropriate when agents are numerous. Assumption (ii) says that the agents face constant prices (i.e., fixed exchange rates between any two goods). Constant prices are motivated by the assumptions that agents are numerous and that retrade cannot be precluded.

To illustrate the rationale for constant prices, suppose the price of some good were increasing in the amount bought and that Alice wanted to buy a lot of this good. Then, multiple agents would gain by buying a small amount each, at lower prices, and then reselling the desired amount to Alice, at a price lower than she would have paid if shopping by herself. The more agents there are to split Alice's trade, the better price they will get for her. Similarly, if the price of a good were decreasing in the amount bought, then an agent could profit by buying in bulk and then selling small amounts to other agents. Thus, any nonlinearity of the amount paid in the quantity purchased can be arbitraged away if there are sufficiently many agents in the economy, so that trades can be split finely, and if retrade is possible, so that agents can act as intermediaries.[6]

In practice, of course, individuals do face quantity discounts, so per-unit prices vary with the amount purchased. Examples of decreasing prices are quantity discounts on Coke® in a supermarket, a fixed fee in all-you-can eat restaurants, a two-part tariff in taxis (which charge a fixed fee for boarding and then per-mile and per-minute rates), and gym membership discounts for long-term contracts. In addition, overtime labor is typically remunerated at a higher wage rate, which means that the implicit price of leisure is decreasing in the purchased amount of leisure. (An individual can be assumed to work 24/7 and then buy back his leisure at the wage rate.) Examples of increasing prices are found in utility bills. Nevertheless, the hope is that nonlinearities are not so widespread and severe as to render our investigation without empirical content.

Formally, a given constant price is denoted by $p \in \mathbb{R}_+^L$. Each agent i chooses a consumption bundle to maximize his utility given his budget constraint:

$$\max_{x^i \in \mathbb{R}_+^L} u^i(x^i) \quad \text{s.t.} \quad p \cdot x^i \leq p \cdot e^i, \quad i \in \mathcal{I}. \tag{1.1}$$

Agent i's wealth is $p \cdot e^i$, which is the amount of money he could get if he sold his entire endowment. His expenditure is $p \cdot x^i$. We denote agent i's **budget set** by

$$\mathcal{B}^i(p) \equiv \left\{ x^i \in \mathbb{R}_+^L \mid p \cdot x^i \leq p \cdot e^i \right\},$$

where the dependence of $\mathcal{B}^i$ on e^i is implicit. Given an arbitrary price p, the set of solutions to agent i's utility-maximization problem is represented by the **demand function**

$$x^i(p) \equiv \arg \max_{x^i \in \mathcal{B}^i(p)} u^i(x^i). \tag{1.2}$$

In general, the demand function can be a set-valued function, also known as a correspondence. (That is, more than one bundle may be optimal at a given price vector.) However, we shall usually make additional assumptions to deliver singleton-valued demand functions (i.e., exactly one bundle is optimal at each price vector). Doing so delivers analytical convenience and simplicity of notation.

---

6. The relationship between the numerosity of agents and the validity of the equilibrium we are about to define is a recurrent theme in general equilibrium theory and will come up twice more in this book (to establish equilibrium existence in "irregular" economies, and to motivate equilibrium outcomes as roughly being equivalent to the core, which is another way to model unfettered exchange.

We now define our main prediction for the outcome of unfettered exchange: Walrasian equilibrium. A Walrasian equilibrium is a vector of prices and an allocation such that each agent's consumption bundle in this allocation maximizes his utility given the prices; and markets clear, meaning that the total demand for each good equals this good's aggregate endowment.

Definition 1.1. A **Walrasian equilibrium** for an exchange economy $\mathcal{E}$ is a price-allocation pair (p, x) such that

1. Each agent maximizes his utility:

$$x^i \in \arg \max_{y^i \in \mathcal{B}^i(p)} u^i(y^i), \quad i \in \mathcal{I}.$$

2. Markets clear:

$$\sum_{i \in \mathcal{I}} x^i = \bar{e}.$$

The set of Walrasian equilibrium allocations is a refinement (i.e., a subset) of the contract set. Indeed, Walrasian allocation is voluntary because each agent likes his equilibrium bundle at least as much as his endowment, or else he would not have traded away from his endowment, which is affordable at all prices. As for the Pareto efficiency of Walrasian allocations, it is established in theorem 1.1.

In definition 1.1, all an agent must "know" is his utility function, his endowments, and the equilibrium price. The agent's problem is "easy" in that he need not know anything about other agents.

In the 1920s and 1930s, a debate raged on the relative merits of the decentralized market economy and the centralized planned economy. Oskar Lange argued that the planned economy was superior simply because it could mimic and, if necessary, improve upon the market economy.[7] Hayek (1945) responded that the information necessary for such planning was immense and dispersed, accessible to no single agent and no planning authority. By contrast, in the market economy, prices (somehow) aggregate all the information necessary to allocate resources.

To corroborate Hayek's point, one might be tempted to appeal to definition 1.1, according to which all coordination (i.e., market clearing) occurs through prices. Nevertheless, the definition does not make Hayek's point precise, for it is mute on the origin of equilibrium prices. These prices just happen to clear the markets by

---

7. Lange's claim is echoed as the **selective intervention puzzle** in the theory of the firm: If a firm can mimic a market (e.g., by administering a market internally) and sometimes improve upon it, why is not the entire economy organized as one large firm? One response is that a firm might be unable to commit to not bailing out its unprofitable division, whereas if this division is an autonomous firm, it simply goes bankrupt. A similar commitment logic favors a market economy over a centrally planned firm.

taking into account everyone's utilities and endowments. But what is this mysterious "market" process that incorporates the information about utilities and endowments into the prices? The definition of the Walrasian equilibrium does not say.

The definition of equilibrium brings out two strong assumptions about the exchange economy. First, agents do not directly care about prices; prices do not enter utility functions. In practice, an agent's enjoyment of a good may well directly depend on its price, as is the case with status goods, such as luxury cars and jewelry. An agent may also enjoy the fact that he can afford certain goods, even if he does not choose to consume them; that is, the agent may have a preference over the size and the shape of his budget set. Second, agents do not care about prices indirectly; prices do not convey information about the quality of goods. In practice, an agent can be unsure about the quality of a good and try to infer this quality from its price. For instance, when looking to buy wine, an individual who knows nothing about wines may prefer a more expensive bottle to a cheaper one, reasoning that the former is more expensive for a reason and is likely to be of higher quality.

1.5 COMMON ASSUMPTIONS

In the remainder of the chapter, we shall repeatedly invoke the following assumptions about the agents' utilities.

U-MONOTONICITY For each agent i, u^i is strictly increasing. That is, $y^i > x^i$ implies $u^i(y^i) > u^i(x^i)$.

U-CONTINUITY For each agent i, u^i is continuous.

U-CONCAVITY For each agent i, u^i is a **strictly concave function**. That is, for all $\alpha \in (0, 1)$ and all $x^i \in \mathbb{R}_+^L$ and $y^i \in \mathbb{R}_+^L$, $x^i \neq y^i$ implies $u^i(\alpha x^i + (1 - \alpha)y^i) > \alpha u^i(x^i) + (1 - \alpha)u^i(y^i)$.

MAINTAINED ASSUMPTIONS: U-MONOTONICITY AND U-CONTINUITY

Assumption u-monotonicity will be maintained henceforth. This assumption rules out situations in which an agent can get satiated in some good (e.g., weekly trips to a movie theater) or when he starts enjoying a good only after his consumption exceeds a certain threshold (e.g., a certain number of pages of a novel). This assumption is stronger than is necessary for all results reported here and is made only to simplify the exposition.

Assumption u-continuity is innocuous and will also be maintained. No finite amount of data can ever contradict it.[8] More than that, no finite amount of data

---

8. One can construct preferences such that an *infinite* amount of data might contradict u-continuity. Safety-first, or **lexicographic**, preferences is a classical example. The agent has safety-first preferences

can ever contradict the hypothesis that an agent's utility function is **smooth**: differentiable as many times as desired. So, u-continuity can be viewed as a convenient technical condition, and smoothness can be assumed in addition to solve the agent's utility-maximization problem (1.1) using calculus.

AN OFTEN-INVOKED ASSUMPTION: *U*-CONCAVITY

Assumption u-concavity is strong but analytically convenient. The ensuing analysis will rely only on its implication, which is that each agent's utility function is such that its every upper contour set is strictly convex. Let us decipher this condition. For any bundle y^i, agent i's corresponding **upper contour set** is defined as

$$UCS^i(y^i) \equiv \left\{ x^i \in \mathbb{R}^L_+ \mid u^i(x^i) \geq u^i(y^i) \right\}.$$

If one assumes u-concavity, then, for any y^i, for any two distinct bundles x^i and $\hat{x}^i$ in $UCS^i(y^i)$, and for any $\lambda \in (0, 1)$,

$$u^i\big(\lambda x^i + (1 - \lambda)\hat{x}^i\big) > \lambda u^i(x^i) + (1 - \lambda)u^i(\hat{x}^i) \geq u^i(y^i),$$

where the strict inequality follows by u-concavity, and the weak inequality follows because x^i and $\hat{x}^i$ are both in $UCS^i(y^i)$. Hence, $u^i(\lambda x^i + (1 - \lambda)\hat{x}^i) > u^i(y^i)$, and, so, under u-concavity, $UCS^i(y^i)$ is a **strictly convex set**.

The strict convexity of upper contour sets means that agents like variety. If indifferent between any two distinct bundles, an agent is better off if he mixes them, in any proportion. The strict convexity thus rules out preferences for addictive consumption, which favors either specialization in the consumption of the addictive good or abstention from it over seeking variety.[9] The strict convexity is more realistic when individual goods correspond to aggregate categories. For instance, an agent might like to split his time between London and San Francisco on the scale of a year, but, on every given day, he would rather be in one city than traveling between the two.

Assumption u-concavity all but implies u-continuity. Indeed, try plotting a utility function that is concave but not continuous. The only discontinuity that u-concavity admits is a jump in the utility as the agent switches from consuming zero amount of some good to consuming an arbitrarily small positive amount. This

---

over cars (more precisely, over bundles of car characteristics) if he cares about safety and prices so that, between any two cars, he prefers the safer one and compares the prices only if the two cars are equally safe. Not only safety-first preferences cannot be represented by a continuous utility function, they cannot be represented by any utility function, as can be shown.

9. Suppose that Alice anticipates *The Americans* (2013–2018) to be an addictive TV series. Then, if indifferent between a subscription to all six seasons of the series and two large boxes of Godiva® chocolate, she will prefer either to a subscription to just three seasons and one box of chocolate.

close relationship between u-concavity and u-continuity notwithstanding, we shall explicitly invoke u-continuity alongside u-concavity, for emphasis.

IMPLICIT ASSUMPTIONS: MAXIMIZATION, ORDINAL UTILITY, AND NARROW SELFISHNESS

We have assumed that each agent's choices can be described by utility maximization.[10] Utility maximization is not a strong assumption as long as the agent behaves in a logically consistent manner (e.g., does not claim to prefer tea to coffee, coffee to wine, and wine to tea).

The analysis in this chapter assumes that utilities are ordinal. An **ordinal** utility encodes how an agent compares bundles but not the intensity of the agent's happiness with each of the bundles. A utility function whose level is identified with the agent's happiness is called **cardinal**. A simple way to test whether analysis exploits cardinality (i.e., assigns meaning to utility levels) is to replace each agent's utility function with an arbitrary positive monotonic transformation of it. If the analysis is unaffected by any such transformation, then this analysis exploits only the ordinal aspects of utility. The computation of the demand function in (1.2) is an example. It is only toward the end of the book that we shall invoke the cardinal interpretation of utility.

Finally, we have made a strong—and unrealistic—assumption that each agent cares only about the bundle that he himself consumes and does not care about others' bundles. This assumption rules out situations in which an individual cares about his social status as captured by his consumption relative to his neighbors', cares about the distribution of consumption in the economy at large, cares about his friends and family, or is bothered by the noise of a neighbor's late-night parties. Nevertheless—except in some end-of-chapter problems—we adhere to this narrow-selfishness assumption, which is a decent approximation in some applications and a useful benchmark in others.

1.6 GRAPHICAL ILLUSTRATIONS IN THE EDGEWORTH BOX

Most general-equilibrium concepts introduced in this chapter can be illustrated in a two-person, two-good exchange economy. An Edgeworth box is a useful graphical tool to study such economies.[11] Figure 1.1(a) depicts one. An Edgeworth box takes

---

10. To get to the central themes fast, this chapter whizzes past such standard topics as choice, preference, utility, and demand. Many a reader will benefit immensely from reading about them in any standard microeconomics textbook, such as Varian (2010), Landsburg (2013), or Nicholson and Snyder (2007).

11. Edgeworth boxes in their modern form were first drawn by Vilfredo Pareto, who was inspired by reading Francis Ysidro Edgeworth.

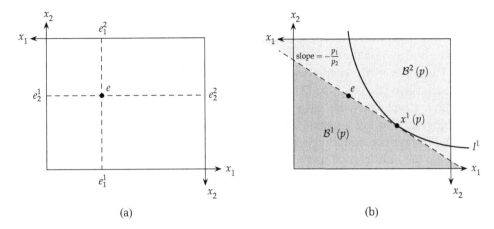

FIGURE 1.1.
The Edgeworth box. The axes along which the endowment and the consumption of goods 1 and 2 are measured are denoted by x_1 and x_2. Agent 1's origin is the bottom left corner. Agent 2's origin is the top right corner.
(a) The agents' endowments e^1 and e^2 are measured from the respective agents' origins and add up to the dimensions of the Edgeworth box.
(b) The relative price p_1/p_2 dictates the slopes of both agents' budget sets, denoted by the shaded triangles labeled as $\mathcal{B}^1(p)$ and $\mathcal{B}^2(p)$, and induces agent 1's optimal consumption bundle, $x^1(p)$, which is the tangency point of his budget line (dashed) and his indifference curve, I^1.

the map of indifference curves for one agent and superimposes upon it the other agent's indifference map that has been rotated 180 degrees and whose origin has been offset appropriately.[12] The origins for the two agents are offset just so that each point in the box can be read as both agent 1's bundle and agent 2's bundle, depending on which origin one uses.

Thus, in figure 1.1(a), the bottom left corner is the origin for agent 1. The bottom horizontal axis measures his consumption of good 1, whereas the leftmost vertical axis measures his consumption of good 2. His endowment, (e_1^1, e_2^1), is at point e. For agent 2, the origin is the top right corner, and the axes are flipped: the top horizontal axis is increasing from right to left and measures his consumption of good 1, whereas the rightmost vertical axis is increasing from top to bottom and measures his consumption of good 2. His endowment, (e_1^2, e_2^2), is the same point e as agent 1's endowment but is measured from agent 2's origin. Each point in the box represents a feasible and nonwasteful (i.e., $\sum_{i \in \mathcal{I}} x^i = \bar{e}$) allocation of the two goods. The dimensions of the Edgeworth box are the aggregate endowments of the two goods.

To illustrate a Walrasian equilibrium, we add prices to the Edgeworth box. In figure 1.1(b), given prices p_1 and p_2 for the two goods, agent 1's budget line is the line that passes through his endowment point e and has the slope $-p_1/p_2$; at any prices, the agent can afford to consume his endowment and can trade away from

12. An agent's **indifference curve** is the set of the bundles all of which give the agent the same specified utility. His **indifference map** is a collection of indifference curves for different utility levels.

his endowment at the constant exchange rate p_1/p_2. The same line is also agent 2's budget line, if viewed from agent 2's origin.

The budget line divides the Edgeworth box into two budget sets, one for each agent. These sets are the shaded triangles $\mathcal{B}^1(p)$ and $\mathcal{B}^2(p)$ in figure 1.1(b). At equilibrium, each agent chooses from his budget set a consumption bundle that maximizes his utility. Graphically, he seeks the indifference curve that is the farthest from his origin and that has a nonempty intersection with his budget set. In the figure, agent 1 demands consumption bundle $x^1(p)$, which is characterized by the tangency condition: the indifference curve is tangent to the budget line.

To formally illustrate the tangency condition in figure 1.1(b), let $u_l^i(x^i) \equiv \partial u^i(x^i)/\partial x_l^i$ denote agent i's **marginal utility** from good l; $u_l^i(x^i)$ is the partial derivative of u^i with respect to x_l^i. Then, the tangency in the figure is captured by the condition

$$\frac{u_1^i(x^i(p))}{u_2^i(x^i(p))} = \frac{p_1}{p_2}, \quad i \in \mathcal{I}. \tag{1.3}$$

Equation (1.3) reads: $u_1^i(x^i(p))/u_2^i(x^i(p))$, the **marginal rate of substitution** of good 1 for good 2, equals p_1/p_2, the relative price. The tangency condition in (1.3) need not characterize an optimal consumption bundle if the agent does not optimally consume a positive amount of each good or if his utility function is not differentiable. Furthermore, the tangency condition may hold for multiple bundles if u-concavity is violated.

To find a Walrasian equilibrium, we must find the prices at which markets for both goods clear, or, graphically, at which both agents choose the same point (but potentially different bundles) in the Edgeworth box. In figure 1.2(a), prices do not clear the markets. Agent 2 wishes to supply less of good 2 than agent 1 wishes to consume; good 2 is in excess demand. Similarly, agent 1 wishes to supply more of good 1 than agent 2 demands; good 1 is in excess supply. Lowering the relative price of good 1 by rotating the budget line counter clockwise about the endowment point e eliminates the excess supply of good 1 and equilibrates both markets, in figure 1.2(b).

In figure 1.2(b), point x is the Walrasian equilibrium allocation. Agent 1 sells good 1 and buys good 2; agent 2 sells good 2 and buys good 1. The Walrasian equilibrium allocation can be equivalently described as the intersection of the two agents' offer curves. An agent's **offer curve** is the set of the agent's demands that are obtained by varying the prices that he faces, as in figure 1.3. The fact that, in Figure 1.2(b), point x lies on each agent's offer curve means that each agent demands a bundle that maximizes his utility given the prices. The fact that x is at the intersection of the agents' offer curves means that the agents demands are compatible; markets clear. Thus, conditions (i) and (ii) of definition 1.1 hold.

Recall that the motivation for Walrasian equilibrium was to refine the contract set as a prediction for the outcome of unfettered exchange. But how much finer is

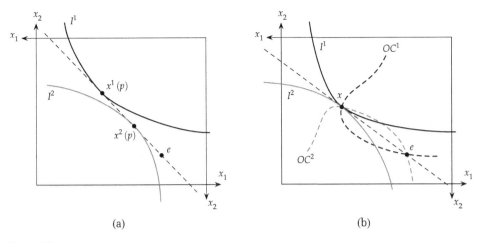

FIGURE 1.2.
Disequilibrium and equilibrium in the Edgeworth box. The unique equilibrium allocation x is the intersection point of the agents' offer curves (OC^1 and OC^2), as well as the tangency point of the agents' indifference curves (I^1 and I^2) to the (dashed) budget line.
(a) Disequilibrium. At the prices corresponding to the dashed budget line, there is excess demand for good 2 and excess supply of good 1.
(b) Equilibrium.

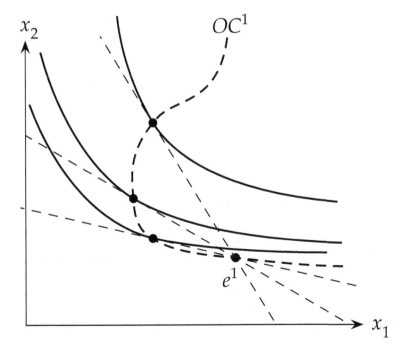

FIGURE 1.3.
Agent 1's offer curve is the dashed curve OC^1. The offer curve traces out the agent's optimal bundles (bold dots) as prices change, causing his (dashed) budget line to pivot around his endowment point, e^1.

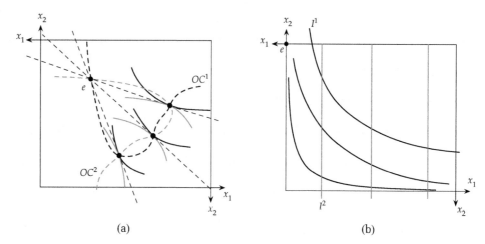

(a)   (b)

FIGURE 1.4.
Equilibria may be multiple or fail to exist.
(a) Multiplicity. The agents' offer curves (OC^1 and OC^2) intersect three times, so three equilibria exist.
(b) Nonexistence. The market for good 1 cannot clear: at any positive price, agent 2 would not sell any of good 1, while agent 1 would always demand some.

the set of Walrasian-equilibrium allocations? (In figure 1.2(b), it is just a point.) In particular, is the Walrasian equilibrium allocation unique? And at the other extreme: Is a Walrasian equilibrium guaranteed to exist?

It turns out that Walrasian equilibrium need not be unique and need not exist. Figure 1.4(a) is an example with multiple equilibria. Given endowment e, the offer curves of the two agents intersect thrice; there are three equilibria.

Note, by the way, that if one draws the agents' offer curves "at random," it is much more likely that they will intersect an odd, rather than even, number of times. There is a general result to this effect: an even number of Walrasian equilibria is nongeneric. A property is **nongeneric** if it holds with probability zero if one draws the economy's parameter values uniformly at random from a sufficiently rich set. A property is **generic** if it holds with probability one if one draws the economy's parameter values uniformly at random from a sufficiently rich set. (Thus, a property may be neither generic nor nongeneric.) The oddness of number of Walrasian equilibria can be shown to be generic under appropriate regularity conditions.

In figure 1.4(b), no Walrasian equilibrium exists. The endowment point e is such that agent 1 is endowed with all of good 2, and agent 2 is endowed with all of good 1. The agents' utility functions are $u^1(x^1) = \ln x_1^1 + \ln x_2^1$ and $u^2(x^2) = x_1^2$.[13] That is, agent 1 cares about both goods and is desperate to consume

---

13. Because the general description of the exchange economy assumes that utility functions are defined on $\mathbb{R}_+^L$, we follow the convention that $\ln 0 = -\infty$.

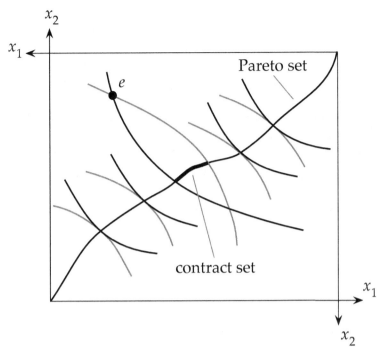

FIGURE 1.5.
The Pareto set and its subset, the contract set. The Pareto set here is the curve that passes from one origin to the other and comprises all the tangency points of the agents' indifference curves. The contract set is the set of Pareto efficient allocations that each agent prefers to his endowment *e*.

at least a little of each, whereas agent 2 cares only about good 1, thereby violating u-monotonicity and u-concavity (recall that the concavity in u-concavity is strict). If an equilibrium with price p exists, then $p \gg 0$; or else agent 1 will demand an infinite amount of a good whose price is zero, and the market for that good will not clear. At any equilibrium with $p \gg 0$, however, agent 2 would choose to consume his endowment, while agent 1 would insist on buying at least a little bit of good 1; the market for good 1 would not clear. Thus, no market-clearing price exists.

Figure 1.5 illustrates the Pareto and the contract sets in the Edgeworth box. In the figure, u-monotonicity, u-continuity, and u-concavity hold, and the Pareto set is the set of points at each of which the agents' indifference curves are tangent, and, so, their upper contour sets intersect only at their boundaries; there is no way to make one agent better off without making the other one worse off. The contract set is a subset of the Pareto set that each agent weakly prefers to his endowment. More generally, the Pareto set may include points on the boundary of the Edgeworth box and (when u-concavity fails) need not even be a curve. (Draw a picture.)

One limitation of the Edgeworth box is immediate. With just two agents, the Walrasian assumption that each agent takes prices as given—instead of trying to influence these prices by being a tough bargainer—is unrealistic. Nevertheless, the realism of price-taking can be salvaged while preserving the Edgeworth box. To do so, assume a large and equal number (ideally, a continuum) of clones of agents 1 and 2 and (quite arbitrarily) restrict attention to allocations in which, if indifferent, same-type clones choose identical bundles. The Edgeworth box is then interpreted to illustrate the behavior of the two agent types.

Furthermore, the Edgeworth box's restriction to two-good economies makes some economic insights inaccessible. Problem 1.4 illustrates one such insight, which is concerned with the stability of equilibria (analyzed in section 1.10).

1.7 THE FIRST WELFARE THEOREM

The Edgeworth box provides intuition for a central result in general-equilibrium theory: any Walrasian equilibrium allocation is Pareto efficient. Indeed, at the Walrasian equilibrium in figure 1.2(b), the budget line separates the agents' upper contour sets with respect to the equilibrium allocation. (This is true regardless of whether u-concavity holds.) Thus, no feasible allocation can make both agents weakly better off and one agent strictly better off than at the Walrasian-equilibrium allocation. In other words, any Walrasian equilibrium is Pareto efficient. This result is known as the **First Welfare Theorem** (**FWT**).

Theorem 1.1 (First Welfare Theorem). *Let $(p, (x^i)_{i \in \mathcal{I}})$ be a Walrasian equilibrium for economy $\mathcal{E}$. If u-monotonicity holds, then the allocation $x \equiv (x^i)_{i \in \mathcal{I}}$ is Pareto efficient.*

Proof. By way of contradiction, suppose that the equilibrium allocation x is Pareto dominated by some feasible allocation $\hat{x}$. That is, $\hat{x}$ is feasible and satisfies $u^i(\hat{x}^i) \geq u^i(x^i)$ for all $i \in \mathcal{I}$, with the inequality being strict for some $i \in \mathcal{I}$.

Take an agent j for whom $u^j(\hat{x}^j) > u^j(x^j)$. Conclude $p \cdot \hat{x}^j > p \cdot e^j$ by revealed preference; that is, the fact that agent j prefers $\hat{x}^j$ to x^j reveals that $\hat{x}^j$ were unaffordable when x^j was chosen.

Moreover, for any $i \in \mathcal{I}$, $p \cdot \hat{x}^i \geq p \cdot e^i$. Indeed, suppose, by contradiction, that $p \cdot \hat{x}^i < p \cdot e^i$ for some $i \in \mathcal{I}$. Construct a new bundle, $\tilde{x}^i \equiv \hat{x}^i + (\varepsilon, 0, ..., 0)$ with $\varepsilon > 0$ such that $p \cdot \tilde{x}^i < p \cdot e^i$, which one can always do by picking a sufficiently small ε. Then, by u-monotonicity, $u^i(\tilde{x}^i) > u^i(\hat{x}^i) \geq u^i(x^i)$. Thus, even though $\tilde{x}^i$ is affordable and is preferred to, x^i, agent i chooses x^i over $\tilde{x}^i$, thereby failing to optimize and contradicting equilibrium. Therefore, the contradiction hypothesis $p \cdot \hat{x}^i < p \cdot e^i$ cannot be true.

Finally, adding up the inequalities established above gives $\sum_{i \in \mathcal{I}} p \cdot \hat{x}^i > \sum_{i \in \mathcal{I}} p \cdot e^i$, or, equivalently,

$$\sum_{l \in \mathcal{L}} p_l \left(\sum_{i \in \mathcal{I}} \hat{x}_l^i - \bar{e}_l \right) > 0.$$

At equilibrium, $p_l > 0$ for all $l \in \mathcal{L}$, by u-monotonicity. (Indeed, if $p_l \leq 0$ for some l, then, each agent will demand an infinite amount of good l, thereby violating market clearing for this good.) Then, the display above implies that, for at least one l, $\sum_{i \in \mathcal{I}} \hat{x}_l^i > \bar{e}_l$. That is, $\hat{x}$ is not feasible and, so, cannot Pareto dominate the equilibrium allocation x. ∎

Coupled with the observation that an agent's endowment is always affordable to him, the FWT immediately implies

Corollary 1.1. *The set of Walrasian equilibrium allocations is a refinement of the contract set.*

The FWT supports Adam Smith's assertion that the individuals who act selfishly end up behaving in a way that is desirable from a societal standpoint. Even though there is no explicit social coordination, the outcome is efficient. Of course, Pareto efficiency says nothing about distributional justice. It can be Pareto efficient for one individual to have everything and for everyone else to have nothing.

The theorem's assumptions seem weak. Given the model of an exchange economy, the only assumption is u-monotonicity: agents prefer more to less. (And even this assumption can be weakened.) Of course, the model itself contains many heroic assumptions, which are unlikely to hold in any real economy:

1. All agents face the same prices. In particular, there are no sales taxes, which would divorce the price the buyer pays from the price the seller receives (problem 1.6). Nor is there any asymmetric information about the quality of any good (e.g., a secondhand car); such asymmetry, too, would divorce the price the buyer believes he pays from the price the seller believes he receives (per unit of quality, say).

2. All agents are price takers. That is, the agents do not believe that their choices of bundles can affect prices (see problem 1.5 and, for a subtler point, problem 1.15). The assumption is plausible in economies with many similar agents but is suspect with few well-endowed agents who dominate the economy.

3. Markets are **complete**—that is, markets exist for all goods, which can be exchanged freely, and all agents can costlessly participate in these markets. At

the other extreme is **autarky**, wherein each agent must consume his endowment, either because markets are absent or because participation in them is prohibitively costly. Except for the special case when the endowment is Pareto efficient, autarky is not Pareto efficient. A typical example of an incomplete market is an economy with missing insurance markets (section 1.11).

4. There is no **externality**, defined as a situation in which an agent's consumption of a good directly affects another agent's utility (problems 1.2 and 1.8).

5. Property rights are well-defined. Alice cannot just grab Bob's goods. Instead, she must convince him to part with these goods in exchange for the goods that Bob values even more.

6. Equilibrium is reached, if it exists. The model says nothing about why, when left to themselves, agents would arrive at an equilibrium.

Furthermore, the FWT's conclusion is vacuous unless equilibrium exists. Existence requires additional assumptions. Therefore, it would be rash to conclude that, as long as individuals prefer more to less, **laissez-faire** (i.e., the policy of economic nonintervention by the government) is justified.

Even when the theorem's hypotheses apply, its conclusion should not be exaggerated. In particular, even though the introduction of markets for all goods weakly Pareto improves on autarky,

1. When markets are incomplete, the introduction of a market for an additional good need not lead to a Pareto improvement and may even lead to a Pareto worsening (problem 1.10).

2. When some agents are excluded from the market, the inclusion of an additional agent need not lead to a Pareto improvement (problem 1.3).

3. Complete markets need not lead to an outcome that is more "fair" or "equitable" than autarky (problem 1.9).

1.8   THE SECOND WELFARE THEOREM

While the FWT says that any equilibrium is efficient, the **Second Welfare Theorem (SWT)** says that any efficient allocation can be supported as an equilibrium allocation by appropriately redistributing the endowments. Now, surely if there is any way to redistribute endowments so, redistributing them all the way to coincide with the target efficient allocation must do the job. That is the approach taken in theorem 1.2.

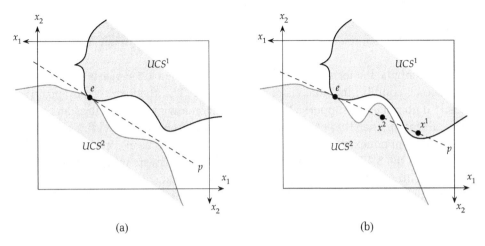

FIGURE 1.6.

Illustrations of the Second Welfare Theorem. Endowment e is Pareto efficient; the agents' upper contour sets, UCS^1 and UCS^2, have only one point in common.

(a) The SWT's conclusion holds. Price p supports endowment e as a Walrasian equilibrium allocation.

(b) No Walrasian equilibrium exists, so the SWT's conclusion does not hold. For instance, at some price p, agent 1 demands x^1, agent 2 demands x^2, and, so, good 1 is in excess demand; markets do not clear at p.

Theorem 1.2 (Second Welfare Theorem). *Let $\mathcal{E}$ be an economy with a Pareto efficient endowment e. If $\mathcal{E}$ has a Walrasian equilibrium, then there exists a price vector $p \in \mathbb{R}_+^L$ such that (p, e) is a Walrasian equilibrium of $\mathcal{E}$.*

Proof. Let (p, x) be a Walrasian equilibrium, which exists by the theorem's hypothesis. Then, each agent i's bundle x^i must be at least as desirable to him as his endowment:

$$u^i(x^i) \geq u^i(e^i) \quad \text{for all } i \in \mathcal{I}.$$

Moreover, no inequality in the display above may be strict or else the Pareto efficiency of e would be contradicted. Therefore, $u^i(x^i) = u^i(e^i)$ for all $i \in \mathcal{I}$.

Because x^i is agent i's optimal bundle at the price p, and $u^i(x^i) = u^i(e^i)$, it must also be that e^i, too, is his optimal bundle at price p. Furthermore, e (trivially) clears the markets. Thus, (p, e) is a Walrasian equilibrium, as desired. ∎

Figure 1.6 illustrates the SWT in an Edgeworth box. Because e is Pareto efficient, the agents' upper contour sets with respect to e may only have boundary points in common, one of which (in this example, the only one) is e. If these two upper contour sets can be separated by a line that passes through e but not through the interior of either set, then this line is the price line that supports e as a Walrasian equilibrium allocation (figure 1.6(a)). If no such line can be drawn, then, at any price, at least one agent would seek to consume in the interior of his upper contour set, and, so, the agents' implied demands would fail to clear the markets (figure 1.6(b)).

Incidentally, the formulation of the SWT in theorem 1.2 suggests an easy way to construct equilibrium nonexistence examples. The theorem's contrapositive reads:[14] if no price can support a Pareto efficient endowment as a Walrasian equilibrium allocation, then the economy has no Walrasian equilibrium at all. This is how the equilibrium nonexistence example in figure 1.4(b) has been constructed.

Why is the SWT economically significant? Two answers will be offered. One has to do with resale proofness, another one with market socialism.

In the SWT's statement, the endowment is redistributed all the way to the target Pareto efficient allocation, and no trade occurs at equilibrium, once markets open. Even then, the planner may value the fact that the target allocation can be supported at a Walrasian equilibrium.[15] In this case, even if the agents can trade in Walrasian markets (perhaps, behind the planner's back), they will not trade away from the target allocation. Thus, the planner's target allocation is resale-proof.

There are other ways to get at the target Pareto efficient allocation than to redistribute the endowment to coincide with this allocation. Any endowment that, at the supporting Walrasian prices, gives each agent the same wealth as he enjoys at the target allocation will set the economy on course for the target allocation. In the Edgeworth box, such endowments lie on the budget line that supports the target efficient allocation.

The SWT thus enables **market socialism**, advocated in the 1930s by Oskar Lange, among others. To illustrate, suppose there are two agents and two goods: labor and stuff, as in figure 1.7. An agent can consume his endowment of labor as leisure or transform some of it into a service (such as a massage, a haircut, or a jazz performance) and sell it in the market. (The labor good allows one to view the exchange economy as possessing a primitive production technology.) Stuff can be viewed as a composite of various material goods. The government believes that the initial endowment of labor and stuff, denoted by e, would lead to an equilibrium allocation, x, that is "unfair," perhaps because it gives too much of every good to agent 1. The government envisions a "fair" allocation, x', which is Pareto efficient.

An omnipotent planner could implement x' directly by redistributing the endowment from e to x'. But suppose the government cannot redistribute labor (perhaps because doing so would amount to slavery, deemed repugnant). Nevertheless, by the SWT, one can draw a supporting price line p' through x'. The

---

14. The **contrapositive** for statement "A implies B" is the equivalent statement "not B implies not A."

15. On these pages, the **planner**, or the social planner, is an impersonal entity that will occasionally pass a normative judgment on the economy, aggregate individual preferences, or be involved in redesigning aspects of the economy to meet some normative desiderata. The planner may be an economic expert, a philosopher, or a democratically elected government. The planner's appearance does not necessarily connote a planned economy.

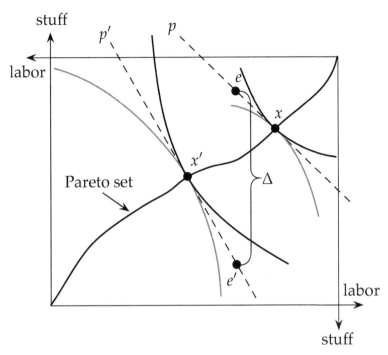

FIGURE 1.7.
Market socialism. The government prefers the Pareto efficient allocation x' to the Walrasian equilibrium allocation x from the initial endowment e. By redistributing amount Δ of "stuff" from agent 1 to agent 2, the government can induce x' as a Walrasian equilibrium allocation from the new endowment e'.

government can then try to redistribute stuff in a way that the new endowment, denoted by e', would lie on p'. (In figure 1.7, such redistribution amounts to transferring amount Δ of stuff from agent 1 to agent 2.) When such redistribution is feasible, the desired allocation x' can be supported as a Walrasian equilibrium (p', x') of the economy with the redistributed endowment e'. In the term "market socialism," the redistribution is "socialism," and the subsequent trading is "market."[16]

We conclude the discussion of the SWT with warnings against two potential misinterpretations:

1. It is tempting to say that, while the FWT shows the sufficiency of Walrasian markets for efficiency, the SWT shows the necessity of markets. Not so. The SWT says only that any efficient allocation can be supported at a Walrasian equilibrium. The theorem does not say that it must be. Indeed, the planner

16. Oskar Lange also envisioned snatching the price discovery away from the invisible hand of the market and placing it into the hands of the government, which, presumably, would be able to arrive at equilibrium prices with greater precision and less drama than plays out, say, in the stock market.

can implement the target efficient allocation directly, without bothering with markets and prices.

2. The SWT may seem to suggest that, in practice as well as in theory, any efficient allocation can be reached by redistributing the agents' endowments and letting the markets play out. But note that, in the SWT, redistribution is **lump-sum**, that is, independent of the agents' choices. Lump-sum redistribution is rarely available in practice.

   To illustrate, suppose that, from the planner's point of view, the Walrasian equilibrium gives too little consumption to short individuals. Then, the planner can redistribute endowments toward short individuals, so that the Walrasian equilibrium starting at the new endowments treats them better. The problem with applying this argument more broadly is that, unlike height, most characteristics on which the planner may want to base redistribution are either agents' private information or are chosen by them. For instance, if the goal is to redistribute from the smart to the less smart, the smart will be tempted to lie about their intelligence by intentionally flunking IQ tests. If the planner chooses to tax university graduates more because they tend to be smarter, then the smart will be less likely to enroll in universities, and the ensuing redistribution will no longer be lump-sum.[17] Pareto efficiency may be compromised.

1.9 EQUILIBRIUM EXISTENCE (AND NONEXISTENCE)

From the positive perspective, the Walrasian model is only useful if it generates a prediction for an outcome of unfettered exchange and if this prediction approximates the observation well. Whether the prediction is a good approximation is largely an empirical question.[18] What one can determine theoretically is whether the Walrasian model predicts at all, and, if so, when. That is, the question is: Under what conditions does a Walrasian equilibrium exist? Existence is necessary to lend relevance to the conclusions of both the FWT and the SWT.

Ideally, one would try to establish equilibrium existence under the weakest conditions possible. To simplify exposition, however, we shall discuss existence only under rather restrictive conditions.

---

17. Redistribution that affects individual behavior is called **distortionary**, in recognition of the fact that it likely distorts individual choices away from Pareto efficiency.

18. A theoretical contribution to this question would be to analyze models with a carefully specified exchange protocol and examine the conditions under which Walrasian equilibrium approximates well the outcomes of these models. Such an analysis is performed, for instance, by Jackson and Manelli (1997).

EXISTENCE

For nearly eighty years after Léon Walras formulated his model of general equilibrium, it was an open question whether such an equilibrium existed. Of course, one
can formulate an economy (e.g., in an Edgeworth box) and then either explicitly
construct an equilibrium or prove that no such construction is possible. The question that tantalized the best minds in economics for almost eighty years was more
ambitious, almost mystical: Can one prove equilibrium existence in a large class of
economies even if one does not know how to construct such equilibria? How does
one even begin to approach a question like this?

Early approaches were heuristic. To illustrate—and to fix some basic ideas
for future reference—assume that each agent's demand function, defined in (1.2),
is singleton-valued (a condition for this will be stated shortly). Then, Walrasian
equilibrium exists if and only if one can find a price vector p such that the value of
the **aggregate excess demand**, defined as

$$z(p) \equiv \sum_{i \in \mathcal{I}} x^i(p) - \bar{e},$$

is zero:

$$z(p) = 0. \tag{1.4}$$

To see that $z(p) = 0$ if and only if $(p, (x^i(p))_{i \in \mathcal{I}})$ is a Walrasian equilibrium, note that
each $x^i(p)$ satisfies the agent-optimization part of definition 1.1, and $z(p) = 0$ if and
only if the market-clearing part holds.

The idea in the early literature (Léon Walras, Vilfredo Pareto, and Francis
Ysidro Edgeworth) was to ascertain that the number of equations and the number of unknowns in system (1.4) are the same. This approach is naive. Even for
a linear system, merely counting equations and unknowns is inadequate.[19] And
system (1.4) is a nonlinear one. Moreover, what if some prices that solve the system
turn out to be complex numbers? Nevertheless, as a warm-up exercise, we begin by
counting equations and unknowns.

Lemma 1.1 collects the observations that come in useful in this counting
exercise and also in the subsequent analysis.

Lemma 1.1. *Let z be an aggregate excess demand function. Suppose u-monotonicity
holds. Then,*

---

19. For instance, for two unknowns a and b, the (trivial) two-equation system $\{a = 1, b = 2\}$ has the unique
solution ($a = 1$ and $b = 2$), system $\{a = 1, a = 2\}$ has no solution, and system $\{a = 1, 2a = 2\}$ has infinitely
many solutions ($a = 1$, and b is anything).

1. Any Walrasian equilibrium price vector p is positive in each component: $p \gg 0$.

2. For any (not necessarily equilibrium) price vector $p \gg 0$, **Walras's law** holds: $p \cdot z(p) = 0$.

3. The aggregate excess demand function z is **homogeneous of degree zero**: for all $\lambda > 0$ and $p \gg 0$, $z(\lambda p) = z(p)$.

4. If the price-allocation pair (p, x) is a Walrasian equilibrium, then so is $(\lambda p, x)$ for any $\lambda > 0$. In particular, one can set

   - $\lambda = 1/p_l$ to normalize the price of some good l to 1;

   - $\lambda = 1/\sum_{l \in \mathcal{L}} p_l$ to normalize the prices to add up to 1; or

   - $\lambda = 1/\sqrt{\sum_{l \in \mathcal{L}} p_l^2}$ to normalize the sum of the squares of all prices to add up to 1.

Proof. To show part 1, suppose, by contradiction, that some good is priced at zero at a Walrasian equilibrium. Then, by u-monotonicity, each agent would wish to consume an arbitrarily large amount of this good, and, so, the market clearing condition will fail, in contradiction to equilibrium.

To show part 2, note that u-monotonicity implies that, at any price vector $p \gg 0$, each agent i optimally spends his entire budget. That is, his budget constraint holds as equality: $p \cdot x^i(p) = p \cdot e^i$. Adding up the agents' budget constraints and rearranging gives $p \cdot z(p) = 0$.

To show part 3, note that the agent's problem in (1.2) is unchanged if the price vector is scaled by any positive number. As a result, each agent i's demand function x^i is homogeneous of degree zero in prices. Then, z is also homogeneous of degree zero in prices.

To show part 4, let p be a Walrasian equilibrium price. Because z is homogeneous of degree zero, $z(p) = 0$ implies $z(\lambda p) = 0$ for all $\lambda > 0$, and, so, λp, too, is a Walrasian equilibrium price. ∎

At first glance, the number of equations and unknowns in (1.4) is the same and equals the number of goods, L. This equality is a heuristic indication that a solution might exist. By part 4 of lemma 1.1, however, one can rescale the prices by setting the price of an arbitrary good equal to 1. In this case, we have L equations but now only $L - 1$ unknowns. Should one then expect equilibrium nonexistence? Not so fast.

To regain the reassurance of the same number of equations and unknowns, we shall deduce that system (1.4) is really $L - 1$ equations, not L. That is, one equation is redundant, implied by the remaining $L - 1$ equations. Let us argue that the market clearing condition for one of the goods—say, good L—can be taken to be redundant.

By part 4 of lemma 1.1, we can look for equilibrium prices among the price vectors with $p_L = 1$. Suppose that we have identified a price vector p with $p_L = 1$ at which markets clear for goods $1, 2, ..., L - 1$: $z_l(p) = 0$ for all $l = 1, 2, ..., L - 1$. Substituting the price normalization, Walras's law (part 2 of lemma 1.1) reads

$$\sum_{l=1}^{L-1} p_l z_l(p) + z_L(p) = 0,$$

and, so, implies the market clearing condition for good L: $z_L(p) = 0$. That is, one (any one) of the equations in (1.4) is redundant. So, we have $L - 1$ equations and $L - 1$ unknowns, which is promising for existence. This is as far as one can get by counting equations and unknowns.

The breakthrough came in 1951, when, in his dissertation, Nash (1951) used a fixed-point theorem to prove the existence of a Nash equilibrium in games. Shortly thereafter, Arrow and Debreu (1954) built on Nash's idea (at first, independently) to prove the existence of a Walrasian equilibrium. McKenzie (1954), too, proved such existence, independently of Arrow and Debreu (and in a different model) and unaware of Nash's work. Theorem 1.3 captures the essence of their findings.

Theorem 1.3 (Existence of Walrasian Equilibrium). *If an economy $\mathcal{E}$ satisfies u-continuity, u-monotonicity, and u-concavity, then a Walrasian equilibrium exists.*

Proof Sketch. See section 1.13. ∎

The assumptions in theorem 1.3 are unnecessarily strong. Even so, the proof is technical and lacks an immediate economic interpretation. Its most interesting bit—the invocation of a fixed-point theorem—is highlighted in section 1.13, which still suppresses some detail. The remainder of this section sketches a graphical existence argument for the special case of two goods. This argument has a transparent economic interpretation and introduces a tool for analyzing further properties of equilibria. Instead of invoking a fixed-point theorem, the argument invokes the **Intermediate Value Theorem**, which says that if a continuous function defined on an interval takes any two values, then it also takes all values in between. (This fact is easy to visualize.)

To begin with, it is useful to establish additional properties of the aggregate excess demand functions under the assumptions of theorem 1.3. First of all, the aggregate excess demand function is indeed a function, not a correspondence (i.e., it is a singleton-valued function, not a set-valued one). Indeed, by u-concavity, the solution to each agent i's utility-maximization problem is unique; his demand function is singleton-valued. As a result, the aggregate excess demand, too, is singleton-valued.

Further, in a two-good economy, we can focus on the aggregate excess demand function for, say, good 1 and forget the other good. Indeed, by part 4 of lemma 1.1, we can set $p_2 = 1$ and reduce the search for equilibrium to the search for a price p_1 (positive, by part 1 of lemma 1.1) that clears the market for good 1: $z_1(p_1, 1) = 0$. Walras's law (part 2 of lemma 1.1) and $z_1(p_1, 1) = 0$ will automatically imply market clearing for good 2: $z_2(p_1, 1) = 0$.

To apply the Intermediate Value Theorem to $z_1(\cdot, 1)$, we show, in lemma 1.2, that $z_1(\cdot, 1)$ is continuous, positive for sufficiently small prices and negative for sufficiently large ones.[20] Though the statement is intuitive, the lemma's proof is technical, and, so, we shall content ourselves with a proof sketch.

Lemma 1.2. *Let $L = 2$. Normalize $p_2 = 1$. Suppose u-continuity, u-monotonicity, and u-concavity hold. Then,*

1. *$z_1(\cdot, 1)$ is continuous on $\mathbb{R}_{++}$;*

2. *$\lim_{p_1 \to 0} z_1(p_1, 1) = \infty$;*

3. *$\lim_{p_1 \to \infty} z_1(p_1, 1) < 0$.*

Proof Sketch. Part 1 follows by applying the Theorem of the Maximum to each agent's utility-maximization problem in (1.2). The version of the **Theorem of the Maximum** that we invoke says that if the maximand, u^i, is continuous in bundle x^i (by u-continuity), if the maximizer, $x^i(p)$, is single-valued for each price vector p (by u-concavity), and if the budget set, $\mathcal{B}^i(p)$, is bounded (by $p \gg 0$), closed (the inequality in the budget constraint in $\mathcal{B}^i(p)$ is weak), and continuous in an appropriate sense in p for $p \gg 0$, then the maximizer, $x^i(p)$, is continuous in p. In particular, $x_1^i(p_1, 1)$ is continuous in p_1, and so is $z_1(p_1, 1) \equiv \sum_{i \in \mathcal{I}} x_1^i(p_1, 1) - \bar{e}_1$. Assumption u-continuity is necessary to guarantee the existence of a utility-maximizing bundle. Assumption u-concavity guarantees that such a bundle is unique and changes smoothly in prices.

For part 2, take any agent who is endowed with a positive amount of good 2 and call him "agent i." Because $p_2 = 1$, his wealth is not going to zero as $p_1 \to 0$. Define the limit bundle $x^* \equiv \lim_{p_1^n \to 0} x^i(p_1^n, 1)$, where the sequence $\{p_1^n\}$ is positive.[21] Suppose, by contradiction, that component x_1^* of the limit bundle $x^* \equiv (x_1^*, x_2^*)$ is finite. Because, by definition, each demand $x^i(p_1^n, 1)$ is affordable at p_1^n, so must be the limit bundle x^* at the limit price $p_1 = 0$. Even though affordable, bundle

---

20. Notation $z_1(\cdot, 1)$ converts z_1 into a function of its first argument, p_1, with the second argument, p_2, fixed at 1.

21. By assuming the existence of the limit, we gloss over some technical detail.

x^* is suboptimal at the limit price $p_1 = 0$ because, say, bundle $\hat{x} \equiv x^* + (1, 0)$ is both affordable at that price and is preferred to x^* (by u-monotonicity):

$$u^i(\hat{x}) > u^i(x^*) \quad \text{and} \quad (0, 1) \cdot \hat{x} \leq (0, 1) \cdot e^i.$$

By u-continuity, one can find a $\lambda \in (0, 1)$ such that

$$u^i(\lambda \hat{x}) > u^i(x^*) \quad \text{and} \quad (0, 1) \cdot \lambda \hat{x} < (0, 1) \cdot e^i.$$

Again, by u-continuity and because $x^i(p_1^n, 1) \to x^*$ as $p_1^n \to 0$, one can find a sufficiently large n such that

$$u^i(\lambda \hat{x}) > u^i\left(x^i(p_1^n, 1)\right) \quad \text{and} \quad (p_1^n, 1) \cdot \lambda \hat{x} < (p_1^n, 1) \cdot e^i,$$

implying that demand $x^i(p_1^n, 1)$ is suboptimal at price p_1^n, which is a contradiction. The contradiction hypothesis that x_1^* is finite must be false.

For part 3, take any agent who is endowed with a positive amount of good 1. Because only relative prices matter,

$$\lim_{p_1 \to \infty} z_1(p_1, 1) = \lim_{p_2 \to 0} z_1(1, p_2).$$

By noting that the argument in part 2 is symmetric with respect to the two goods, conclude that $\lim_{p_2 \to 0} z_2(1, p_2) = \infty$. Then, by Walras's law, as $p_2 \to 0$,

$$z_1(1, p_2) + \underbrace{p_2}_{\to 0} \underbrace{z_2(1, p_2)}_{\to \infty} = 0 \quad \Longrightarrow \quad z_1(1, p_2) < 0,$$

or, equivalently, $\lim_{p_1 \to \infty} z_1(p_1, 1) < 0$. ∎

Figure 1.8(a) illustrates the role that u-concavity plays in ensuring that each agent's demand function—and, hence, the aggregate excess demand—is continuous. When u-concavity fails, and upper-contour sets are not guaranteed to be convex, the agent's demand can jump in response to a small change in relative prices; the conclusion of part 1 of lemma 1.2 can fail. Figure 1.8(b) illustrates that part 2 of the lemma does not say that, as a good becomes cheaper, an agent demands more of the good. Instead, the claim is that only eventually, as the price of the good becomes sufficiently cheap, the agent starts demanding an arbitrarily large amount of it.

We can now prove theorem 1.3 for the special case of $L = 2$. As has been noted, to solve (1.4), one must find a p_1 such that $z_1(p_1, 1) = 0$. Figure 1.9 plots a $z_1(\cdot, 1)$ that satisfies the properties listed in lemma 1.2. Because it is positive for a small p_1, negative for a large p_1, and continuous, $z_1(\cdot, 1)$ must intersect zero at least once,

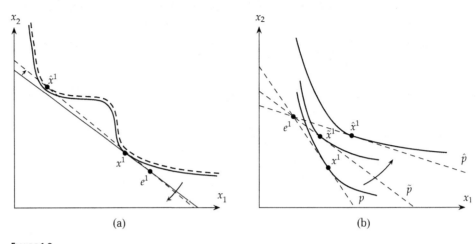

FIGURE 1.8.

An agent's responses to price changes illustrate the logic behind lemma 1.2.

(a) The agent's upper-contour sets are not convex. As a result, a small change in relative prices (from the solid to the dashed budget lines) leads to a large change in demand (from x^1 to $\hat{x}^1$).

(b) The demand for a good may be nonmonotone in its price. As the budget line pivots counterclockwise—from p, to $\tilde{p}$, to $\hat{p}$—about the agent's endowment e^1, good 1 becomes relatively cheaper. In response, the agent first consumes less of good 1 (as he switches from bundle x^1 to $\tilde{x}^1$) but eventually consumes more of that good (bundle $\hat{x}^1$).

maybe several times. The necessity of the intersection is apparent graphically and follows formally from the Intermediate Value Theorem. Thus, at least one Walrasian equilibrium price vector exists.

NONEXISTENCE

What if no Walrasian equilibrium exists? In practice, in the situations that the Walrasian model is designed to capture, something surely happens whatever the characteristics of the economy. Once the researcher revisits the room with a dozen traders, one shall observe some outcome of their exchange. So, in theory, too, one must seek a prediction, a notion of equilibrium, that would exist under broad conditions. Danilov and Sotskov (1990) summarize this philosophy:

> The leading idea was expressed by Hilbert (1904): "Every problem in the calculus of variation has a solution provided the word 'solution' is suitably understood." In the economic context this means that economic equilibrium always exists provided that it is suitably understood. Young (1969) adds: "What this statement means is that existence theorems do not require the machinery of proofs as much as proper definitions."

For example, one way to extend Walrasian equilibrium to cover some instances of equilibrium nonexistence is not to insist on market clearing and instead to minimize

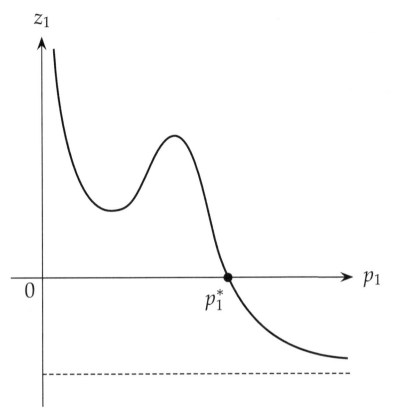

FIGURE 1.9.
Existence of Walrasian equilibrium price vector $(p_1^*, 1)$ for the case of two goods. The value of the aggregate excess demand z_1 is zero at every equilibrium price p_1, with $p_2 = 1$ being the normalization.

the imbalances across all markets. Thus, assuming again that all excess demands are functions, a price vector is an **approximate-Walrasian-equilibrium** price if it minimizes some measure of overall excess demand:

$$\inf_{p \in \mathbb{R}_+^L} \sum_{l \in \mathcal{L}} z_l(p)^2. \tag{1.5}$$

This newly defined equilibrium concept coincides with Walrasian equilibrium whenever the latter exists. Whenever the latter does not exist, approximate Walrasian equilibrium requires some rationing, wastage, or both.

An alternative way to operationalize an approximate Walrasian equilibrium is to retain exact market clearing but weaken utility maximization. For instance, a price-allocation pair can be called approximate-equilibrium if markets clear, and no agent sacrifices more than ε units of utility by choosing the bundle prescribed

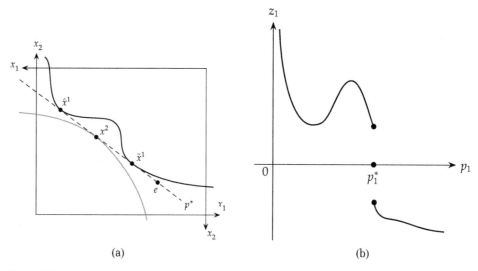

FIGURE 1.10.

An Edgeworth box economy with one or two copies of each agent type. Walrasian equilibrium at price vector $p^* = (p_1^*, 1)$ exists with two copies but not with one.

(a) With one agent of each type, p^* is not a Walrasian-equilibrium price. At p^*, agent 2 chooses x^2, whereas agent 1 chooses either $\hat{x}^1$ or $\tilde{x}^1$; in either case, markets do not clear. With two agents of each type, p^* is an equilibrium price. At p^*, each copy of agent 2 chooses bundle x^2; one copy of agent 1, while indifferent, chooses $\hat{x}^1$, whereas the other copy, also indifferent, chooses $\tilde{x}^1$. Markets clear: $(\hat{x}^1 + \tilde{x}^1)/2 + x^2 = \bar{e}$.

(b) The aggregate excess demand function (set-valued at p_1^*) for good 1 in an economy with two types of each agent. The function "jumps" at p_1^* because u-concavity fails. If, at p_1^*, both copies of agent 1 either choose bundle $\tilde{x}^1$ or choose bundle $\hat{x}^1$ (not shown), then the value of the aggregate excess demand is either positive or negative, respectively. If each copy of agent 1 chooses a distinct bundle, then the aggregate excess demand is zero, and p_1^* is an equilibrium price.

to him by the allocation instead of his optimal bundle. If one insists on treating utility as ordinal, then one can alternatively define an approximate-equilibrium price-allocation pair by requiring that no agent overpay more than ε units of, say, good 1 to obtain the utility induced by consuming the bundle prescribed by that allocation. Then, one can seek a price that minimizes the value of ε for which an approximate equilibrium as described in this paragraph exists. If such an ε is zero, then the approximate equilibrium is an (exact) Walrasian equilibrium.

Walrasian nonexistence problem is alleviated when agents are numerous. We illustrate this point in an Edgeworth box economy that violates u-concavity. In that economy, a disequilibrium price becomes an equilibrium price if one increases the number of agents.

Figure 1.10 illustrates the construction. When upper contour sets are nonconvex, situations such as the one depicted in figure 1.10(a) may arise. At a given price, agent 1 is indifferent between two bundles, consuming neither of which would clear the markets. However, consuming the average of these two bundles would. Consuming the average bundle, of course, is suboptimal for agent 1. What one can do, though, is to clone both agents and instruct half of type-1 agents (the clones of the original agent 1) to choose one bundle and instruct the other half to choose the other bundle. All type-2 clones would consume the same bundle, which is uniquely optimal for them. As a result, the markets would clear.[22] Figure 1.10(b) illustrates the argument in terms of the aggregate excess demand function for good 1.

More generally, if, at some price, the market clearing bundle for some agent is a weighted average (with rational weights) of two bundles between which he is indifferent at that price, then one can keep cloning the agents until the desired weights are attained by instructing an appropriate fraction of the indifferent clones to choose the intended bundle. Furthermore, one can dispose of the instructions on how to break the indifference if the cloning technology is imperfect, so that each cloned agent has a tiny preference in favor of either bundle. Then, tiny price adjustments can make the intended fraction of the clones choose the intended bundle.

1.10 UNIQUENESS, STABILITY, AND COMPARATIVE STATICS

We have shown that, under somewhat general conditions, the set of Walrasian equilibrium allocations is nonempty and refines the contract set. We now discuss three questions, which are broadly concerned with how suitable a refinement the Walrasian equilibrium is.

1. How many Walrasian equilibria are there?

2. Would a reasonable dynamic adjustment process converge to a Walrasian equilibrium? If so, which process and to which equilibrium?

3. How do changes in the economy's primitives change equilibria? Do they do so in an "intuitive" way?

In answering these questions, we assume that all aggregate excess demand functions are continuous, singleton-valued, and satisfy Walras's law, and that equilibrium prices are positive.

GLOBAL UNIQUENESS
The Edgeworth box in figure 1.4(a) illustrates that Walrasian equilibrium need not be (globally) unique. Figure 1.11 illustrates the same situation in the space of prices and aggregate excess demands; the aggregate excess demand function for good 1 has three zeros—at p'_1, at p''_1, and at p'''_1—each of which corresponds to a Walrasian

---

22. Figure 1.10(a) can be made more dramatic (but less typical) by moving the endowment point e to coincide with point x^2. In this case, the contrapositive to the formulation of the SWT in theorem 1.2 will imply that no price (not just p^*) clears the markets.

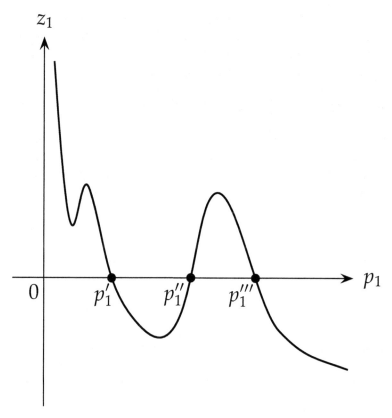

FIGURE 1.11.
Multiple Walrasian equilibria exist, at prices $(p_1', 1)$, $(p_1'', 1)$, and $(p_1''', 1)$.

equilibrium. Even though multiple equilibria need not always arise, they cannot be dismissed as nongeneric.

LOCAL UNIQUENESS

Even if there are multiple Walrasian equilibria, it may still be the case that each of them is **locally unique** in the sense that there is no other (normalized) Walrasian equilibrium price vector within a small enough neighborhood of the original equilibrium price vector. Local uniqueness of equilibrium prices implies local uniqueness of equilibrium allocations (under the maintained assumption that individual demands are singleton-valued).

It turns out that, in "well-behaved" economies (roughly speaking, when excess demand functions are smooth), generically, Walrasian equilibria are locally unique, and, so, the number of equilibria is finite. To informally illustrate this idea in the two-good case of figure 1.12, normalize $p_2 = 1$ and look for the values of p_1 that satisfy $z_1(p_1, 1) = 0$. In figure 1.12(a), $z_1(p_1, 1)$ is zero on the interval of prices

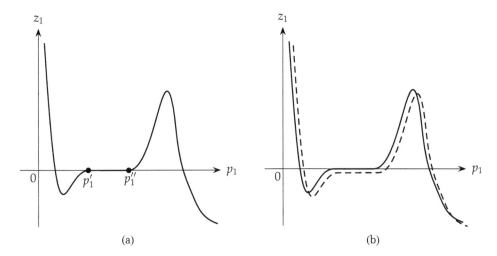

FIGURE 1.12.
The genericity of the local uniqueness of equilibria.
(a) Equilibria are locally nonunique. Any price vector $(p_1, 1)$ with $p_1 \in [p'_1, p''_1]$ is an equilibrium price vector.
(b) Perturbing slightly the excess demand function of figure 1.12(a) (from the solid curve to the dashed curve) eliminates the local nonuniqueness of equilibria.

$[p'_1, p''_1]$; there is a continuum of equilibria. In figure 1.12(b), a small perturbation of function $z_1(\cdot, 1)$, such as the one that might arise from a small change in endowments or utilities, restores a finite number of locally unique equilibria.

Figure 1.12 also suggest that, generically, there is an odd number of equilibria. Indeed, because $z_1(\cdot, 1)$ starts above zero and finishes below zero, generically, it must cross zero an odd number of times. This generic oddness of number can also be shown for more than two goods. Besides being a curious tidbit in itself, this oddness of number alerts the researcher who has discovered an even number of equilibria to the presence of at least one more equilibrium.

TÂTONNEMENT STABILITY

When asked to bet on a coin toss, it is wise to bet on either heads or tails, which can be viewed as stable equilibria of the physical system. It is unwise to bet that the coin would balance on its edge (an unstable equilibrium) or remain suspended in midair (not an equilibrium at all). Can it be that Walrasian equilibria, too, come in two kinds: stable and unstable? If so, the Walrasian prediction can be further refined, with unstable equilibria dismissed and stable ones gaining stronger justification.

The problem with discussing the stability of a Walrasian equilibrium is that the Walrasian equilibrium is an inherently static concept, defined without any reference to a dynamic adjustment process. By contrast, the equilibrium position of a tossed coin can be ascertained by perturbing the coin a little and then checking whether physical forces help or hinder the coin regain its original position. There is no analogue for the gravitational, frictional, and normal forces in the Walrasian model. Walrasian equilibrium is not defined as a rest point of a dynamic system.

To operationalize the notion of stability in the Walrasian model, we introduce an ad hoc dynamic system whose rest points coincide with the Walrasian equilibria of the corresponding exchange economy. Ad hoc "market forces" will play the part of physical forces. These market forces commonly go by the name of the law of supply and demand. One may hear: "If oil becomes scarce relative to other goods, the law of supply and demand implies that the price of oil will tend to rise." It is this "tend to rise" assertion that we postulate as market forces. (We shall see that "tend to rise" need not be the same as "will eventually rise.")

The ad hoc dynamic price-adjustment process, suggested by Léon Walras, is called **tâtonnement**. According to this process, agents meet in a public square. A fictional oracle called the **Walrasian auctioneer** announces a price vector. After he does so, every agent calls out (truthfully, we assume) his demand at those prices. Instead of attempting to execute trades at the announced prices, however, the auctioneer adjusts the prices according to some rule (which embodies "market forces") and announces a new price vector. The process continues until the price vector is called out at which the aggregate demand coincides with, or at least is sufficiently close to, the aggregate supply. At this point, the auctioneer stops, announces the final price vector, and trade occurs at this price vector.

In practice, of course, markets do not operate like this. (Oskar Lange envisioned that this is how the government would set prices in market socialism.) Therefore, a leap of faith is required of the reader to suppose that the described tâtonnement process has descriptive relevance. What is required of the researcher is to test the empirical validity of this leap of faith (a task to which we shall return).

To operationalize the workings of the Walrasian auctioneer, it is convenient to model tâtonnement in continuous time, indexed by $t \geq 0$. The initial announced price vector, denoted by $p(0)$, is arbitrary, and the time-t price vector is denoted by $p(t)$. The price-adjustment rule is governed by the system of L differential equations

$$\frac{\mathrm{d}p(t)}{\mathrm{d}t} = z(p(t)), \quad t \geq 0. \tag{1.6}$$

This system requires the auctioneer to raise the price for each good whose aggregate excess demand is positive and to lower the price for each good whose aggregate excess demand is negative. This rule—an assumption, in no way an implication of the Walrasian equilibrium—formalizes the equilibrating force implicit in the proverbial **law of supply and demand**. The stationary points of the rule in (1.6) are all prices p at which $z(p) = 0$. These are the Walrasian equilibrium prices.

An equilibrium price vector p is said to be **locally stable** if, under tâtonnement, prices converge to p from anywhere in a sufficiently small neighborhood of p. If an equilibrium is not locally stable, it is said to be **locally unstable**. A unique

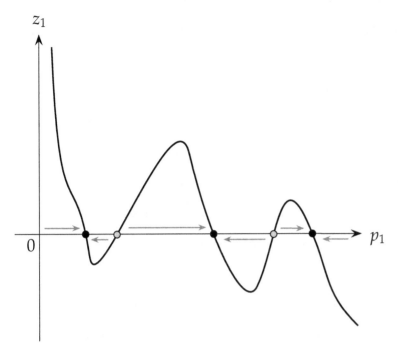

FIGURE 1.13.
In the underlying two-good economy, the extreme and the middle Walrasian equilibria (solid dots) are locally stable, as is indicated by the arrows, which point in the direction of the tâtonnement price change. The remaining two equilibria (shaded dots) are not locally stable.

equilibrium price vector p is said to be **globally stable** if, under tâtonnement, prices converge to p from any initial price vector $p(0)$.[23]

Figure 1.13 illustrates three locally stable and two locally unstable equilibria in a two-good economy. The figure uses the fact that, with two goods, the stability conclusions are unchanged if tâtonnement in (1.6) is replaced by a version that normalizes the price of good 2 to $p_2 = 1$ and sets $dp_1(t)/dt = z_1(p_1(t), 1)$.[24] As a result, stability can be read off the figure.

23. Defined analogously in the model of a coin toss, local stability would claim heads and tails, and local instability would claim being perched on the edge. Neither heads nor tails would be globally stable; if sufficiently perturbed away from heads, the coin may never revert to heads and would instead settle on tails.

24. Indeed, with two goods, only the evolution of the relative price matters. Tâtonnement in (1.6) implies

$$\frac{d}{dt}\left(\frac{p_1(t)}{p_2(t)}\right) = z_1(p(t))\left(\frac{1}{p_2(t)} + \frac{p_1(t)^2}{p_2(t)^3}\right),$$

where use has been made of Walras's law. Thus, the direction of the change in the relative price $p_1(t)/p_2(t)$ is given by the sign of $z_1(p(t))$. Because, for the question of stability, the exact rate of the change in the relative price is irrelevant, one can normalize $p_2 = 1$ and set $dp_1(t)/dt = z_1(p_1(t), 1)$.

Even though intuitive, Walrasian tâtonnement has its limitations:

1. If agents reasoned strategically, they would not find it in their interest to announce their true demands to the Walrasian auctioneer. Instead, each agent would seek to exploit tâtonnement so as to nudge equilibrium prices in his favor. (For instance, an agent might understate his demand for a good, so that the auctioneer would lower that good's price.) This criticism echoes the criticism of the price-taking, or competitive, assumption in the definition of the Walrasian equilibrium.

2. Scarf (1960) provides examples with more than two goods in which tâtonnement cycles and never converges to the unique Walrasian equilibrium. (The tossed coin remains suspended in the air, as it were.) In one such example (problem 1.4), unless one begins at the equilibrium price, tâtonnement prices orbit as in figure 1.14.

Limitation 1 above suggests that not only tâtonnement, but any attempt to construct an equilibration process may be an ill-defined project. To illustrate, suppose that, in their interactions with the auctioneer, we model agents as strategic. In this case, the equilibration process itself becomes an equilibrium object, an outcome of a dynamic strategic interaction. In pursuit of deeper understanding of equilibration, one may further ask: How should one model the convergence to the strategic equilibrium of the equilibration process for the Walrasian equilibrium? The answer, presumably, would lead to a strategic equilibration process for the strategic equilibration process for the Walrasian equilibrium. And so on, ad infinitum. As a result, the modern approach (e.g., in macroeconomics) is to model a dynamic equilibrium in a model of a dynamic economy, which evolves over time, and to refrain from posing questions about the equilibration process.

Limitation 2 may suggest discarding tâtonnement because it may fail to deliver convergence to any equilibrium. This attitude is appropriate for someone who has the same confidence in the infallibility of the Walrasian equilibrium as he does in the event that a tossed coin drops instead of remaining suspended in the air. Absent this confidence, tâtonnement's failure to converge may be a feature, not a bug—a criticism of Walrasian equilibrium, not of tâtonnement. If an equilibrium is impossible to approach by means of a natural—albeit ad hoc—adjustment process, why should one expect this equilibrium to prevail? Indeed, tâtonnement could be a starting point for constructing an alternative equilibrium prediction, especially in the cases in which no Walrasian equilibrium exists. Nevertheless, economics has evolved to give precedence to equilibrium concepts over ad hoc heuristics; limitation 2 is typically construed as a blow to the ad hoc tâtonnement, not to the Walrasian equilibrium.

A further blow to tâtonnement comes from the discovery that examples of instability such as Scarf's can be constructed when and only when the number

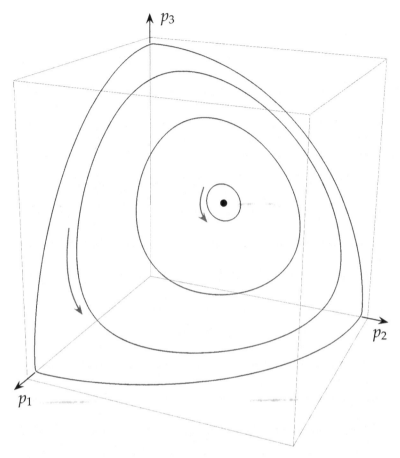

FIGURE 1.14.
An economy with three goods and three agents in which Walrasian tâtonnement fails to converge to the unique equilibrium price (denoted by the dot at the center). Normalized to lie on a sphere, the tâtonnement prices orbit the equilibrium price counterclockwise (problem 1.4).

of goods is odd. This fragility of the construction with respect to the parity of the number of goods—the parity having no economic content whatsoever—can be construed as a weakness of tâtonnement. This adverse interpretation is warranted, however, only if one has good reason to believe that the price dynamics in real-world economies ought to be independent of seemingly trivial aspects of the economy. There are examples in physics (e.g., the double-rod pendulum) and biology (e.g., population growth) in which dynamics are sensitive to small changes in the initial conditions—the fragility similar in spirit to the sensitivity of price-adjustment dynamics to the parity of the number of goods.

Even if one doubts the plausibility of tâtonnement as the process that captures the spirit of what unravels behind the scenes and delivers a Walrasian equilibrium, one can still contemplate tâtonnement as a mechanism for computing equilibria. In such a **Walrasian tâtonnement mechanism**, each agent would report his excess demand at the price announced by the auctioneer until tâtonnement converges, whereupon the auctioneer reallocates the goods so that each agent consumes his Walrasian equilibrium bundle. Such a mechanism has inspired auction formats that have been used in practice, such as the simultaneous ascending auction analyzed by Milgrom (2000).

If, instead of a decentralized unfettered exchange, one can resort to a centralized mechanism to arrive at a Walrasian equilibrium, then why take the roundabout route of tâtonnement? In the **direct Walrasian mechanism**, each agent reports his entire excess demand function, whereupon the mechanism immediately computes a Walrasian allocation. Financial exchanges that are driven by the limit-order book resemble the direct Walrasian mechanism because a sequence of limit orders submitted by a trader can be constructed to approximate an excess demand function that he may wish to report. (A **limit order** is an order to buy or sell a security at a specified price or better.)

A relative disadvantage of the direct Walrasian mechanism is that excess demand *functions* are infinitely-dimensional objects, whose communication may be costlier than the communication of finitely many excess demand *values* in the Walrasian tâtonnement mechanism. Both mechanisms are deficient in that agents may strategically misreport their true excess demands. As a result, the mechanisms' outcomes may not be Walrasian equilibria with respect to the agents' true utilities and true endowments.

UNIQUENESS AND STABILITY WITH GROSS SUBSTITUTES

One response to the tâtonnement cycles in figure 1.14 and their seemingly arbitrary dependence on the parity of the number of goods is to look the other way. Doing so is appropriate if such tâtonnement indignity occurs only on the periphery of the modeling universe and, so, is irrelevant for practical applications. That, in turn, depends on how much of the modeling universe one is willing to consign to the periphery. In particular, if one is content not to venture beyond so-called gross substitutes economies, then one can breathe the pure oxygen of a unique equilibrium, convergent tâtonnement, and the intuitive response of equilibrium objects to changes in the economy's parameters (as will be illustrated).

Goods k and $l \neq k$ are said to be gross substitutes if two conditions hold: an increase in the price of good k increases the demand for good l, and an increase in the price of good l increases the demand for good k. Being explicit about the symmetry of the two goods in the definition is essential; one can conceive of examples in which the demand for good l increases in the price of good k, but the demand for good k does not increase in the price of good l.[25] It is also essential that the demand respond as described in the definition to all price changes and at all prices, not just locally.

The entire demand function is said to satisfy the gross substitutes property if any two goods are gross substitutes. We highlight the definition of gross substitutes for the aggregate excess demand function, for it is the definition invoked in the subsequent equilibrium analysis:

Definition 1.2. For a given endowment e, the aggregate excess demand function z satisfies the **gross substitutes** property if, for any good k and any two price vectors p and p', $p'_k > p_k$ and $p'_{-k} = p_{-k}$ imply $z_l(p') > z_l(p)$ for all $l \neq k$.[26]

To see why the property in definition 1.2 is called "substitutes," one needs to appreciate that the gross substitutes property implies that each good's aggregate excess demand is decreasing in that good's own price. This is seen using the function z's homogeneity of degree zero (part 3 of lemma 1.1), which, when $p_l > 0$, implies $z_l(p_l, p_{-l}) = z_l(1, p_{-l}/p_l)$. As a result, increasing p_l while holding the remaining prices fixed has the same effect on z_l as does holding p_l fixed and reducing all other goods' prices. By the gross substitutes property, as other goods' prices decrease one by one, z_l decreases at each step.

To summarize, when the gross substitutes property holds, as the price of one good rises, the demand for it falls, whereas the demand for an arbitrary other good increases. That is, the demands for the two goods move in opposite directions, which is the kind of behavior one would normally associate with the idea that the goods are substitutes.

With this interpretation, it becomes apparent that the gross substitutes property is quite restrictive. While one can conceive of goods that are substitutes (e.g., a night at the opera and a night at the ballet), one can equally well conceive of goods that are not (e.g., a gym membership and workout attire). The profit of this restrictive assumption is the uniqueness result:

Theorem 1.4. *If the aggregate excess demand function z satisfies gross substitutes and u-monotonicity holds, then the economy has at most one Walrasian equilibrium—that is, $z(p) = 0$ has at most one (normalized) solution.*

---

25. For example, Bob works at a bank and must wear a suit. If the price of jeans rises, then Bob buys more suit trousers and also wears them casually. However, if the price of suit trousers rises instead, then Bob buys fewer jeans because he is now poorer; he spends more on suit trousers, which he needs for work.

26. Notation $p'_{-k} = p_{-k}$ means $p'_l = p_l$ for all $l \neq k$.

Proof. By way of contradiction, suppose that $z(p) = z(p') = 0$ for two price vectors p and p' that are not collinear.[27] By the homogeneity of degree zero of z (part 3 of lemma 1.1) and by u-monotonicity (which implies $p \gg 0$ and $p' \gg 0$), we can normalize the two price vectors so that $p'_l \geq p_l$ for all l and $p'_k = p_k$ for some k. Then, we can move from p to p' in $L-1$ steps, at each of which we weakly increase the price of one of $l \neq k$ goods from p_l to p'_l. At each step at which a price increases strictly (and there must be at least one such step because p' is not collinear to p), the aggregate demand for good k must increase, implying $z_k(p') > z_k(p) = 0$, which is a contradiction. ∎

Theorem 1.5 shows that if the gross substitutes property holds, Walrasian tâtonnement converges to the unique equilibrium. The proof relies on the following lemma, which says that any aggregate bundle that is chosen by the agents at a disequilibrium price is not affordable to the agents at the equilibrium price.

Lemma 1.3. *Suppose that the aggregate excess demand function z satisfies gross substitutes, that p^* is an equilibrium price, and that u-monotonicity holds. Then, for any price p that is not collinear to p^*, $p^* \cdot z(p) > 0$.*

Proof Sketch. We shall only prove the case of $L = 2$.
Normalize the price of good 2: $p_2^* = p_2 = 1$. Then,

$$
\begin{aligned}
p^* \cdot z(p) &= (p^* - p) \cdot z(p) \\
&= (p^* - p) \cdot z(p) - (p^* - p) \cdot z(p^*) \\
&= (p^* - p) \cdot \big(z(p) - z(p^*)\big) \\
&= \big(p_1^* - p_1\big)\big(z_1(p) - z_1(p^*)\big) > 0,
\end{aligned}
$$

where the first equality uses Walras's law (i.e., $p \cdot z(p) = 0$, by u-monotonicity), the second equality uses the fact that p^* is an equilibrium price (i.e., $z(p^*) = 0$), the third equality rearranges, and the final equality uses the price normalization $p_2^* = p_2 = 1$. The inequality follows by the gross substitutes property: if $p_1 > p_1^*$, then $z_1(p) < z_1(p^*)$, and if $p_1 < p_1^*$, then $z_1(p) > z_1(p^*)$. ∎

To prove the tâtonnement convergence, it is convenient to normalize the prices to lie on the $(L-1)$-dimensional sphere

$$
P^S \equiv \left\{ p \in \mathbb{R}^L \mid \sum_{l \in \mathcal{L}} p_l^2 = 1 \right\}.
$$

---

27. Positive price vectors p and p' are **collinear** if one is a scalar multiple of the other—that is, $p' = \lambda p$ for some $\lambda > 0$.

This normalization has the property that if the initial price vector $p(0)$ is in P^S, then, in the course of tâtonnement, the price vector $p(t)$ remains in P^S:

$$\frac{d}{dt} \sum_{l \in \mathcal{L}} p_l(t)^2 = 2p(t) \cdot z(p(t)) = 0,$$

where the first equality is by the specification of tâtonnement in (1.6), and the second equality is by Walras's law.

Theorem 1.5. *Suppose that the aggregate excess demand function z satisfies gross substitutes, that u-monotonicity holds, and that p^* in P^S is a Walrasian equilibrium price vector. Then, for any initial price vector $p(0) \gg 0$ in P^S, the price path $\{p(t) | t \geq 0\}$ generated by the tâtonnement adjustment rule*

$$\frac{dp(t)}{dt} = z(p(t))$$

converges to p^* as $t \rightarrow \infty$.

Proof. We shall show that the distance between $p(t)$ and p^* vanishes as time goes by. Let $D(p) \equiv \sum_{l \in \mathcal{L}} (p_l - p_l^*)^2/2$ denote the distance between vectors p and p^*. Then,

$$\frac{dD(p(t))}{dt} = (p(t) - p^*) \cdot \frac{dp(t)}{dt}$$
$$= (p(t) - p^*) \cdot z(p(t))$$
$$= -p^* \cdot z(p(t)) \leq 0,$$

where the third equality uses Walras's law, and the inequality, which follows from lemma 1.3, is strict unless $p = p^*$. Because the distance $D(p(t))$ is weakly decreasing in t for all $t \geq 0$ and is bounded below by zero, $D(p(t))$ must converge, either to zero or to some positive number. In the former case, $p(t) \rightarrow p^*$. In the latter case, $p(t) \rightarrow p \neq p^*$ for some p in P^S, which, by lemma 1.3, implies $\lim_{t \rightarrow \infty} dD(p(t))/dt = dD(p)/dt < 0$, thereby contradicting the convergence of $D(p(t))$. Hence, $p(t) \rightarrow p \neq p^*$ is impossible; $p(t) \rightarrow p^*$ is necessary. ∎

Theorem 1.5 is not a proof of equilibrium existence. The theorem's premise is that an equilibrium exists, and the convergence proof relies on this premise.

COMPARATIVE STATICS

Comparative statics is concerned with comparing equilibria as one varies the economy's parameters (e.g., endowments or utility functions). "Statics" emphasizes that what is being compared are "static" equilibria in alternative economies; the exercise has nothing to say about the dynamic adjustment path an economy would take in search of a new equilibrium if its parameters were altered. In particular, for an altered economy, equilibria are computed from the initial endowment, instead of taking an equilibrium allocation of the original economy as the new endowment point.

The question about how an equilibrium changes in response to a change in some parameter is delicate when equilibria are multiple. When the equilibria are locally unique (which is true generically), one can focus on a neighborhood of an equilibrium and assume that small parameter changes will keep the economy at the corresponding local equilibrium. The Walrasian model contains no justification for this assumption. This assumption's implicit logic is that if there is some systematic reason for why, say, the equilibrium with the cheapest good 1 must prevail in the original economy, then the equilibrium with the cheapest good 1 may also prevail in the perturbed economy. (Perhaps, the agents who happen to consume a lot of good 1 also happen to be good at coordinating the economy on their preferred equilibrium.)

To illustrate, assume that there are two goods and normalize $p_2 = 1$. Assume also that, for agent 1, good 1 is a **normal good**, meaning that, as the agent's wealth rises, his demand for this good rises. Consider an increase in agent 1's endowment of the other good, good 2. At any price p_1, his wealth will rise and so will his demand for good 1, a normal good. As a result, the aggregate excess demand for good 1 will also rise, say, from z_1 to $\hat{z}_1$ in figure 1.15(a). The figure illustrates the induced comparative statics in an economy with three equilibria, indexed by good-1's prices p'_1, p''_1, and p'''_1. The comparative statics for equilibria p'_1 and p'''_1 are intuitive; a rise in the aggregate endowment of good 2 causes its relative price to fall. The comparative statics for equilibrium p''_1 is counterintuitive; as good 2 becomes more plentiful, its relative price rises.

Can equilibrium p''_1 be somehow ruled out? Enter the **correspondence principle**: in two-good economies, equilibria that have counterintuitive comparative statics are also the ones that are locally unstable. Equilibrium p''_1 is locally unstable and, so, can be dismissed as unlikely.

Alternatively, one can adopt an agnostic stance and confine oneself to statements about the sets of equilibria, instead of individual equilibria. An economy may fail to jump to the closest equilibrium. Unstable equilibria may fail to unravel. In this case, we say that a set of equilibria increases if its smallest and its largest elements both increase. Then, in the economy of figure 1.15(a), the set of equilibrium prices for good 1 increases if good 2 becomes more plentiful. In two-good economies, comparative statics for sets tend to be intuitive because, generically, the smallest and the largest equilibria are stable and, so, have intuitive comparative statics.

With gross substitutes, comparative statics is no longer delicate. Equilibrium, if it exists, is unique, stable, and has intuitive comparative statics. In particular, in figure 1.15(b), any change that raises the excess demand for a good increases the equilibrium price of that good.

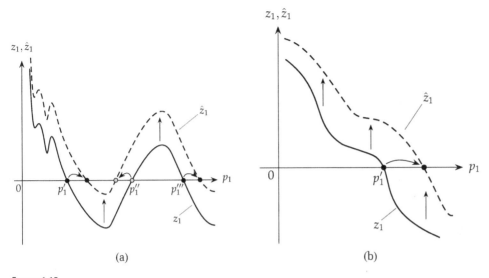

FIGURE 1.15.
Comparative statics in two-good economies. The aggregate excess demand for good 1 increases from z_1 (the solid curve) to $\hat{z}_1$ (the dashed curve). Equilibria are assumed to move in the direction indicated by the bent arrows.
(a) Stable equilibria (solid dots) have intuitive comparative statics, whereas the unstable one (the shaded dot) has counterintuitive comparative statics.
(b) With gross substitutes, equilibrium is unique, and comparative statics are intuitive.

1.11   TIME AND UNCERTAINTY

Among the many simplifications of the Walrasian model that we have studied so far are the restrictions to static and to deterministic economies. Upon reflection, however, these are not restrictions at all. To accommodate dynamics and uncertainty, it suffices to reinterpret the model.

A TRIVIAL REINTERPRETATION
Time is introduced by observing that ice cream today is not the same as ice cream tomorrow. It is not just the lifetime amount of ice cream consumed that matters; one's utility is affected by how ice cream consumption is distributed over time. Ice cream today and ice cream tomorrow are distinct goods. That is, we identify a good not just with its physical characteristics but also with its consumption date.

Uncertainty is handled similarly. Ice cream consumed when it is sunny and hot is not the same as ice cream consumed when it is rainy and cold. Thus, in addition to being described by its physical characteristics, a good is also described by a **state of the world**, which is a complete description of the date and the circumstances under which the good is consumed.

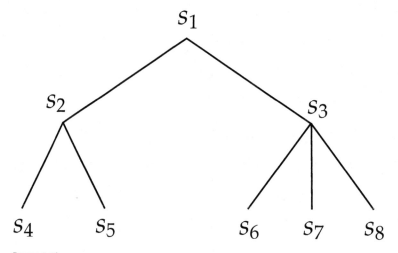

FIGURE 1.16.

An event tree. State s_1 occurs at time $t = 1$. Either s_2 or s_3 occurs at $t = 2$. At $t = 3$, s_2 is followed by s_4 or s_5, whereas s_3 is followed by s_6, s_7, or s_8.

Apart from reinterpreting goods, the Walrasian model requires no modification to accommodate time and uncertainty. One may—but need not—speak of impatience and of probability by specializing and appropriately interpreting the agents' utility functions. Even if one does, the agents need not be equally impatient or agree on probabilities.

Formally, to accommodate time and uncertainty, we introduce a state space $S \equiv \{s_1, s_2, \ldots, s_S\}$ of finite cardinality S. Each state s describes the time and circumstances of consumption or of endowment realization. An economy with L **basic goods** (i.e., ice cream or a Zumba® class) becomes an economy with LS **contingent goods**. At state s, agent i's endowment vector is denoted by $e^i(s) \in \mathbb{R}^L_+$ and his consumption bundle is denoted by $x^i(s) \in \mathbb{R}^L_+$. The agent's utility function is $u^i : \mathbb{R}^{LS}_+ \to \mathbb{R}$. All agents agree on S; that is, all agree on which states are possible.

Figure 1.16 depicts an event tree that illustrates a state space $S \equiv \{s_1, s_2, \ldots, s_8\}$. In the figure, s_1 is interpreted as the state at time $t = 1$ (i.e., there is no uncertainty about what happens at $t = 1$); s_2 and s_3 are the possible states at time $t = 2$; s_4 and s_5 are time $t = 3$ states that can follow time $t = 2$ state s_2; and s_6, s_7, and s_8 are time $t = 3$ states that can follow time $t = 2$ state s_3. The utility function of agent i is simply $u^i(x^i) = u^i(x^i(s_1), x^i(s_2), \ldots, x^i(s_8))$, where $x^i \equiv (x^i(s))_{s \in S}$.

The interpretation of the Walrasian equilibrium in this model is that all trade occurs at "time zero," before any uncertainty has been realized. No retrade can occur after that. If u-continuity, u-monotonicity, and u-concavity hold, then Walrasian equilibria exist and are Pareto efficient. The additional assumption of gross

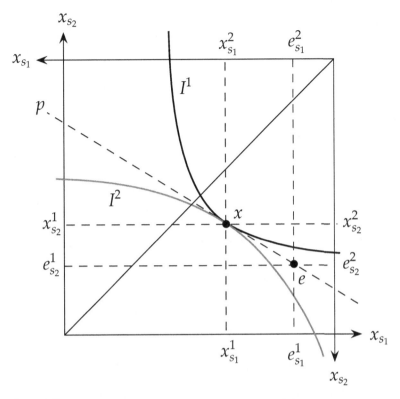

FIGURE 1.17.

An Edgeworth box economy reinterpreted. In the dynamic interpretation, s_1-contingent good is time $t = 1$ consumption, and s_2-contingent good is time $t = 2$ consumption. At $t = 1$, agent 1 lends amount $e^1_{s_1} - x^1_{s_1}$ to agent 2, who repays amount $e^2_{s_2} - x^2_{s_2}$ at time $t = 2$; the gross interest rate is the negative of the slope of the price line p. In the uncertainty interpretation, the s_1-contingent good is the consumption when agent 2 has an accident, whereas agent 1 does not, and the s_2-contingent good is the consumption when agent 1 has an accident, whereas agent 2 does not; the equilibrium allocation x reflects the outcome of the agents' trade in insurance contracts.

substitutes delivers equilibrium uniqueness and tâtonnement convergence. There is nothing new here, except for the interpretation.

AN EDGEWORTH BOX EXAMPLE

Let us consider the special case of two agents and two contingent goods that are derived from a single basic good: $I = 2$, $L = 1$, and $S = 2$. This case fits into an Edgeworth box, in figure 1.17. Agent i's state-s contingent consumption is denoted by x^i_s.[28] The state-contingent endowments are indexed analogously and, in this example, are assumed to satisfy $e^1_{s_1} + e^2_{s_1} = e^1_{s_2} + e^2_{s_2}$. This specification is agnostic about

---

28. Because there is just one basic good, the subscript is freed up to index consumption by state.

whether the states correspond to two calendar dates (the dynamic interpretation) or two mutually exclusive events (the uncertainty interpretation).

In the dynamic interpretation, $x_{s_1}^i$ is agent i's time $t=1$ consumption, and $x_{s_2}^i$ is his time $t=2$ consumption. At equilibrium allocation x, agent 1 lends amount $e_{s_1}^1 - x_{s_1}^1$ to agent 2 at time $t=1$; agent 2 repays amount $e_{s_2}^2 - x_{s_2}^2$ at time $t=2$. The **gross interest rate** is defined to be the relative price p_1/p_2, which, at equilibrium, equals $(e_{s_2}^2 - x_{s_2}^2)/(e_{s_1}^1 - x_{s_1}^1)$, as can be read off figure 1.17. The **net interest rate** is defined to be $p_1/p_2 - 1$ (multiply by 100 for percentage points).

The aggregate endowment is time-invariant: $e_{s_1}^1 + e_{s_1}^2 = e_{s_2}^1 + e_{s_2}^2$; that is, there is no growth (positive or negative). Hence, it is feasible for each agent to consume the same amount at both dates or, in other words, to **fully smooth consumption** over time. Nevertheless, the agents' preferences are such that, at equilibrium, each agent consumes more on the date when his endowment of the basic good is higher. Graphically, the equilibrium allocation x lies off the diagonal that connects the agents' origins in the Edgeworth box and toward the endowments. Consumption smoothing does not occur, for each agent enjoys consumption more when he is more "productive" (e.g., because this is when he is at his prime).

In the uncertainty interpretation, $x_{s_1}^i$ is agent i's consumption when agent 2 has an accident, whereas agent 1 does not; and $x_{s_2}^i$ is agent i's consumption when agent 1 has an accident, whereas agent 2 does not. Thus, the agents' accidents are perfectly negatively correlated. (The accident interpretation is motivated by the assumptions that $e_{s_2}^1 < e_{s_1}^1$ and $e_{s_1}^2 < e_{s_2}^2$.) The equilibrium allocation x reflects the outcome of the agents' trade in insurance contracts. In particular, agent 1 promises to transfer amount $e_{s_1}^1 - x_{s_1}^1$ (his **insurance premium**) to agent 2 if state s_1 occurs in return for receiving amount $e_{s_2}^2 - x_{s_2}^2$ (his insurance payout less his insurance premium) from agent 2 if state s_2 occurs. Symmetrically, $e_{s_2}^2 - x_{s_2}^2$ is agent 2's insurance premium, and $e_{s_1}^1 - x_{s_1}^1$ is his insurance payout less the premium.

There is no uncertainty about the aggregate endowment: $e_{s_1}^1 + e_{s_1}^2 = e_{s_2}^1 + e_{s_2}^2$; that is, there is no aggregate risk. Hence, it is feasible for each agent to consume the same amount at every state or, in other words, to **insure fully**. Nevertheless, the agents' preferences are such that, at equilibrium, each agent underinsures. Graphically, the equilibrium allocation x lies off the diagonal that connects the agents' origins in the Edgeworth box, and toward the endowments. Underinsurance occurs because each agent enjoys consumption more when he experiences no accident (e.g., because he is healthier at that state).

There is nothing special about underinsurance in this example, just as there is nothing special about the lack of full consumption smoothing. There is no accounting for tastes. Generally, an agent would tend to seek extra consumption at the states at which he values consumption more. For instance, he may value consumption more if his car is stolen, and, so, he must spend extra on taxis or must replace his car. In this case, he may buy insurance against the accident, possibly partial insurance, as in figure 1.17. The agent may also value consumption more when his favorite team wins and he is eager to celebrate. In this case, he may bet on his team's victory, which is the opposite of insurance in its informal, everyday sense.[29]

THE NONTRIVIAL LIMITATIONS OF THE REINTERPRETATION

The Walrasian model has no problem in capturing all the intertemporal and insurance markets that can possibly exist. This achievement is also the model's limitation. In particular,

1. The Walrasian model assumes the existence of complete markets, meaning markets for all contingent goods. In the stochastic context, the sources of uncertainty are so numerous (i.e., the state space S is so large) that markets for all contingent goods are impractical to set up; incomplete markets is the rule. For instance, complete markets would require markets for insurance against having a headache on the day of one's job interview, against missing one's dental appointment because of an unexpected traffic jam, and against failing to enjoy a movie.

2. In the presence of time and uncertainty, simply declaring a subset of goods as nontradable and then applying the Walrasian model to the remaining goods is an economically uninteresting way to model incomplete markets. For instance, when agents can lend and borrow but cannot trade insurance, no single good is nontradable. Instead, some contingent goods can be traded only as a bundle, as will be explained in an example.

3. The Walrasian model assumes perfect and costless enforcement of trades. In the static and deterministic interpretation, it may be realistic to imagine, say, two individuals who meet in a room and simultaneously swap some of their endowments, so that few, if any, enforcement issues arise. In a dynamic context, however, the lender would legitimately worry that, in the absence of enforcement (which is costly), the borrower may abscond without having repaid his debt, especially if the repayment date is far in the future. With uncertainty, an agent willing to buy disability insurance against severe back pain may have trouble finding a willing underwriter. Such insurance would be hard to enforce because pain is notoriously difficult to demonstrate; the insured would be tempted to lie in order to claim the insurance payout.

4. The Walrasian model assumes that all trades are executed at time zero; there is no retrade as time progresses. The restriction to no retrade calls for implausibly

---

29. In figure 1.17, each agent betting on the accident failing to materialize would correspond to an equilibrium allocation south east of the endowment point. It is not hard to draw the indifference curves that would rationalize this outcome.

complex time-zero trades: complete contingent plans. From the practical point of view, it may be simpler to trade sequentially. One would buy insurance only for the events that can occur tomorrow, in the expectation that one would optimally invest tomorrow (depending on which event occurs) in the insurance for the day after tomorrow, and so on.

5. The Walrasian model has no language to speak of time-varying preferences. For instance, on Monday, Alice may prefer working out on Tuesday to working out on Wednesday, whereas on Tuesday, she may change her mind and prefer working out on Wednesday to working out on Tuesday, even if no new information arrives between Monday and Tuesday. (Such a change in preference is indicative of a tendency to procrastinate.) Time-varying preferences create demand for sequential trading.

6. In the Walrasian model, market-clearing prices depend on the agents' utilities and endowments. (Of course.) Even though each agent takes the prices as given when deciding which consumption bundle to buy, he does not revise his utility function in light of what he learns from the prices about others' utilities and endowments. While natural in the deterministic interpretation of the model, in the stochastic interpretation, this neglect of the information contained in the prices is restrictive unless all agents have the same information about the likelihoods of states and, thus, have nothing to learn from each other. For instance, if Alice observes that the prices of all goods in some state are surprisingly high, she will infer that the demand from other agents is high, meaning that they probably deem the state quite likely, and so she will revise her utility (i.e., revise her beliefs about the likelihoods of states) to reflect that fact.

A model of incomplete markets, developed by Radner (1972), addresses the first two limitations on the list above.[30] This **incomplete markets** model restricts markets to predetermined bundles of goods, so that some goods can be traded only in certain proportions. Such predetermined bundles are called (financial) **securities**. The special case that identifies a security with each contingent good is the Walrasian model. Another special case occurs when some goods are nontradable, whereas all others are freely tradable in the Walrasian manner. A subtler special case is developed in the following example.

An Example with Incomplete Markets

Let $S \equiv \{s_1, s_2, s_3\}$, where state s_1 occurs at time $t = 1$, and states s_2 and s_3 correspond to two possible states at time $t = 2$. There are two agents, $I = 2$, and a single basic

---

30. The remaining limitations are also addressed in the literature.

good, $L = 1$. The agents' utilities are identical:[31]

$$u\left(x^i_{s_1}, x^i_{s_2}, x^i_{s_3}\right) \equiv \ln x^i_{s_1} + \frac{1}{2} \ln x^i_{s_2} + \frac{1}{2} \ln x^i_{s_3}, \quad i = 1, 2.$$

The agents' state-contingent endowment vectors are $e^1 = (1, b, c)$ and $e^2 = (1, c, b)$ for some positive b and c with $b > c$. Only two securities can be exchanged: (i) a security that pays a unit of the basic good at state s_1 (e.g., one avocado at time $t = 1$), and (ii) a security that pays a unit of the basic good at state s_2 and a unit of the basic good at state s_3 (e.g., one avocado for sure at time $t = 2$). The security described in (ii) is a **risk-free bond**: s_2- and s_3-contingent goods can be traded only as a bundle.

Each agent i chooses an amount $a^i \in \mathbb{R}$ of the bond to exchange for the time-1 good. Normalize the price of the time-1 good to 1, and let p denote the price of the bond. An **incomplete markets equilibrium** for the described economy is a tuple (a^1, a^2, p) such that each agent buys an optimal amount of the bond given its price,

$$a^i \in \arg\max u\left(e^i_{s_1} - pa^i, e^i_{s_2} + a^i, e^i_{s_3} + a^i\right), \quad i = 1, 2,$$

and the market for the bond (which is in zero net supply, meaning that the agents trade the bond only with each other) clears:

$$\sum_{i \in \mathcal{I}} a^i = 0.$$

One can verify that the tuple $(a^1, a^2, p) = (0, 0, (b+c)/(2bc))$ is an equilibrium; each agent consumes his endowment. Intuitively, both agents are equally well-endowed at $t = 1$ and equally well-endowed at $t = 2$. Hence, given the prevailing equilibrium price of the bond, none of them wants to transfer consumption across time, which is what the bond is good for. Instead, ideally, each agent would like to insure by transferring consumption across states s_2 and s_3. However, the agents have no access to a security that would enable them to do so. As a result, the conclusion of the FWT fails. (The theorem's premise fails; markets are incomplete.) The equilibrium allocation is Pareto dominated by the allocation that achieves

---

31. If one insists on reading impatience and probability into the model, one can rearrange agent i's utility as

$$u\left(x^i_{s_1}, x^i_{s_2}, x^i_{s_3}\right) \equiv \ln x^i_{s_1} + \underbrace{1}_{\substack{\text{discount factor} \\ \approx 1 - \text{discount rate}}} \left(\underbrace{\frac{1}{2}}_{\text{probability}} \ln x^i_{s_2} + \underbrace{\frac{1}{2}}_{\text{probability}} \ln x^i_{s_3} \right)$$

and interpret states s_2 and s_3 as equiprobable and the discount rate (approximately one minus the discount factor) as zero.

full insurance:

$$x^1 = x^2 = \left(1, \frac{b+c}{2}, \frac{b+c}{2}\right).$$

1.12   CONCLUDING REMARKS

The usefulness of the Walrasian paradigm is largely predicated on two hypotheses:

1.   The outcome of unfettered exchange is well approximated by a Walrasian equilibrium.

2.   When equilibria are multiple, the locally stable equilibria are the empirically relevant ones.

One way to test these hypotheses is to construct a Walrasian model of an actual economy (e.g., a model with the focus on international trade or on business cycles), estimate the model's parameters, and then test the model's predictions against the data. The problem with this test is that it confounds the invalidity of the Walrasian paradigm with model misspecification. The latter is likely. In this case, the divergence between the model's predictions and data would not implicate the Walrasian paradigm beyond reasonable doubt.

Alternatively, one may seek to legitimize the Walrasian model by showing that it can explain the qualitative features of a hitherto unexplained phenomenon. The **transfer paradox** (whereby an agent becomes better off as he transfers a part of his endowment to another agent; see problem 1.13) and the **immiserizing growth paradox** (whereby an agent becomes worse off as his endowment grows; see problem 1.14) are good candidates for such phenomena. In either case, the paradox occurs because, as an agent's endowment of a good increases, the equilibrium price of this good falls (i.e., moves against him). Unfortunately, these paradoxes remain theoretical curiosities, observed in the Edgeworth box but elusive in the wild.[32]

---

32. This is not quite true. There is some suggestive evidence of immiserizing growth. Sawada (2009) reports historical instances when the growth of the real per capita gross domestic product in some country would be accompanied by a decline in the welfare of the country's so-called representative consumer. This consumer's welfare is said to decline if the aggregate bundle of goods that the country consumes this period was affordable already last period, and yet, last period, the country chose a different bundle, which it therefore must prefer to this period's bundle. The existence of a representative consumer, who has preferences over the entire country's consumption bundles, is a heroic assumption; it is only justified under rather restrictive conditions on individual preferences. Moreover, because the countries in the sample are small and, so, unlikely to perceptibly affect world prices, the mechanism responsible for the documented immiserizing growth is likely to differ from the one exhibited in the Edgeworth box of problem 1.14. Similarly, while the evidence for the transfer paradox for aid-receiving small countries is reported by Yano

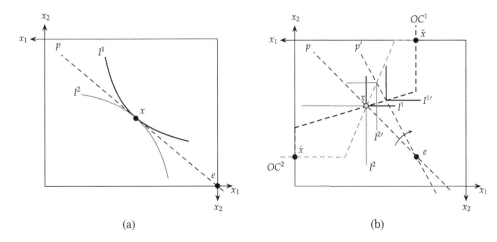

FIGURE 1.18.

Two experimental tests of the Walrasian model.

(a) The Edgeworth box economy has a unique equilibrium, (p, x), from the endowment point e. Gjerstad (2013) finds that unfettered competition, modeled as a continuous double auction, leads to the convergence to the equilibrium.

(b) The Edgeworth box economy has three equilibria, at the intersections of the piecewise-linear offer curves OC^1 and OC^2. Equilibrium (p, x) occurs where the agents' angular indifference curves I^1 and I^2 touch the budget line p that passes through the endowment point e. This equilibrium is unstable: if the relative price for good 1 rises to p', then the excess demand for good 1 becomes positive, and the relative price for good 1 rises even further, away from p. The extreme equilibria $((0, 1), \hat{x})$ and $((1, 0), \bar{x})$ are stable. The experiments of Crockett et al. (2011) strongly favor the extreme equilibria, even though, in either of them, one agent type is as well off as he would be consuming his endowment, whereas the other type reaps the entire gains from trade.

Direct evidence on the validity of the Walrasian paradigm is experimental. Gjerstad (2013) studies a twelve-agent Edgeworth box economy in a laboratory setting. The economy is Edgeworth box in the sense that it comprises six identical copies of agent 1 and six identical copies of agent 2. Agent 1 has all of good 1 and none of good 2; agent 2 has all of good 2 and none of good 1. The Walrasian equilibrium is unique. With just two agent types, one can depict each type's indifference curves and each type's average consumption bundle in the standard Edgeworth box. Figure 1.18(a) illustrates. In the experiment, subjects (undergraduate students) engage in unfettered exchange over several sequential replications of the economy.

Each replication is called a period. Within each period, unfettered exchange is operationalized as a **continuous double auction**, in which agent 1 can repeatedly submit a bid, and agent 2 can repeatedly submit an ask, for a unit of good 2 in terms of good 1. A unit is traded once a bid and an ask cross—that is, once the bid exceeds the ask. The transaction price can be either the ask or the bid. Having traded a unit, any agent may submit another request to buy (a bid) or sell (an ask) a unit

---

and Nugent (1999), the mechanism for the documented paradox is likely to differ from the one posited in problem 1.13.

of good 2. Thus, time permitting, each agent may attempt to trade as many units as he likes.[33] Gjerstad (2013) finds that the final transaction prices at the end of each period converge to Walrasian equilibrium prices. The experiment lends support to hypothesis 1 above.

Crockett, Oprea, and Plott (2011) find support for hypothesis 2 above in an environment in which the deck is intentionally stacked against that hypothesis. The Edgeworth box economy that they study, depicted in figure 1.18(b), has three equilibria: an unstable equilibrium and two stable ones. Each of the stable equilibria is "counterintuitive" in that the price of one of the goods is zero, and all of the gains from trade accrue either to type 1 agents or to type 2 agents; each agent of the other type is as well off at equilibrium as he would be consuming his endowment.

Nevertheless, Crockett et al. (2011) find that, in the course of unfettered exchange, subjects (undergraduate students, once again) converge to the counter-intuitive but stable equilibria, as Walrasian tâtonnement would have it—unless the initial price vector happens to be right at the unstable equilibrium, in which case the economy remains at that equilibrium. In their experimental design, six to ten agents are type 1, and the same number are type 2. The unfettered competition is operationalized as a continuous double auction.[34] The parameters are chosen so that the sum of all the agents' utilities is the same at all three equilibria. This way, the researcher can be sure that an equilibrium is not selected because of the salience of its payoffs.

Both experimental papers assume (uncontroversially) that subjects prefer more money to less. Both papers structure the agents' payoffs so as to induce intended utility functions over the consumption bundles. As a result, each subject is motivated to behave as if he were indeed maximizing the induced utility function. But do individuals in the wild, outside the lab, behave as if they were maximizing some utility function?

To ascertain the validity of the Walrasian approach, it remains to ascertain that, when no utility function is explicitly induced by the experimenter, individuals nonetheless make choices as if they were maximizing some utility function. Empirically, utility maximization amounts to the consistency of observed choices. If Bob chooses life in the countryside over life in a city, chooses life in a city over life in the suburbs, and chooses life in the suburbs over life in the countryside, then he is being inconsistent; no utility function that assigns numerical values to each of the listed options can be maximized to generate Bob's circular choices. By contrast,

---

33. The described continuous double auction is essentially the protocol used in financial exchanges driven by the transparent limit-order book, such as the one used at the London Stock Exchange.

34. One would not want to literally administer tâtonnement instead of the continuous double auction. The research question is not whether subjects compute their demands correctly and report them truthfully in response to the queries of the Walrasian auctioneer. Rather, the question is whether tâtonnement is an empirically relevant equilibrium-selection device.

if Bob's choices are not susceptible to the cycles of the kind described, then, under a rather weak additional condition of the continuity of preferences, Bob's choices can be described by utility maximization. Cox (1997) has demonstrated how utility maximization can be tested by observing individual choices and has found empirical evidence in its favor.

1.13   APPENDIX: A PROOF SKETCH OF THEOREM 1.3

In economics, most equilibrium-existence proofs that are nonconstructive share a pattern. First, the existence problem is reduced to showing that a carefully constructed function f from some set Y into itself has a **fixed point**, which is to say that one can find a $p^* \in Y$ such that $p^* = f(p^*)$. Second, the existence of a fixed point is established by appealing to one of many fixed-point theorems. This is how John Nash proved the existence of Nash equilibrium in 1951; and this is how Kenneth Arrow, Gérard Debreu, and Lionel McKenzie proved the existence of Walrasian equilibrium in 1954. This method of proof is short on economic insight and long on mathematical details. Nevertheless, the proof is worth exploring for its ingenuity, its historical significance, and the elegance of the mathematics involved.

BROUWER'S FIXED-POINT THEOREM
We shall attack (but not quite conquer in every detail) theorem 1.3 by using Brouwer's fixed-point theorem, which we do not prove.

Theorem 1.6 (Brouwer's Fixed-Point Theorem).   *Any continuous function $f : Y \to Y$ that maps a nonempty, compact (i.e., bounded and closed), and convex subset Y of a Euclidean space into itself has a fixed point in Y; that is, there exists a $p^* \in Y$ such that $p^* = f(p^*)$.*

The subset of the Euclidean space that we shall work with is $Y \subset \mathbb{R}_+^L$, which is a set of prices for L goods. For $Y = [0, 1]$, the theorem's conclusion is apparent from figure 1.19(a).

For a physical illustration in $\mathbb{R}$ or $\mathbb{R}^2$, suppose that, in the evening, a (one-dimensional or two-dimensional) sheet is neatly laid out on a (respectively, one-dimensional or two-dimensional) bed. (See figure 1.19(b) top for a one-dimensional example.) Then the bed is slept on. As a result, in the morning, the sheet may have wrinkles and folds; it can even be stretched or compressed in places, if made from an elastic material. (See figure 1.19(b) bottom.) Brouwer's fixed-point theorem says

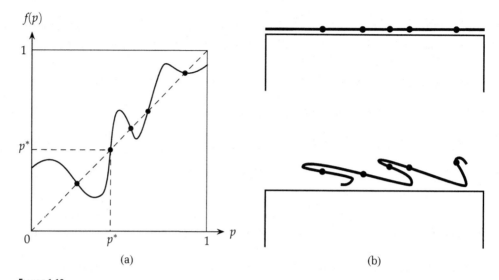

FIGURE 1.19.

Brouwer's fixed-point theorem.

(a) A continuous function from [0, 1] to [0, 1] must cross the 45-degree (dashed) line at least once. Here, it does so five times, with p^* being one such point, a fixed point of the function.

(b) A sheet neatly laid out on a bed in the evening (top) will be wrinkled and creased (bottom), but at least one point (here, five points, marked by dots) will have the same coordinates as in the evening.

that, in the morning, at least one spot on the sheet will not have changed its location from the previous evening provided:

- The bed has no holes in it and is otherwise conventionally shaped (Y is convex).

- The bed's dimensions are finite (Y is bounded).

- The bed contains its boundary points (Y is closed).

- In the evening, the sheet covers the entire surface of the bed without spilling over (the domain of f is Y).

- In the morning, the sheet does not spill over the bed (the range of f is contained in Y) but need not cover the entire surface of the bed (the range of f need not coincide with Y).

- In the morning, the sheet has no holes torn in it (f is continuous).

For the one-dimensional version of the sheet example in figure 1.19(b), figure 1.19(a) maps the location of a point on the sheet in the evening (the horizontal axis) into the location of a point on the sheet in the morning (the vertical axis). A three-dimensional analog of the sheet example is a mug of coffee. Brouwer's fixed-point theorem ensures that, however diligently one stirs, at least one molecule will end up where it started.

PROOF SKETCH OF THEOREM 1.3

The argument supplied here is a sketch, not a proof, of theorem 1.3 because we *pretend* that (i) the aggregate excess demand function, denoted by z, is a continuous function, defined on the set $P^\Delta \equiv \{p \in \mathbb{R}_+^L \mid \sum_{l \in \mathcal{L}} p_l = 1\}$ of normalized prices; and (ii) $p_l = 0$ implies $z_l(p) > 0$. This pretense is not far from the truth.

Regarding (i), in the interior of P^Δ, z is indeed continuous (by u-continuity and u-concavity), as can be shown by analogy with part 1 of lemma 1.2. The trouble is that z is not defined on the boundary of P^Δ; when a price of some good is zero, no agent will be satisfied with consuming a finite amount of that good (by u-monotonicity). Instead, one can show, by analogy with part 2 of lemma 1.2, that, as some prices approach zero, the aggregate excess demand for at least one of the goods whose price approaches zero must approach infinity (by u-continuity and u-monotonicity). So, by assuming (i), we implicitly fudge the true aggregate excess demand function by capping it near, and at, the boundary of P^Δ in the hope that this fudge is of no adverse consequence for the existence argument because equilibrium price vectors are in the interior of P^Δ (by u-monotonicity). Regarding (ii), it disciplines our fudge by incorporating the spirit of the limit behavior of the true aggregate excess demand function as prices approach the boundary of P^Δ.

In addition, we assume that (fudged) z satisfies Walras's law everywhere on P^Δ.

The idea of the existence proof is to posit a discrete-time tâtonnement-like adjustment process whose stationary points—just as those of tâtonnement in (1.6)—are Walrasian equilibrium prices. Specifically, given the current-period price $p \in P^\Delta$, let the next-period price $\psi(p)$ be

$$\psi(p) \equiv \arg\max_{p' \in P^\Delta} \left\{ p' \cdot z(p) - \sum_{l \in \mathcal{L}} (p'_l - p_l)^2 \right\}. \tag{1.7}$$

The mapping ψ is a function by the Weierstrass theorem, which says that any continuous function that maps a nonempty, bounded, and closed set into a subset of real numbers attains a maximum on that set. Indeed, the maximand in (1.7) is continuous in p' and the maximizer is chosen from a nonempty, bounded, and closed set, P^Δ. As a result, ψ is nonempty-valued. Furthermore, ψ is singleton-valued because the maximand is strictly concave.

By construction, ψ maps P^Δ into itself.

As tâtonnement would, the process implied by (1.7) raises the prices for the goods in excess demand while lowering the prices for the goods in excess supply.

The quadratic term in (1.7) can be interpreted as the auctioneer's cost of price adjustment. We first show that the process has a stationary, or fixed, point and then argue that this point is actually a Walrasian equilibrium price.

To show that ψ has a fixed point, denoted by p^*, in theorem 1.6, take f to be ψ and take Y to be P^Δ. It is immediate that P^Δ satisfies the requisite nonemptiness, compactness, and convexity conditions. To conclude that ψ is continuous, appeal to the Theorem of the Maximum, which guarantees continuity because the maximand in (1.7) is jointly continuous in p and p' and because the maximizer is unique. Thus, Brouwer's fixed-point theorem applies: a $p^* \in Y$ with $p^* = \psi(p^*)$ exists.

The argument that shows that $p^* = \psi(p^*)$ implies that p^* is a Walrasian equilibrium price has two parts: first, show that $p^* = \psi(p^*)$ implies $z(p^*) \le 0$ and then rule out $z_l(p^*) < 0$ for any $l \in \mathcal{L}$, to conclude that $z(p^*) = 0$.[35] So, suppose that $p^* = \psi(p^*)$. Then, for all $p' \in P^\Delta$,

$$p^* \cdot z(p^*) \ge p' \cdot z(p^*) - \sum_{l \in \mathcal{L}} \left(p'_l - p^*_l\right)^2,$$

which, by Walras's law (i.e., $p^* \cdot z(p^*) = 0$), becomes

$$\sum_{l \in \mathcal{L}} \left(p'_l - p^*_l\right)^2 \ge p' \cdot z(p^*).$$

The inequality above must hold for any $p' \in P^\Delta$ and, in particular, for $p' = \varepsilon p + (1 - \varepsilon)p^*$ with any $p \in P^\Delta$ and any $\varepsilon \in (0, 1)$. As a result,

$$\varepsilon^2 \sum_{l \in \mathcal{L}} \left(p_l - p^*_l\right)^2 \ge \varepsilon p \cdot z(p^*),$$

where, again, use has been made of Walras's law (i.e., $p^* \cdot z(p^*) = 0$). Because the inequality in the display above must hold for all $\varepsilon \in (0, 1)$, including arbitrarily small ones, it must be that $0 \ge p \cdot z(p^*)$ for all $p \in P^\Delta$, which is possible only if $z(p^*) \le 0$.

To conclude that the fixed point p^* is a Walrasian equilibrium price, it remains to rule out $z(p^*) < 0$. By contradiction, suppose that $z_l(p^*) < 0$ for some l. Then, for both $p^* \cdot z(p^*) = 0$ (Walras's law) and $z(p^*) \le 0$ to hold, it must be that $p^*_l = 0$. However, by the assumption on z (motivated by u-monotonicity), $p^*_l = 0$ implies $z_l(p^*) > 0$, thereby contradicting $z_l(p^*) < 0$. To summarize, $p^* \in \psi(p^*)$ implies $z(p^*) = 0$.

---

35. The converse is also true; every Walrasian-equilibrium price is a fixed point of ψ. Indeed, if $z(p^*) = 0$, then the maximand in (1.7), which becomes $-\sum_{l \in \mathcal{L}} (p'_l - p^*_l)^2$, is maximized at $p' = p^*$.

1.14   BIBLIOGRAPHICAL NOTES

This chapter has evolved from the Stanford lecture notes compiled in 2006 by Jonathan Levin (appended by Ilya Segal, preceded by Felix Kubler's notes). It is hard to be original about the topic so traditional and so superbly exposed by Mas-Colell, Whinston, and Green (1995, part four), on whose narrative Levin's notes are based. The main difference in the present exposition is in the assumptions that ensure that correspondences can be replaced by functions, for simplicity.

Duppe and Weintraub (2014) describe the intellectual atmosphere that gave rise to the seminal papers in the modern general equilibrium theory: McKenzie (1954) and Arrow and Debreu (1954). The latter paper has not only proved existence of equilibrium but has also done it in the model that has become the standard paradigm in economics. The FWT and the SWT are formally established by Arrow (1951) and Debreu (1951).

The formulation of the SWT in theorem 1.2 is nonstandard and is due to Maskin and Roberts (2008, theorem 3); it is also reported by Varian (1992, p. 329). Theorem 1.4 is proposition 17.F.3 of Mas-Colell et al. (1995, p. 613). Lemma 1.3 is proved in the general case by Kenneth J. Arrow and Hurwicz (1959, lemma 5), and its two-good version is exercise 17.F.7 of Mas-Colell et al. (1995, p. 646). Theorem 1.5 is theorem 17.H.1 of Mas-Colell et al. (1995, p. 623). The elegant equilibrium existence proof of theorem 1.3, in section 1.13, is due to Geanakoplos (2003, section 4.1). This proof omits some detail by taking the aggregate excess demand function as a primitive. A detailed proof is reported by Jehle and Reny (2011, theorem 5.5, p. 211). A notion of an approximate Walrasian equilibrium is discussed by Postlewaite and Schmeidler (1981).

The Theorem of the Maximum (invoked in the proof of part 1 of lemma 1.2 and in the proof of theorem 1.3) is ubiquitous in economic analysis and is reported, for instance, by Jehle and Reny (2011, theorem A2.21, p. 602) and Mas-Colell et al. (1995, theorem M.K.6, p. 963). Part 2 of lemma 1.2 is proved by Jehle and Reny (2011, theorem 5.4, p. 209–211). Brouwer's fixed-point theorem (invoked in the proof of theorem 1.3) is also ubiquitous and is reported by Jehle and Reny (2011, theorem A1.11, p. 523) and Mas-Colell et al. (1995, theorem M.I.1, p. 952). The Weierstrass theorem (invoked in the proof of theorem 1.3) is the extreme value theorem and is reported by Rudin (1976, theorem 4.16, p. 89).

Most end-of-chapter problems are bound not to be original, either by choice or by accident, owing to the established nature of general equilibrium theory and its instruction. Problem 1.4 is based on an example by Scarf (1960). Problem 1.7 is a variation on problem 17.C.3 of Mas-Colell et al. (1995). The concept of envy-freeness studied in problem 1.9 is due to Foley (1967) and is surveyed by Thomson and Varian (1984). The observation that adding a market when markets are incomplete need not lead to a Pareto improvement is due to Newbery and Stiglitz (1984), and problem 1.10 is a variation on this theme. Problem 1.12 is inspired by Sobel (2007). Problem 1.13 is essentially problem 15.B.10 of Mas-Colell et al. (1995). The possibility of immiserizing growth, studied in problem 1.14, was first pointed out by Bhagwati (1958). Problem 1.15 is an instance of a more general manipulability problem described by Postlewaite (1979).

PROBLEMS

Problem 1.1 (A Logarithmic Economy). Consider an economy with two agents, in $\mathcal{I} \equiv \{1, 2\}$, and two goods, in $\mathcal{L} \equiv \{1, 2\}$. Each agent i's utility from consuming bundle x^i is

$$u^i(x^i) \equiv \sum_{l \in \mathcal{L}} \alpha_l \ln x_l^i,$$

where all α_l are positive and $\sum_{l \in \mathcal{L}} \alpha_l = 1$.

1. Solve for the agents' demands at positive prices, argue that the economy satisfies the gross substitutes property, and find the Walrasian equilibrium.

2. Compute $z_1(\cdot, \alpha_2/\bar{e}_2)$, the aggregate excess demand for good 1 as a function of p_1 under the normalization $p_2 = \alpha_2/\bar{e}_2$. Plot this function and illustrate the tâtonnement process (in the price of good 1) by plotting the evolution of $p_1(t)$ over time.

3. Identify the Pareto set and plot it in the Edgeworth box.

4. Suppose that the planner solves

$$\max_{(x^1, x^2) \in \mathbb{R}_+^4} \sum_{i \in \mathcal{I}} \omega^i u^i(x^i) \quad \text{s.t.} \quad (\forall l \in \mathcal{L}) \sum_{i \in \mathcal{I}} x_l^i = \bar{e}_l,$$

where each ω^i is nonnegative and $\omega^1 + \omega^2 = 1$. Show that, as one varies ω^1, the solution to the planner's problem in the above display traces out the set of Pareto efficient allocations. What should the weights ω^1 and ω^2 be for the planner to choose the Walrasian equilibrium allocation? Conclude that the Walrasian market acts as a benevolent social planner who chooses a Pareto efficient allocation by maximizing a weighted sum of the agents' utilities while putting a greater weight on the better endowed agent.

Problem 1.2 (Inefficient Markets). Consider an economy with two agents and two goods. The agents' endowments are $e^1 = (1, 2)$ and $e^2 = (2, 1)$. The agents' utility functions are

$$u^1(x^1, x^2) = \ln x_1^1 + \ln x_2^1 - \ln x_2^2$$
$$u^2(x^2, x^1) = \ln x_1^2 + \ln x_2^2 - \ln x_1^1.$$

Thus, agent i is hurt when the other agent consumes more of the good in which agent i is better endowed.

1. Define Walrasian equilibrium.

2. Compute a Walrasian equilibrium.

3. Are the agents better off at the Walrasian equilibrium or in autarky?

4. How is your answer consistent with the FWT?

Problem 1.3 (Gradual Trade Liberalization). Consider an economy with three agents—Alice, Bob, and Carol—and two goods. Assume that the assumptions of the FWT hold.

1. Forget about Carol for now, and suppose that Alice and Bob engage in Walrasian trade. Call this arrangement AB. Are Alice and Bob better off in AB than in autarky?

2. Suppose that Carol joins Alice and Bob and now all three engage in Walrasian trade from their initial endowments. Call this arrangement ABC. Using the argument mimicking the proof of the FWT, prove that it cannot be that, for Alice and Bob, their allocation in AB Pareto dominates their allocation in ABC.

3. By example, show that Alice can be better off in AB than in ABC. For instance, you can consider a two-good economy with endowments $e^{Alice} = (1, 2)$, $e^{Bob} = (2, 1)$, and $e^{Carol} = (\frac{3}{2}, y)$, and the log utility $u^i(x^i) = \ln x_1^i + \ln x_2^i$ for each $i \in \{Alice, Bob, Carol\}$ and then show that one can find a $y > 0$ such that Alice is better off in AB than in ABC.

4. Suggest a way to redistribute the endowments of Alice and Bob among themselves so that each is weakly better off in ABC than in AB.

5. What practical implications can you draw from this example for the political economy of the liberalization of international trade? You can interpret Alice, Bob, and Carol as "representative consumers" of three distinct countries, or you can interpret Alice and Bob as representing two types of consumers in one country and Carol as representing consumers in another country.

Problem 1.4 (Instability). This problem shows that tâtonnement may fail to converge even if the Walrasian equilibrium is unique. The calculations in this problem underly figure 1.14. Consider an exchange economy with three agents, $\mathcal{I} = \{1, 2, 3\}$, and three goods, $\mathcal{L} = \{1, 2, 3\}$. The agents' utilities are

$$u^1(x^1) = \min\left\{x_1^1, x_2^1\right\}$$
$$u^2(x^2) = \min\left\{x_2^2, x_3^2\right\}$$
$$u^3(x^3) = \min\left\{x_3^3, x_1^3\right\}.$$

That is, each agent cares only about two out of three goods. The agents' endowments are

$$e^1 = (1, 0, 0)$$
$$e^2 = (0, 1, 0)$$
$$e^3 = (0, 0, 1).$$

The price-adjustment rule is Walrasian tâtonnement:

$$\frac{\mathrm{d}p(t)}{\mathrm{d}t} = z(p(t)), \quad t \geq 0, \tag{1.8}$$

where z is the aggregate excess demand function. Normalize the initial price vector $p(0)$ to lie in the set $P^S \equiv \left\{p \in \mathbb{R}_{++}^3 \mid \sum_{l \in \mathcal{L}} p_l^2 = 3\right\}$.

1. Show that, for any initial price $p(0)$ in P^S and for any $t > 0$, the Walrasian tâtonnement price $p(t)$ is also in P^S.

2. Compute each agent's demand as a function of prices.

3. Compute the aggregate excess demand function, denoted by z.

4. For each of the following assumptions, please indicate whether the economy satisfies it: u-continuity, u-monotonicity, u-concavity, and gross substitutes.

5. Identify a Walrasian equilibrium price in P^S.

6. Show that the equilibrium you have identified in part 5 is unique.

7. Show that, for any initial price vector $p(0) \in P^S$ and for any $t > 0$, the Walrasian tâtonnement price vector $p(t)$ satisfies $p_1(t)p_2(t)p_3(t) = p_1(0)p_2(0)p_3(0)$.

8. Argue that part 7 implies that the unique equilibrium is locally unstable.

9. Section 1.10 proposes a coin toss as a metaphor for tâtonnement settling on a Walrasian equilibrium. Please propose a physical metaphor for an economy in which Walrasian equilibrium is unique and yet tâtonnement never converges to this equilibrium.

Problem 1.5 (Monopoly). It is naive to expect two individuals who meet to exchange their endowments to take prices as given instead of trying to influence these prices. Perhaps, the individual who looks more menacing, is better politically connected, or is more patient and skillful at negotiating will be able to influence the prices in his favor. This question is concerned with analyzing the consequences of such influence.

Assume two agents, $\mathcal{I}=\{1,2\}$, two goods, $\mathcal{L}=\{1,2\}$, and that u-continuity, u-monotonicity, and u-concavity hold. Agent 1's demand, x^1, maximizes his utility, u^1, for each prevailing price:

$$x^1(p) = \arg\max_{y^1 \in \mathcal{B}^1(p)} u^1(y^1),$$

where $\mathcal{B}^1(p)$ is his budget set. In contrast to agent 1, agent 2 does not take the prices as given. Instead, he is a monopolist; he makes a take-it-or-leave-it offer of a price, denoted by p^M, to agent 1. At this price, agent 1 trades the amount that he finds optimal, $x^1(p^M)$. Thus, agent 2 optimally chooses p^M so as to maximize his utility:

$$p^M \in \arg\max_{p \in \mathbb{R}^2} \left\{ u^2(e^1 + e^2 - x^1(p)) \mid e^1 + e^2 - x^1(p) \geq 0 \right\}.$$

Thus, agent 2's consumption at the price p^M is $e^1 + e^2 - x^1(p^M)$, which is the aggregate endowment less agent 1's demand.

Study the monopolist's problem analytically by making, if necessary, any functional form assumptions you like, or graphically, in the Edgeworth box, to answer the following questions.

1. What does the unique monopoly outcome $(x^1(p^M), x^2(p^M), p^M)$ look like?

2. Is the monopoly outcome a Walrasian equilibrium?

3. Is the monopoly outcome Pareto efficient?

4. Suppose that, instead of presenting agent 1 with a price, agent 2 makes a take-it-or-leave-it offer to agent 1 to exchange his endowment for some bundle. Agent 1 is assumed to accept this offer if and only if he is not made worse off by this exchange compared to consuming his endowment. Does agent 2 optimally propose the monopoly allocation $x^1(p^M), x^2(p^M)$? Is the allocation agent 2 optimally proposes Pareto efficient?

Problem 1.6 (Taxation). Assume two agents, $\mathcal{I}=\{1,2\}$, two goods, $\mathcal{L}=\{1,2\}$, u-continuity, u-monotonicity, and u-concavity, and smooth utility functions (which imply smooth indifference curves). A government must collect $g > 0$ units of good 1 in order to appease an Alien Monster. Assume that $g < e_1^1 + e_1^2$, so that the appeasement is feasible. The government imposes a **sales tax** $t > 0$ on trade in good 1; that is, whenever an agent sells some amount $\Delta > 0$ of good 1 to the other agent, that other agent receives only $\Delta(1 - t)$ units of the good, with Δt units going to the government (and then to the Alien Monster). The government sets t just so as to collect the requisite g units of good 1 at the Walrasian equilibrium induced by t.

A price-allocation pair (p, x) is a Walrasian equilibrium of economy $((u^i, e^i)_{i \in \mathcal{I}}, g, t)$—an endowment economy with government spending g and a sales tax t—if each agent i's bundle x^i maximizes his utility subject to a budget constraint,

$$x^i \in \arg \max_{y^i \in \mathbb{R}^2_+} u^i(y^i)$$

$$\text{s.t. } p_1 \max \left\{0, y_1^i - e_1^i\right\} + p_1(1 - t) \min \left\{0, y_1^i - e_1^i\right\} + p_2 \left(y_2^i - e_2^i\right) \leq 0, \qquad (1.9)$$

and if the market clearing conditions hold:

$$x_1^1 + x_1^2 + g = \bar{e}_1 \qquad (1.10)$$
$$x_2^1 + x_2^2 = \bar{e}_2.$$

The government's budget constraint is

$$t \max \left\{e_1^1 - x_1^1, e_1^2 - x_1^2\right\} = g. \qquad (1.11)$$

1. Explain agent i's budget constraint (1.9), the market clearing condition (1.10), and the government's budget constraint (1.11) term by term. In what sense can one say that agents face different prices?

2. Suppose that the government addresses the agents thus: "You want high government expenditure on appeasing the Alien Monster? You want low taxes? No problem. We can do both!" Comment on the plausibility of the government's assertion.

3. Give a graphical example (in the Edgeworth box) of an economy $((e^i, u^i)_{i \in \mathcal{I}}, g, t)$ and its Walrasian equilibrium.

4. Show that, in your graphical example in part 3, the Walrasian equilibrium is not Pareto efficient. That is, there exists an alternative feasible allocation at which one agent is better off, another agent is no worse off, and the Alien Monster is appeased.

Problem 1.7 (Redistributive Taxation).   Assume two agents, $\mathcal{I} = \{1, 2\}$, two goods, $\mathcal{L} = \{1, 2\}$, u-continuity, u-monotonicity, u-concavity, and smooth utility functions (which imply smooth indifference curves). As in problem 1.6, the government collects $g > 0$ units of good 1 to appease an Alien Monster, where $g < e_1^1 + e_1^2$. The government imposes a sales tax $t > 0$ on trade in good 1. The magnitude of t is set so as to collect the requisite g at the Walrasian equilibrium induced by t.

In the current problem, the Alien Monster has mellowed and requires no appeasement. The government, however, is reluctant to relinquish its ability to tax. Instead, the government's goal is to collect the same g, but now, instead of giving g to the Alien Monster, the government promises to unconditionally transfer g to agent 1. (Such an unconditional transfer—a transfer that is independent of the agent's choices—is called lump-sum transfer.[36])

A price-allocation pair (p, x) is a Walrasian equilibrium of economy $((u^i, e^i)_{i \in \mathcal{I}}, g, t)$ if each agent i's bundle x^i maximizes his utility subject to the budget constraint,

$$x^i \in \arg \max_{y^i \in \mathbb{R}^2_+} u^i(y^i) \quad \text{s.t.}$$

$$p_1 \max \{0, y_1^i - e_1^i - \mathbf{1}_{\{i=1\}} g\} + p_1 (1 - t) \min \{0, y_1^i - e_1^i - \mathbf{1}_{\{i=1\}} g\}$$
$$+ p_2 (y_2^i - e_2^i) \leq 0 \tag{1.12}$$

(where $\mathbf{1}_{\{i=1\}}$ is the indicator function, which equals 1 if $i = 1$ and equals 0 otherwise), and if the market clearing conditions hold:

$$x_1^1 + x_1^2 = \bar{e}_1 \tag{1.13}$$
$$x_2^1 + x_2^2 = \bar{e}_2.$$

The government's budget constraint is

$$t \max \{e_1^1 + g - x_1^1, e_1^2 - x_1^2\} = g. \tag{1.14}$$

1. Explain each agent i's budget constraint (1.12), the market clearing condition (1.13), and the government's budget constraint (1.14) term by term, and why they differ from the corresponding conditions (1.9), (1.10), and (1.11) in problem 1.6.

2. Give a graphical example (in the Edgeworth box) of an economy $((e^i, u^i)_{i \in \mathcal{I}}, g, t)$ and its Walrasian equilibrium.

3. Show that, in your graphical example in part 2, the Walrasian equilibrium is not Pareto efficient. That is, there exists an alternative feasible allocation at which one agent is better off and the other agent is no worse off. Propose a

---

36. A **lump-sum tax** is defined analogously; it is a payment that is independent of the agent's choices. In this problem, the tax is not lump-sum. Agent i's tax payment, $t \max \{0, e_1^i + \mathbf{1}_{\{i=1\}} g - x_1^i\}$, depends on his choice of x_1^i.

way to quantify the inefficiency arising due to the taxation and illustrate this measure in the Edgeworth box.

Problem 1.8 (Externality). Assume two agents, $\mathcal{I} = \{1, 2\}$, and two goods, $\mathcal{L} = \{1, 2\}$. Assume that there is an externality from agent 2 onto agent 1 in the sense that agent 2's consumption, x^2, directly enters agent 1's utility function, $u^1(x^1, x^2)$. Assume that agent 2's utility, $u^2(x^2)$, depends only on his own consumption.

1. Define Walrasian equilibrium assuming that, when choosing his consumption bundle x^1, agent 1 takes agent 2's consumption bundle x^2 as given. In this model, what difficulty do you face when trying to analyze Walrasian equilibria in the Edgeworth box?

2. Solve for a Walrasian equilibrium assuming

$$u^1\left(x_1^1, x_2^1, x_1^2\right) = \ln x_1^1 + \ln x_2^1 + \ln x_1^2$$
$$u^2\left(x_1^2, x_2^2\right) = \ln x_1^2 + \ln x_2^2$$
$$e^1 = e^2 = (1, 1).$$

3. Prove that the equilibrium that you have identified in part 2 is not Pareto efficient. How is your conclusion consistent with the FWT?

4. Identify at least one Pareto efficient allocation.

Problem 1.9 (Envy). Assume two agents, $\mathcal{I} = \{1, 2\}$, two goods, $\mathcal{L} = \{1, 2\}$, and that u-continuity, u-monotonicity, and u-concavity hold.

1. In a Walrasian equilibrium of some economy $(u^i, e^i)_{i \in \{1, 2\}}$, can it be that some agent **envies** the consumption bundle of another? That is, can it be that, at some equilibrium (x^1, x^2, p),

$$u^1(x^2) > u^1(x^1) \quad \text{or} \quad u^2(x^1) > u^2(x^2)?$$

2. Can it be that, at some equilibrium (x^1, x^2, p),

$$u^1(x^2) > u^1(x^1) \quad \text{and} \quad u^2(x^1) > u^2(x^2)?$$

3. Suppose that an economy $(u^i, e^i)_{i \in \{1, 2\}}$ is such that $e^1 = e^2$. Can it be that, at a Walrasian equilibrium, either agent envies the other?

4. An allocation is **envy-free** if no agent envies the consumption bundle of another. Consider an economy $(u^i, e^i)_{i \in \{1, 2\}}$ in which the endowment profile is envy-free. Show that a corresponding Walrasian equilibrium allocation can fail to be envy-free.

5. How would you define an envy-free allocation (x^1, x^2) in an environment with consumption externalities, in which the agents' utilities are $u^1(x^1, x^2)$ and $u^2(x^2, x^1)$?

Problem 1.10 (Incomplete Markets with Scavenging). In a Walrasian model with a twist, this problem illustrates that making more goods tradable need not mono-tonically increase each agent's equilibrium utility. Two agents, in $\mathcal{I} = \{1, 2\}$, are roommates. Each one consumes three goods, from the set $\mathcal{L} = \{1, 2, 3\}$. Goods 1 and 2 are cereal and chocolate, whereas good 3 is "me-time." For Alice, agent 1, the me-time is practicing her grand piano in the living room. For Bob, agent 2, the me-time is lounging about whenever Alice is not practicing her piano. Alice and Bob are at home always at the same time, for one unit of time. This unit of time—me-time—is Alice's endowment. Bob is endowed with no me-time. Formally, the agents' endow-ments are $e^1 = (a, 0, 1)$ and $e^2 = (b, \frac{1}{2}, 0)$, for some $a > 0$ and $b > 0$ that are sufficiently large so that no agent ever consumes a negative quantity of good 1 at any of the allocations considered in this problem. The agents' utility functions are

$$u^1(x^1) = x_1^1 + x_2^1 - (x_2^1)^2 + x_3^1 - (x_3^1)^2 + x_2^1 x_3^1 \qquad (1.15)$$
$$u^2(x^2) = x_1^2 + x_2^2 - (x_2^2)^2 + 10(x_3^2 - (x_3^2)^2).$$

There is **free disposal**, meaning that each agent can freely discard any amount of any good. There is also **free scavenging** (a neologism), meaning that whatever one agent discards, the other one can collect and consume. In particular, if Alice discards some of her me-time, then Bob can consume some or all of the discarded time.

1. Motivate the functional forms of the agents' utilities in (1.15).

2. Compute each agent's consumption and utility in autarky assuming that the agents may exercise free disposal and free scavenging.

3. Suppose that a Walrasian market opens in goods 1 and 2 but not in good 3.

    (a) Define a Walrasian equilibrium for this case of incomplete markets assuming that Bob takes Alice's equilibrium consumption of good 3 as given.

    (b) Compute the agents' demands as functions of positive prices. Assume interior solutions to the agents' maximization problems.

    (c) Compute a Walrasian equilibrium (restricted to trade in goods 1 and 2) and report each agent's utility in this equilibrium.

    (d) Note that, relative to autarky, Alice is better off and Bob is worse off. How is this result consistent with the FWT?

4. Suppose that a Walrasian market opens in all goods.

(a) Compute the agents' demands as functions of positive prices. Assume interior solutions to the agents' maximization problems.

(b) Compute a Walrasian equilibrium and report each agent's utility in this equilibrium.

(c) Note that, relative to the incomplete markets (i.e., when only goods 1 and 2 are tradable) of part 3, both agents are better off with complete markets (i.e., when all goods are tradable). Nevertheless, agent 2 is still worse off than in autarky. How can this be consistent with the FWT?

Problem 1.11 (Sunspot Equilibria). Consider a Walrasian exchange economy with two agents, $\mathcal{I} = \{1, 2\}$, and two goods, $\mathcal{L} = \{1, 2\}$. The set of all Pareto efficient allocations induces a **utility possibility frontier (UPF)**:

$$\mathcal{P} \equiv \left\{ \left(u^1(x^1), u^2(x^2) \right) \in \mathbb{R}^2 \mid (x^1, x^2) \text{ is Pareto efficient} \right\}.$$

Figure 1.20 plots the UPF for the economy. In the figure, the three dots denote the utility levels corresponding to three equilibria, indexed by equilibrium prices p, p', and p''.

1. Plot the agents' offer curves and the induced equilibria in an Edgeworth box in a manner consistent with the UPF in figure 1.20.

2. Define a **sunspot equilibrium** as a lottery parameterized by an arbitrary random variable $\tilde{p}$ with values in the set of the Walrasian equilibrium prices $\{p, p', p''\}$. In a sunspot equilibrium, the agents observe a realization of the random variable $\tilde{p}$ and then coordinate on the Walrasian equilibrium corresponding to that realization. As a result, each agent i's ex-ante utility at the sunspot equilibrium is given by

$$\mathbb{E}\left[u^i(x^i(\tilde{p})) \right],$$

where the expectation is over $\tilde{p}$. Draw the set of all possible sunspot-equilibrium ex-ante utilities.

3. We say that a lottery over feasible allocations ex-ante Pareto dominates another lottery over feasible allocations if each agent's ex-ante utility is at least as high with the former lottery as it is with the latter, and the inequality is strict for at least one agent. Does there exist a sunspot equilibrium that ex-ante Pareto dominates some (not necessarily each) Walrasian equilibrium?

4. How is your answer in part 3 consistent with the FWT?

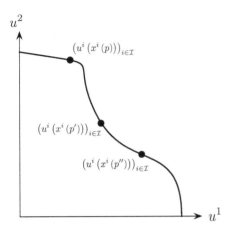

FIGURE 1.20.
The utility possibility frontier.

5. Consider a sunspot equilibrium that is not ex-ante Pareto dominated by any other sunspot equilibrium. Must this sunspot equilibrium be ex-ante Pareto efficient?

Problem 1.12 (Tastes versus Values). Consider a Walrasian exchange economy. Each agent i is endowed with a vector $e^i \in \mathbb{R}^L_+$ of goods. Arrow (1963) observes that markets are good at uncovering tastes but not values. This assertion is somewhat cryptic. In order to operationalize tastes and values, let them denote different components of a utility function. In particular, let agent i's utility from allocation $x \in \mathbb{R}^{IL}_+$ be

$$u^i(x) = t^i(x^i) + v^i(x^{-i}), \tag{1.16}$$

where $x^i \in \mathbb{R}^L_+$ is agent i's consumption bundle (chosen by agent i) and $x^{-i} \in \mathbb{R}^{L(I-1)}_+$ is everyone else's consumption bundle, with $x \equiv (x^i, x^{-i})$. Call the function $t^i : \mathbb{R}^L_+ \to \mathbb{R}$ agent i's **taste**, and call the function $v^i : \mathbb{R}^{L(I-1)}_+ \to \mathbb{R}$ his **values**. For instance, v^i may capture agent i's aversion to consumption inequality, to rampant gratuitous violence, and to polluted environment. By contrast, t^i may betray his taste for consuming a lot of everything, being gratuitously violent, and polluting with abandon. The goal is to show that Walrasian equilibrium outcomes depend on tastes, not values. As a result, it is impossible to infer values from market outcomes.

1. Define Walrasian equilibrium.

2. Argue that the set of Walrasian equilibria is independent of agents' values.

3. Does the conclusion of the FWT hold?

4. The assertion in part 2 is counterintuitive. Indeed, suppose that Bob does not like it when Alice smokes. Suppose that Alice cares about Bob. It is natural to surmise that she will smoke less than she would if she did not care about Bob. Yet part 2 says that someone (e.g., agent i) who cares about others (i.e., $v^i \neq 0$) does not let his values affect his choices. What is "wrong" with the smoking Alice example?

5. Suppose that each agent i's utility function, instead of being (1.16), is

$$u^i(x) = v^i\big(t^i(x^i), x^{-i}\big), \tag{1.17}$$

where the function $t^i : \mathbb{R}^L_+ \to \mathbb{R}$ is called "tastes," and the function $v^i : \mathbb{R} \times \mathbb{R}^{L(I-1)}_+ \to \mathbb{R}$ is increasing in its first argument and is called "values." Interpret the preferences represented by (1.17) and argue that the assertion in part 2 remains true if (1.16) is replaced with (1.17).

6. Suppose that each agent i's utility function, instead of being (1.16) or (1.17), is

$$u^i(x) = t^i\big(v^i(x^{-i}), x^i\big), \tag{1.18}$$

where the function $v^i : \mathbb{R}^{L(I-1)}_+ \to \mathbb{R}$ is called "values," and the function $t^i : \mathbb{R} \times \mathbb{R}^L_+ \to \mathbb{R}$ is increasing in its first argument and is called "tastes." Interpret the preferences represented by (1.18) and argue that the assertion in part 2 is false if (1.16) is replaced with (1.18).

Problem 1.13 (The Transfer Paradox).   After WWI, the Allies asked Germany to pay huge reparations. John Maynard Keynes objected. He argued that these reparations were even more burdensome for Germany than they seemed and that the humiliated Germany would be a politically unstable, dangerous place. In particular, Keynes argued that the price of German exports would have to fall for the rest of the world to be willing to buy them and that Germany would suffer further from this fall. Bertil Ohlin denied the logical necessity of Keynes's conclusion. The goal of this problem is to illustrate that Ohlin was right and that, moreover, the **transfer paradox** could have occurred: the prices of German exports could have risen (instead of falling, as Keynes believed) so much that Germany would have actually been better off as a result of the reparations.[37] The argument will be made in a two-agent ($I = 2$), two-good ($L = 2$) exchange economy, in an Edgeworth box.

1. Show graphically, in an Edgeworth box, that there exist utilities $u \equiv (u^1, u^2)$ and initial endowments $e \equiv (e^1, e^2)$ such that agent 1 may be better off at an equilibrium of an economy (u, e) than at an equilibrium of an economy (u, e'), where $e' \equiv \big(e^1_1 + \delta, e^1_2, e^2_1 - \delta, e^2_2\big)$ for some $\delta > 0$. In other words, paradoxically,

---

37. In the end, Germany ended up paying little of the requested reparations.

agent 1 may be worse off if, before trading, he receives a transfer of good 1 from agent 2. Explain intuitively the described transfer paradox.

2. Argue that no transfer paradox can occur if the utilities are such that equilibrium multiplicity is ruled out for all endowments.

3. Can the transfer paradox occur in an economy in which the initial endowment e is Pareto efficient? What does your answer imply for the likelihood of observing the transfer paradox in practice?

4. This part requires you to imagine what the agents' offer curves must look like when the transfer paradox occurs. First, show that, at the initial endowment e, multiple equilibria must exist. (This observations strengthens the assertion in part 2.) Then show that the pretransfer equilibrium implicated in the transfer paradox can be either stable or unstable. Finally, show that if one starts with the pretransfer equilibrium at which agent 1 is worst off (incidentally, this equilibrium is stable), then no transfer paradox ensues as agent 1's endowment is increased from e to e'. The last result discredits the transfer paradox (in the Edgeworth box), which is shown to rely on an arbitrary selection of the initial equilibrium.

Problem 1.14 (Immiserizing Growth). The goal is to show the possibility of **immiserizing growth** in the Walrasian model: at equilibrium, an agent can be worse off if his endowment increases. (Equivalently, an agent may gain by destroying a part of his endowment before engaging in trade.) There are two agents and two goods. Agent i's utility from consuming bundle $(x_1^i, x_2^i) \in \mathbb{R}_{++}^2$ is

$$u(x_1^i, x_2^i) = \frac{(x_1^i)^{1-\sigma} + (x_2^i)^{1-\sigma} - 2}{1 - \sigma},$$

for some $\sigma > 0$ with $\sigma \neq 1$.

1. Show that $\lim_{\sigma \to 1} u(x_1^i, x_2^i) = \ln x_1^i + \ln x_2^i$. (*Hint*: Use L'Hôpital's rule.)

2. Argue that, in some sense, when σ is larger, the two goods are poorer substitutes. In particular, consider the following experiment. Suppose that p_1/p_2, the relative price of good 1, rises by one percent. Approximately by how much will x_1^i/x_2^i, the relative consumption of good 1, fall? The answer is $1/\sigma$, which goes by the name of the **elasticity of substitution** between the two goods. To arrive at this answer, show that the bundle (x_1^i, x_2^i) that solves the agent's utility maximization problem must satisfy

$$\left(\frac{x_1^i}{x_2^i}\right)^{-1} = \left(\frac{p_1}{p_2}\right)^{\frac{1}{\sigma}}. \tag{1.19}$$

3. Compute agent i's demands x_1^i and x_2^i as the functions of the price vector (p_1, p_2).

4. Find an equilibrium price vector. Is the equilibrium allocation unique?

5. Find the equilibrium utility of agent i. This utility depends only on the agents' endowments, once the allocation and prices have been substituted out.

6. Assume that $e_1^1 = a$, for some $a > 0$, and $e_2^1 = e_1^2 = e_2^2 = \frac{1}{2}$. Plot (on a computer) the equilibrium utility of agent 1 as a function of a. Do so for different values of $\sigma > 0$. Identify numerically a value of σ for which the equilibrium utility is decreasing in a on some interval. Explain intuitively this equilibrium phenomenon; you may draw an Edgeworth box, if you like.

7. Now assume that $e_1^1 = \frac{1}{2} - b$, $e_1^2 = \frac{1}{2} + b$, for $b \in (-\frac{1}{2}, \frac{1}{2})$, and $e_2^1 = e_2^2 = \frac{1}{2}$. Can you find a value of σ for which agent 1's equilibrium utility is increasing in b on some interval? Relate your answer to problem 1.13.

Problem 1.15 (Endowment Withholding).   Assume two agents, $\mathcal{I} = \{1, 2\}$, and two goods, $\mathcal{L} = \{1, 2\}$. Let $(u^i, e^i)_{i \in \mathcal{I}}$ be an economy satisfying u-continuity, u-monotonicity, and u-concavity. A planner is charged with enforcing the (assume unique) Walrasian outcome. Agent 1 is called Alice. The planner knows all the aspects of the economy except Alice's endowment, e^1. So, he asks. First, Alice reports (possibly untruthfully) to the planner some nonnegative endowment $\hat{e}^1$, after which the planner enforces the Walrasian equilibrium trades for the economy $((u^1, \hat{e}^1), (u^2, e^2))$.

1. In an Edgeworth box, construct an example in which Alice benefits from withholding some of her endowment by reporting an $\hat{e}^1 < e^1$, thereby guaranteeing herself consumption $e^1 - \hat{e}^1$ in addition to the trade that the planner subsequently enforces.[38]

2. Suppose Alice withholds (not necessarily optimally) a part of her endowment to her benefit. Must the induced outcome be Pareto efficient with respect to the actual endowments (e^1, e^2)?

---

38. The question focuses on withholding, not overstating, because it is easier to catch Alice overstating (the planner can simply ask Alice to show her reported endowment) than withholding (Alice can hide her endowment).

CHAPTER 2

MARKETS AND MORALS I

2.1 INTRODUCTION

Are markets moral? This question is easy to answer in a well-defined model, such as that of chapter 1. If equilibrium outcomes possess the sought normative properties (e.g., Pareto efficiency and some notion of equity), then markets can be said to be moral and to motivate the participants to act in a moral way. Otherwise, markets are immoral; they nudge participants to act immorally in the sense of promoting an outcome that defies the specified normative objectives. For instance, if all that one normatively cares about is Pareto efficiency, then markets are moral under the conditions of the FWT (theorem 1.1) but immoral, say, in the presence of externalities (problems 1.2 and 1.8). If, instead, all that one cares about is envy-freeness, then markets are immoral even under the ideal assumptions of the FWT (problem 1.9).

However, the question of the morality of markets is typically raised (by philosophers, journalists, an occasional economist) in everyday contexts, outside formal models. As befits most seemingly straightforward but vaguely defined questions, it rouses passions and polarizes. Taking this question seriously is a valuable exercise in translating nebulous concepts into the language that is precise enough for measurement. Such translations help sharpen interesting questions and help interpret empirical findings, which, in turn, suggest which models one should examine next.

To begin answering whether markets are moral in practice, one must conceptualize "markets" and "moral." The proximity to the Walrasian model is a decent test for whether an observed exchange is a market. Morality can be identified with the advancement of a collection of mutually compatible normative goals. If one of these goals is Pareto efficiency, then one would regard as immoral, say, the act of surreptitiously unplugging a vending machine, thereby denying the vendor and its customers the benefit of trade and, thus, leading to a Pareto inferior outcome. Often, however, the Pareto criterion is not discerning enough. For example, is it moral for Alice to gratuitously punch Bob if she expects to enjoy doing so? Most moral comparisons are of this kind: there are both winners and losers from the act.

As an empirical matter, it is compelling to postulate that an act is **immoral** if the inflicted suffering *clearly* exceeds the perpetrator's gain, where the qualifier "clearly" must be explained. In addition to being normatively compelling, the proposed definition seems to capture the way most individuals tend to think about morality most of the time, whether they explicitly acknowledge doing so or not. We say that an act is **moral** if it is not immoral.

How can Alice tell whether Bob's pain from being punched *clearly* exceeds her pleasure from punching him? There is a venerable tradition in moral philosophy and economics of inviting a decision-maker behind the so-called veil of ignorance, as proposed by Harsanyi (1955) and Rawls (1971), among others. Behind this **veil of ignorance**—or in the so-called **original position**—the decision-maker is unaware of his position in the society; he can be the unwilling recipient of the punch or the one to administer it. If, behind the veil, *most* decision-makers (whose opinions may differ) would refuse to endorse punching, then we say that the suffering of the punched *clearly* exceeds the gain of the puncher, and, so, it is immoral to punch.

Note that, in order to recognize punching as immoral, we do not require an individual to refrain from punching in practice. We do not even require the individual to refuse to endorse punching behind the veil of ignorance. We only ask that the individual—who, for all we know, might be a masochist—recognize that most decision-makers in the original position would refuse to endorse punching.

In this chapter, we discuss morality in the context of three experimental studies. The goal of the discussion is to learn to recognize markets and to attempt to operationalize morality in applications. The first study, by Milgram (1963), a psychologist, has nothing to do with markets. Instead, it sets the stage for thinking about immoral behavior. In addition, the study helps one appreciate the distinguishing methodological feature of experimental economics (as opposed to experimental psychology): the economists' commitment to refraining from deception by commission. The second study, by economists Falk and Szech (2013a), operationalizes markets and immoral conduct in the lab and argues that markets promote immorality. The third study, by economists and anthropologists Henrich et al. (2001), combines experimental and field data to argue the opposite: markets promote morality. No reconciliation of the last two studies' conflicting conclusions is offered.

2.2   OBEDIENCE TO AUTHORITY LEADS TO IMMORAL BEHAVIOR

THE EXPERIMENT

In the aftermath of WWII, researchers wondered how so many people could so easily obey the authority of the few to conduct atrocious, immoral acts. In the 1960s, Yale psychologist Stanley Milgram set out to find out. For his **obedience experiment**, Milgram (1963) enlisted volunteers from different walks of life to be human subjects (i.e., participants) in an experiment, purportedly a Yale experiment designed to study the effects of punishment on learning. Each participant's task was to be a teacher and administer an electrical shock to the learner each time the learner gave an incorrect answer or failed to respond. Unbeknownst to the participants, the learner was the experimenter's confederate (i.e., an accomplice), who received no electrical shock. As the learner would groan, moan, plead, and then fall silent, the teacher was encouraged to proceed with the punishment. Each participant was paid a flat $4.50 fee (about four times the hourly minimum wage) just for participating.

The experimenter's authority induced the subjects to administer increasingly powerful electrical shocks in the belief that they contributed to the study on learning. Each time the learner made a mistake, the teacher was required to jack up the voltage. Sixty-five percent of participants delivered the maximal shock, marked "450 volts," exceeding "danger: severe shock" level. The subjects' obedience diminished somewhat, but did not disappear when the hoax experimenter had been stripped of his Yale credentials in a companion experiment, described by Milgram (1965); 48% of participants delivered the maximal shock in that experiment.

In related experiments, Milgram (1965) documents the **dilution of responsibility**. In one experiment, a subject, who played the part of a teacher, was put into the same room with other teachers, all of whom were the experimenter's confederates. If the teacher-confederates delivered higher shocks, the subject was more likely to do so, too. In another related experiment, a subject was assigned to assist a teacher-confederate with subsidiary tasks without having to directly deliver the shock. In this case, the subjects were more likely to assist in delivering the highest voltage than the subjects in the original experiment were to deliver the shocks directly. In both cases, one can interpret the peer effect the confederate teacher exerted on the subject as the dilution of the subject's sense of responsibility.

FURTHER INTERPRETATION

The subjects' delivery of the maximal shock can be regarded as immoral, according to our definition of morality. Indeed, at the start of the experiment, subjects were effectively prompted to imagine themselves behind the veil of ignorance as it was revealed to them that a random draw would determine their role: either the learner or the teacher. To assess morality, however, the veil of ignorance must be even more comprehensive than that.

The appropriate thought experiment in the original position would have the subject imagine himself, with some probabilities, in one of four positions: the experimenter, the general public that would benefit from the purported experiment on learning, the teacher, and the learner. For most, the public benefit from this study would probably not outweigh the gratuitous suffering of both the electrically shocked learner and (consistent with the experimental records) the distressed teacher.[1] Thus, the subjects must have realized that they behaved immorally when administering the shocks.

The pessimistic interpretation of the study is that Americans (of New Haven, in the 1960s) are gullible and can easily be manipulated by an authority figure. The optimistic interpretation is that Americans trust each other and, in particular, trust experts and institutions. Both trust and trustworthiness are essential for society (in general) and markets (in particular) to function effectively. For instance, the FWT implicitly assumes that any agent can be trusted to honor any trade he has chosen to execute. Trustworthiness is especially important in the environments in which monitoring and enforcement are costly, such as environments with time and uncertainty.

A REMARK ON METHODOLOGY: DECEPTION

The main problem with the methodology in the obedience experiment is its reliance on deception. Deception undermines the validity of subsequent studies. For instance, Milgram asks each subject to participate in a lottery to determine whether he is a teacher or a learner, but the lottery is rigged; each subject is assigned to be the teacher for sure. The study on learning, advertised to the subjects, is a hoax. The learner is a confederate, who acts out agony, while no electrical shock is ever delivered. The fellow teachers introduced in some experiments are confederates, too. Moreover, the subjects are secretly recorded, observed through one-way mirrors, and occasionally photographed. As studies based on deception become well-known—as the obedience experiment has done—subjects in new experiments come to expect deception and attempt to second-guess the experimenter. The subjects' behavior thus becomes impossible to interpret because the researcher can never tell how the subjects view the experimental setting.

Experimental economics is careful to distance itself from experimental psychology, which uses deception to this day. Economists never plant confederates and never lie (at least not by commission) about the experimental procedures. Whether

---

1. The teachers indeed loathed inflicting pain. For instance, in a related experiment in which the experimenter gave instructions by phone, the subjects' compliance decreased to one-third of the compliance observed when the experimenter was present in the same room. Moreover, the subjects lied to the experimenter by claiming that they administered a higher level of shock than they actually did (Milgram, 1965).

owing to the culture of no deception, to lesser demand for sensational findings, or just to luck, economics experiments withstand the tests of replication better than the competition does.[2]

Experimental economics took off after the golden age of experimental social psychology (exemplified by the work of Milgram). By that time, ethics review committees were already widespread. These committees would think twice before letting researchers submit subjects to the emotional distress of the kind experienced in the obedience experiment. As a result, economics experiments are rarely as dramatic as the early social psychology experiments. The economics experiment we turn to next is a cleverly conceived exception.

2.3   MARKETS LEAD TO IMMORAL BEHAVIOR

THE EXPERIMENT

Falk and Szech (2013a) hypothesize that—and set out to test experimentally whether—markets lead to immoral behavior. According to the authors, "[m]arkets are institutions where sellers and buyers interact and can trade items." In the lab, the authors operationalize markets as a bilateral bargaining situation. They define behavior as immoral if it inflicts disproportionate suffering on a third party, a party that does not participate in the bargaining.

The **mouse experiment** of Falk and Szech (2013a) has two leading experimental **treatments**, or versions, to be compared and contrasted. In the **individual treatment**, the experimenter gives €10 (a bit over an hourly minimum wage) to a subject if and only if the subject consents to having a mouse gassed to death. If the subject rejects the offer, the mouse lives on in comfort until it dies of natural causes.

In the **bargaining treatment**, the subjects are partitioned into pairs, and each pair engages in a continuous double auction for the life of a mouse. In particular, in the **continuous double auction**, one member of the pair, say, Alice, is the seller of the life of a mouse, whereas the other member, say, Bob, is a potential buyer, provisionally endowed by the experimenter with €20 (about two and a half hours at the minimum wage). Alice may repeatedly submit an ask, which is a number between zero and €20, and Bob may repeatedly submit a bid, which is a number in the same range. As soon as the ask and the bid cross (i.e., the bid exceeds the ask), trade occurs at Bob's latest bid, denoted by x. Alice gets x euros, Bob keeps

2. Camerer et al. (2016) successfully replicate eleven out of eighteen (i.e., 61%) experiments published in top economics journals. The corresponding figures (reported in "A far from dismal outcome." *The Economist*, March 5, 2016) are 36% for psychology and 11% for pharmaceutical studies. (See also Open Science Collaboration. "Estimating the reproducibility of psychological science." *Science*, August 28, 2015; and Nave, Gidi. "Is the replication crisis in Psychology real?" *The Neuroeconomist* (blog), March 2, 2016, http://theneuroeconomist.com/2016/03/is-the-replication-crisis-in-psychology-real/.)

$20 - x$ euros, and the mouse is gassed to death. If either Alice or Bob refuses to transact, the mouse lives, and Alice and Bob each get zero; Bob's €20 go back to the experimenter.

The experimental economists' commitment to avoiding lies by commission is exemplified by this passage from the instructions that Falk and Szech (2013a) distributed to the experimental subjects:

> Please note: All statements made in these instructions are true. This holds for all experiments carried out by the Bonn Econ Lab, and also for this experiment. In particular, all actions to be taken will be implemented exactly in the way they are described. If you want to, you will be able to verify the correctness of all statements made in these instructions after the experiment.

It requires imagination to place oneself behind the veil of ignorance and imagine being born a mouse, the experimental subject, or someone else who is directly or indirectly concerned with the experiment. It is conceivable, however, that, having performed this exercise, most would regard the prospect of gassing a mouse for the sake of €10 or even €20 changing hands as a gratuitous act of violence, an immoral act. Yet Falk and Szech (2013a) find that

- 46% of subjects kill a mouse for €10 in the individual treatment; and

- 72% of subjects kill a mouse for €10 or less in the bargaining treatment.

Under the assumption that each subject prefers more money to less, those who kill for less than €10 would also kill for €10. Thus, subjects are more eager to kill in the bargaining treatment than in the individual treatment.

One may be tempted to explain the difference between the two treatments by observing that, in the bargaining treatment, killing a mouse generates the total of €20 for both subjects, compared to just €10 per gassed mouse in the individual treatment. Then, behind the veil of ignorance, killing a mouse in the bargaining treatment is more compelling than in the individual treatment, provided the decision-maker imagines himself in the position of a mouse or a human subject but never of the taxpayer who finances the experiment (lest the transfer be a wash). This explanation is challenged by the **price-list treatment** (described in problem 2.1), which elicits the amount of money at which a subject is just indifferent between letting a mouse live and killing the mouse while keeping the money. The price-list treatment indicates that, in order to raise the killing rate in the individual treatment to 72%, which is the killing rate in bargaining treatment, the posted price in the individual treatment must be nearly €50, which is well above the €20 shared by the killers in the bargaining treatment:

- 72% of subjects kill a mouse for €47.50 in the price-list treatment.

It is hard to imagine that a subject would prefer sharing €20 to getting nearly €50 all by himself. Something else must be going on.

The view that it is the difference between €10 in the individual treatment and €20 in the bargaining treatment that is responsible for the difference in the two treatments' outcomes is also challenged by the **augmented individual treatment**. In this treatment, whenever a subject accepts the posted price of €10 from the experimenter, some other subject is also given €10. Thus, the total of €20 is at stake, just as in the bargaining treatment. Still,

- 45% of subjects kill a mouse for €10 in the augmented individual treatment.

That is, in the augmented individual treatment, subjects kill at roughly the same rate as in the individual treatment. The authors conclude that this is the difference in protocols—posted-price versus the continuous double action—that is responsible for the difference in the observed killing rates.

FURTHER INTERPRETATION

Falk and Szech (2013a) suggest the following reasons for why bargaining—which they identify with markets—leads to a higher incidence of mouse killings than a posted price.

- By making multiple experimental subjects complicit in an outcome, markets dilute responsibility. (In the individual treatment, the experimenter, who posts the price, likely dilutes the responsibility as well, but, perhaps, by not as much as a fellow subject in the bargaining treatment.)

- The mere existence of a market can be construed as an endorsement of the market transaction by the authority that has created the market. That is, the experimental subject may bring from outside the lab the notion that the existence of a market signals the morality of the transaction.

- Markets may nudge participants to focus on the materialistic aspects of a transaction. This subconscious association of markets with materialistic aspects comes from experiences outside the lab.

Taking the first bullet point seriously, we formally explore responsibility and its dilution shortly.

The phenomenon in the second bullet point is discussed in section 6.2 in the context of the experiment of Gneezy and Rustichini (2000).

The phenomenon in the third bullet point is illustrated by the **screen saver experiment** of Vohs, Mead, and Goode (2006, experiments 7 and 9). In one treatment of that experiment, the subjects are seated in front of a computer to perform some simple tasks and are shown a screen saver with floating fish. In another treatment, the screen saver has floating banknotes instead. In the former treatment, the subjects are more eager to cooperate with another participant (experiment 9) and more eager to sit closer to another participant in a get-acquainted session (experiment 7). On the basis of this and related experiments (which measure contributions to charity and the willingness to help an experimenter's confederate to collect "accidentally" scattered pencils), Vohs et al. (2006) conclude that markets make individuals less helpful and less willing to solicit help—less moral, in a sense.

A REMARK ON METHODOLOGY: P-HACKING

The screen saver experiment is intriguing. It belongs to the genre of experiments in which exposing participants to money makes them narrowly selfish and also accepting of inequality (Caruso, Vohs, Baxter, and Waytz, 2013; Vohs, 2015). In fact, the experimental results are so intriguing that the screen saver experiment would probably not have been published if its findings had been negative (i.e., with both treatment groups equally eager to cooperate and be socially intimate with others). Such a **publication bias** toward positive results can lead to the publication of spurious findings: roughly speaking, if researchers perform a hundred experiments, about five of these are likely to produce results that are statistically significant at the 5% level (i.e., with p-value $= 0.05$) even if no underlying relationship exists in any of these experiments. These five experiments would then be published and reported as statistically significant.

The anticipation of the publication bias encourages **p-hacking**: the practice of exercising the researcher's creative freedom in designing experiments, in dynamically selecting the sample size, and in altering the measurement procedure until an effect with the desired p-value emerges. The smoking gun for both the publication bias and the p-hacking are the p-values that statistically improbably bunch at just under 0.05, the received criterion for statistical significance (see Brodeur, Lé, Sangnier, and Zylberberg, 2016; Masicampo and Lalande, 2012; and Nuzzo, Regina. "Scientific method: statistical errors." *Nature*, February 12, 2014).

Can the results of the screen saver experiment be but a statistical fluke due to the publication bias or the p-hacking? Rohrer, Pashler, and Harris (2015) do some detective work. They notice that p-values in the experiments of Vohs et al. (2006) are bunched below 0.05, with none above 0.05. This suggests that some experiments with no effect of money cues on the subjects' behavior may have been suppressed. Indeed, Rohrer et al. (2015) report that the authors of the screen saver experiment conducted, but did not report, two (unpublished) studies that found no effects and performed, but did not report, additional, measurements that were not statistically significant. Further, Rohrer et al. (2015) try and fail to replicate a series of experiments that test the effects of the exposure to money cues on morality.

The mouse experiment of Falk and Szech (2013a) and the companion experiments reported by Falk and Szech (2013b) contain no smoking gun; p-values do not bunch improbably. Indeed, the p-values that support the main conclusions are below 0.01, thereby meeting a higher standard for statistical significance.

MODELING THE DILUTION OF RESPONSIBILITY

Both Milgram (1963) and Falk and Szech (2013a) appeal to the dilution of responsibility to explain why subjects are more willing to engage in immoral behavior as their peer-group size increases. Let us formalize the idea. Defining responsibility formally is of interest both for normative reasons, to establish guilt in the court of law, and for positive reasons, to describe how the subjective feeling of guilt may vary with the group size.

Consider a majority-voting problem. A voter is **pivotal ex-post** if his vote affects the outcome; had he voted differently, the outcome would have been different. Suppose that a society wants to avert some outcome, denoted by X. Suppose that Alice is pivotal and outcome X prevails. Then, it is natural to say that Alice is responsible for X.

Now, suppose that Alice is not pivotal. Still, she has voted for X, and X has prevailed. Is Alice not responsible because she is not pivotal?[3] If responsibility is defined as being pivotal (ex-post), conditional on how others have voted, then indeed Alice is not responsible. Moreover, if Alice is not pivotal in the majority vote, then no one is pivotal and, so, no one is responsible.

Alternatively, one can identify responsibility with the extent to which an agent is **pivotal ex-ante**, before others have cast their votes. In particular, Alice's responsibility can be defined as the probability that her vote will be pivotal, computed before others' votes have been observed. This probability could be computed, say, under the assumption that all others cast their votes uniformly at random or under some other assumption informed by the history of past votes.

The notion of responsibility derived from pivotality ex-ante naturally leads to the dilution of responsibility: the larger the population of voters, the less likely it is that any individual agent will end up being pivotal and, hence, responsible. As a result, individuals may feel less compunction when acting in larger groups. This logic applies well to the obedience experiment. The subject in the role of the teacher's underling may feel less responsible than a lone subject for approving an electrical shock if he believes that there is a positive probability that the teacher vetoes his approval. This probability of the veto discounts the subject's emotional burden of responsibility while leaving the gratification from obeying the authority intact, thereby making the subject more eager to approve. By contrast, the dilution of responsibility explains less well the subjects' eagerness to transact in the bargaining treatment of the mouse experiment relative to the individual treatment. In the

---

3. Arendt (1963) asks: Was an individual who was complicit in Nazi crimes responsible for them, even if his choices have not affected the course of history?

bargaining treatment, the counterparty's potential refusal to transact discounts not only the responsibility for instigating the death of the mouse but also the expected monetary gain from the transaction.

EXTERNAL VALIDITY

To conclude from the mouse experiment that markets tend to make individuals immoral, one must accept that the bargaining treatment is a better metaphor for the markets outside the lab than the individual treatment is. One could argue the opposite. Let us attempt to identify the features of the market that market designers tend to (or ought to) have in mind when designing an exchange mechanism with appealing normative properties. (Thus, we are not after a market cornered by a monopolist or plagued by insider trading.) Then we shall compare these features to the treatments in the mouse experiment. For both normative (by the FWT) and positive (to reflect the common usage of the term "market") reasons, it is natural to look to the Walrasian paradigm for pointers to the essential features of a **market**:

- *Anonymity*: A transaction between agents is unaffected by whether they knew each other before this transaction and whether they expect to transact with each other in the future. In a dynamic environment, a transaction is taken to mean an entire contract (e.g., an insurance contract or a cell phone plan).

- *(Private) Property Rights*: Each agent is free to refrain from trading; no one is coerced to part with his endowment.

- *Bilateral Transactions*: Whether a pair of agents transact is up to this pair alone.

- *Price-Taking*: Each agent takes the terms of the transaction as given. Even if he affects these terms (perhaps, ever so slightly), he behaves as if he does not realize that he affects them.

- *Universal Access*: No agent is precluded from transacting, and all agents transact on the same terms.

- *Enforcement*: No agent can renege on the terms of the transaction that he has agreed to.

Both the individual treatment and the bargaining treatment respect anonymity, property rights (here, the freedom not to transact), the bilateral nature of the transaction (i.e., the mouse has no say in whether trade occurs), universal access, and enforcement. However, only the individual treatment satisfies price-taking. So, in a sense, the individual treatment can be interpreted as the more accurate metaphor for a market. If so, then the mouse experiment suggests that markets make individuals more moral, not less.

Furthermore, if one wishes to interpret the killing rates seen in the experimental lab as being valid externally, outside the lab, one would have to admit the possibility that the subjects saw through certain aspects of the experimental design. A savvy subject may think: "Sure, gassing a mouse sounds awful. But it cannot be too awful or else the ethics review committee would have never approved the experiment. So, there must be a catch; it is probably O.K. to kill a mouse." And he would be right.

There is a catch indeed. The mice killed in the experiment are so-called surplus mice, bred for medical experiments but deemed unfit, even though healthy. Such mice are routinely killed to save money for their upkeep. What Falk and Szech (2013a) have done is to pay for the upkeep of the mice that the subjects in their experiment have refused to kill. Had the subjects known that the society deems it desirable to kill the surplus mice, they might have reconsidered their objections to killing, on the grounds of morality. Perhaps, some guessed that much.

Thus, by suppressing the fact that the default option for the mice is death, the authors of the experiment have lied by omission (as opposed to lying by commission, as Milgram, 1963, did). Even though this lie might have affected the incidence of mouse deaths, there are no a-priori grounds to believe that this lie would affect the difference in killings rates between the individual and the bargaining treatments. It is this difference, not the individual magnitudes, that is the focus of the study.

2.4   MARKETS LEAD TO MORAL BEHAVIOR

THE EXPERIMENT

Henrich, Boyd, Bowles, Camerer, Fehr, Gintis, and McElreath (2001) test the hypothesis that markets cause moral behavior. This hypothesis can be motivated by the observation of Herbert Gintis: "Movements for religious and lifestyle tolerance, gender equality, and democracy have flourished and triumphed in societies governed by market exchange, and nowhere else."[4] Henrich et al. (2001) further conjecture that "the more frequently people experience market transactions, the more they will also experience abstract sharing principles concerning behaviors toward strangers [...]." The hypothesis that market interactions make individuals kinder has a long pedigree; it goes back to the Enlightenment view of **doux commerce** (gentle commerce).

To explore the plausibility of their hypothesis, Henrich et al. (2001) conduct the **small-scale societies (SSS)** experiment. Instead of recreating market and non-market experimental treatments in a laboratory (as Falk and Szech, 2013a, do), Henrich et al. (2001) borrow market, nonmarket, and a variety of intermediate treatments from field observations. These field observations are of UCLA undergraduates

---

4. See Gintis, Herbert. "Forum response: how markets crowd out morals." *Boston Review*, June 25, 2012, http://www.bostonreview.net/gintis-giving-economists-their-due.

and fifteen small-scale societies (foragers, horticulturalists, nomadic herders, and agriculturalists) living under varying degrees of market integration in twelve countries across five continents. A society's **market integration** is measured by averaging its ranks in each of three categories: (i) the degree of engagement in market exchange (e.g., hired labor, the amount of land devoted to crops for sale, and the prevalence of the national language, as opposed to local dialects, which is a proxy for the exposure to markets), (ii) the settlement size (which varies from about a hundred to a thousand individuals), and (iii) sociopolitical complexity (roughly the amount of decision-making that occurs above the household level). The rankings within each of the three categories are subjective,[5] and the choice to average across these categories is arbitrary. Categories (ii) and (iii) bear no direct relationship to markets and are only presumed to be correlated with market prevalence. For instance, exchange between households is presumed to be mediated by markets, and so larger settlements must rely on markets that are more expansive, thereby motivating category (ii). Category (iii) can be motivated by presuming that more complex markets require more complex regulation, which calls for more complex institutions.

The SSS experiment defines moral behavior as generosity toward one's opponent in the ultimatum game. The **ultimatum game** has two players: a proposer and a responder. The proposer is provisionally given a "dollar" (a day's or two days' wages in the small-scale societies), of which he chooses amount x to offer to the responder. If the responder accepts, the proposer keeps $1 - x$, and the responder keeps x. If the responder rejects, the proposer and the responder each get zero. The degree of the proposer's morality is identified with the magnitude of x, the generosity of the proposer's offer. Indeed, it is plausible that, behind the veil of ignorance, not knowing whether he will be a proposer or a responder, a decision-maker would seek to insure by making the proposer split the dollar: $x = \frac{1}{2}$.

Strictly speaking, one would wish to identify with morality the difference between the hypothetical proposer's offers behind the veil of ignorance and with this veil lifted. We take the latter to be zero. The rationale is the **backward induction** principle, which instructs the proposer to put himself into the shoes of the responder and imagine the responder's reaction to every possible offer of the proposer. The proposer then is to choose the offer that will generate the most favorable reaction by the responder. "To maximize his monetary payoff," reasons the proposer, "the responder can do no better than to accept any offer; the alternative is getting zero. I shall therefore maximize my monetary payoff by offering $x = 0$."[6] Backward induction thus implies that any positive offer indicates that the proposer cares not only

---

5. Henrich et al. (2005) describe the construction of the rankings of the small-scale societies, or groups: "Then the field researchers lined up and sorted themselves by repeatedly comparing the group they studied with those of their two neighbors in line, switching places as necessary, and repeating the process until no one needed to move."

6. To make sure the responder (strictly) prefers to accept his offer, the proposer can offer some small positive amount (e.g., one cent).

about his monetary payoff but also about the responder's and, so, is being generous, or moral.

Now, in practice, responders' behavior does not conform with the backward induction principle, but we shall argue that this nonconformity does not subtract from the proposer's morality. In experimental data gathered over decades and across the globe (e.g., Roth, Prasnikar, Okuno-Fujiwara, and Zamir, 1991), a substantial fraction of responders refuse to maximize their monetary payoffs; small offers are emphatically rejected, perhaps, because they are deemed unfair. As a result, the proposer's observed reluctance to make small offers may indicate not his generosity but his narrow self-interest, the desire to maximize his monetary payoff by avoiding the responder's retributive rejection. Formally, assume that the responder accepts an offer x with probability $F(x)$, where function F is continuous, increasing, and satisfies $F(0) = 0$ and $F(1) = 1$. The proposer knows F. Let x^* denote the offer that maximizes the proposer's expected monetary payoff:

$$x^* \in \arg \max_{x \in [0,1]} F(x)(1 - x). \qquad (2.1)$$

For example, if $F(x) = x^\gamma$ for some $\gamma > 0$, then $x^* = \gamma / (1 + \gamma)$; the more likely the responder is to reject low offers (i.e., the higher γ), the more will be offered by the proposer. Then, the proposer can be said to be generous if and only if he offers $x > x^*$. Proposers' offers in the experiments conducted on university students suggest that $x \approx x^*$ (Roth et al., 1991), whereas Henrich et al. (2001) document $x > x^*$ in several small-scale societies.

Should one then plot market integration against $x - x^*$ (as the second-pass approach suggests), instead of x (as the first-pass approach suggests), in order to uncover the relationship between market integration and generosity? Not so fast. Imagine that Alice and Bob live in a kindly town whose denizens customarily hold doors for each other. If Bob fails to hold the door for Alice as she exits a Starbucks®, the door will hit the startled Alice and cause her to spill her drink. To avoid such an embarrassment, Bob always holds doors. Does Alice's expectation of kindness undo Bob's kindness? Is an act kindly only if it exceeds the expectation of kindness? In the long run, as long as individuals learn, it is not even statistically possible for the acts of kindness to systematically exceed expected kindness; the expectation of kindness will catch up with reality. Surely the expectation of kindness itself must be a testament to the town where Alice and Bob live being a kindly town.

So, the third and the final pass at defining generosity in the ultimatum game recognizes that the high expectation of generosity embedded into the responder's propensity to reject low offers is itself a measure of the population generosity. So let us designate x^* as a measure of expected generosity and designate $x - x^*$ as a correction for the proposer's unanticipated generosity. Let the overall generosity be $x^* + (x - x^*) = x$, which coincides with the measure of the generosity motivated by the first pass at the problem and adopted by the authors of the SSS experiment.

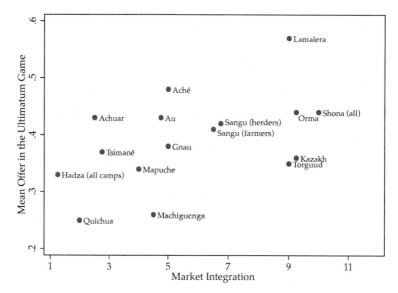

FIGURE 2.1.
The plot of mean offers against market integration. *Source*: the same as figure 5 of Henrich et al. (2005).

Figure 2.1 plots *x* against market integration. The apparent positive statistical relationship is interpreted as causal by the authors. The interpretation is that the more an individual experiences market transactions, the more he experiences Pareto improving trades, thereby witnessing his trade partners gain. These experiences help the individual discover his latent taste for pleasing others (the taste believed by Singer, 1981, to be accessible through the exercise of reason) and for vicariously partaking in others' pleasures (perhaps via mirror neurons, as popularized by Ramachandran, 2011, chapter 4). This is doux commerce at work.

FURTHER INTERPRETATION

When interpreting the correlation in figure 2.1, one ought to exercise caution. The plot reports correlation, not causation. This correlation can be the result of market integration affecting generosity, of generosity (or, rather, its likely correlates: trust and trustworthiness)[7] affecting market integration, or of some third, unobserved, cause affecting both generosity and market integration. This third factor could be the capacity for abstract reasoning, as measured, for instance, by nonverbal IQ scores. Let us elaborate.

Higher IQ helps societies design and operate more complex markets.

---

7. Trust is an especially valuable resource for the functioning of markets in dynamic and stochastic settings. The lender should trust the borrower to repay. The insurer should trust the insuree not to fake the accident.

Higher IQ individuals also behave more cooperatively in strategic, positive-sum settings, in a manner consistent with the morality derived from behind the veil of ignorance.[8] Thus, Burks, Carpenter, Goette, and Rustichini (2009) study experimentally a **trust game** (also known as the **sequential prisoner's dilemma**). In this game, the first mover is free to transfer some of his monetary endowment to the second mover, with the transfer doubled by the experimenter upon receipt. Then the second mover is free to transfer some of his monetary endowment to the first mover, with the transfer doubled by the experimenter upon receipt. Backward induction suggests that all transfers be zero. Experiments usually generate positive transfers. What Burks et al. (2009) find on top of that is that trucker trainees (the human subjects in their experiments) with higher nonverbal IQ test scores tend to make more generous offers when they are first movers and tend to reward the first mover's generosity more when they are second movers.

Moreover, higher IQ individuals are more likely to recognize positive-sum games in the first place. In particular, Caplan and Miller (2010)—whose measure of intelligence is a vocabulary test—report survey evidence according to which the individual propensity to "think like economists" is better predicted by intelligence than by education.[9] Proto, Rustichini, and Sofianos (2015) find that students with higher nonverbal IQ test scores are more likely to cooperate in an **infinitely repeated prisoner's dilemma** (with stochastic termination after each repetition). In the experiment, cooperation (which is one of many equilibrium outcomes) may be caused by the subjects' ability to recognize, and coordinate on, a positive-sum play.

To summarize, variation in IQ may directly cause variation in market complexity and in moral behavior. As a result, markets and morals would covary, even if one did not directly affect the other.

If present, IQ differences are likely to be caused, at least in part, by culture and wealth.[10] If so, however, the IQ differences themselves are likely to be indirectly caused by the differences in market integration, which affects wealth, which affects nutrition, education, and culture, which affect IQ. Furthermore, higher IQ individuals are likely to be more productive, thereby contributing to wealth. Thus, there is a positive feedback loop between wealth and IQ. In addition, wealth is likely to contribute to market complexity and moral behavior directly, for wealth cushions

8. We say that a situation is a **positive-sum game** if at least one pair of feasible outcomes can be strictly Pareto ranked, meaning that one outcome Pareto dominates the other. By contrast, in a **zero-sum game**, no two feasible outcomes can be Pareto ranked, meaning that if, in one outcome, one agent is better off than in another outcome, then the opposite must hold for some other agent.

9. Vocabulary is likely to be a strong marker for social class, so its use as a proxy for IQ is problematic.

10. In Western cultures, the secular rise in IQ during the past century—the so-called **Flynn effect**—is likely to be due to the increasing pervasiveness of abstract, scientific thinking in education and popular culture (Pinker, 2011, chapter 9) as well as improved nutrition (Feyrer, Politi, and Weil, 2017), not due to natural selection, which operates on a time scale longer than the Flynn effect.

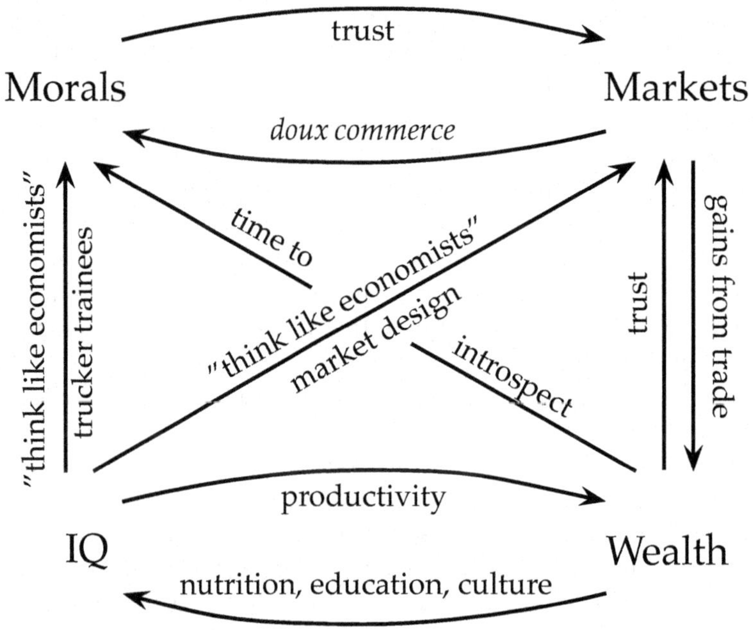

FIGURE 2.2.
The challenge of identifying the causal effect of markets on morals in the presence of common causes (IQ and wealth). Each arrow points from a cause to an effect.

the betrayal of trust and makes generosity, and the time spent contemplating morals behind the veil of ignorance, more affordable.

Figure 2.2 summarizes the discussion above and thus illustrates the challenges of causal inference. The identification of each causal effect separately would call for intricate experimental designs or the application of sophisticated econometric techniques. In addition, the figure points out a nuance in the formulation of the exact question one is after. When interested in the effect of markets on morals, is one interested only in the direct effect, labeled "doux commerce" in the figure, or is one interested in the total effect, which is the sum of the direct effect and the indirect effect that operates through wealth, IQ, and (through a positive feedback loop) morals themselves? From the policy point of view, the total effect is of primary interest.

2.5   CONCLUDING REMARKS

The reported experiments on markets and morals exhibit statistically significant results and admit compelling causal interpretations. But what are the channels through which markets affect morality? What is it that the experiments pick up?

It is plausible and likely that exposure to markets would influence preferences and social norms.[11] But would one expect this influence to emerge over decades or generations (as it might in the SSS experiment), in the course of an hour (as it might in the mouse experiment), or after a minute (as it might in the screen saver experiment)? What seems likely is that the SSS experiment picks up the long-term causal effect of institutions on social norms; the mouse experiment picks up the **framing** effect, whereby one of the two rather similar mouse-killing scenarios is designed to resemble a market setting, thereby triggering the *conscious* adoption of the market norms developed outside the lab; and the screen saver experiment picks up the **priming** effect, whereby floating dollar bills *nonconsciously* invoke the emotions and attitudes that prevail when the individual operates in a market, and these emotions and attitudes affect subjects' behavior in the lab.[12] Thus, the reported experiments not only differ in their methodology and the precise formulation of the question they address, but they also measure different causal mechanisms.

Just as it is delicate to determine what exactly the market variables pick up in the experiments, it is also delicate to determine what exactly the measures of morality correspond to. In the mouse experiment, do those who refuse to accept €10 for killing a mouse follow their moral compass or are they instinctively reacting to the social opprobrium that they would face if they endorsed the killing in their daily lives? In the SSS experiment, are the proposers who offer to share a dollar guided by the morality of equitable distribution or do they borrow behavioral norms from their daily lives, in which the failure to share today may trigger retaliation tomorrow? That is, in their heart of hearts, are the individuals who behave morally in the reported experiments inherently moral or merely strategic and calculating? It is nigh to impossible to tell. And, for most practical purposes, it does not matter much.

2.6   BIBLIOGRAPHICAL NOTES

Sections 2.2, 2.3, and 2.4 describe the experiments conducted, respectively, by Milgram (1963), by Falk and Szech (2013a), and by Henrich (2000); Henrich, Boyd, Bowles, Camerer, Fehr, Gintis, and McElreath (2001); Henrich et al., eds (2004); Henrich et al. (2005). Bowles (2016) offers a book-length examination of the morality of markets.

---

11. It is also plausible and likely that preferences and social norms would affect the incidence of markets.

12. In psychology and economics, a **frame** comprises the payoff-irrelevant aspects of the presentation of a problem that an experimental subject faces. In the mouse experiment, the difference between the two leading treatments is more than just a difference in frames; the strategic aspects of the treatments differ. However, our comparison of these two treatments hones in on the same dilemma: whether to kill a mouse for €10. The similarity of the subjects' behavior in the individual and the augmented individual treatments suggests that the strategic aspects of the two leading treatments are quite similar.

Identifying responsibility with some variation on pivotality, as in section 2.3, has been a part of folklore at least since David Hume.[13] Chockler and Halpern (2004) introduce an ex-post measure of responsibility along the lines of problem 2.2. The broad appeal of ex-post measures of responsibility is corroborated by the experiments of Zultan, Gerstenberg, and Lagnado (2012). Ex-ante pivotality has been studied in political science in the context of the measures of voter power. For instance, Philip D. Straffin (1977, theorems 1 and 2) examines the ex-ante pivotality in which the votes are cast independently and another version, in which the votes are correlated, and shows that these versions are equivalent to two commonly used indices of voter power (viz., Banzhaf and Shapley-Shubik indices).

PROBLEMS

Problem 2.1 (Price-List Treatment).   Consider the following experiment. Bob, the experimenter, calls upon Alice, the subject, to whom he announces: "I have secretly written a positive number on a sheet of paper that is hidden in my pocket. Denote this number by x. Please tell me any number y. If $y \leq x$, then I shall pay you x euros and kill a mouse. If $y > x$, then I shall pay you nothing, and the mouse will live. Which number y do you choose, Alice?" The described procedure is essentially the price-list treatment of Falk and Szech (2013a). Assume that, because Alice cares for mice, Alice experiences a disutility equivalent to $v > 0$ euros if Bob kills a mouse. Which number y should Alice choose, and why?

Problem 2.2 (Pivotal Ex-Post).   There are I voters, each of whom casts a vote in favor of or against outcome X. Let I be odd. The outcome is determined according to the simple majority rule: X is chosen if and only if at least $(I+1)/2$ votes are in favor. Suppose that the votes have been cast. Call a voter pivotal at distance $d \in \{0, 1, 2, \ldots\}$ if at least k others must flip their votes for him to become pivotal (i.e., for his vote to determine the outcome).

1.   What is the highest value distance can take for a voter?

2.   Show that any voter in the majority has a smaller distance (i.e., is closer to being pivotal) than any voter in the minority.

3.   Define a voter's (ex-post) responsibility to be $1/(1+d)$, where d is his distance from being pivotal. Define the aggregate responsibility to be the sum of individual responsibilities. For a given I, when is the aggregate responsibility maximal and when is it minimal? What happens to individual responsibility as the number of voters increases?

13. In *An Enquiry Concerning Human Understanding*, Hume writes: "[W]e may define a cause to be an object, followed by another, [...] if the first object had not been, the second never had existed."

Problem 2.3 (Pivotal Ex-Ante). There are I voters, each of whom casts a vote in favor of or against outcome X. Let I be odd. The outcome is determined according to the simple majority rule: X is chosen if and only if at least $(I+1)/2$ votes are in favor. Suppose that it is commonly believed that each voter votes in favor of X with probability p and that the votes are cast independently of each other.

1. What is the ex-ante probability that any individual is pivotal?

2. If one adds up the probabilities in part 1 over all voters, how does the sum depend on I? (If you cannot derive a formal answer, then plot the function on a computer.)

3. Show that the probability in part 1 is decreasing in I. (Again, if you cannot derive a formal answer, then plot the function on a computer.)

4. What do your answers to parts 2 and 3 tell you about the propriety of equating responsibility with the property of being ex-ante pivotal?

Problem 2.4 (The Ultimatum Game). Assume that, in the ultimatum game, the responder accepts an offer of amount x with probability $F(x)$, where $F(x) = x^\gamma$ for some $\gamma > 0$. The proposer knows F. The proposer is risk averse in the sense that his payoff from retaining amount $1 - x$ with probability $F(x)$ is captured by the expected utility

$$F(x)u(1 - x) + (1 - F(x))u(0),$$

where u is some increasing and strictly concave function. Let $\hat{x}$ denote the offer that maximizes the proposer's expected utility:

$$\hat{x} \in \arg \max_{x \in [0,1]} \{F(x)u(1 - x) + (1 - F(x))u(0)\}.$$

1. Show graphically that the proposer is strictly worse off if he faces the lottery that pays $1 - x$ with probability $F(x)$ and 0 with probability $1 - F(x)$ than if he for sure receives this lottery's expectation, $F(x)(1 - x)$. Conclude that the concavity of u captures aversion to risk.

2. Assume that $u(y) = y^\alpha$ for all $y \geq 0$ and for some $\alpha \in (0, 1)$ and show that $\hat{x} > x^*$, where $x^* \equiv \gamma/(1 + \gamma)$ is the optimal offer of a risk neutral proposer, who maximizes his expected monetary payoff. Conclude that, in the lab, the proposer's offer conflates his generosity with his attitude toward risk.

3. In the context of the small-scale societies experiment, can you speculate why risk aversion could be positively correlated with market integration? Can you speculate why generosity could be positively correlated with market integration?

CHAPTER 3

FROM THE JUNGLE TO DESIGN ECONOMICS

3.1 INTRODUCTION

Walrasian equilibrium is Pareto efficient (by the FWT). So is equilibrium in the jungle, where relative power, not wealth, determines each agent's budget set. So, if a normative argument in favor of Walrasian outcomes is to be advanced, it cannot be on the merits of efficiency alone.

In applications, its ominous connotations notwithstanding, the jungle may be preferred to the market. For instance, the college students who apply for on-campus housing do not bid to rent the most desirable dorm rooms. Instead, they "fight" (by digital proxies, in the course of the execution of a room-assignment algorithm) for the rooms; the students' relative powers are determined by their relative seniority and by draws from a random-number generator.

When both the market and the jungle are deemed subpar, alternative exchanges can be contemplated. An alternative exchange may be inspired by the Walrasian ideal when the decentralized market is believed not to approximate this ideal well enough. For instance, trading in human organs, such as kidneys for cash, is deemed objectionable by some and is illegal in most countries, including the United States. (A legal market for kidneys exists in Iran.) What occurs instead in the United States is a centralized kidney exchange based on an algorithm that resembles the top trading cycles (TTC) algorithm, introduced later in this chapter. It will be shown that the TTC allocation coincides with the unique Walrasian equilibrium allocation of a suitably defined exchange economy.

Given the equivalence between the TTC and Walrasian outcomes, what is then so objectionable about an unfettered exchange—a market—for human organs that is not objectionable about the kidney exchange based on TTC? One possibility is that TTC guarantees the attainment of the Walrasian ideal, whereas unfettered exchange does not. Another possibility, which will be explored in some detail, is that these are instances of exchange across certain classes of goods that are deemed objectionable by the public, not markets per se. For instance, it may be deemed repugnant to exchange one's labor for a kidney but not repugnant to exchange one's spouse's kidney for another donor's kidney and to exchange one's own labor for others' labor. This sentiment of repugnance can be rationalized by aversion to inequality, as will be explained.

In some cases, the distinction between an agent and a good is blurred. If so, Walrasian exchange is not directly applicable. For instance, suppose the goal is to partition, say, twelve police officers into pairs of partners. Each officer is an agent seeking a partner, a good, but he is also a good himself, a partner evaluated by all other officers. It is dubitable that decentralized deliberation would give rise to officer prices, as in a Walrasian exchange. Nor is it likely (or desirable) that the most powerful policeman would unilaterally choose a partner for the duration of his service—and would get away with that, as in the jungle economy. This chapter introduces an alternative equilibrium concept—stability—which is tailored to the environments that exhibit the described agent–good duality.

3.2 THE JUNGLE ECONOMY

The jungle economy differs from the exchange economy by replacing private endowments of goods with a social endowment and a power ranking of agents. While, in Walrasian equilibrium, greater private endowments translate into larger budget sets, in jungle equilibrium, a higher position in the power ranking enables an agent to consume more by expropriating those below him in that ranking. Examples of jungle economies are a troop of monkeys, all ranked according to dominance and seeking to divide a pile of fruit, or a firm's employees, all ranked according to seniority and seeking to allocate offices in a new building.

THE JUNGLE

A jungle economy comprises a set $\mathcal{L} = \{1, 2, ..., L\}$ of goods; the **social endowment** vector $\bar{e} \equiv (\bar{e}_1, \bar{e}_2, ..., \bar{e}_L) \in \mathbb{R}_{++}^L$ of these goods; a set $\mathcal{I} = \{1, 2, ..., I\}$ of agents; for each agent $i \in \mathcal{I}$, a binary preference relation $\succ^i$ that strictly ranks any pair of distinct bundles in his finite **consumption set** $X^i \subset \mathbb{R}^L_+$, which contains 0;[1] and a binary **power relation** $\rhd$ that strictly ranks any pair of distinct agents i and j, so that $i \rhd j$ means that agent i can expropriate—and, so, is more powerful than—agent j. The **jungle economy** is $\mathcal{J} \equiv ((\succ^i, X^i)_{i \in \mathcal{I}}, \bar{e}, \rhd)$. Henceforth, without loss of generality, we label the agents so that agent 1 is the most powerful agent, agent 2 is the second most powerful agent, and so on, with agent I being the least powerful.

The consumption set X^i captures the bounds on agent i's ability to consume. For example, an element x^i of X^i can be a house where agent i may choose to live, an individual whom he may choose to marry, or a set of cars that he may choose to own. Because it is finite, X^i is bounded; it bounds agent i's ability to consume, either for legal reasons (e.g., it may be illegal to have more than one spouse) or technological reasons (e.g., the agent may find it infeasible to protect and maintain more than a dozen cars).

To illustrate the notation, consider example 3.1.

Example 3.1 (Job Allocation).   Let $\mathcal{L}$ be a set of jobs. The social endowment $\bar{e} = (1, 1, ..., 1)$ specifies that a single copy of each job is available. For each agent $i \in \mathcal{I}$, the consumption set

$$X^i = \{(0, 0, ..., 0), (1, 0, ..., 0), (0, 1, 0, ..., 0), ..., (0, ..., 0, 1)\}$$

means that each agent can consume at most one job and cannot consume a fraction of a job.   △

A **feasible allocation** is a vector $x \equiv (x^1, x^2, ..., x^I)$ of nonnegative bundles such that $x \in X^1 \times X^2 \times ... \times X^I$ and $\sum_{i \in \mathcal{I}} x^i \le \bar{e}$. Call the residual $x^0 \equiv \bar{e} - \sum_{i \in \mathcal{I}} x^i$ the **unclaimed bundle**. The unclaimed bundle may be zero, but it is natural to allow it to be nonzero because the indivisibilities inherent in finite consumption sets may make it impossible to allocate $\bar{e}$ without a residual. For instance, whenever $L > I$ in example 3.1, feasibility requires a nonzero unclaimed bundle.

Remark 3.1.   Each agent's (strict) preference relation $\succ^i$ on X^i can be equivalently represented by an (ordinal) utility function, $u^i : \mathbb{R}^L_+ \to \mathbb{R}$, as in the Walrasian model of chapter 1. To do so, just set $u^i(x^i)$ equal to the negative of the agent's rank of x^i in X^i according to $\succ^i$. Furthermore, one can obviate the need for X^i by letting u^i be punitively small on $\mathbb{R}^L_+$ outside X^i, so that the agent would never choose anything outside X^i even if he could. Utility representation has no advantage over working with the preference relation directly, however. When X^i is finite, one cannot use

---

1. Formally, $\succ^i$ is a **linear order**, just as the "greater-than" relation is on the set of real numbers. In particular, $\succ^i$ is **transitive** ($a \succ^i b$ and $b \succ^i c$ imply $a \succ^i c$), **asymmetric** ($a \succ^i b$ and $b \succ^i a$ cannot hold at the same time), and **complete** (if a and b are distinct, then either $a \succ^i b$ or $b \succ^i a$).

calculus to characterize optimizing behavior. One cannot even draw indifference curves, as, by assumption, no agent is ever indifferent between any two alternatives in X^i.

JUNGLE EQUILIBRIUM

Consider unfettered competition in the jungle. Because agents can expropriate each other, private endowments would have had no bearing on the final allocation and, so, we have not even introduced them; all endowment is social. Unfettered competition for the social endowment is likely to lead to an outcome in which each agent ends up with a bundle that contains nothing that any agent who is more powerful than him would desire. Definition 3.1 captures this idea.

Definition 3.1. A **jungle equilibrium** for a jungle economy $\mathcal{J}$ is a feasible allocation x such that no agent can assemble a more preferred bundle than his assigned bundle x^i in x by combining his own assigned bundle, the bundles in x held by the agents less powerful than him, and the unclaimed bundle. Formally, for each agent $i \in \mathcal{I}$, his equilibrium bundle x^i must satisfy

$$\underbrace{\left\{ y^i \in X^i \mid y^i \succ^i x^i \right\}}_{\text{strict upper contour set}} \cap \underbrace{\left\{ y^i \in X^i \mid y^i \leq x^i + \sum_{j \in \mathcal{I}: i \rhd j} x^j + x^0 \right\}}_{\text{budget set}} = \varnothing.$$

It is instructive to contrast a jungle economy and its jungle equilibrium to a related exchange economy and its Walrasian equilibrium. Take a jungle economy $\mathcal{J} \equiv \left((\succ^i, X^i)_{i \in \mathcal{I}}, \bar{e}, \rhd \right)$. A related exchange economy $\mathcal{E} \equiv (\succ^i, X^i, e^i)_{i \in \mathcal{I}}$ replaces the social endowment vector $\bar{e}$ and the power relation $\rhd$ with private endowments $e \equiv (e^1, e^2, \ldots, e^I)$ such that $\sum_{i \in \mathcal{I}} e^i = \bar{e}$.[2] Of course, many a matrix e adds up to $\bar{e}$, and, so, one can construct many exchange economies that are related to $\mathcal{J}$.

Let us equivalently redefine Walrasian equilibrium in a manner parallel to the definition of jungle equilibrium, with preference relations instead of utilities. A Walrasian equilibrium for an exchange economy $\mathcal{E} = (\succ^i, X^i, e^i)_{i \in \mathcal{I}}$ is a price-allocation pair (p, x) such that markets clear, and no agent can find in his budget set a more preferred bundle than his bundle in x. Formally, $\sum_{i \in \mathcal{I}} x^i = \bar{e}$, and, for each agent $i \in \mathcal{I}$, his equilibrium bundle x^i must satisfy

$$\underbrace{\left\{ y^i \in X^i \mid y^i \succ^i x^i \right\}}_{\text{strict upper contour set}} \cap \underbrace{\left\{ y^i \in X^i \mid p \cdot y^i \leq p \cdot e^i \right\}}_{\text{budget set}} = \varnothing.$$

---

2. Because any pair $(\succ^i, X^i)$ can be equivalently replaced by an appropriately specified utility function u^i (recall remark 3.1), we use the same symbol $\mathcal{E}$ for an exchange economy here as in chapter 1.

Even though $\mathcal{E}$ has no exogenously specified power relation of $\mathcal{J}$, a similar (but not equivalent) role in $\mathcal{E}$ is played by a combination of private endowments and equilibrium prices, which together determine each agent's wealth. A wealthier agent has a larger budget set. Because Walrasian equilibrium need not be unique, the ranking of individual wealths need not be unique either. Another distinction between Walrasian and jungle models is that Walrasian equilibrium insists on market clearing, whereas jungle equilibrium admits a nonzero unclaimed bundle. In environments with indivisibilities, however, it is natural to replace market clearing with the weak inequality $\sum_{i\in\mathcal{I}} x^i \leq \bar{e}$, which admits an unclaimed bundle. In the only application of Walrasian equilibrium to the jungle economy that we shall look at in this chapter, market clearing will hold; therefore, we keep the definition of Walrasian equilibrium unchanged from chapter 1.

EXISTENCE AND UNIQUENESS

Algorithm 1 will be used in the constructive proof of equilibrium existence. The algorithm is also of independent interest. For the algorithm, recall that the agents are indexed in the decreasing order of their power.

Algorithm 1 (Serial Dictatorship, SD). *The algorithm constructs an allocation* $x = (x^1, x^2, \ldots, x^I)$ *in I rounds, indexed by $i = 1, 2, \ldots, I$.*

1. *At round 1, set x^1 to be agent 1's most preferred bundle in the set $\{y^1 \in X^1 \mid y^1 \leq \bar{e}\}$ of all feasible bundles that can be assembled from the social endowment.*

2. *At each round $i \geq 2$, set x^i to be agent i's most preferred bundle in the set $\left\{y^i \in X^i \mid y^i \leq \bar{e} - \sum_{j\in\mathcal{I}:j\rhd i} x^j\right\}$ of the bundles that can be assembled after $i-1$ most powerful agents have claimed their bundles.*

Note that the assignment at each round of SD is possible because, by assumption, $0 \in X^i$ for all $i \in \mathcal{I}$. Also note that, at each round, the assignment is unique because the preferences are strict. Hence, SD is well-defined: it selects a unique allocation in a finite number of steps.[3]

Theorem 3.1. *A jungle equilibrium exists and is unique.*

Proof. Let x be the allocation selected by SD. The proof proceeds by induction.
For the inductive base, notice that x^1 is agent 1's uniquely optimal bundle, and, in any equilibrium, he must have this bundle or else he will expropriate someone.

---

3. "Serial dictatorship" is a somewhat misleading label for an algorithm in which, at round i, agent i chooses his preferred bundle but does not directly dictate the bundles that others must consume. **Sequential priority** is a more appropriate—albeit less memorable—label for SD.

For the inductive step, suppose that, in any equilibrium, the agents who are more powerful than agent i receive their SD bundles $(x^1, x^2, ..., x^{i-1})$. Then, x^i is agent i's uniquely optimal jungle equilibrium bundle, by construction of x in SD.

Combining the two steps implies that x is the unique equilibrium. ∎

Theorem 3.1 is both simpler and stronger than its counterpart for exchange economies. In exchange economies, the existence proof relies on a fixed-point argument (section 1.13), equilibrium is hard to compute, and equilibrium uniqueness is guaranteed only under additional, strong, assumptions (e.g., the gross substitutes assumption in theorem 1.4).

EFFICIENCY

Theorem 3.2 (Jungle Welfare Theorem). *The jungle equilibrium is Pareto efficient.*

Proof. Recall from the proof of theorem 3.1 that the unique jungle equilibrium allocation is the unique SD allocation. At this allocation, agent 1 gets his uniquely preferred bundle and, hence, cannot be made better off. Agent i ($i \geq 2$) could be made better off only if the bundles of some of the more powerful agents were altered, in which case at least one of them would be worse off because each of them holds the uniquely optimal bundle conditional on keeping the bundles of the agents more powerful than him fixed. Thus, no agent can be made better off without making some other agent worse off. ∎

Theorem 3.2, an analogue of the FWT, relies on the fact that no agent is indifferent between any two bundles. The jungle economy has no analogue of the SWT (problem 3.2).

Jungle equilibrium selects but one from, generally, many Pareto efficient allocations. This selection may or may not be compelling on normative grounds, depending on the application.

CONVERGENCE

Just as in the Walrasian model, one can study the problem of convergence to an equilibrium. While these are the equilibrium prices that come out of nowhere in the Walrasian model, it is the equilibrium allocation itself that does so in the jungle model. Short of an auctioneer who would centralize an economy by executing SD, what decentralized adjustment process would lead an economy to a jungle equilibrium? A natural adjustment process would start with the social endowment lying around as an unclaimed bundle and then, each period, would call upon a randomly chosen agent to attempt to expropriate weaker agents. Problem 3.1 discusses when this process converges to the jungle equilibrium.

3.3   JUNGLE VERSUS WALRASIAN MARKET

This section compares jungle equilibrium and Walrasian equilibrium in a simple exchange economy, called the house allocation problem. Just as SD (an algorithm that computes the jungle equilibrium allocation) is of independent interest, top trading cycles (TTC), the algorithm introduced later in this section to compute the Walrasian equilibrium allocation, is also of independent interest. Both SD and TTC are used in centralized exchanges when decentralized exchanges, jungles or markets, cannot be relied upon to arrive at an equilibrium. The analysis of these algorithms is therefore a gateway into market design, a kind of economics engineering.

THE HOUSE ALLOCATION PROBLEM

The **house allocation problem with private endowments** comprises agents in $\mathcal{I} = \{1, 2, ..., I\}$ and the same number $L = I$ of houses in $\mathcal{L} = \{1, 2, ..., L\}$. Each agent i's consumption set admits any bundle that contains exactly one house. Henceforth, for notational brevity, when referring to each agent i's bundle, we shall simply refer to a house in $\mathcal{L}$ and define his preference relation $\succ^i$ directly on $\mathcal{L}$. Each agent is endowed with a house. Normalize the names of agents and houses so that each agent i is endowed with house $l = i$. The house allocation problem with private endowments is thus an exchange economy.

In order to compare Walrasian and jungle equilibrium outcomes, we define a jungle economy related to the house allocation problem with private endowments. Replace the private endowments by the social endowment of one unit of each house in $\mathcal{L}$ and by an arbitrary power relation for the agents. This related jungle economy is the **house allocation problem with social endowment**.

An agent's private endowment can be interpreted literally, as ownership, or figuratively, to register his entitlement to an outcome that is at least as good (for him) as his endowment. Power can also be interpreted literally, as an agent's ability to expropriate others, or figuratively, as a priority that reflects the agent's seniority or need for housing.

JUNGLE EQUILIBRIUM

The jungle equilibrium of the house allocation problem with social endowment is found by applying SD.

WALRASIAN EQUILIBRIUM

A Walrasian equilibrium of the house allocation problem with private endowments is constructed by, first, guessing a Walrasian equilibrium allocation and then seeking supporting prices. Inspired by the FWT (just inspired—u-monotonicity does not hold), let us seek a Walrasian equilibrium allocation among Pareto efficient ones. Some Pareto efficient allocation can be identified by postulating an arbitrary power relation and then executing SD with respect to this relation.[4] However, such an allocation need not possess the property that any Walrasian equilibrium allocation must possess: it need not be voluntary.[5]

A voluntary efficient allocation can be found using algorithm 2. First the algorithm identifies the groups of agents (so-called "trading cycles") whose first choice is to reallocate their houses among themselves. After these (so-called "top") groups have been housed, the procedure is repeated for the remaining, still unhoused, agents and their houses.

Algorithm 2 (Top Trading Cycles, TTC). *Let $r = 1, \ldots, R$ index the algorithm's round, where R denotes an endogenously determined final round.*

1. *At round $r = 1$, each agent i creates a list that ranks all houses according to his preference relation.*

2. *Each agent points to the highest-ranked house on his list.*

3. *Each house l points to its owner, agent $i = l$. This creates a graph, with agents and houses as nodes.*

4. *Cycles in the graph are identified.[6] At least one cycle—called trading cycle—exists. Each agent in a cycle is assigned the house to which he is pointing. Let $\mathcal{L}_r \subset \mathcal{L}$ and $\mathcal{I}_r \subset \mathcal{I}$ denote the sets of houses and agents, respectively, assigned at round r. (Note that an agent is assigned a house if and only if his house is assigned to someone.)*

5. *Each agent who has not been assigned a house removes the houses that have been assigned (i.e., all houses in $\mathcal{L}_r$) from his list.*

6. *If any agent is still unhoused, increment r by 1 and return to step 2. Otherwise, set $R = r$.*

Assignments at each round of TTC are unique because the agents' preferences are strict. Hence, TTC is well-defined: it selects a unique allocation in a finite number of steps.

Example 3.2 illustrates TTC.

---

4. Indeed, it can be shown that any efficient allocation in the house allocation problem can be obtained by postulating an appropriate power relation and executing SD (Abdulkadiroğlu and Sönmez, 1998, lemma 1).

5. Recall from section 1.3 that an allocation is voluntary if each agent weakly prefers his assigned bundle to his endowment.

6. A **cycle** is a collection of nodes (agents and houses) such that each node is eventually visited no matter at which node of the cycle one starts as long as one proceeds to visit the nodes by following directed links (from houses to their owners and from agents to their most preferred houses).

Example 3.2 (TTC in the House Allocation Problem). Let $\mathcal{I} = \mathcal{L} = \{1, 2, 3, 4, 5\}$. Recall that, by convention, each agent i is endowed with house $l = i$. Let the agents' preferences $(\succ^i)_{i \in \mathcal{I}}$ satisfy

$$3 \succ^1 \ldots$$
$$1 \succ^2 \ldots$$
$$2 \succ^3 \ldots$$
$$3 \succ^4 2 \succ^4 4 \succ^4 \ldots$$
$$4 \succ^5 1 \succ^5 5 \succ^5 \ldots,$$

where each ellipsis (...) indicates that the preference ordering can be completed in an arbitrary way. The TTC assignment can be verified to be the collection of agent-house pairs:

$$\{(1, 3), (2, 1), (3, 2), (4, 4), (5, 5)\}.$$

In particular, the agents assigned at rounds 1, 2, and 3 of the algorithm are, respectively, $\mathcal{I}_1 = \{1, 2, 3\}$, $\mathcal{I}_2 = \{4\}$, and $\mathcal{I}_3 = \{5\}$. The graphs induced by each round of TTC are plotted in figure 3.1. △

Theorem 3.3 ascertains that TTC satisfies the two properties we expect a Walrasian equilibrium allocation to satisfy.

Theorem 3.3. *The allocation selected by TTC is voluntary and Pareto efficient.*

Proof. The proof proceeds in two steps. Step 1 shows that the TTC allocation is voluntary. Step 2 shows that it is Pareto efficient.

Step 1 (*Until one is housed, one cannot lose one's endowment to another agent*). Indeed, an agent's house is in a cycle if and only if the agent himself is in that same cycle, for his house always points at him. At each round, each agent points either to his endowment or to a house that he prefers to his endowment. As a result, no agent is ever assigned a house that he likes less than his endowment.

Step 2 (*The proof of Pareto efficiency is by induction on round r in TTC*).
For the inductive base, note that each agent $i \in \mathcal{I}_1$, assigned a house at round 1, gets his most preferred house and, because his preference is strict, would only be made worse off if asked to exchange houses with someone else. Hence, if a Pareto-improving reallocation of houses exists, no agent assigned a house in round 1 can be a party to such a reallocation.

For the inductive step, suppose that, for $r \leq R - 1$, no agent who was assigned a house at round r or earlier can be a party to a Pareto-improving reallocation. It

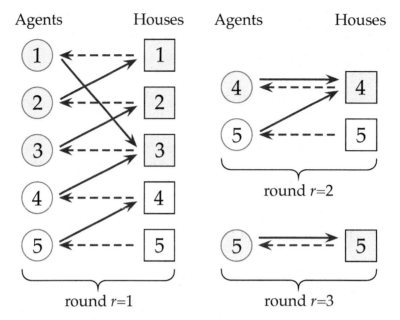

FIGURE 3.1.

The graphs induced by TTC in example 3.2. The agents are denoted by circles and their endowments of houses by squares. Each dashed arrow points from a house to its owner. Each solid arrow points from an agent to his most preferred house among the houses still available at a given round. The agents and the houses that comprise a trading cycle are shaded.

will be shown that no agent who gets his assignment at round $r+1$ can be a party to a Pareto-improving reallocation either. Indeed, each agent in $\mathcal{I}_{r+1}$ gets his most preferred house among the houses in $\cup_{s=r+1}^{R}\mathcal{L}_s$, and no one in $\cup_{s=1}^{r}\mathcal{I}_s$ would wish to exchange a house with him, by the inductive hypothesis.

Then, by induction, no agent in $\mathcal{I}$ can be a party to a Pareto-improving reallocation. That is, the TTC allocation is Pareto efficient. ∎

By theorem 3.3, the TTC allocation is a promising candidate for a Walrasian equilibrium allocation. We proceed to construct house prices $p=(p_1,p_2,...,p_L)$ that support this allocation at an equilibrium. In particular, to each house $l\in\mathcal{L}_r$, allocated at round r of the TTC, assign the same price

$$p_l=\frac{1}{r}. \tag{3.1}$$

What is crucial is that the houses allocated at later rounds be cheaper, and all houses allocated at the same round have the same price. Theorem 3.4 shows that p in (3.1) supports the TTC allocation as an equilibrium allocation and that there is no other equilibrium allocation.

Theorem 3.4. *The TTC allocation and the corresponding price vector constructed above comprise a Walrasian equilibrium of the house allocation problem with private endowments. Conversely, any Walrasian equilibrium allocation is the TTC allocation.*

Proof. Let the TTC allocation and the prices defined in (3.1) comprise a conjectured Walrasian equilibrium. At the conjectured equilibrium prices, no agent can afford a house that has been awarded at a round before he received his TTC assignment; that house is more expensive than his endowment, by construction of the prices. To any house allocated at or after the round at which he got his assignment, the agent prefers his assignment, as TTC would have it.[7] Hence, at the conjectured equilibrium prices, each agent optimally chooses his TTC assignment. Thus, at the conjectured equilibrium, agents optimize and markets clear.

For the converse, take an arbitrary Walrasian equilibrium. The most expensive houses are bought by the owners of the most expensive houses, each of whom can afford, and therefore must get, his first choice. (Indeed, if the owner of a most expensive house bought a cheaper house, then at least one of the most expensive houses would remain unsold, thereby contradicting market clearing.) So, there must be a trading cycle (or multiple) comprised of the most expensive houses, their owners, the arrows that point from these houses to their original owners, and the arrows that point from these owners to their first choices, which they buy. So, the equilibrium allocation of the most expensive houses is as in the first round of TTC.

With the most expensive houses and their owners out of the way, we can construct an analogous argument for the owners of the houses that are most expensive among the remaining ones. The trading cycle obtained for them is a trading cycle either in the first round or the second round of TTC. (Why?) The analogous argument for the remaining houses and agents completes the proof; any Walrasian equilibrium allocation coincides with the TTC allocation and, hence, is unique. ∎

Theorems 3.4 and 3.3 immediately imply a version of the the FWT:

Theorem 3.5. *In the house allocation problem with private endowments, the unique Walrasian equilibrium allocation is Pareto efficient.*

COMPARING JUNGLE AND WALRASIAN EQUILIBRIA

Both jungle and Walrasian equilibria in the house allocation problem are Pareto efficient. Jungle equilibrium favors more powerful agents. Walrasian equilibrium favors the agents with more expensive houses. If an agent's house is popular (i.e.,

---

7. No agent would ever wish to save money by opting for a cheaper, but less preferred, house because he would have no use for the extra money.

is high up in others' rankings), then it is likely to be expensive. TTC illustrates the intuition. An agent who points at an arbitrary house is more likely to get this house early if others are more likely to point at his house early. The houses assigned at an early round of TTC are the expensive ones at the Walrasian equilibrium.

Should a society strive to favor the wealthy or the powerful? This depends on whether it is wealth or power that reflects the merit that the society would like to reward. The society may wish to reward one or the other depending on the allocation problem and may vary the distribution of one or the other across allocation problems. A blanket prescription is not required.

One argument for favoring the wealthy might be that, in practice, wealth generation is a positive-sum game, whereas power generation is zero-sum. This argument is inaccurate, however. Power generation need not be zero-sum.[8] The society may admire power—be it physical strength, beauty, or intelligence—for its own sake or because it contributes to the social endowment. For instance, if a better student gets a higher priority when choosing his dorm room, his investment in academic excellence in the pursuit of the higher priority has social value. In the model of the jungle, the social value of power is unaccounted for. In the Walrasian model, by contrast, wealth is expressed in terms of endowments of goods, which have value because agents prefer consuming more to less.

Nor does wealth generation need to be positive-sum in practice. While the Walrasian model assumes that agents take prices and endowments as given, one can conceive of a richer model in which agents would attempt to influence both. In particular, agents could steal others' endowments, with some resources wasted in the process. Moreover, agents may seek to destroy others' or even their own endowments (as is suggested by problem 1.14) in order to influence equilibrium prices in their favor.

Another argument in favor of the wealth-rewarding Walrasian economy is that resources are lost in conflict when power is exercised, but no resources are lost in voluntary exchange. This argument is also inaccurate. The exercise of power need not breed conflict. When it is clear who is the stronger agent, the weaker one is better off surrendering immediately and being expropriated rather than fighting, being beaten up, and then being expropriated anyway. Moreover, voluntary exchange need not be costless. It is necessary to expend resources to enforce the contracts that would ensure that each party delivers its trade as promised. Contract enforcement is likely to be especially costly when goods are traded over time, in which case future delivery in exchange for today's receipt of a good (i.e., debt repayment) must be enforced; or across states of the world, in which case the relevant states of the world must be verified and the delivery of corresponding goods must be enforced.

---

8. Recall from footnote 8 in chapter 2 that, in zero-sum situations, one agent's gain is necessarily accompanied by another agent's loss.

For instance, costly investigation is needed to rule out arson in order to enforce an insurance contract.

The costly exercise of power (e.g., wars, armed robberies, or battery) may occur when the agents' power relation is not commonly known. A wasteful conflict can be a means to discover this power relation. Resources can be similarly wasted in an exchange economy governed by voluntary exchange when individual endowments and preferences are not commonly known. The ignorance of endowments and preferences (and technology) could be a reason for the observed lengthy and wasteful disagreements in bargaining (e.g., workers' strikes), especially when the agents are few.

In the house allocation problem, the distributional consequences of jungle equilibrium do not look extreme. They would if an agent could consume multiple houses and preferred consuming more houses to fewer. Then, at the jungle equilibrium, the most powerful agent would take all the houses and others would remain unhoused. Of course, endowing a single agent with all houses in an exchange economy would lead to an equally extreme outcome.

It seems, however, that while the Walrasian equilibrium admits more or less inequality of consumption, depending on the inequality of endowments, the jungle equilibrium insists on (in some sense) the maximal inequality of power and, as a result, on maximal inequality of consumption. In the jungle, inequality is maximal in the sense that either Alice expropriates Bob or Bob expropriates Alice; Alice cannot be just ever so slightly more powerful than Bob, thereby expropriating him just a little. In principle, one can conceive of a modified jungle economy in which power is a matter of degree and equilibrium allocation is continuous in power.

A simple way to model fine gradations of power is to assume that the power relation is a random variable, whose probability distribution can be adjusted finely, to favor certain agents. This way, the expected jungle equilibrium allocation (viewed before the power relation has been realized) can be finely adjusted as well. Algorithm 3 describes a jungle equilibrium allocation in this modified economy.

Algorithm 3 (Random Serial Dictatorship, RSD).

1.   *Draw a power ordering of agents at random.*

2.   *Apply SD (algorithm 1).*

What has been altogether omitted from the foregoing comparison of the jungle and the Walrasian market is the importance of having clearly defined rules of exchange in the first place. It is conceivable that having either arrangement (market or jungle) is Pareto preferred to tolerating the uncertainty regarding which arrangement will prevail. One argument for clearly defined rules is that, in the absence of such rules, each agent may engage in wasteful influence activities, each fighting for the rules that would favor him. Another argument for clearly defined rules is that they enable one to plan ahead (problem 4.5).

DESIGN ECONOMICS AT WORK

Both SD and TTC are ubiquitous in centralized exchanges in practice. In the planned economy of the Soviet Union, jobs would be allocated by inviting university graduates to enter a room in the descending order of their grades (i.e., according to their power relation in SD) and pick the most preferred job from the list of remaining jobs.[9] In Mexico City, public high school seats are allocated using SD, with priorities determined by students' scores in a standardized test. At the University of Chicago in 2002, faculty offices at the then newly completed Booth School of Business building were allocated according to SD. The power of each faculty member was influenced by his seniority and merit as perceived by the Deputy Dean for Faculty (Thaler, 2015, chapter 28). RSD and TTC have been proposed to allocate residence permits to refugees, night shifts to doctors, and public housing to tenants.

When there is no obvious merit the society would like to reward, RSD with the power relation drawn uniformly at random can be used instead of SD in house allocation problems with social endowments. Examples are the allocation of offices to employees, over subscribed courses to students, and dormitory rooms to college freshmen. RSD is a natural choice when agents have no endowments of the objects that are being allocated.

TTC is typically used when agents join the exchange with endowments. An algorithm related to TTC is used to exchange kidneys among the patients who join the kidney exchange with their donors.[10] TTC is also used to reallocate rooms among the college students, some of whom already live on campus. (Those who do not yet live on campus can be provisionally assigned a random room as their endowment, and then TTC can be executed.)

Given that TTC delivers the Walrasian allocation, why use TTC instead of a decentralized market? One practical consideration stems from the popular opposition to some goods being traded in decentralized markets. For example, exchanging human organs in a decentralized market is considered repugnant (as discussed by Roth, 2007). In response, Roth, Sönmez, and Ünver (2004) proposed an alternative to the market in which kidneys are traded freely and openly. In particular, the team proposed TTC, a variant of which has been accepted and is widely used. Ironically, TTC is not considered repugnant even though (by theorem 3.4) the allocation that it selects is Walrasian, or "market." Why not?

---

9. Or such was the official story. In practice, one's power relation was also affected by one's connections.

10. Practical considerations limit the size of trading cycles. All surgeries in the cycle must occur simultaneously in order to preclude any donor from reneging on his promise to donate. As a result, the literal application of TTC is infeasible.

The Walrasian outcome delivered by TTC in the context of kidney exchange may not be repugnant because it has equitable distributional consequences due to the equitable distribution of the wealth that TTC earmarks for the purchase of a kidney. This earmarked wealth is derived from the value of the donor's kidney (each patient comes with a possibly incompatible donor), not from the value of the patient's property or the balance in his bank account. Thus, objections to a market in organs can be understood not as objections to markets per se (e.g., because markets "commodify," "objectify," or "deal in sacrilege") but as objections to the market's distributional consequences when the wealth used in the market is comprehensive in the sense of having been derived from a broad set of endowments. We shall revisit this point.

Furthermore, TTC may fail to be deemed repugnant not in spite of its Walrasian outcome but thanks to it. TTC guarantees the Walrasian allocation. By contrast, expecting the Walrasian allocation to emerge in the course of unfettered exchange, in which agents are left to their own devices to exchange kidneys, requires a leap of faith. This leap may be suspect. Some may be deceived or intimidated to trade at unfavorable prices. Even without foul play, agents may find it hard to determine whether all gains from trade have been realized—harder than in the well-behaved economies of chapter 1 (problem 3.5).

Sometimes, however, TTC's equivalence to a Walrasian market is TTC's undoing. School choice in Boston is an example. In the **school choice problem**, students can choose (subject to constraints) which public school to attend. In 2003 in Boston, an algorithm had to be redesigned because the old (so-called Boston) algorithm encouraged students to strategically misreport their preferences, thereby disadvantaging the students who were poor at strategy. One of the desiderata in the design of a new algorithm (led by Atila Abdulkadiroğlu, Parag A. Pathak, Alvin E. Roth, and Tayfun Sönmez) was to help students with siblings at a particular school attend the same school. Initially, TTC was proposed.

Under TTC, schools would have been treated as houses in the house allocation problem. A student's endowment would have been the school that his sibling attended. (If a student has no sibling in school, assign the nearest or an arbitrary school to that student as his endowment.) The school superintendent objected (Abdulkadiroğlu, Pathak, Roth, and Sönmez, 2006, p. 26):

> It may be argued, however, that certain priorities—for instance, sibling priority— apply only to students for particular schools and should not be traded away.

What the superintendent meant must have been the following: TTC is too blunt an instrument if the goal is to nudge a student's consumption toward a certain bundle (i.e., to enable him to attend the school that his sibling attends) without affecting this student's welfare "excessively." Ideally, the sibling priority would insure the family against the state in which it must, at a great cost, transport its children to multiple schools. What TTC would have done by assigning endowments according to the sibling priority is to have affected the student's chances of getting not only into the school that his sibling attends but also into other schools, thereby affecting the student's welfare excessively.

Here is an example. Suppose there are three schools: the Worst School, the Middling School, and the Best School. The Best School is the most popular one, whereas the Worst School is the least popular one. If Alice's sibling is, say, at the Best School, the school superintendent would want to make it easier for Alice to get into the Best School without necessarily making it easier for her to get into the Middling School. In TTC, if school priority is modeled as endowment, then it is easy for a student endowed with the Best School also to get into the Middling School. Similarly, if Bob's sibling attends the Worst School, the superintendent does not wish this fact to handicap Bob's ability to get into the Middling School or the Best School.

As a result of the superintendent's criticism, TTC was rejected in favor of the so-called deferred acceptance (DA) algorithm, analyzed later in this chapter.

Historically, a natural arena for design had been the Soviet Union. Central planning sought, among other objectives, Pareto efficient allocation of resources. For ideological reasons, however, the problem of coordinating economic activity could not be delegated to the impersonal market. In late 1930s, Leonid Kantorovich developed optimization techniques for planning. Ironically—just as in the case of the TTC in the house allocation problem with private endowments—Kantorovich's techniques prescribed allocations that could be supported by market prices. Because, in the Soviet Union, market prices were considered repugnant, Kantorovich had to defend himself against the accusations that his intentions were to sabotage the socialist system.[11]

3.4   A METAPHOR FOR TTC IN WALRASIAN CONTEXT

This section explores why it may be regarded as repugnant to exchange human organs for money, whereas kidney-for-kidney exchange in TTC is not regarded as repugnant. A repugnant transaction differs from an immoral one in the sense of chapter 2 in that a repugnant transaction first and foremost *feels* wrong. One can readily give the reasons for the immorality of punching a stranger or stealing a neighbor's cat. By contrast, the repugnance of serving horse meat (illegal in California), tasting lactoderm, selling retinae, or tipping one's mother-in-law for an excellent dinner are harder to rationalize. They just feel wrong. The underlying

---

11. Spufford (2012, part II, chapter 1) is a fictional account, based on the historical sources cited therein, of Kantorovich's confrontation with the Communist Party ideologues. Vershik's (2007) is a nonfictional account.

rationalization may be subtle or unavailable. In the latter case, the attitude of repugnance is but basic disgust. This section's focus is on the former case.

Trade in human organs is the leading example. The Pope, medical doctors, and much of the general public regard markets in human organs as repugnant. The kidney exchange, based on TTC, is not regarded as repugnant, however, even though the TTC allocation is a Walrasian equilibrium allocation. Why not? The thesis in this section is that, with TTC, the kidney market is isolated from all other markets in the economy. As a result, economy-wide wealth inequality does not spill over into the kidney market and, so, does not amplify health inequality. For unexamined reasons, the society has a lower tolerance for health inequality than for other kinds of consumption inequality.

This section illustrates the spillovers-inspired reasoning in a general-equilibrium setting. Consider an exchange economy of chapter 1 but now assume that goods are partitioned into submarkets and can be exchanged within these submarkets but not across. The interpretation is that one submarket comprises goods exchanged for money, whereas the remaining submarkets comprise goods (e.g., kidneys, babysitting hours, and various favors among friends) exchanged for some points of moral standing. The society cares about the inequality in the consumption of certain goods and has evolved to partition the markets with this concern in mind.

A SIMPLE ECONOMY

The model's basic elements are those of the standard exchange economy of chapter 1: I agents, indexed by $i \in \mathcal{I}$, trade L goods, indexed by $l \in \mathcal{L}$. Agent i's endowment is $e^i \in \mathbb{R}_+^L$, and his consumption bundle is $x^i \in \mathbb{R}_+^L$. His utility from bundle x^i is

$$u(x^i) \equiv \sum_{l \in \mathcal{L}} \alpha_l \ln x_l^i. \tag{3.2}$$

where $\alpha_l > 0$ for each $l \in \mathcal{L}$. We denote the economy by $\mathcal{E} \equiv (u, (e^i)_{i \in \mathcal{I}})$.

Note that we assume that agents differ in their endowments but, for simplicity, have identical preferences. The critical assumption about preferences is the separability across goods. That is, an agent's ranking of a subset of goods in his bundle is independent of the levels at which the remaining goods in his bundle are kept fixed.

What is new relative to the Walrasian economy of chapter 1 is the partition of the set of goods into K nonempty **submarkets**, each indexed by $k \in \mathcal{K} \equiv \{1, 2, ..., K\}$ and comprising the goods in $\mathcal{L}_k \subset \mathcal{L}$. The partition is denoted by $\mathcal{P} \equiv (\mathcal{L}_1, \mathcal{L}_2, ..., \mathcal{L}_K)$. The goods can be exchanged within each submarket but never across submarkets. **Repugnance** is defined as the sentiment that (perhaps, in conjunction with law) proscribes the exchange of goods across submarkets. We denote the partitioned exchange economy by $(\mathcal{E}, \mathcal{P})$.

EQUILIBRIUM

The equilibrium concept is Walrasian except that goods cannot be exchanged across submarkets. It is as if each submarket had its own currency with no two currencies being exchangeable for each other.

Definition 3.2. **Walrasian partition equilibrium** for an economy $(\mathcal{E}, \mathcal{P})$ is a price-allocation pair (p, x) such that

1. Each agent i maximizes his utility function

$$x^i \in \arg \max_{y^i \in \mathbb{R}_+^L} u(y^i)$$

subject to K budget constraints

$$\sum_{l \in \mathcal{L}_k} p_l y_l^i \leq \sum_{l \in \mathcal{L}_k} p_l e_l^i, \quad k \in \mathcal{K}. \tag{3.3}$$

2. Markets clear:

$$\sum_{i \in \mathcal{I}} x^i = \bar{e}.$$

The Walrasian partition equilibrium of definition 3.2 differs from the Walrasian equilibrium of definition 1.1 in assuming that each agent faces K budget constraints instead of one comprehensive constraint. Each budget constraint indexed by k stipulates that only the wealth derived from the endowments in goods class $\mathcal{L}_k$ can be spent on the goods in that class. Walrasian equilibrium is a special case when $\mathcal{P} \equiv \{\mathcal{L}\}$.

The separability of preferences inherent in the additive specification of the utility function in (3.2) and the independence of each agent's submarket-specific budget constraints in (3.3) imply that each agent's utility maximization problem is separable across submarkets. That is, one can solve agent i's utility maximization problem by maximizing his utility in each submarket k separately:

$$\max_{(y_l^i)_{l \in \mathcal{L}_k}} \sum_{l \in \mathcal{L}_k} \alpha_l \ln y_l^i \quad \text{s.t.} \quad \sum_{l \in \mathcal{L}_k} p_l y_l^i \leq \sum_{l \in \mathcal{L}_k} p_l e_l^i.$$

The implied demands can be verified to be

$$x_l^i = \frac{\alpha_l}{\sum_{l' \in \mathcal{L}_k} \alpha_{l'}} \frac{\sum_{l' \in \mathcal{L}_k} p_{l'} e_{l'}^i}{p_l}, \quad l \in \mathcal{L}_k. \tag{3.4}$$

Substituting the demand functions (3.4) into the market clearing condition $\sum_{i \in \mathcal{I}} x^i = \bar{e}$, one can verify equilibrium prices:

$$p = \left(\frac{a_l}{\bar{e}_l} \right)_{l \in \mathcal{L}}. \tag{3.5}$$

Crucially for the ensuing argument, this price vector is independent of the partition $\mathcal{P}$.

The equilibrium price vector is unique subject to normalization. One can freely scale the price vector, not only overall, but also independently in each submarket because the relative prices across submarkets are meaningless; no exchange across submarkets is permitted. As a result, one can view prices in each submarket as being denominated in a distinct, nonconvertible currency. Subject to normalization, however, the equilibrium price vector is unique because the aggregate demands satisfy the gross substitutes property (verified for logarithmic utilities in part 1 of problem 1.1), and, so, the uniqueness conclusion of theorem 1.4 applies (with appropriate modifications for the Walrasian partition equilibrium): the equilibrium allocation is unique.

A METAPHOR FOR KIDNEY EXCHANGE

Theorem 3.6 shows that, in the context of the general equilibrium model introduced above, one cannot justify making human organs nontradable on the grounds of Pareto efficiency alone. In particular, merging any two submarkets leads to a Pareto improvement. Thus, equilibrium in an economy with a **comprehensive market**, in which any two goods are exchangeable, Pareto dominates an economy with a **segmented (or partitioned) market**, in which goods are partitioned into two or more submarkets.

Theorem 3.6. *Suppose that partition $\mathcal{P}'$ is obtained from $\mathcal{P}$ by merging some of the submarkets in $\mathcal{P}$. Then, each agent is weakly better off at the Walrasian partition equilibrium of $(\mathcal{E}, \mathcal{P}')$ than at the Walrasian partition equilibrium of $(\mathcal{E}, \mathcal{P})$.*

Proof. The Pareto ranking of the two equilibrium allocations is implied by two facts: (i) the equilibrium prices in (3.5) are the same for any $\mathcal{P}$, and (ii) the budget constraints (3.3) for $\mathcal{P}$ imply the budget constraints (3.3) for $\mathcal{P}'$. That is, each budget constraint in $(\mathcal{E}, \mathcal{P}')$ either coincides with some constraint in $(\mathcal{E}, \mathcal{P})$ or can be obtained by adding up two or more constraints in $(\mathcal{E}, \mathcal{P})$. A sum of constraints is less demanding than all of the constituent constraints taken together. Therefore, each agent's utility maximization problem is weakly more restrictive—and, so, each agent is weakly worse off—with $\mathcal{P}$ than with $\mathcal{P}'$.[12]　　　■

---

12. Fact (i) is essential for the conclusion and relies on the model's strong functional form assumptions. One can construct examples in which fact (i) fails, and the theorem's conclusion no longer holds.

The planner may have other considerations in mind, apart from Pareto efficiency. For instance, the planner may be concerned with equitable distribution of a particular subset of goods, such as health. In this case, partitioning markets in the manner accomplished by TTC may address these additional concerns. Example 3.3, which we analyze in the remainder of this subsection, illustrates.

Example 3.3 (Kidney Exchange in General Equilibrium). Two agents, $\mathcal{I} = \{1, 2\}$, exchange five goods, $\mathcal{L} = \{1, 2, 3, 4, 5\}$. The agents' endowments are $e^1 = (4, 0, 0, 0, 2)$ and $e^2 = (0, 4, 6, 6, 6)$, and their utility functions are identical: $u(x^i) = \sum_{l \in \mathcal{L}} \ln(x_l^i)$, $i \in \mathcal{I}$. △

In example 3.3, goods 1 and 2 can be interpreted as blood-type-A and blood-type-B kidneys, whereas goods 3, 4, and 5 are food, clothing, and shelter. Each agent is a household comprised of four individuals. In household 1, two individuals are healthy and have a pair of type-A kidneys each, whereas the other two individuals are on dialysis and in need of type-B kidneys. This interpretation follows from the observation that the household would prefer two kidneys of each type to four kidneys of the same type. Analogously, in household 2, two individuals are healthy and have a pair of type-B kidneys each, whereas the other two individuals are on dialysis and in need of type-A kidneys. The household utility function is interpreted as the outcome of (unmodeled) intrahousehold bargaining among the household members.

In the example, equilibrium prices (for any partition) are $(\frac{1}{4}, \frac{1}{4}, \frac{1}{6}, \frac{1}{6}, \frac{1}{8})$. In the comprehensive market, all goods are exchangeable, and the households' equilibrium bundles can be verified to be

$$x^1 = \left(1, 1, \frac{3}{2}, \frac{3}{2}, 2\right) \quad \text{and} \quad x^2 = \left(3, 3, \frac{9}{2}, \frac{9}{2}, 6\right).$$

Thus, household 1 consumes one of each type of kidney, whereas household 2 consumes three of each type. What has happened is that household 1 has sold three type-A kidneys to buy one type-B kidney, some food, and clothing. Because household 2 is better endowed with nonkidney goods than household 1 is, household 2 sells only one type-B kidney, some food, and clothing to buy three type-A kidneys.

Each household is better off with trade than with autarky, and the equilibrium outcome is Pareto efficient. Nevertheless, the planner may be concerned about the health inequality that has emerged. In particular, household 1 has ended up with two kidneys, which have been allocated between two household members, who lead healthy lives, whereas the remaining two household members are on dialysis. By contrast, household 2 has ended up with six kidneys, and, so, all four household members lead healthy lives.[13] The planner may favor a more equitable allocation of kidneys, even though this is not what the households themselves want.

One way to achieve an equitable allocation of kidneys is to ban any trade in kidneys altogether without restricting trade in the remaining goods. Then, each household will consume its endowment of kidneys while optimally trading the remaining goods. This outcome is bad: each household's utility is negative infinity.[14]

Another way to achieve an equitable allocation of kidneys, one that Pareto improves on no-trade in kidneys, is to partition the market into two submarkets: one for the kidneys of both types and another one for the remaining goods. Formally, the partition is $\mathcal{P} = \{\{1, 2\}, \{3, 4, 5\}\}$. The induced equilibrium bundles are

$$x^1 = \left(2, 2, \frac{1}{2}, \frac{1}{2}, \frac{2}{3}\right) \quad \text{and} \quad x^2 = \left(2, 2, \frac{11}{2}, \frac{11}{2}, \frac{22}{3}\right).$$

The equilibrium allocation can be interpreted to say that each member of each household ends up with one healthy kidney, either after having sold one or after having bought one. This allocation corresponds to the TTC outcome with four participants: two couples from each household. Each couple from household 1 is endowed with an extra type-A kidney and needs a type-B kidney. Each couple from household 2 is endowed with an extra type-B kidney and needs a type-A kidney. Each couple can be interpreted to comprise a husband and a wife; the husband needs a kidney, whereas his wife has two healthy kidneys, one of which is available for exchange.

The idea of seeking equity in the consumption of some goods, possibly at the cost of Pareto efficiency, goes by the name of **specific egalitarianism** (Tobin, 1970). (The view that goods in general should be distributed more equally is **general egalitarianism**.) The analysis of example 3.3 illustrates that one need not shut down markets completely in order to achieve specific egalitarianism in health outcomes. In the example, partitioning markets serves specific egalitarianism in health outcomes because, across households, kidneys are distributed more equally than nonkidney goods. In this case, partitioning precludes the wealth spillover from nonkidney goods to kidney goods.

One can conceive of an alternative economy that, in contrast to example 3.3, is characterized by greater inequality in kidney endowments than in nonkidney

13. The interpretation is that one household-1 member has been harvested of both his kidneys (and is now on dialysis), and one household-2 member has been transplanted two kidneys, even though only one suffices to lead a healthy life.

14. With no trade in kidneys, two members of each household remain on dialysis. Now, the comprehensive market, too, leaves two—but different—household-1 members on dialysis. Perhaps, different household members have different probabilities of survival on, or tolerance for, dialysis, and, so, it matters to the households who ends up on dialysis.

endowments. In this case, specific egalitarianism in health outcomes would be promoted by the comprehensive market, not a partitioned one. In particular, while TTC in kidneys may fail to find a compatible donor for some individual, this individual may be able to sell his house and buy a kidney in the comprehensive market.

Specific egalitarianism notwithstanding, theorem 3.6 assures that both households prefer the comprehensive market to a partitioned one. Nonetheless, one could try to justify specific egalitarianism as reflecting the fact that individuals are directly affected by, but cannot directly affect, the health of others in the economy or as a paternalistic response to the households' tendency to undervalue the importance of health.[15]

3.5   MATCHING AGENTS TO AGENTS

In both jungle and Walrasian economies, agents have preferences over goods, but goods have no preferences over agents. Agents' preferences matter for welfare analysis. In addition, agents have agency: when we ask what will happen when two dozen agents and some goods are locked in a room, we assume that these are the agents, not the goods, who will take the initiative in the exchange that ensues.

Some allocation problems admit no distinction between agents and goods, however. Sometimes, agents—such as friends, romantic partners, employers and employees, and roommates—are also goods at the same time. Each such agent can be interpreted as his own endowment and has preferences over other agents. From both positive and normative perspectives, jungle and Walrasian models are poor frameworks for thinking about the allocation problems in which agents are matched to other agents, not to goods. This section introduces an alternative framework to think about such problems.

Objectifying one side of the market (e.g., women or employees) by ignoring their preferences while respecting the preferences of other side (men or employers) and postulating either jungle equilibrium or Walrasian equilibrium as a solution concept does not appear to be a viable recipe for forging relationships (romantic or employment). This recipe prescribes slavery—unjust and, in the long term, inefficient.[16] Indeed, the objectified side of the market is denied even the basic liberty of staying away from the exchange, the liberty available to any agent in both Walrasian

---

15. In particular, the planner may disagree with the aggregation that emerges as the outcome of the intra-household bargaining that motivates the utility specification in example 3.3.

16. Here, the allusion to inefficiency is in seeming contradiction to theorems 3.2 and 3.3, which continue to maintain efficiency of jungle and Walrasian outcomes in the house allocation problem even if objects are granted preferences (problem 3.8). Instead, the allusion to inefficiency speculates about the properties of a richer, unspecified model in which violence and injustice lead to the loss of resources and stunted innovation and economic growth.

equilibrium (an agent's endowment is always affordable to him) and the jungle equilibrium (the null bundle is always available).

Even with normative objections put aside, jungle and Walrasian models are poor frameworks for thinking about the outcome of unfettered matching of agents to agents. An object cannot hide or elope with another agent, whereas an enslaved and abducted agent can. This section takes inspiration from the Walrasian model to propose a new equilibrium concept that respects the individual liberty of all parties to the match. Even then, in special cases, the equilibrium outcome may fail to improve on the objectification outcome (parts 3 and 4 of problem 3.9).

THE ROOMMATES PROBLEM

The focus is on an economy in which no distinction between agents and goods exists, and the goal is to match agents into pairs or leave them alone. Applications are matching police detectives or patrol officers into pairs of partners and matching individuals into pairs of roommates. The latter application gives the problem its name.

A **roommates problem** comprises a finite set $\mathcal{I}$ of I agents, with typical elements i, j, and k. A **match**, denoted by x, is a partition of $\mathcal{I}$ into pairs and singletons. A pair is interpreted as roommates, matched to each other, whereas a singleton is an agent who is unmatched or, as we shall sometimes say, matched to himself.[17]

A match, x, is the analogue of an allocation in the exchange economy. The analogue of a consumption bundle is an agent's partner in the match.

Each agent i is described by a binary preference relation $\succ^i$ on all agents in $\mathcal{I}$, including himself. Relation $\succ^i$ strictly ranks any two distinct elements in $\mathcal{I}$. As in the jungle economy, the strictness of $\succ^i$ is natural because the set of alternatives, $\mathcal{I}$, is finite. The interpretation of $j \succ^i k$ is that agent i prefers being matched with agent j to being matched with agent k. The interpretation of $i \succ^i j$ is that agent j is **unacceptable** for agent i, who prefers being alone to being with j. Any agent j with $j \succ^i i$ is said to be **acceptable** for i. Note that each agent cares only about his own partner (if any); he does not care about who others are matched to. The analogous assumption in the exchange and jungle economies is that each agent cares only about his own consumption bundle.

STABILITY

We would like to predict the outcome of unfettered matching and rematching in the roommates problem. We imitate the exercise conducted in the analysis of the exchange economy in section 1.3. We invite a couple dozen police officers into

---

17. Alternatively, one can interpret the setup as a monogamous gay-marriage problem, with agents being either all men or all women. A match, then, is a partition of the agents into romantic couples and the unmatched.

a room and encourage them to freely match and rematch in an attempt to find a partner. What do we expect the final outcome to be?

In designing our prediction, an equilibrium concept, we imitate the construction of the contract set for the exchange economy. In particular, we assume that:

1. No agent is worse off as a result of unfettered matching than he would have been by simply consuming his endowment, which is himself. That is, there is no coercion; the final match is **voluntary** in the sense that no agent is matched to an unacceptable partner.

2. All bilateral gains from matching and rematching have been exhausted. That is, there exists no pair of agents—called a **blocking pair**—who are not matched to each other and who each would prefer being matched to the other instead of his current partner.

The absence of blocking pairs is not quite the same as Pareto efficiency in the definition of the contract set. The absence of blocking pairs is motivated by the assumption that if two individuals like each other, nothing can prevent them from being together. Because those left behind by the members of the blocking pair cannot object, the satisfaction of a blocking pair need not be a Pareto improvement. Furthermore, the absence of blocking pairs does not explicitly insist on looking for the gains from rematching that would involve more than two agents.

Combining the two principles of unfettered matching described above, we obtain a stable match, a roommates-problem counterpart of an allocation in the contract set and, as we shall see, of the Walrasian equilibrium allocation in the exchange economy.

Definition 3.3. A match x is **stable** if it is voluntary and contains no blocking pair.

To see the analogy between Walrasian equilibrium and a stable match, note that, in the Walrasian model, an agent's endowment and equilibrium prices determine his budget set, from which he then chooses his preferred bundle. In that economy, roughly speaking, if an agent has ample endowment of a good that is scarce and liked by many, then this good will be expensive, the agent will be wealthy, and his budget set will be large. The agent's budget set depends not only on his own characteristics but also on those of others, through equilibrium prices.

One can define an agent's **budget set** in the roommates problem analogously. Fix a match x. Agent i's budget set $\mathcal{B}^i(x) \subset \mathcal{I}$ is defined to contain agent i's partner in x, agent i himself, and all other agents (if any) who would prefer being matched with agent i to their partners in x.[18] Thus, roughly, $\mathcal{B}^i(x)$ is larger if agent i is more popular (i.e., is higher up in other agents' preference rankings).

With the definition of agent i's budget set $\mathcal{B}^i(x)$ in hand, one can postulate an analog for the utility-maximization part of the definition of the Walrasian equilibrium. At a match x, agent i's optimally chooses his most preferred partner in $\mathcal{B}^i(x)$ according to his preference $\succ^i$. This chosen partner is exactly agent i's partner in x, for every $i \in \mathcal{I}$, if and only if x is a stable match. The budget sets at a stable match are said to be **supporting** for that match.

Stability imposes rather weak restrictions on a match. Nevertheless, example 3.4 illustrates that a stable match need not exist.

Example 3.4 (No Stable Match Exists). Let $\mathcal{I} = \{1, 2, 3, 4\}$. The agents' preferences are

$$2 \succ^1 3 \succ^1 4 \succ^1 1$$
$$3 \succ^2 1 \succ^2 4 \succ^2 2$$
$$1 \succ^3 2 \succ^3 4 \succ^3 3,$$
$$\ldots \succ^4 4,$$

where agent 4's preference is arbitrary as long as he finds all partners acceptable. Because all partners are acceptable, no match involving an unmatched agent is stable. Among the remaining three matches, no stable match exists because whoever is matched with agent 4 wants to change and can find a willing partner. Indeed, in match $x \equiv \{(1, 2), (3, 4)\}$, pair $(2, 3)$ is a blocking pair; in match $x' \equiv \{(1, 4), (2, 3)\}$, pair $(1, 3)$ is a blocking pair; and in match $x'' \equiv \{(1, 3), (2, 4)\}$, pair $(1, 2)$ is a blocking pair. $\triangle$

One can take at least three stances toward the nonexistence of a stable match.

1. One may wonder whether example 3.4 is in any way atypical. Sure, nonexistence in example 3.4 suggests that gay marriages, rooming arrangements, best-buddy cliques, and partner assignments in police departments are sometimes doomed to be unstable. But does example 3.4 illustrate a pervasive problem?

   It turns out that it does. Suppose one draws the agents' preferences uniformly at random assuming that all partners are acceptable. What is the probability that no stable match exists? Pittel and Irving (1994) prove that, as the number

---

18. We overload notation $\mathcal{B}^i$ by using $\mathcal{B}^i(x)$ and $\mathcal{B}^i(p)$ to denote agent i's budget sets, respectively, in the roommates problem and in the Walrasian model. Notation $\mathcal{B}^i(x)$ will not be used in the formal analysis. It is presented here only to facilitate the analogy with the Walrasian model.

of agents converges to infinity, the probability that a stable match exists does not exceed $\sqrt{e}/2 \approx 0.82$. This upper bound is nowhere near tight. Numerical simulations suggest that the probability that a stable match exists is decreasing in I and is 0.96 for $I = 4$, 0.64 for $I = 100$, 0.39 for $I = 1,000$, and 0.23 for $I = 10,000$. This probability has been conjectured to be of order $I^{-\frac{1}{4}}$ and to converge to zero as $I \to \infty$ (Mertens, 2005, section 3.1). Thus, nonexistence is by no means exceptional.

2. One can redefine equilibrium. For instance, one can postulate that equilibrium is not a single match but a cycle of matches, such as cycle $x \to x' \to x'' \to x$ in example 3.4. That is, cycles are identified by satisfying blocking pairs in some order.[19] Multiple cycles may exist, each of which would then be an equilibrium.

   For yet another equilibrium concept, one can postulate that the members of a blocking pair foresee when their rematch is vulnerable to further rematches and, as a result, refrain from the initial rematch. This foresight-based logic may compel one to designate each individual match in the set $\{x, x', x''\}$ in example 3.4 as an equilibrium, with the interpretation that any match in the set can happen and that the equilibrium concept is agnostic about the likeliest one.

   Another option is to weaken stability by recognizing that the requirement that all blocking pairs be ruled out is unnecessarily stringent. Each agent may not be acquainted with all other agents and their preferences. As a result, he may fail to find a willing partner with whom to form a blocking pair. Unfortunately, this weakening also undermines the predictive appeal of stability; the agents may be insufficiently informed to arrive at a (redefined) stable match.

3. One can focus on economies in which preferences are restricted to be such that a stable match is guaranteed to exist. One such application is the so-called marriage problem, in which agents are partitioned into men and women, and the preferences are restricted to be such that no agent finds it acceptable to be matched with any agent of the same sex except himself.

THE MARRIAGE PROBLEM

Let $\mathcal{M}$ (with typical elements m and m') be the set of men and $\mathcal{W}$ (with typical elements w and w') be the set of women. The set of all agents is thus $\mathcal{I} \equiv \mathcal{M} \cup \mathcal{W}$. The **marriage problem** consists in matching men and women into heterosexual pairs, while possibly leaving some agents unmatched (i.e., matched with themselves).

---

19. A loose analogy in the Walrasian model would amount to identifying the set of equilibria in the economy of figure 1.14 with the set of price cycles that tâtonnement draws at and around the unique Walrasian equilibrium.

The only difference from the roommates problem is that the domain of preferences is restricted. In addition to marriage and dating, this restriction on the domain is appropriate in modeling school and college admissions, fraternity and sorority rushes, and employer and employee matching when individual wages are nonnegotiable.

EXISTENCE AND (NON)UNIQUENESS OF A STABLE MATCH

In examples with a handful of agents, all possible matches can be enumerated and directly checked for stability.

Example 3.5 (Two Stable Matches).   There are two men, m and m', and two women, w and w'. All partners of the opposite sex are acceptable. Let $w \succ^m w'$, $w' \succ^{m'} w$, $m' \succ^w m$, and $m \succ^{w'} m'$. The stable matches can be verified to be $\{(m, w), (m', w')\}$ and $\{(m', w), (m, w')\}$.   △

Example 3.5 illustrates that multiple matches can be stable; uniqueness is not guaranteed.

Does a stable match always exist? Algorithm 4 identifies a match that theorem 3.7 shows to be stable. Thus, we have a constructive proof of the existence of a stable match.

Algorithm 4 (Deferred Acceptance, DA).   *The **man-proposing deferred acceptance algorithm** proceeds in steps:*

1.   *Each man creates a list that ranks all acceptable women.*

2.   *Each man proposes to the top woman on his list.*

3.   *Each woman compares the men who have proposed to her to the man whom she is currently holding (if any), and tentatively holds on to the one whom she likes most and who is acceptable to her, if such a man exists.[20] She rejects the remaining men.*

4.   *Each rejected man removes the rejecting woman from his list.*

5.   *If at least one man has been rejected at step 3, go to to step 2; otherwise, match each woman to the man whom she is currently holding.*

Algorithm 4 is called deferred acceptance because each woman defers her final acceptance of any proposal until the very end of the algorithm. Until then, each woman tentatively holds the best man who has proposed to her so far. Note that, at each iteration of the algorithm, each man's optimal proposal is unique, and each

---

20. Initially, no woman is holding a man.

woman's optimal response is unique because the preferences are strict. Moreover, the algorithm terminates in a finite number of steps because, as long as some men keep getting rejected, their lists shrink. These lists cannot shrink forever, so the algorithm is guaranteed to terminate in finite time. Thus, DA is well-defined.

Theorem 3.7. *In the marriage problem, a stable match always exists. In particular, the match selected by the man-proposing deferred acceptance algorithm is stable.*

Proof. In the match selected by the man-proposing DA, no man is matched to an unacceptable woman because he would never propose to an unacceptable woman to begin with. No woman is matched to an unacceptable man because she would never accept a proposal from an unacceptable man. Thus, all partners are acceptable.

Suppose that man m prefers woman w to his current partner (possibly himself). Then, at some round of the algorithm, m proposed to w, and she rejected him in favor of someone whom she prefers—which is either herself (in which case, m is unacceptable to her, and, so, (m, w) cannot be a blocking pair) or another man. If she rejected m in favor of another man, then she is either eventually matched to that other man or is matched to a man whom she likes even more, implying that (m, w) cannot be a blocking pair. Thus, no blocking pair can be found. The selected match is stable. ∎

DEFERRED ACCEPTANCE AS TÂTONNEMENT

DA resembles Walrasian tâtonnement. In tâtonnement, budget sets adjust as prices vary until the adjustment process converges (in the limit) to an equilibrium, with its supporting budget sets. In DA, there are no prices. Still, in the course of the execution of DA, the budget sets adjust until the adjustment process converges (in a finite number of steps) to a stable match.

To be precise, **DA interpreted as tâtonnement** begins at round $r = 1$ by presenting each man with the largest budget set possible: the list of all women out there plus himself. Once each man has reported his demand (i.e., his preferred woman) to the "auctioneer" (i.e., the executor of DA), each woman's budget set is set to be the set of men who have just demanded her plus herself. As a result, some women can be in excess demand and others not demanded at all. So, the auctioneer adjusts the budget sets. The adjustment shrinks each rejected man's budget set by removing the woman who has rejected him.

At the beginning of each round $r \geq 2$ of DA, each man's budget set is the set of women who have not rejected him at earlier rounds plus himself. At the end of each round $r \geq 2$, each woman's budget set is the set of men who have ever proposed to her plus herself. The agents' reported demands are, first, each man's selection from his budget set, and then, each woman's selection from hers. Once the adjustment process terminates—that is, the budget sets no longer change—a stable match is reached.

In the described interpretation of DA as tâtonnement, each woman's final budget set is the supporting budget set introduced in the discussion that follows definition 3.3. Each man's final budget set requires some pruning before qualifying as supporting. From each man's list of women who have never rejected him one must remove those who prefer their matched partners to him. Voilá!

EFFICIENCY AND OPTIMALITY

Theorem 3.8 is an analogue of the FWT.

Theorem 3.8 (The Roommates Welfare Theorem). *In the roommates problem and, a fortiori, in the marriage problem, any stable match is Pareto efficient.*

Proof. By contradiction, suppose that a stable match x is not Pareto efficient. Then, one can find an agent—say, Alice—who can be made better off without making anyone else worse off.

If Alice is made better off by being unmatched, then, in x, she must have been matched to an unacceptable partner, thereby contradicting the hypothesis that x is stable.

If Alice is made better off by being matched to, say, Bob, then the Pareto improvement requires that Bob be no worse as a result of being matched to Alice. Indeed, Bob must be (strictly) better off because, by the strictness of preferences, he cannot be indifferent. If so, however, Alice and Bob form a blocking pair in x, thereby contradicting the theorem's hypothesis that x is stable. ∎

The marriage problem imposes additional structure on the roommates problem and thereby encourages one to ask the comparative welfare question: At a stable match, how do women fare relative to men? By symmetry of men's and women's roles in the problem, the answer must depend on which stable match one is talking about. There are two matches that are easy to compute and analyze: the match selected by the man-proposing DA and the match selected by the woman-proposing DA. The latter version of DA simply switches the roles of men and women in the man-proposing DA. The two versions of DA yield different matches as long as matches are multiple (e.g., as in example 3.5).

The tâtonnement interpretation of DA contains a hint for the comparison of the matches selected by the man-proposing and woman-proposing DA. In the man-proposing DA, men start with the largest (in the set-inclusion sense) possible budget sets, and women start with the smallest ones. Then men's budget sets shrink, and women's budget sets grow, until a stable match is encountered. So, roughly speaking, the man-proposing DA finds the stable match supported by the largest budget sets for men and smallest ones for women. Because each agent is better off when choosing from a larger budget set, the stable match selected by the man-proposing DA must be pretty good for men and pretty bad for women and mutatis mutandis for the stable match selected by the woman-proposing DA. Theorem 3.9 validates this intuition.

To compare stable matches, we introduce an additional term. A match is **man-optimal** if it is stable and if there is no other stable match that some man prefers. Note that man-optimality is defined with respect to the set of stable matches, not all matches. Note also that it is not immediate that a man-optimal match should exist; the definition requires all men to agree on the best match. If it exists, however, the man-optimal match is unique. (Indeed, because men's preferences are strict, all men can be indifferent between two matches only if each man has the same assignment in both matches, thereby implying that the two matches are actually the same match.)

Theorem 3.9. *In the marriage problem, the man-proposing deferred acceptance algorithm selects the man-optimal match.*

Proof. Let us say that woman w is **possible** for man m if there exists a stable match at which w and m are paired to each other. It will be shown that, in the course of the execution of DA, no woman rejects a man for whom she is possible. As a result, each man is either matched to his most preferred possible woman or remains unmatched; the selected match is man-optimal.

Proceed by induction. For the inductive base, note that, at round 1, no woman rejects a man for whom she is possible. By contradiction, suppose that, at round 1, w rejects m, for whom she is possible, in favor of m', thereby revealing $m' \succ^w m$. Because m' proposes to w at round 1, w is the first choice for m'. Hence, in any match that pairs m and w, (m', w) is a blocking pair. Therefore, w is not possible for m.

For the inductive step, suppose that neither at nor before some round $r \geq 1$ has a woman rejected a man for whom she is possible. Suppose also that, in some stable match x, w is matched with m (so, w is possible for m), and m' is either single or matched with w' (in which case, w' is possible for m'). By contradiction, suppose that, even though w is possible for m, she rejects him at round $r + 1$ in favor of m', thereby revealing $m' \succ^w m$. (Woman w cannot reject m in favor of remaining single because, by hypothesis, w is possible for m.)

If, in match x, m' is single, then the fact that he has proposed to w at round $r + 1$ reveals $w \succ^{m'} m'$.

If, in match x, m' is matched with w', then surely w' did not reject him at or before round r, for, by hypothesis, no woman has rejected a man for whom she is possible at or before round r. Nor was w' holding m' at the end of round r, for then m' would not have proposed to w at round $r + 1$. Instead, either m' was held by w at the end of round r or he was rejected by someone else at the end of round r. Either way, m' must have proposed to w before he proposed to w', thereby revealing $w \succ^{m'} w'$.

Combining the revealed preferences $m' \succ^w m$ and either $w \succ^{m'} m'$ or $w \succ^{m'} w'$, we conclude that (m', w) is a blocking pair in x, contradicting the supposed stability of x and, hence, also the supposition that w, who rejects m at round $r+1$, is possible for m. To conclude, no woman ever rejects a man for whom she is possible. ∎

By analogy to man-optimality, a match is defined to be **woman-optimal** if it is stable and if there is no other stable match that some woman prefers. By the symmetry of the environment, theorem 3.9 implies that the match selected by the woman-proposing DA is woman-optimal. The theorem has another immediate implication: corollary 3.1. In the corollary, a match is **woman-pessimal** if it is stable and if there is no other stable match that some woman likes less.

Corollary 3.1. *In the marriage problem, the man-proposing deferred acceptance algorithm selects the woman-pessimal match.*

Proof. Note that no woman can be unmatched in the man-proposing DA match and be worse off in some other stable match. So, by contradiction, suppose that woman w is matched with man m in the man-proposing DA match and that, in some other stable match, denoted by x, she is worse off. By man-optimality of the man-proposing DA match (theorem 3.9), m must prefer w to his assignment in x. Then, pair (m, w) blocks x, thereby contradicting the stability of x. ∎

Theorem 3.9 and corollary 3.1 suggest that the common social convention—which resembles the man-proposing DA, and in which men are on the proactive side of courtship—favors men over women. However, this conclusion relies on the assumption that agents do not act strategically. Example 3.6 illustrates that, by strategically misrepresenting their preferences, women can turn the tables and induce the man-proposing DA to select the woman-optimal match.

Example 3.6 (Lying Pays). The agents and their preferences are as in example 3.5. If each agent reports his or her true preference relation, then the man-proposing DA terminates in one round and selects the man-optimal match, $\{(m, w), (m', w')\}$. Now, suppose that w misrepresents her preference by pretending that m' is her only acceptable man. Everyone else reports truthfully. Then, at the first round of DA, w rejects m, while w' tentatively accepts m'. At the second round, w' tentatively accepts m and releases m', who then proposes to w at the third and final round and is accepted. The final match is the woman-optimal one, $\{(m', w), (m, w')\}$. △

What woman w in example 3.6 does is play hard-to-get. She understates her interest in men by truncating her preference list of acceptable men. This strategy of understating one's demand is typical for buyers with market power in various contexts. For instance, an art collector may understate his interest in a piece of art that he eyes in a gallery in order to improve his bargaining position with the gallery owner. The only employer (e.g., a mine) in a small town may understate its demand for labor in order to drive down the wages. The understatement of demand by a woman can also be seen as a supply restriction, of herself. Such restrictions of supply are typical for sellers with market power. The mechanism through which w benefits from strategically truncating her preference list is subtle and relies on general-equilibrium effects: w rejects a man in anticipation that he would then propose to someone else and trigger a chain of rejections and proposals that would eventually benefit w.

The ability of a woman to profitably manipulate the man-proposing DA in example 3.6 requires her to know others' preferences. If women know everyone's preferences and can coordinate their strategies for lying, then they can lie so as to induce any match that is stable with respect to true (as opposed to reported) preferences, as problem 3.10 shows. In particular, women can always lie so as to induce the woman-optimal match. One can show generally and verify in example 3.6 that no man can benefit by lying, regardless of whether women lie (part 1 of problem 3.9).

CONVERGENCE

By analogy to the jungle economy, one can ask about the roommates problem: What decentralized adjustment process would guarantee convergence to a stable match, if such a match exists? For the marriage problem, in which the stable match always exists, the answer is that the natural adjustment process that you have probably just thought of accomplishes convergence. This process picks a pair of (possibly nondistinct) agents at random and asks whether they would like to abandon their current partners (if any) and elope with each other. If they would, they do, leaving their former partners (if any) behind, unmatched. This sequential process of satisfying a randomly chosen pair is guaranteed to converge to a stable match, as Roth, and Vande Vate (1990) show.

DESIGN ECONOMICS AT WORK, ONCE AGAIN

Recall that the Boston school superintendent rejected TTC. The algorithm that was eventually adopted is the man-proposing DA. In DA's application to school choice, school seats are "women" and students are "men." If a school has a quota of q students to fill, then this school enters the exchange as q school seats. Any two seats that belong to the same school rank students the same. (That is, each school has preferences over individual students and not over the composition of its classes.) Each school ranks higher those students who have siblings at that school or those who live nearby. Students rank the schools as they wish as long as their rankings are strict. The ranking over schools is extended to the ranking over school seats by ensuring that if a student prefers school A to school B, then he prefers any seat at school A to any seat at school B.

Because DA requires strict preferences, we must ensure that no school (and, hence, no school seat) is indifferent between any two students. Any such indifference is resolved through randomization. For instance, suppose that all students live near some school, but some have a sibling at the school, while others do not. In this case, the school assigns a uniformly distributed random number from $(1, 2)$ to a student with a sibling at the school and a uniformly distributed random number from $(0, 1)$ to a student with no sibling at the school. The school then ranks the students in the descending order of the numbers they have drawn. (This indifference-breaking approach is ad hoc and has no claim to normative appeal.) Then the student-proposing DA is executed with students and school seats as participants and the preferences formed as described above.

By theorem 3.9, the match selected by the student-proposing DA is student-optimal with respect to reported preferences, which are also the true preferences as long as no one lies. Schools cannot lie by design; they cannot falsify a sibling or a student's home address. School lying would have been harder to detect if schools were permitted to express richer preferences (e.g., to reflect how well a student or his parents did on an admissions interview), but such rich preferences are ruled out by the philosophy that public schools are there to serve students, not the other way around. In contrast to schools, students can lie. Recall, however, the fact that we have supplied without a proof: the side that proposes in DA cannot gain by lying. So, students should not lie either.

To see why the Boston school superintendent preferred DA to TTC, note that, in DA, if some school ranks a student particularly highly, this student's chances of getting into some other school are not directly improved—in marked contrast to TTC. Roughly, when the equilibrium concept is stability (selected by DA), if a student is liked more by some school, his budget set weakly increases (Balinski and Sönmez, 1999, theorem 5), but only in the "direction" of that school. By contrast, when the equilibrium concept is Walrasian equilibrium (selected by TTC), if a student is liked more by some school, his budget set increases in the direction of all schools. Equivalently, a school priority assigned as an endowment in TTC can be interpreted as an **ownership right**, whereas a school priority assigned as the school's preference in DA can be interpreted as a **use right** (which cannot be sold).

Why insist on stability when schools can be simply proscribed from renegotiating a match by forming blocking pairs with students? It turns out that a threat to a match is not so much a school–student blocking pair as a litigious parent. What stability rules out is **justified envy**, expressed in the following (fictional) complaint of a parent:

> My boy Bob has gotten into school 1, even though he prefers school 2, and even though his sibling attends school 2. At the same time, Alice, the Fergusons' middle daughter, has gotten into school 2 even though she has no sibling there. This

is unfair. As a result, we envy Alice and think that our envy is justified. We shall therefore sue the school board.

Note that a stable match admits no justified envy if and only if it is stable.

The elegance and simplicity of DA notwithstanding, not every situation in which agents seek agents would benefit from centralization. For instance, one might think that DA would have been applied to solve the dating, if not the actual marriage, problem. In particular, DA could have been deployed at speed-dating events and on dating websites. But it has not been. At speed dating events, instead of being asked to rank the interviewed partners, each participant is asked to partition the partners into two classes: the acceptable and the unacceptable. Then the organizers share Alice's email with Bob and Bob's email with Alice if and only if Alice and Bob both list each other as acceptable. As a result, each participant may end up being matched with multiple partners.

There is a good reason why DA is not used to form romantic couples. A monogamous match right at the end of a speed-dating night might not be desirable. Much uncertainty remains after a series of four-minute speed dates. One may hesitate to base the final match recommendations on the information revealed during such brief encounters. Instead, it is useful to go on further dates, with multiple partners, to get to know them better, and only then to settle on a single person to date.

3.6 CONCLUDING REMARKS

For jungle equilibrium, for Walrasian equilibrium in the house allocation problem with private endowments, and for stability in the marriage problem, we have exhibited centralized algorithms (SD, TTC, and DA) that deliver equilibrium outcomes without relying on the unspecified magic of the agents' decentralized interactions. The planner may favor these centralized algorithms over laissez-faire (unregulated exchange) not because he dislikes laissez-faire but precisely because he likes it so much that he would not like to leave its outcome to chance.

Here is why chance may not work in an exchange economy. It may be hard for agents to realize that gains from trade have not yet been fully exploited. That is, it may be hard to diagnose Pareto inefficiency. For instance, in the house allocation problem with endowments, no bilaterally beneficial exchange may exist. Instead, it may require all agents to gather together in order to identify a mutually beneficial chain of exchanges. We say that diagnosing Pareto inefficiency is hard if doing so may require more than bilateral interactions. Whether diagnosing is hard depends on the features of the economy (problem 3.5).

There are situations, however, in which the unspecified magic of an informal matching procedure is a feature, not a bug, and should be cherished. That is, not every centralized matching procedure would benefit from being straightjacketed into SD, TTC, DA, or some such formal algorithm. Matching a young Mormon to a mission and then to a mission companion is an example. To illustrate, suppose that the last place Elder Price wants to go to on a mission is Uganda, and the last companion he wants to have is Elder Cunningham.[21] Suppose that RSD were used to allocate missions and then a simple lottery were used to find each missionary a companion. Then, if Elder Price were to find himself in Uganda with Elder Cunningham, he would feel doubly demoralized by his poor luck and would decry the arbitrariness of the algorithm.[22]

In practice, the procedure that the Mormon Church uses to deploy sisters and elders (young Mormons) to missions is quite a bit less mechanical than the one described above. Mission assignments are made by divine revelation to the ecclesiastical leader. Then each mission's president forms companionships under the guidance of the Holy Spirit. Matched according to this procedure, in Uganda and with Elder Cunningham as his companion, Elder Price will likely seek God's lesson in his assignment and will strive to make the most of it. Thus, before seeking to improve upon a prevailing allocation mechanism, it is a good practice to first ascertain that it is broken and that its idiosyncratic features are not an optimal response to some special features of the environment.

3.7   BIBLIOGRAPHICAL NOTES

The model in section 3.2 is due to Piccione and Rubinstein (2007). Section 3.4 draws on ongoing joint work with Patrick Harless. Roth and Sotomayor (1990, Part I) is the classical textbook treatment of the material covered in section 3.5. Example 3.4 is example 3 of Gale and Shapley (1962). Abdulkadiroğlu and Sönmez (2013) survey the material covered in sections 3.3 and 3.5 and assign credit to each result.

TTC is due to David Gale and is reported by Shapley and Scarf (1974). DA is due to Gale and Shapley (1962). The interpretation of DA as tâtonnement is articulated (in a more general framework than the marriage problem) by Hatfield and Milgrom (2005). The idea of redefining stability in a forward-looking fashion when no match exists that is stable in the conventional sense is Chwe's (1994). For the roommates problem, an algorithm that finds a stable match whenever it exists has been proposed by Irving (1985). This algorithm is more intricate than those presented in this chapter and, so, is not discussed here.

Problems 3.3 and 3.4 are based on lemma 1 of Abdulkadiroğlu and Sönmez (1998). Part 2 of problem 3.5 is an example due to Goldman and Starr (1982).

---

21. All characters and incidents are fictional and taken from the musical *The Book of Mormon*.

22. And if, instead, the assignments of missions and companions somehow took into account missions' and prospective companions' preferences, then Elder Price would be doubly upset to find out how underappreciated he was.

The strategy-proofness of TTC reported in problem 3.7 is established by Roth (1982). Part 1 of problem 3.9 is implied by theorem 4.7 of Roth and Sotomayor (1990). Part 4 of problem 3.9 is inspired by Ashlagi, Kanoria, and Leshno (2015). Problem 3.10 is implied by theorem 4.15 of Roth and Sotomayor (1990). Problem 3.11, on obviously strategy-proofness, is based on the work of Li (2017); Li (2017) and Schmelzer (2017) provide experimental evidence that obvious strategy-proofness favors truthful behavior. Problem 3.13 is inspired by Balinski and Sönmez (1999, section 8).

PROBLEMS

Problem 3.1 (Convergence to Jungle Equilibrium). This question is concerned with a decentralized adjustment process in the jungle. Consider the house allocation problem with houses initially allocated randomly among the agents. Each agent's preference ordering over houses is drawn uniformly at random.

In each period of the adjustment process, call upon an agent chosen uniformly at random. Permit this agent to discard the house that he is currently holding (if any) in exchange for any house in the unclaimed bundle or for the house expropriated from another agent (if less powerful) chosen uniformly at random. Repeat. Is the described adjustment process guaranteed to converge to the unique jungle equilibrium? Define what you mean by "converge."

Problem 3.2 (The Second Welfare Nontheorem). Consider a jungle economy $\mathcal{J} = ((\succ^i, X^i)_{i \in \mathcal{I}}, \bar{e}, \rhd)$.

1. How many power relations on $\mathcal{I}$, the set of agents, can one construct?

2. Consider the following **Second Welfare Nontheorem**: Any Pareto efficient allocation can be supported as a jungle equilibrium for some power relation. Prove that the Second Welfare Nontheorem is not a theorem. (*Hint*: Consider a graphical proof by counterexample. Let $I = 2$ and $L = 2$. In how many ways can one allocate power? How many equilibria can there be for each allocation of power? In an Edgeworth box, depict an economy that has more Pareto efficient allocations than there are ways to allocate power.)

Problem 3.3 (Wealth is Power). Consider an exchange economy corresponding to the house allocation problem with private endowments. In this chapter, we constructed a Walrasian equilibrium for this economy by appealing to TTC. Prove that the identified Walrasian equilibrium allocation can be obtained as the jungle equilibrium allocation in the corresponding jungle economy (which neglects individual endowments and considers only the social endowment) once the power relation has been

chosen appropriately. (*Hint*: Find the Walrasian equilibrium in the exchange economy by executing TTC. Rank the agents in the descending order of the prices of their
houses. Having appropriately broken any ties, make this order the power relation.)

Problem 3.4 (Power is Wealth). Fix a power relation and consider a jungle economy
corresponding to the house allocation problem with social endowment. Prove that
the jungle-equilibrium allocation can be obtained as the Walrasian equilibrium allocation in the corresponding exchange economy (which neglects the power relation)
once the individual endowments have been chosen appropriately. (*Hint*: Find the
jungle equilibrium in the jungle economy by executing SD. Define the corresponding exchange economy by letting each agent's endowment be the house allocated to
him in the jungle equilibrium.)

Problem 3.5 (Pairwise versus Pareto Efficiency). This question is concerned with
whether, in an exchange economy, local interactions suffice to detect Pareto inefficiency. Only if they do, does it seem plausible that agents would be able to arrive
at a Pareto efficient allocation in a decentralized manner. Call an allocation **pairwise efficient** if no two agents can benefit from further exchange with each other.
Pareto efficiency implies pairwise efficiency. This problem is concerned with the
converse.

1. Argue that, in the house allocation problem with private endowments, pairwise efficiency does not imply Pareto efficiency.

2. Consider an exchange economy with three goods, in $\mathcal{L} = \{1, 2, 3\}$, and three
   agents, in $\mathcal{I} = \{1, 2, 3\}$, whose utility functions are

   $$u^1(x^1) = 2x_1^1 + x_2^1, \qquad u^2(x^2) = 2x_2^2 + x_3^2, \qquad u^3(x^3) = 2x_3^3 + x_1^3.$$

   Let the aggregate endowment be $\bar{e} = (2, 2, 2)$. Consider the allocation $x \equiv$
   (x^1, x^2, x^3) where $x^1 = (1, 1, 0)$, $x^2 = (0, 1, 1)$, and $x^3 = (1, 0, 1)$. Conclude that
   pairwise efficiency does not imply Pareto efficiency.

3. Consider an arbitrary exchange economy with differentiable utility functions that satisfy *u*-monotonicity and *u*-concavity. Suppose that allocation x
   exhausts the aggregate endowment (i.e., $\sum_{i \in \mathcal{I}} x^i = \bar{e}$) and is interior (i.e., $x \gg 0$)
   and pairwise efficient. Argue that x is Pareto efficient.
   Here is a long *hint*: Allocation x is Pareto efficient if and only if it solves
   problem P (why?):

   $$P: \quad \max_{y \in \mathbb{R}_+^{IL}} u^1(y^1)$$

   $$\text{s.t. } u^i(y^i) \geq u^i(x^i) \quad \text{for all } i \in \mathcal{I} \setminus \{1\}$$

   $$\text{s.t. } \sum_{i \in \mathcal{I}} y^i \leq \bar{e}.$$

An allocation x is pairwise efficient if, for all i and j, it solves problem P^{ij}:

$$P^{ij}: \quad \max_{(y^i, y^j) \in \mathbb{R}^{2L}_+} u^i(y^i)$$

$$\text{s.t. } u^j(y^j) \geq u^j(x^j)$$

$$\text{s.t. } y^i + y^j \leq x^i + x^j.$$

Now use the Lagrangian (aka Kuhn-Tucker) approach to constrained optimization (see, e.g., appendix five of Kreps, 2012) to conclude that x solves P if x solves P^{ij} for all $i, j \in \mathcal{I}$. If the Lagrangian approach does not speak to you, then at least try to argue intuitively that pairwise efficiency equates the marginal rates of substitution between any two goods for any two agents, which is also what Pareto efficiency requires.

Problem 3.6 (Top Trading Cycles). Consider an exchange economy corresponding to the house allocation problem with private endowments comprised of four agents, $\mathcal{I} = \{1, 2, 3, 4\}$, and four houses, $\mathcal{L} = \{A, B, C, D\}$. Agent 1 owns A, agent 2 owns B, agent 3 owns C, and agent 4 owns D. Agent 1 prefers C to A to B to D; agent 2 prefers A to D to B to C; agent 3 prefers A to B to C to D; and agent 4 prefers C to B to A to D.

1. Find a Walrasian equilibrium of this economy.

2. Suppose that agent 3 leaves the economy before the houses have been allocated and bequeaths his endowment, house C, to agent 2. Thus, agent 2 is now endowed with two houses, B and C. Each agent still derives utility from just one house; if anyone ends up with multiple houses, he lives in the one that he likes most and is neither burdened nor pleased by the possession of his other house or houses. Define and identify a Walrasian equilibrium in this economy. Is the identified equilibrium allocation Pareto efficient? How is your answer consistent with the FWT?

Problem 3.7 (Strategy Proofness). With each of the algorithms SD, TTC, and RSD, one can associate a **direct mechanism**, which asks each agent i to report (possibly untruthfully) his preference relation $\succ^i$ and then maps the agents' reports into an outcome by executing the corresponding algorithm. Call the mechanisms so obtained from algorithms SD, TTC, and RSD, respectively, direct SD mechanism, direct TTC mechanism, and direct RSD mechanism. A direct mechanism is **strategy-proof** if no agent can gain by lying about his preferences regardless of what the remaining agents choose to do. Strategy-proofness is a valuable property because it makes it easy for agents to behave optimally, thereby reducing their cognitive participation costs; less sophisticated agents are not at a disadvantage of committing strategic errors; and agents' resources are not wasted in an attempt to benefit from spying on others' preferences, beliefs, beliefs about beliefs, and so on.

1. Argue that the direct SD mechanism is strategy-proof.

2. Argue that the direct RSD mechanism is strategy-proof.

3. Argue that the direct TTC mechanism is strategy-proof.

Problem 3.8 (The Efficiency of Objectification). Consider the house allocation problem, but now assume that houses, too, have strict preferences over agents. All houses are acceptable to any agent, and all agents are acceptable to any house.

1. Ignore houses' preferences and execute SD for some power ordering of the agents. (That is, these are the agents who choose in SD, and the houses are treated as objects.) Argue that the outcome selected by SD is Pareto efficient even when the houses' preferences are taken into account along with the agents' preferences.

2. Ignore each house's preference except for its first choice. Let the houses whose first choices are not in conflict point at their first-choice agents. Let the houses whose first choices are in conflict point at arbitrary agents so that, in the end, each agent has exactly one house point at him. Execute TTC while treating each house that points at an agent as this agent's endowment. Argue that the outcome selected by TTC is Pareto efficient even when the houses' preferences are taken into account along with the agents' preferences.

3. Consider a house that, in part 2, gets to point at its most preferred agent. Can this house be worse off at the TTC outcome than at a SD outcome induced by some power ordering?

4. In spite of the Pareto efficiency of SD and TTC, what could be the reasons for objecting to SD (i.e., a jungle economy) and TTC (i.e., a Walrasian economy) as ways to solve the marriage problem obtained by interpreting the house allocation problem's agents as men and its houses as women?

Problem 3.9 (Five Easy Pieces: The Marriage Problem). Each question below is concerned with a different marriage problem.

1. There are two men, m and m', and two women, w and w'. All partners of the opposite sex are acceptable to each agent. Let $w \succ^m w'$, $w' \succ^{m'} w$, $m' \succ^w m$, and $m \succ^{w'} m'$. Show that, in the man-proposing DA, no man can benefit from lying about his preferences.

2. Prove that if the man-proposing DA and the woman-proposing DA select the same match, then the stable match is unique.

3. Assume that all women rank all men the same, whereas men's preferences can be arbitrary. Prove that the unique stable match coincides with the unique SD outcome in the related economy in which women are objectified and the men's power ordering coincides with the women's common ranking of men.

4. This question illustrates that a small change in the gender balance may lead to a stark change in the agents' welfare. To begin with, there are three men, m, m', and m'', and three women, w, w', and w''. All partners of the opposite sex are acceptable. Consider the cycle $m \to w'' \to m' \to w \to m'' \to w' \to m$. Each agent ranks the agents of the opposite sex in the descending order as he travels the cycle once, starting from his own position. For instance, the preferences of man m' are

$$w \succ^{m'} w' \succ^{m'} w''.$$

Show that if an arbitrary agent drops out (thereby causing gender imbalance), then the unique stable match in the marriage problem with the remaining five agents corresponds to the unique SD outcome in the related economy in which the (three) agents on the long side of the markets are objectified and those (two) on the short side are endowed with an arbitrary power ordering.

5. The number of men and women is the same and is denoted by n. Give an upper bound on the number of the proposal rounds in which DA must terminate.

Problem 3.10 (The Scope for Lying in DA). Consider the marriage problem. Take any stable match and denote it by x. Execute the man-proposing DA while assuming that each man reports his preferences truthfully, whereas each woman lies by reporting her assignment (if any) in x as her only acceptable partner. Argue that the algorithm selects x. That is, by coordinating their lies, women can induce the man-proposing DA to select whichever stable (with respect to the agents' true preferences) match they please.

Problem 3.11 (Obviously Strategy-Proof Mechanisms). The conclusion of part 1 of problem 3.9 can be generalized: the direct mechanism corresponding to the man-proposing DA is strategy-proof for men.[23] With this strategy-proofness in mind, Hassidim, Romm, and Shorrer (2016) describe applicants' behavior in the Israeli Psychology Match, which connects prospective students and master's programs by means of the man-proposing DA:

> Applicants participating in the match were advised on multiple occasions to submit their true preferences, and were told that reporting false preferences could only hurt them compared to telling the truth. This advice was communicated in all emails and letters received from the automated matching system or

---

23. Direct mechanisms and strategy proofness are defined in problem 3.7.

from the departments themselves. Furthermore, the matching system's website included a Frequently Asked Questions section that addressed this issue in multiple forms [...]. The details of DA and its strategy-proofness were carefully explained to all applicants who inquired about the mechanism (those applicants also received a link to a YouTube video of a lecture on DA in Hebrew).

Nevertheless, about 19% of applicants reported preference for admission without a scholarship to admission to the same program but with a scholarship, which cannot reflect a true preference as long as the true preference values the money and the prestige associated with the scholarship. In the same spirit, Chen and Sönmez (2002, result 6) find that over a quarter of subjects lie about their preferences in the direct mechanisms corresponding to RSD and TTC, each of which is strategy proof (problem 3.7). So, if strategy-proofness, carefully explained, does not suffice to motivate truthfulness, what would? Obvious strategy-proofness might.

A mechanism is **obviously strategy-proof** if, the first time any participant contemplates deviating from truth telling, he realizes that the most he can achieve by any deviation cannot exceed the least he can achieve by remaining truthful. The qualifiers "most" and "least" reflect the agent's ignorance of others' reports, which—he assumes—can be arbitrary. For each of the mechanisms listed below, is the mechanism obviously strategy-proof?

1. The direct mechanism corresponding to SD.

2. The direct mechanism corresponding to RSD.

3. The direct mechanism corresponding to TTC.

4. The sequential mechanism corresponding to SD in which the agents are approached in the decreasing order of their power. Upon being approached, an agent is asked to choose from the remaining objects.

5. The sequential mechanism corresponding to RSD in which the agents are approached in a random order. Upon being approached, an agent is asked to choose from the remaining objects.

6. The sequential mechanism corresponding to TTC in which, at each round, each agent attempts to choose a house from the remaining houses as in the description of the TTC algorithm.

Problem 3.12 (Repugnance).   Consider the following transactions, regarded as repugnant by some, and see whether you can come up with economic—as opposed to it-just-feels-wrong—justifications for proscribing these transactions. The point of this exercise is not (or at least not only) to discredit it-just-feels-wrong arguments but to show that feelings-based arguments may have evolved to reflect societal concerns about efficiency and equity. These transactions are trading in human organs for cash, prostitution, tossing dwarfs for a fee, serving horse meat in restaurants (illegal in California), privately owning and trading capital (Karl Marx objected), indentured servitude, trading indulgences (Martin Luther objected), and trading complex financial derivatives (popular press objected).

Problem 3.13 (Immiserizing Growth in Marriage). Consider a marriage problem with two men, m and m', and two women, w and w'. All partners are acceptable, all preferences are strict, and the preference relation of man m is $w' \succ^m w$.

1. Complete the specification of the problem to construct an example of **immiserizing growth in the marriage problem**: woman w becomes worse off at the match selected by the man-proposing DA if man m moves her up in his ranking (e.g., as a result of her transformative investment in a gym membership): $w \succ^m w'$. What happens to the welfare of woman w'? What practical dating advice can you give to women on the basis of this example?

2. Show that one cannot construct an example in which man m becomes worse off at the match selected by the man-proposing DA if some woman moves him up in her ranking.

CHAPTER 4

MARXISM, SOCIALISM, AND THE RESILIENCE OF MARKETS

4.1 INTRODUCTION

This chapter discusses ideas inspired by the work of Karl Marx: distributive justice and political constraints on economic outcomes. Marx's emphasis on distributive justice aligns well with the modern view that economics possesses normative insights that extend beyond the truism that if a Pareto improvement is accessible, it should be pursued. Marx's refusal to take economic institutions as immutable aligns with the contemporary interest in market design.

4.2 EXPLOITATION IN A PRODUCTION ECONOMY

The term "exploitation" refers to inequitable allocation of resources, whether or not Pareto efficient. What exactly inequitable means is in the eye of the beholder. According to Marx, a worker is exploited if his reward is smaller than the value of the output whose production he enables. We operationalize the notion of exploitation in a simple economy with production.

A SIMPLE ECONOMY WITH PRODUCTION

The economy has two factors of production, capital and labor, and a single consumption good, which we call "stuff." There are two types of agents: workers and a single capitalist. Each agent's utility function is strictly increasing in stuff and, so, without loss of generality, is assumed to be the identity function. (That is, $u^i(x^i) = x^i$ for each agent i, where $x^i \in \mathbb{R}_+$ is the agent's consumption of stuff.)

Each worker is endowed with some amount of labor, which he can supply to the capitalist. The capitalist is endowed with K units of capital, which he can transform one-to-one into stuff. Alternatively, the capitalist can combine capital with labor to produce stuff by using a **Leontief technology**: given some coefficients $a \in (0, 1)$ and $b > 0$, k (*k*apital) units of capital and h (*h*ours) units of labor can be transformed into

$$f(k, h) \equiv \min \left\{ \frac{k}{a}, \frac{h}{b} \right\} \tag{4.1}$$

units of stuff.[1] Lower coefficients a and b correspond, respectively, to capital- and to labor-biased technological progress.

Suppose that each worker receives w (*w*age) units of stuff per each unit of labor that he supplies. The utility of the capitalist who engages k units of capital and h units of labor in the Leontief technology is

$$\underbrace{f(k, h) - wh - k}_{\text{profit}} + K,$$

where the bracketed term is the profit. The display above assumes that if k units of capital are employed in the Leontief technology, then the remaining $K - k$ units are directly transformed into stuff.

To define exploitation according to Marx (and to enrich our Marxian vocabulary), we introduce some jargon first. When operating Leontief technology by employing k units of capital and h units of labor, the capitalist produces $f(k, h)$ gross units of output. Equivalently, he produces $f(k, h) - k$ net units of output. To produce exactly one net unit of output, he requires

$$\lambda \equiv \frac{b}{1 - a}$$

---

1. Even though convenient to illustrate ideas, Leontief technology is limited in that it does not recognize the possibility of substitution between labor and capital. For example, in response to a delay in the delivery of IBM computers, the team working on the Manhattan project in Los Alamos during WWII managed to imitate the performance of the ordered computers by equipping a team of low-skilled workers with mechanical calculators and tasking each worker with the execution of a particular step in the computer program (Feynman, 1997, part 3). The converse—the replacement of labor with capital—is the essence of technological progress.

hours of labor (and $a/(1-a)$ units of capital). The amount λ is called **labor embodied in a unit of capital**. (The amount of labor necessary to produce w units of stuff, which is what a worker earns an hour, is $w\lambda$ and is called **socially necessary labor time**. The difference $1 - w\lambda$ between an hour of labor supplied by a worker and the socially necessary labor time is called **surplus labor time**.)

Now on to the definition of exploitation. Suppose that a worker supplies a unit of labor. If the amount of labor embodied in his wage w is less than the amount of labor that he supplies, then the worker is said to be **exploited**. That is, the worker is exploited if $w\lambda < 1$. (The ratio $(1 - w\lambda)/(w\lambda)$ is called the **rate of exploitation**.) This charged language of exploitation is motivated by the arbitrary presumption that any just allocation of output entitles the worker to consume the entire fruit of his labor; because the capitalist contributes no labor, he is not entitled to any reward.

There is an equivalent way to define exploitation that cuts through the Marxist jargon. The capitalist's profit from producing a net unit of output is $1 - w\lambda$. This profit is positive if and only if $w\lambda < 1$, which is also the condition for the worker to be exploited. To summarize,

Observation 4.1. The capitalist's profit is positive if and only if workers are exploited.

EQUILIBRIUM

Observation 4.1 makes exploitation seem likely, if not necessary. It need not be. To see under what conditions exploitation occurs, let us complete the specification of the environment and solve for equilibrium wages and profit. As before, there is a single capitalist, endowed with K units of capital, and all prices are denominated in the units of stuff.

We assume a continuum of workers. This eccentric idea is analogous to modeling a fluid as consisting of a continuum of particles; it is analytically convenient to model fluids so. The assumption of the continuity of workers captures the idea that each worker is economically "small" and that workers are many. A worker in the continuum is indexed by $i \in W \equiv [0, W]$. One can think of a worker as a point on a line of length W, or of **measure** W. Each worker is endowed with a unit of labor in the sense that the aggregate labor endowment integrates to W: $\int_W 1 di = W$.

One way to think of the continuum of workers is to imagine that there are W/ε workers, each of whom can supply $\varepsilon > 0$ hours of labor. All worker-specific quantities—endowment, wages, consumption—are measured per hour. For instance, the amount of labor a worker can supply per hour is one. The aggregate measure of labor in the economy is $(W/\varepsilon) \times \varepsilon = W$, independent of ε. The continuum of workers can be thought of as the limit when $\varepsilon \to 0$.

Let $\gamma > 0$ denote a worker's exogenously given subsistence level of consumption, which is the amount of stuff that he can obtain if he remains on a farm, instead of becoming a member of the **proletariat** by seeking employment in the city, with the capitalist. Each worker maximizes his utility by choosing whether to work for the capitalist or on the farm. If the going wage is $w > \gamma$, the worker works for the capitalist; if $w < \gamma$, the worker remains on the farm; and if $w = \gamma$, the worker is indifferent and may do either. Henceforth, we assume $\gamma < 1/\lambda$, which ensures that there exists a wage that makes both a worker and the capitalist better off working together than pursuing their respective outside options.

For a given wage $w > 0$, the capitalist maximizes his profit (and, a fortiori, his utility) by choosing the measure h of workers to employ and the amount k of capital to allocate to the Leontief technology:

$$\max_{h \geq 0, k \in [0,K]} \{f(k, h) - wh - k\}.$$

If $w > 1/\lambda$, the capitalist optimally does not use the Leontief technology and, instead, directly transforms his endowment of capital into stuff: $k = h = 0$. If $w < 1/\lambda$, the capitalist optimally employs the amount of labor necessary to operate all K units of capital: $k = K$ and $h = bK/a$. When $w = 1/\lambda$, the capitalist optimally employs any amount $k \in [0, K]$ of capital and the corresponding amount $h = bk/a$ of labor in the Leontief technology, with the remaining $K - k$ units of capital being directly transformed into stuff.

In the described environment, a **Walrasian equilibrium with production** can be succinctly defined as a wage, each worker's optimal occupational-choice decision, and the capitalist's optimal production plan such that the labor market clears, meaning that the amount of labor the capitalist wants to hire equals the measure of workers who seek employment with the capitalist; and such that the market for stuff clears, meaning that the total amount of stuff that the agents consume equals the total amount of stuff produced, either directly from capital or with the help of labor. By Walras's law (which can be verified to hold), one can focus on labor-market clearing, which would imply stuff-market clearing.

Whether, in equilibrium, workers end up exploited depends on the existence of the workers (so-called **reserve army of labor**) in excess of the number required to productively operate the available capital.

Theorem 4.1.

1. *Suppose that $W/b > K/a$. That is, there are more workers than can be productively used to operate the available capital. Then, at the unique Walrasian equilibrium, the wage is $w = \gamma$, and the capitalist employs bK/a workers, all of whom are exploited.*

2. *Suppose that $W/b < K/a$. That is, there are fewer workers than can be productively used to operate the available capital. Then, at the unique Walrasian equilibrium, the wage is $w = 1/\lambda$, and the capitalist employs W workers, none of whom is exploited.*

3. *Suppose that $W/b = K/a$. That is, there are exactly as many workers as can be productively used to operate the available capital. Then, there is a continuum of Walrasian equilibria, indexed by a wage $w \in [\gamma, 1/\lambda]$, at each of which the capitalist employs W workers, who are exploited unless $w = 1/\lambda$.*

Proof. For part 1, assume that $W/b > K/a$. If $w > \gamma$, then all W workers choose to work for the capitalist, whereas the capitalist demands at most bK/a workers, which, by hypothesis, is less than W. Thus, the labor market does not clear. If $w < \gamma$, then all workers choose to stay on the farm, whereas the capitalist demands bK/a workers. Hence, the labor market does not clear. Finally, if $w = \gamma$, then each worker is indifferent between staying on the farm and working for the capitalist; in particular, it is optimal for bK/a workers to work for the capitalist. At the same time, the capitalist finds it uniquely optimal to demand bK/a workers, which is the amount required to operate K units of capital with the Leontief technology. Thus, the labor market clears. As a result, $w = \gamma$ is the unique equilibrium wage, and each worker employed by the capitalist is exploited.

For part 2, assume that $W/b < K/a$. If $w < 1/\lambda$, then the capitalist demands bK/a, whereas at most W workers are available. Thus, the labor market does not clear. If $w > 1/\lambda$, then all workers choose to work for the capitalist, whereas the capitalist demands none. Thus, the labor market does not clear. Finally, if $w = 1/\lambda$, then the capitalist is indifferent among all employment levels; in particular, it is optimal for him to demand W. At the same time, each worker finds it uniquely optimal to work for the capitalist. Thus, the labor market clears. As a result, $w = 1/\lambda$ is the unique equilibrium wage, and no worker is exploited.

For part 3, assume that $W/b = K/a$. The analysis of the counterfactuals $w < \gamma$ and $w > 1/\lambda$ above implies that any candidate equilibrium wage must be in the set $[\gamma, 1/\lambda]$. At any wage $w \in [\gamma, 1/\lambda]$, each worker weakly or strictly prefers to work for the capitalist, the capitalist weakly or strictly prefers to employ all workers, and at least one of the preferences (the workers' or the capitalist's) is strict. Thus, any wage $w \in [\gamma, 1/\lambda]$ is an equilibrium wage, at which the capitalist employs all workers. However, only at the equilibrium with $w = 1/\lambda$ are the workers not exploited. ∎

Note that, in the knife-edge case $W/b = K/a$ of theorem 4.1, there is a continuum of equilibria, which can be ranked. Workers prefer equilibria with higher wages, while the opposite is true for the capitalist. The worker-optimal equilibrium, which is also capitalist-pessimal, has $w = 1/\lambda$, whereas the capitalist-optimal equilibrium, which is also worker-pessimal, has $w = \gamma$. The existence of optimal and pessimal equilibria for each side of the market (workers and the capitalist) has a counterpart in the marriage problem (cf. theorem 3.9). Indeed, one can compute the worker-optimal equilibrium by appealing to a variation on the worker-proposing DA (algorithm 4).

The rough adaptation of DA to the problem with wages goes like this: Each worker drafts a rank list of all the contracts that he cares about. Such a contract indicates which capitalist he would work for and the wage he would receive. The contract's first component is trivial because there is just one capitalist, but the approach readily generalizes to multiple capitalists. Possible wages are uncountably many, so discretize the set of wages somehow so that it is finite and includes wages $w = \gamma$ and $w = 1/\lambda$, among others. Because each worker prefers earning more to less, all workers would have the same rank list of contracts. At the first round of the worker-proposing DA, each worker proposes his most preferred—that is, the highest-wage—contract on his list. If that contract specifies a wage that exceeds $w = 1/\lambda$, then the capitalist rejects the contract because he cannot possibly make a nonnegative profit from it. Once the workers start proposing $w = 1/\lambda$, the capitalist starts provisionally accepting. When $W/b \leq K/a$, the capitalist never rejects anyone, and the worker-optimal equilibrium is selected. When $W/b > K/a$, the rejected workers start asking for lower wages, leading to a chain of rejections and provisional acceptances that culminates in the selection of the worker-pessimal equilibrium.[2]

The continuum of equilibria in the knife-edge case $W/b = K/a$ is nongeneric. Should the model's parameters be perturbed ever so slightly, $W/b \neq K/a$ ensues, and equilibrium uniqueness prevails. However, one should not equate mathematical nongenericity with economic irrelevance. For instance, in a richer, dynamic, model, $W/b \neq K/a$, instead of $W/b = K/a$, may be a special case. For instance, when $W/b > K/a$, the high profit may motivate and enable the capitalist to invest in capital, thereby countervailing the inequality. Similarly, case $W/b < K/a$ may motivate immigration, investment in human capital, and fertility, thereby, again, countervailing the inequality. Thus, in this richer model, equilibrium may require $W/b = K/a$.

DISCUSSION

By theorem 4.1, the Marxian presumption that the capitalist exploits workers depends critically on the abundance of labor. As a result, the capitalist may have an incentive to withhold or destroy (or at least restrict the accumulation of) capital in order to maintain his bargaining position (cf. problems 1.14 and 1.15). Of course, by a similar logic, workers may have an incentive to restrict the labor force. Indeed, this is what labor unions do. Similarly, if numerous, capitalists would need an industry association (a counterpart of a labor union) to enforce the restrictions on the accumulation of capital.

---

2. Problem 4.4 further compares Walrasian equilibria to the stable matches selected by DA.

Except in the knife-edge case of $W/b = K/a$, theorem 4.1 delivers extreme outcomes. Either the worker is exploited to the extent that his consumption is at the subsistence level or the worker captures the entire surplus from production. Marx focused, justifiably, on the former outcome: the Industrial Revolution had ushered in the technological progress that replaced skilled artisans with factory machines, whose operation required fewer and unskilled workers. (Formally, such a technological progress corresponds to a lower value of coefficient b in the production function (4.1).) As a result, to capitalists, who owned the machines, the workers appeared to be an abundant, homogenous, unskilled mass.

The extreme distributional outcome of theorem 4.1 relies on Leontief technology, according to which labor and capital are perfect complements. If capital and labor were substitutes to some extent, a less extreme allocation of surplus from production would prevail at equilibrium.

Even when the worker is not held down to his subsistence consumption level, his wage need not be regarded as just. Marx did not regard it as just. Marxism holds that any positive reward to capitalists is unjust because capitalists do not contribute anything to the production process. Capitalists merely control a scarce production factor: capital.

A Marxist solution to exploitation is to allocate by force the ownership of capital—the so-called means of production—to workers. A rationale for this intervention (a **revolution**) is the assumption that capital will not be owned by workers without the intervention. For instance, workers would not own shares in firms. Marxism maintains (as an empirical matter) that capital is held in the hands of a few capitalists, thereby giving rise to the class structure that cleanly separates hired labor from those who hire labor.

Marx's broad thesis is this. The distribution of wealth in an economy depends on the relative scarcity of different factors of production. This relative scarcity need not reflect the relative merits of the worker and the capitalist. Hence, the distribution of wealth is fundamentally unjust.

This thesis relies (at least in part) on a limited view of the economy. According to a richer view, market participants do have a say in how scarce the resources that they command are. For example, a capitalist can invent a new, more productive type of capital, which will initially be scarce by nature of its novelty and, so, command a high return. Similarly, a worker can invest in a new skill, thereby rendering himself hard to replace, and so improve his bargaining power. It is exactly this prospect of altering the distribution of surplus that motivates (possibly excessive) innovation and leads to (possibly excessive) economic growth.

The main idea to take away from this section is that Walrasian equilibrium tends to favor the owners of the scarce resource. The comprehension of this idea does not require the mastery of Marxian jargon (viz., labor embodied in a unit of capital, socially necessary labor time, surplus labor time, exploitation, rate of exploitation, reserve army of labor, and the proletariat).

4.3   THE PREVALENCE OF MARKETS: THE CORE

In a market economy, workers may be exploited in the sense of appropriating only a tiny fraction of the output whose production they make possible merely because labor happens to be more abundant than capital in the economic system that rewards scarcity. This inequitable distribution of the gains from trade is illustrated in its extreme form in theorem 4.1 for a production economy. This inequitable distribution can also be seen in chapter 1's exchange economy, which similarly tends to reward the agents who are well-endowed in scarce goods. If scarcity is arbitrary, economic rewards are arbitrary and, hence, in some sense, unjust. Why would workers (or anyone, for that matter) ever put up with an unjust economic system?

A Marxist answer is that workers do not realize that they are not getting a fair deal; they are ignorant of the intricate workings of the market economy, which is much more complex than the feudal economy that preceded it. Workers may also be ignorant of their common interests and of their ability to coordinate on changing their situation; they lack **class consciousness**. (A Marxist label for this worker ignorance is **false consciousness**.) The presumption is that if only a young revolutionary alerted workers to the inequitable distributional consequences of Walrasian equilibrium, then he would be able to amass a coalition for a revolt.

It turns out that a dissenting coalition is not as easy to assemble as one might have thought. In exchange economy, no dissenting coalition can be assembled, provided that agents cannot steal endowments from each other.[3] Why this is so is the first central insight of this section. The second insight is that, in a sense that will be made precise, Walrasian outcomes are essentially the only ones against which it is hard to assemble a dissenting coalition. These two positive insights suggest that one would expect market outcomes to prevail even if no normative arguments for markets existed.

But normative arguments for markets do exist; we briefly list some before turning to the positive insights concerned with dissenting coalitions. The setting for this section's analysis is the exchange economy of chapter 1.

AN EXCHANGE ECONOMY
An exchange economy $\mathcal{E} \equiv (u^i, e^i)_{i\in\mathcal{I}}$ comprises I agents, indexed by $i \in \mathcal{I}$, and L goods, indexed by $l \in \mathcal{L}$; each agent i has a utility function $u^i : \mathbb{R}_+^L \to \mathbb{R}$ and an endowment vector $e^i \in \mathbb{R}_+^L$ and consumes a bundle, typically denoted by x^i, in $\mathbb{R}_+^L$; the vector of aggregate endowments is $\bar{e}$, the matrix of individual endowments is $e \equiv (e^i)_{i\in\mathcal{I}}$, and the allocation is $x \equiv (x^i)_{i\in\mathcal{I}}$.

---

3. The theoretical impossibility of a peaceful revolt against Walrasian outcomes is consistent with the Marxist emphasis on a violent one: "They [communists] openly declare that their ends can be attained only by the forcible overthrow of all existing social conditions" (taken from *The Manifesto of the Communist Party*).

SOME NORMATIVE ARGUMENTS FOR WALRASIAN OUTCOMES

- Walrasian equilibrium outcomes are voluntary and, under u-monotonicity, Pareto efficient (by the FWT).

- Under u-concavity, Walrasian equilibrium treats equals equally in the sense that only individual preferences and endowments matter, not agents' names. That is, Walrasian equilibrium does not lead to "arbitrary" ex-post inequality in consumption for ex-ante identical agents. (This conclusion follows from the observation that, under u-concavity, each agent's optimal bundle is unique.)

- If endowments are equal for all agents, then the equilibrium allocation is envy-free (problem 1.9).[4]

- For all endowments, Walrasian equilibria are envy-free in trades (problem 4.9).

THE CORE

It is possible that agents get stuck at a Walrasian equilibrium, not because it is normatively appealing but simply because they cannot agree on what to abandon it for. Indeed, by the FWT, a revolutionary would be unable to amass unanimous support from all agents by promising a move away from a Walrasian allocation and toward an alternative allocation that would make some better off while leaving others equally well off.

However, the FWT does not rule out secession by a subset of agents. **Secession** occurs when some agents abscond with their endowments and redistribute these endowments among themselves so that some absconders are better off and no absconder is worse off. (The agents left behind by the absconders may be worse off.) By proving a theorem (theorem 4.2) that strengthens the FWT, it will be shown that no secession away from a Walrasian allocation can occur. That is, every prospective coalition of secessionists must have a discontent. Walrasian outcomes are hard to break away from.

The definition of secession makes a strong assumption: secessionists must respect nonsecessionists' property rights to their private endowments. As a result, secession is tamer than revolution, which deals in expropriation.

To formalize the idea of an allocation's immunity to secession, we define the core for the exchange economy. In the definition, for any coalition $\mathcal{S} \subset \mathcal{I}$ of $S \equiv |\mathcal{S}|$ agents, we define $X^{\mathcal{S}} \subset \mathbb{R}_+^{LS}$ to be the set of allocations that this coalition's members can obtain for themselves by redistributing their own endowments among themselves:

$$X^{\mathcal{S}} \equiv \left\{ (x^i)_{i \in \mathcal{S}} \in \mathbb{R}_+^{LS} \mid \sum_{i \in \mathcal{S}} x^i \leq \sum_{i \in \mathcal{S}} e^i \right\}.$$

---

4. Of course, equal endowments are unlikely to prevail in practice, except by design, as in market socialism.

Definition 4.1. Let $\mathcal{E}$ be an exchange economy. An allocation $x \in X^{\mathcal{I}}$ (feasible for the coalition of all) is a **core allocation** if one cannot find a coalition $\mathcal{S} \subset \mathcal{I}$ and an allocation $\hat{x}^{\mathcal{S}} \equiv (\hat{x}^i)_{i \in \mathcal{S}} \in X^{\mathcal{S}}$ (feasible for $\mathcal{S}$) such that each agent in $\mathcal{S}$ weakly prefers his bundle in $\hat{x}^{\mathcal{S}}$ to his bundle in x, with the preference being strict for some agent. The set of all core allocations of $\mathcal{E}$ is called the **core**.

Definition 4.1 thus says that no coalition can abscond with their endowments and Pareto improve for themselves upon—or **block**—the core allocation. Definition 4.1 readily applies to the house allocation problem with private endowments, introduced in section 3.3 (problem 4.7). The definition can also be straightforwardly adapted to the roommates and, a fortiori, the marriage problems of section 3.5; one only needs to recognize that each agent is his own endowment, and the consummation of couples corresponds to the exchange of endowments (problem 4.8).

That any core allocation is Pareto efficient follows from setting $\mathcal{S} = \mathcal{I}$ in definition 4.1; an allocation must be Pareto efficient for the coalition of all to be unable to block it. Thus, in particular, in the Edgeworth box economy, the core lies in the Pareto set. Furthermore, with just two agents, the only coalitions besides $\{1, 2\}$ (the coalition of all) are $\{1\}$ and $\{2\}$. For these two coalitions, definition 4.1 stipulates that the allocation be voluntary (i.e., each agent be weakly better off at a core allocation than consuming his endowment). Thus, in the Edgeworth box, the core coincides with the contract set, as figure 4.1 illustrates. It is therefore immediate that the core need not be a singleton. It is also immediate that, at least in the Edgeworth box, each Walrasian equilibrium allocation is in the core because each Walrasian equilibrium allocation is in the contract set.

WALRASIAN EQUILIBRIA ARE IN THE CORE

The Edgeworth box intuition carries over to exchange economies with an arbitrary number of agents and an arbitrary number of goods; Walrasian equilibrium allocations are in the core, as theorem 4.2 shows and the Venn diagram in figure 4.2(a) summarizes.

Theorem 4.2 (Core $\supset$ Equilibria). *Let x be a Walrasian equilibrium allocation of an exchange economy $\mathcal{E}$. If u-monotonicity holds, then x is in the core of $\mathcal{E}$.*

Proof. The proof, left as an exercise (problem 4.6), follows nearly verbatim the proof of the FWT (theorem 1.1), with the coalition of all replaced by an arbitrary coalition. ∎

IN "LARGE" ECONOMIES, NOT MUCH ELSE IS IN THE CORE

By showing "Core $\supset$ Equilibria" (where "Equilibria" stands for "Walrasian equilibrium allocations"), theorem 4.2 explains why it may be hard for the agents to abandon a Walrasian equilibrium allocation. Had the converse inclusion "Core $\subset$ Equilibria"

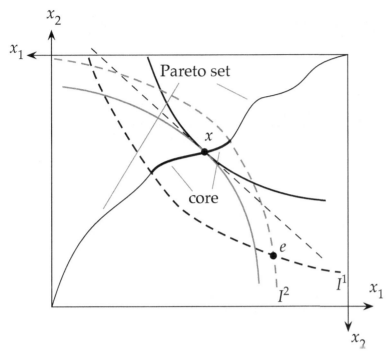

FIGURE 4.1.

The core in the Edgeworth box. The thin curve connecting the two origins is the Pareto set. The thick segment of the curve confined between the agents' indifference curves I^1 and I^2, both going through the endowment point e, is the contract set, which is also the core. Allocation x is in the core but is not a Walrasian equilibrium allocation, for the (dashed) line that passes through x and is tangent to the indifference curves does not pass through e. This line is the only candidate for the equilibrium budget line.

been also true (thereby implying "Core = Equilibria"), one would have been able to conclude that Walrasian allocations had no competition as far as the core was concerned; all impossible-to-secede-from allocations would have been Walrasian. But the converse inclusion fails. It suffices to inspect the Edgeworth box to ascertain that, in general, the set of Walrasian equilibria is a proper subset of the core. So why do Walrasian allocations, not some other elements of the core, seem to persist?

It turns out that, with an appropriately defined asymptotic-inclusion operator $\overset{a}{\subset}$, one can claim an asymptotic version of the converse inclusion: "Core $\overset{a}{\subset}$ Equilibria." So, in the sense of the corresponding asymptotic equality $\overset{a}{=}$ (defined as $\overset{a}{\subset}$ and $\supset$ holding at the same time[5]), one can argue that "Core $\overset{a}{=}$ Equilibria"; each core allocation is either Walrasian or is "close" to some Walrasian allocation,

---

5. Note that, in the relevant definition of asymptotic equality $\overset{a}{=}$, inclusion $\overset{a}{\subset}$ must be asymptotic, whereas inclusion $\supset$ can be taken to be exact, by theorem 4.2.

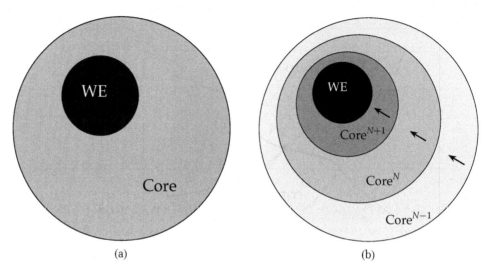

FIGURE 4.2.

Venn diagrams that summarize the relationship between Walrasian allocations and the core. WE denotes the set of (equal-treatment) Walrasian equilibrium allocations, which is independent of N, the number of replications. $Core^N$ (with $Core = Core^1$) denotes the set of (equal treatment) core allocations, which depends on, and is weakly decreasing (in the set-inclusion sense) in, N.

(a) Core inclusion. The set of Walrasian equilibrium allocations is in the core.

(b) Core convergence. The set of core allocations converges to the set of Walrasian equilibrium allocations as the economy is replicated.

and each Walrasian allocation is in the core. Equivalence of the core and Walrasian allocations is asymptotic in the sense that it holds "approximately" when the agents in the economy are "many," and the approximation is better the more agents there are.

The asymptotic shrinkage of the set of core allocations down to the set of Walrasian allocations as the number of agents grows—that is, "Core $\overset{a}{\subset}$ Equilibria"—is called **core convergence** (theorem 4.3). Informally, as the number of agents grows, the number of coalitions that can be formed (this number is $2^I - 1$) grows exponentially, and allocations become easier to block; the core shrinks. Less informally, it is hard to visualize what is supposed to be going on. One can see the core in the Edgeworth box, but, as one keeps adding agents, the dimensionality of the core and the set of Walrasian allocations explodes. How can one even speak of the convergence of sets (of core allocations) if their dimensionality is not held fixed?

To formalize and prove core convergence in a way that can be visualized, we first introduce additional notation and definitions. Take an exchange economy $\mathcal{E} = (u^i, e^i)_{i \in \mathcal{I}}$. An N-**replica** of $\mathcal{E}$, denoted by $\mathcal{E}^N$, is comprised of $N \geq 1$ identical copies (i.e., clones) of each agent in $\mathcal{E}$. Thus, $\mathcal{E}^N$ has IN agents, each of whom is double-indexed by in, where $i \in \mathcal{I}$ indexes the agent's **type**, which is his utility-endowment pair (u^i, e^i), and $n \in \mathcal{N} \equiv \{1, 2, ..., N\}$ indexes the **copy** of that type. Thus, as N grows, $\mathcal{E}^N$ grows in a type-balanced manner, with no type coming to dominate the economy.

For every replica economy $\mathcal{E}^N$, we restrict attention to allocations that satisfy equal treatment. An allocation $x^N \equiv (x^{in})_{i \in \mathcal{I}, n \in \mathcal{N}} \in \mathbb{R}_+^{INL}$ satisfies the **equal treatment of equals** (or, simply, **equal treatment**) if, for any two copies n and n' of any type i, $x^{in} = x^{in'}$. As before, $x \equiv (x^i)_{i \in \mathcal{I}} \in \mathbb{R}_+^{IL}$ denotes an allocation in $\mathcal{E}$. We shall also sometimes refer to x as an allocation in $\mathcal{E}^N$ to mean the equal treatment allocation x^N with $x^{in} = x^i$ for all $i \in \mathcal{I}$ and all $n \in \mathcal{N}$.

We would like to see what happens to both the set of Walrasian equilibrium allocations and the core as N increases.

As N increases, the set of Walrasian equilibrium allocations (in $\mathbb{R}_+^{IL}$, each of which induces an allocation in $\mathbb{R}_+^{INL}$) remains unchanged. In order to see this, take any two positive integers M and N. An allocation $x \in \mathbb{R}_+^{IL}$ induces an equal-treatment Walrasian-equilibrium allocation in $\mathcal{E}^M$ if and only if it induces an equal-treatment Walrasian-equilibrium allocation in $\mathcal{E}^N$. Indeed, each agent's problem is the same in both $\mathcal{E}^M$ and $\mathcal{E}^N$ because one can take the supporting prices to be the same, and markets clear in $\mathcal{E}^N$ if and only if they clear in $\mathcal{E}^M$ because both the aggregate demand and the aggregate supply in $\mathcal{E}^N$ are N/M times the corresponding objects in $\mathcal{E}^M$.

As N increases, the set of core allocations either stays the same or shrinks in the set-inclusion sense (i.e., sheds elements). In order to see this, take any two positive integers M and N with $N > M$. Note that, for any allocation x in $\mathcal{E}$, if the equal treatment allocation x^M induced by x is not in the core of $\mathcal{E}^M$, then the equal treatment allocation x^N induced by x is not in the core of $\mathcal{E}^N$. Indeed, the same agents (down to their type and copy number) who block x^M in $\mathcal{E}^M$ also block x^N in $\mathcal{E}^N$. Furthermore, because $\mathcal{E}^N$ has more agents than $\mathcal{E}^M$ does, more coalitions, potentially blocking, can be constructed in $\mathcal{E}^N$ than in $\mathcal{E}^M$, and the allocations unblocked in $\mathcal{E}^M$ may be blocked in $\mathcal{E}^N$. Thus, the core is weakly decreasing in N in the set-inclusion sense.

Because the core is weakly decreasing in N and (by theorem 4.2) is bounded below by the set of Walrasian allocations (which is independent of N), the core must converge to some limit set.[6] The Venn diagram in figure 4.2(b) summarizes the convergence claim. The remaining question is whether the core converges to the set of Walrasian allocations or to some other limit, a superset of Walrasian allocations. Theorem 4.3 establishes that the core converges to the former.

---

6. To convince yourself of the logic that a weakly decreasing sequence that is bounded below must converge, you may draw a weakly decreasing function that is bounded below. This function must converge, either to the said lower bound or to some number greater than that bound.

Theorem 4.3 (Core $\overset{a}{\subset}$ Equilibria). *Take an exchange economy $\mathcal{E}$ and assume that u-monotonicity and u-concavity hold and that each agent's utility function is continuously differentiable. Suppose that an interior allocation $x \in \mathbb{R}_{++}^{IL}$, for every $N \geq 1$, induces an equal treatment allocation x^N that is in the core of $\mathcal{E}^N$. Then, for every $N \geq 1$, x^N is a Walrasian equilibrium allocation of $\mathcal{E}^N$; that is, **core convergence** obtains.*

Proof Sketch The basic idea of the proof applies to any number of agents and any number of goods. For expositional clarity, we focus on the Edgeworth box economy and provide a graphical argument.

Let $\mathcal{I} = \{1, 2\}$ and $\mathcal{L} = \{1, 2\}$, and let allocation $x \equiv (x^1, x^2)$ satisfy the theorem's hypothesis. Because x is in the core, it is feasible (i.e., $\sum_{i \in \mathcal{I}} x^i \leq \bar{e}$) and Pareto efficient. By u-monotonicity, Pareto efficiency implies that no good is wasted: $\sum_{i \in \mathcal{I}} x^i = \bar{e}$. That is, x satisfies market clearing and, hence, can be depicted in the Edgeworth box. Interior and Pareto efficient, x is a tangency point of the agents' indifference curves. Figure 4.3 illustrates.

To validate x as a Walrasian equilibrium allocation in $\mathcal{E}$, it remains to find supporting prices. With the price of good 2 normalized to $p_2 = 1$ (by u-monotonicity, this can be done), the only viable candidate for the equilibrium price p_1 is the one that makes the budget line tangent to the agents' indifference curves at x:

$$p_1 = \frac{u_1^i(x^i)}{u_2^i(x^i)}, \tag{4.2}$$

which is independent of $i \in \mathcal{I}$. By u-monotonicity, p_1 in (4.2) is well-defined and positive.

To ascertain that the constructed price vector $p = (p_1, 1)$ indeed supports x, one must show that the corresponding budget line that passes through x also passed through the endowment point e; that is $p \cdot x^i = p \cdot e^i$ for each $i \in \mathcal{I}$. If so, u-concavity and the tangency of each agent's indifference curve to this budget line would imply that each agent i maximizes his utility by choosing x^i at p.

By contradiction, suppose that the budget line corresponding to p does not pass through e. Then, it must be that, for some agent—say, agent 1—$p \cdot x^1 > p \cdot e^1$, as in figure 4.3. Because agent 1 consumes more than he can afford, it is tempting to hypothesize that, in some replica economy $\mathcal{E}^N$, all agents except for one copy of agent 1 could gain by seceding, thereby contradicting the theorem's hypothesis that the equal treatment allocation x^N induced by x is in the core of $\mathcal{E}^N$.

With one copy of type-1 agent excluded, redistribute his trade vector $x^1 - e^1$ equally among the remaining agents—whose coalition is denoted by $\mathcal{S}$—to construct

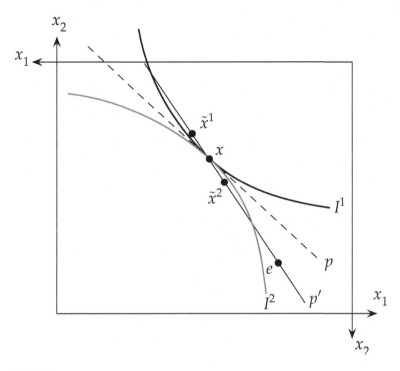

FIGURE 4.3.

A step in the proof of theorem 4.3. If x, a core allocation in $\mathcal{E}$, is unaffordable to agent 1 at the price vector p, then x cannot be in the core of $\mathcal{E}^N$ for a sufficiently large N. The argument proceeds by forming a (blocking) coalition $\mathcal{S}$ of all agents except one copy of agent 1, whose trade at x is shared equally among the members of $\mathcal{S}$, thereby leading to a new allocation $\tilde{x} \equiv (\tilde{x}^1, \tilde{x}^2)$, which everyone in $\mathcal{S}$ prefers to x. Indeed, allocation $\tilde{x}$ lies on the line p', which captures the terms on which agent 1 exchanges good 1 for good 2 to arrive at x. Bestowing a small fraction of this trade on any agent in $\mathcal{S}$ (i.e., moving away from x along p') makes this agent better off because p' is steeper than p.

a candidate blocking allocation $\tilde{x} \in \mathbb{R}_+^{IL}$:

$$\tilde{x}^i \equiv x^i + \frac{1}{IN - 1}(x^1 - e^1), \quad i \in \mathcal{I}. \tag{4.3}$$

If N is sufficiently large, then $\tilde{x} \equiv (\tilde{x}^1, \tilde{x}^2)$ is feasible because x is interior.

By construction, the bundles $(\tilde{x}^1, \tilde{x}^2)$ lie on what in figure 4.3 is line p', which goes through the endowment e and the original allocation x. By the contradiction hypothesis $p \cdot x^1 > p \cdot e^1$, line p' is steeper than the tangent line p. The larger the N, the closer are $\tilde{x}^1$ and $\tilde{x}^2$ to x. Hence, if N is large enough, then $\tilde{x}^1$ is in type 1's upper contour set, and $\tilde{x}^2$ is in type 2's upper contour set, and, hence, each agent in $\mathcal{S}$ prefers $\tilde{x}$ to x; $\mathcal{S}$ is a blocking coalition. Because $\mathcal{S}$ blocks x^N, x^N is not in the core of $\mathcal{E}^N$, which contradicts the theorem's hypothesis. Thus, $p \cdot x^1 > p \cdot e^1$ is impossible.

As a result, $p \cdot x^i = p \cdot e^i$ for all $i \in \mathcal{I}$, which (together with u-concavity and the tangency of the budget line) ensures that each agent i maximizes his utility by choosing x^i at p. Coupled with the market clearing, utility maximization implies that (p, x) is a Walrasian equilibrium of $\mathcal{E}$, and so x^N is a Walrasian equilibrium of $\mathcal{E}^N$, for any $N \geq 1$, as desired. ∎

Remark 4.1. One can show that u-concavity implies that any allocation x^N that is in the core of $\mathcal{E}^N$ for every $N \geq 1$ is an equal treatment allocation (problem 4.10; proposition 15.10 of Kreps, 2012; or chapter 21 of Varian, 1992). Moreover, u-concavity implies that any Walrasian equilibrium allocation is an equal treatment allocation because each agent's optimal bundle is unique. Hence, the theorem's focus on equal treatment allocations entails no loss of generality.

DISCUSSION

Theorem 4.3 says that the set of Walrasian equilibrium allocations approximates the core. This approximation is good only in the limit, as the number of agents grows. But then Walrasian equilibrium itself is "good" only in the limit, at which it is plausible to assume that each agent takes prices as given and does not try to influence them with his choice of trades. So, in some sense, the core and Walrasian allocations are equivalent. It is a remarkable, and not at all obvious, fact that the two leading conceptualizations of unfettered exchange—the core and Walrasian equilibrium—are essentially equivalent.

The core is indeed a plausible conceptualization of unfettered exchange. By insisting on Pareto efficiency, the core insists that no money be left on the table. The core also insists on the allocation being voluntary. Thus, the core is a subset of the contract set. In addition, the core requires that no subset of agents be able to gain by contracting among themselves on the side. This freedom to contract on the side bites off bits and pieces of the contract set to leave but a core.

When the number of agents is small, the core's agnostic nature, which often delivers a continuum of allocations while Walrasian equilibrium delivers one or a handful of allocations, can advantage the core over Walrasian equilibria. Having narrowed the set of likely outcomes down to the set of core allocations, one may be uncomfortable imposing stronger, Walrasian, assumptions. The stronger Walrasian assumptions may seem gratuitous when the number of agents in the economy is small and the price-taking behavior is hard to justify.

Nevertheless, there is a tendency in economics to seek singleton predictions. If a theory is agnostic about what exactly is going to happen, while observation tells us that invariably something does happen, then the theory is incomplete, and the scientist is compelled to complete it. Because they deliver sharper results and are often easier to compute, Walrasian equilibria figure more prominently in economic analysis than does the core.

Walrasian equilibrium and the core can be (informally) viewed as dual concepts. Walrasian equilibrium postulates a market clearing price vector and prescribes how to derive allocations from this price vector by appealing to utility maximization. By contrast, the core postulates core allocations, from which one can (but need not) derive the exchange rates, or prices, consistent with the implied trades away from the endowments and toward a core allocation. Walrasian agents need to know nothing about each other's preferences and endowments, but the supporting equilibrium prices must "know" all of that to clear the markets. By contrast, in order to verify a core allocation, agents must know each other's preferences and endowments, which is necessary to assess whether forming seceding coalitions is profitable. To the extent that it is more natural to assume that the knowledge of the economy is possessed by agents rather than prices, the core is a more literal conceptualization of unfettered competition—a market economy—-than Walrasian equilibrium.

The core is an ode to individual sovereignty and the freedom of contracting, which are the fundamental tenets of the market economy. The complete freedom of contracting that underlies the core is crucial. The core assumes that any subset of agents can form a coalition at no cost and then divide their endowments in any manner, also at no cost. In particular, the assumption that the coalition of all can be formed is responsible for the conclusion that the core allocation is Pareto efficient.[7]

The implicit presumption that contracting is costly in practice is responsible for the intuition—which clashes with the Pareto efficiency of the core—that unconstrained cartels (e.g., coalitions of oil producers) lead to Pareto inefficient outcomes. This intuition about inefficiency relies on the assumption that cartel members cannot form costless coalitions with their customers by signing arbitrary and costless contracts with them. In practice, it may be costly to identify all potential customers and tailor and enforce individual (e.g., price-discriminatory) contracts. If it is impossible to ensure that all possible coalitions can be costlessly formed, then permitting more coalitions need not lead to a better outcome—just as opening new markets need not lead to a Pareto improvement when complete markets are out of reach.

The conclusion of theorem 4.3 relies on the assumption that the economy grows by adding agents in a "balanced" manner. This assumption ensures that no agent dominates the economy. For instance, one can imagine growing an economy by postulating two agents with huge endowments and adding only

---

7. In addition, the proof of theorem 4.3 uses the fact that the coalition of all but one agent can be formed. The proof still goes through, however, as long as, for some $\alpha \in (0, 1)$, any coalition comprising up to αN agents can be formed.

agents with vanishing endowments. Then, the growing economy of any size will essentially remain a two-agent economy, and the core will not converge to Walrasian allocations.

Because of the intimate connection between the core and Walrasian equilibrium, the core is susceptible to the two theoretical criticisms that also afflict Walrasian equilibrium. In a Walrasian equilibrium, the equilibrating price vector comes out of nowhere to induce an equilibrium allocation. In a core, the core allocation itself comes out of nowhere. Furthermore, the Walrasian model provides no definitive argument (tâtonnement is an attempt) for why an economy would converge to equilibrium if initial prices are disequilibrium prices. Similarly, the core supplies no negotiation protocol whereby agents would negotiate toward a core allocation. In examples, however, one can construct decentralized protocols that would lead to Walrasian or core outcomes.

4.4   SOCIALISM

Section 4.2 emphasized the arguably arbitrary and (with Leontief technology) extreme distributional consequences of private ownership in a market economy. There, the private ownership is of the disembodied means of production, which are physical capital and the technology that converts physical capital and labor into output. The socialist ideal aims to combine the collective ownership of the disembodied means of production with the limited private ownership of the embodied means of production (i.e., human capital) to deliver an equitable distribution of consumption. To analyze this ideal, we consider another economy with production.

It is a priori not obvious what the appropriate notions of collective ownership and limited private ownership should be. Indeed, it is not clear at all how to think about ownership unless it is absolute, as in the Walrasian model. To circumvent the problem of operationalizing the concept of collective ownership, notice that what ultimately matters to the agents is not the ownership structure per se but the properties of the mapping from the data of the environment (i.e., preferences, endowments, and production technology) into allocations. This mapping is called **social choice function**. A tentative vision of the ownership structure can motivate the social choice function, but conditional on this function, the details of the underlying ownership structure are irrelevant (as long as one is a consequentialist, which one ultimately ought to be).[8]

8. There is no moral justification for foregoing a desirable outcome in order to favor one mechanism over another. If nevertheless one insists on doing so, then, tautologically, one can regard the mechanism's details that one cares about as components of the outcome and thus remain a consequentialist. A consequentialist may come across as a nonconsequentialist when working with an incomplete model. For instance, in the house allocation problem with private endowments, one may prefer executing TTC to

Thus, the ownership-design approach taken in this section is, first, to postulate the conditions, or desiderata (also called "axioms"), that a benevolent designer, inspired by his vision of an ideal ownership structure, may like a social choice function to satisfy and then to describe the set of social choice functions that satisfy these conditions. It will be shown that seemingly innocuous conditions jointly restrict the set of admissible social choice functions to a singleton that mandates that the agents' utilities be equalized. This approach of studying the implications of conditions imposed on a social choice function is the essence of the axiomatic approach to normative economics.

To briefly illustrate the axiomatic approach, consider the familiar example: the house allocation problem with private endowments (section 3.3). Suppose that the designer seeks a social choice function that maps the individual endowments of houses and preferences over these houses into allocations that are in the core. (The core requirement is the axiom in this application of the axiomatic approach.) Then, one can show that there exists a unique social choice function with this property. This function can be shown to always select the TTC allocation.[9]

ANOTHER ECONOMY WITH PRODUCTION

A production economy has two goods (stuff and leisure), indexed by $l \in \mathcal{L} = \{1, 2\}$, and two agents, indexed by $i \in \mathcal{I} = \{1, 2\}$. Both agents have the same utility function $u : \mathbb{R}_{++} \times X^i \to \mathbb{R}$. Agent i's utility $u(s^i, x^i)$ is a function of his skill $s^i \in \mathbb{R}_{++}$, amount $x_1^i \in \mathbb{R}_+$ of stuff that he consumes, and amount $x_2^i \in [0, 1]$ of leisure that he consumes. Thus, agent i's consumption set is $X^i = \mathbb{R}_+ \times [0, 1]$. Agent i is endowed with no stuff and with one unit of leisure. Any leisure that he does not consume, he supplies as $h^i \equiv 1 - x_2^i$ hours of labor. A weakly increasing production function $f : \mathbb{R}_+ \to \mathbb{R}_+$ transforms $h \equiv \sum_{i \in \mathcal{I}} h^i$ units of aggregate labor into $f(h)$ units of stuff. A constant, or **social-endowment**, production function f would induce a so-called social-endowment economy, with social endowment $f(0)$, not initially assigned to any agent. Because utility functions and (private) endowments are the same for all agents and do not vary in the analysis, a production economy is abbreviated to $\mathcal{P} \equiv (s^1, s^2, f)$.

Henceforth, we assume that the agents' common utility function, u, satisfies

***U*-MONOTONICITY** u is (strictly) increasing in each component of x^i. That is, as in chapter 1, the more an agent consumes, the happier he is.

COMPENSATION For all $s^i \in \mathbb{R}_{++}$ and all $x_2^i \in [0, 1]$, the range of function $u(s^i, \cdot, x_2^i)$ is $\mathbb{R}$. That is, the effect of any change in skill or leisure on the utility can be completely offset by an appropriate change in the consumption of stuff.

---

letting an unfettered exchange play out in the hope that this unfettered exchange would converge to the unique Walrasian allocation, which is also the TTC allocation.

9. One can prove this result in two steps (part 2 of problem 4.7). First show that TTC selects a core allocation. Then show that there exists only one core allocation.

SKILL-MONOTONICITY u is weakly increasing in s^i. That is, holding a consumption bundle x^i fixed, a more skilled agent is weakly happier.

SKILL–CONSUMPTION NEUTRALITY $u(s^i, x_1^i, 1)$ is independent of s^i for any x_1^i. That is, if agent i supplies no labor (i.e., $x_2^i = 1$), then his skill does not affect his utility, no matter how much stuff he consumes.

Skill–consumption neutrality requires that if an agent consumes his entire endowment of leisure (i.e., supplies no labor), then his enjoyment of stuff is not enhanced by his skill. Hence, it is inappropriate to interpret s^i as a parameter that raises agent i's overall happiness. Instead, it is natural to interpret an increase in s^i as a decrease in the agent's disutility of labor, which is one way to think about higher productivity.[10]

The utility function in example 4.1 satisfies each of the assumptions listed above.

Example 4.1 (An Admissible Utility Function). Let

$$u(s^i, x_1^i, x_2^i) \equiv \ln x_1^i - \frac{1 - x_2^i}{s^i},$$

where $1 - x_2^i$ is the amount of labor supplied; a higher s^i means that it is less painful for the agent to supply labor. The range of $u(s^i, \cdot, x_2^i)$ is $\mathbb{R}$, for any s^i and x_2^i. $\triangle$

An allocation $x \equiv (x^1, x^2) \in X^1 \times X^2$ is **feasible** if the aggregate consumption of stuff does not exceed its production:

$$\sum_{i \in \mathcal{I}} x_1^i \leq f\left(\sum_{i \in \mathcal{I}} (1 - x_2^i)\right).$$

A social choice function F maps any production economy $\mathcal{P}$ into some feasible allocation x in $X^1 \times X^2$. As a matter of notation, when $F(\mathcal{P}) = x$, define $F^1(\mathcal{P}) = x^1$ and $F^2(\mathcal{P}) = x^2$ to be the bundles that the social choice function assigns to agents 1 and 2, respectively, where $x \equiv (x^1, x^2)$. In the following illustrative examples of social choice functions, $\mathbf{1}_{\{\}}$ denotes an indicator function, whose value is 1 if the condition in the braces is true and is 0 otherwise.

- If $F(\mathcal{P}) = ((0, 1), (0, 1))$ for all $\mathcal{P}$, then each agent consumes his endowment. No production occurs. Any social endowment $f(0)$, if positive, is wasted.

---

10. This is not the only way. An alternative formulation would model a greater skill as a greater time endowment, which does not vary across agents in the present formulation.

- If $F(\mathcal{P}) = \mathbf{1}_{\{s^1 \geq s^2\}} \left(\left(f(1), \frac{1}{2} \right), \left(0, \frac{1}{2} \right) \right) + \mathbf{1}_{\{s^1 < s^2\}} \left(\left(0, \frac{1}{2} \right), \left(f(1), \frac{1}{2} \right) \right)$ for all $\mathcal{P}$, then each agent works half-time, and the more skilled agent consumes all the fruits of the joint labor.

- If $F(\mathcal{P}) = \mathbf{1}_{\{f' \equiv 0\}} \left(\left(\frac{1}{2} f(0), 1 \right), \left(\frac{1}{2} f(0), 1 \right) \right) + \mathbf{1}_{\{f' \neq 0\}} \left(\left(\frac{1}{2} f(1), 0 \right), \left(\frac{1}{2} f(1), 0 \right) \right)$, then the agents supply no labor if the economy is social-endowment economy, and each agent supplies the maximal amount of labor otherwise, with stuff shared equally.

DESIDERATA

We shall impose a collection of efficiency and fairness desiderata on the social choice function. In addition to being interesting in their own right, these desiderata taken together capture what seem to be the essential properties of collective ownership of the means of production. This way, we shall be able to say something about the implications of the nebulous concept of collective ownership without committing to a detailed description of how collective ownership is to be operationalized. Because collective ownership is a defining feature of socialism, the posited desiderata are collected under the rubric "socialism."

Condition 4.1 (Pareto Efficiency). F selects a Pareto efficient allocation. That is, for no economy $\mathcal{P}$ can one find a feasible allocation $x \in X^1 \times X^2$ such that

$$u(s^i, x^i) \geq u\left(s^i, F^i(\mathcal{P}) \right), \quad i \in \mathcal{I},$$

with at least one inequality being strict.

Condition 4.1 is uncontroversial in most settings, socialist or not.

Condition 4.2 (Equal Treatment of Equals).   If agents have identical skills, then they must enjoy identical utility levels. That is, for any economy $\mathcal{P}$,

$$s^1 = s^2 \implies u\left(s^1, F^1(\mathcal{P}) \right) = u\left(s^2, F^2(\mathcal{P}) \right).$$

While condition 4.2 seems natural, it is easy to construct examples in which it would appear gratuitous.[11] For instance, suppose that a society is endowed with antibiotics in the amount just enough to treat one patient. Then, insisting on splitting the antibiotics equally and thereby treating no one, as condition 4.2 (equal treatment) would have it, seems wrong, perhaps, because incompatible with condition 4.1 (Pareto efficiency). To obtain the incompatibility formally, one must assume that the utility is independent of the amount of antibiotics consumed until

---

11. The routing problem SM2LA, in section 8.3, is one such example.

this amount exceeds some threshold. In the present model, this independence is ruled out by u-monotonicity. Nevertheless, the criticism stands: Would one be willing to sacrifice the sure rescue of Alice from near-certain death for the sake of an arbitrarily small chance of Bob's survival?[12] Such dramatic scenarios would be ruled out by assuming that the utility is concave (which we neither assume nor rule out); concavity guides the intuition that favors sharing instead of extreme allocation.

In condition 4.3, s^i and s^{*i} denote two possible skills for an arbitrary agent $i \in \mathcal{I}$, and s^{-i} denotes the skill of the other agent, agent $-i \equiv \mathcal{I} \setminus i$.

Condition 4.3 (Limited Private Ownership of the Embodied Means of Production). An agent becomes weakly better off if he becomes more skilled. That is, for any two economies $\mathcal{P} - (s^i, s^{-i}, f)$ and $\mathcal{P}^* - (s^{*i}, s^{-i}, f)$,

$$s^{*i} > s^i \implies u\big(s^{*i}, F^i(\mathcal{P}^*)\big) \geq u\big(s^i, F^i(\mathcal{P})\big).$$

It seems compelling to make a more skilled agent work more. Condition 4.3 rules out the situations in which a more skilled agent is made to work so much more without being appropriately compensated with stuff that he ends up being worse off. The condition can also be justified on positive grounds: in a richer model, an agent would be inclined to underinvest in, or even destroy, his skill if, in violation of condition 4.3, greater skill were penalized.

If Alice becomes more skilled, should Bob be allowed to be worse off as a result? The following condition, socialist in spirit, objects to the possibility that Bob is worse off.

Condition 4.4 (Solidarity). An agent becomes weakly better off if the other agent becomes more skilled. That is, for any two economies $\mathcal{P} = (s^i, s^{-i}, f)$ and $\mathcal{P}^* = (s^{*i}, s^{-i}, f)$,

$$s^{*i} > s^i \implies u\big(s^{-i}, F^{-i}(\mathcal{P}^*)\big) \geq u\big(s^{-i}, F^{-i}(\mathcal{P})\big).$$

Condition 4.4 can be interpreted as limited collective ownership of the embodied means of production. The condition is motivated by the attitude according to which one cannot take full credit for one's skill. Some win the gene lottery and happen to be born stronger, smarter, and more patient. Those who trained and studied hard to become stronger, smarter, and more patient did so, in part, thanks to institutions that enabled them to develop their talents. Therefore, the society at large deserves a share in the success of each individual.

---

12. An objector to the formulation of equal treatment in condition 4.2 may entertain weakening it while preserving some of its spirit by letting a coin toss determine the recipient of the antibiotics, thereby treating equals equally ex-ante, before the outcome of the coin toss is known.

Finally, for the quintessentially socialist condition that follows, define $f^* \geq f$ to be the shorthand for $f^*(h) \geq f(h)$ for all h.

Condition 4.5 (Collective Ownership of the Disembodied Means of Production). As technology improves, each agent becomes weakly better off. That is, for any two economies $\mathcal{P} = (s^1, s^2, f)$ and $\mathcal{P}^* = (s^1, s^2, f^*)$,

$$f^* \geq f \implies u\big(s^i, F^i(\mathcal{P}^*)\big) \geq u\big(s^i, F^i(\mathcal{P})\big), \qquad i \in \mathcal{I}.$$

Definition 4.2. Conditions 4.1–4.5 comprise **socialism**. A social choice function that satisfies these conditions is **socialist**.

To summarize the scope of the conditions that comprise socialism, recall that the set of agents, their private endowments, and the utility function are all fixed, while skills and the production function vary. Each condition must hold for any skill profile and for any weakly increasing production function. The conditions would be weaker if they were required to hold only for a particular production function or a class of production functions (e.g., only strictly increasing ones) or only for some skill pairs. In particular, if the set of admissible production functions were a singleton, then condition 4.5 (collective ownership) would be vacuous. If one is ever surprised by an implication of seemingly innocuous conditions, one should verify that this implication is not driven by some exotic element in the conditions' domain.[13]

SOCIALISM REQUIRES EGALITARIANISM

How about adding to the list of socialist conditions equal treatment of *unequals*, which would require that both agents' utilities be equalized regardless of whether the agents' skills are equal? Would that be too much egalitarianism? Logically, equal treatment of unequals is not in contradiction with socialism. But it seems gratuitously demanding.

In fact, equal treatment of unequals is implied by the socialist conditions that we have already imposed.

Theorem 4.4 (Egalitarianism). *Suppose that a social choice function F is socialist. Then, F must select an outcome that equalizes the agents' utilities. That is, for any economy* $\mathcal{P}$, $u\big(s^1, F^1(\mathcal{P})\big) = u\big(s^2, F^2(\mathcal{P})\big)$.

Proof. Fix an arbitrary skill profile (s^1, s^2). Fix a socialist social choice function F. The proof proceeds in three steps, signposted in figure 4.4.

Step 1 (As one varies f, the allocations selected by F are weakly Pareto ranked— that is, can be compared according to the Pareto criterion).

---

13. A condition's **domain** is the set of all economies $\mathcal{P}$ for which the condition must hold.

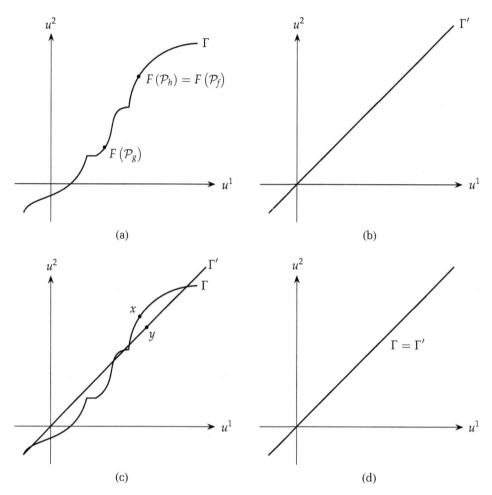

FIGURE 4.4.

Claims in the steps in the proof of theorem 4.4, illustrated in the utility space. Fix a skill profile and a social choice function and vary the production function.

(a) Step 1: For any two production functions *f* and *g*, the utility profiles induced by allocations $F(\mathcal{P}_f)$ and $F(\mathcal{P}_g)$ must lie on a nondecreasing curve, denoted by Γ. $\mathcal{P}_h$ is the auxiliary economy used in the proof.

(b) Step 2: In the economies in which the production function is social-endowment, the agents' utilities are equal and, as the social endowment varies, trace out the entire 45-degree line, denoted by Γ'.

(c) Step 3: If an allocation *x* is in Γ but not in Γ', then one can find an allocation *y* in Γ' that is not in Γ, which contradicts $\Gamma' \subset \Gamma$.

(d) Synthesis: The set of all possible utility profiles is the 45-degree line; that is, $\Gamma = \Gamma'$.

In an economy $\mathcal{P} = (s^1, s^2, f)$, vary the (weakly increasing) production function f to define the set of agents' payoffs induced by the social choice function F:

$$\Gamma \equiv \left\{ \left(u\left(s^1, F^1(\mathcal{P})\right), u\left(s^2, F^2(\mathcal{P})\right)\right) \mid f : \mathbb{R}_+ \to \mathbb{R}_+ \right\}. \tag{4.4}$$

It will be shown that graph Γ lies on a weakly increasing curve in the utility space, and, hence, the underlying allocations are Pareto ranked.

Take any two production functions, f and g. Define a new production function $h \equiv \max\{f, g\}$, which is a pointwise maximum of f and g. Denote the economies corresponding to production functions f, g, and h by $\mathcal{P}_f$, $\mathcal{P}_g$, and $\mathcal{P}_h$, respectively. We must show that both agents will either agree that $F(\mathcal{P}_f)$ is weakly preferred to $F(\mathcal{P}_g)$ or the other way around. Figure 4.4(a) illustrates what we need to show.

Allocation $F(\mathcal{P}_h)$ is feasible either in $\mathcal{P}_f$ or in $\mathcal{P}_g$ or in both economies. (Why?) Without loss of generality, assume that $F(\mathcal{P}_h)$ is feasible in $\mathcal{P}_f$.[14] On the one hand, because $F(\mathcal{P}_h)$ is feasible in $\mathcal{P}_f$ but F chooses $F(\mathcal{P}_f)$, condition 4.1 (Pareto efficiency) implies that $F(\mathcal{P}_h)$ cannot Pareto dominate $F(\mathcal{P}_f)$. On the other hand, condition 4.5 (collective ownership) implies that each agent weakly prefers $F(\mathcal{P}_h)$ to $F(\mathcal{P}_f)$. Hence, it must be that each agent is indifferent between $F(\mathcal{P}_h)$ and $F(\mathcal{P}_f)$.

Condition 4.5 (collective ownership) also implies that each agent weakly prefers $F(\mathcal{P}_h)$ to $F(\mathcal{P}_g)$. Because each agent is indifferent between $F(\mathcal{P}_h)$ and $F(\mathcal{P}_f)$, it must be that each agent weakly prefers $F(\mathcal{P}_f)$ to $F(\mathcal{P}_g)$.

To summarize, for any f and g, either $F(\mathcal{P}_h)$ is feasible in $\mathcal{P}_f$, and each agent weakly prefers $F(\mathcal{P}_f)$ to $F(\mathcal{P}_g)$, or $F(\mathcal{P}_h)$ is feasible in $\mathcal{P}_g$, and each agent weakly prefers $F(\mathcal{P}_g)$ to $F(\mathcal{P}_f)$, or both. Either way, $F(\mathcal{P}_f)$ and $F(\mathcal{P}_g)$ are weakly Pareto ranked; Γ lies on a weakly increasing curve.

Step 2 (*In social-endowment economies, egalitarianism must prevail*).
Without loss of generality, assume that the fixed skill profile (s^1, s^2) is such that $s^1 \geq s^2$.[15]

Consider an economy $\mathcal{P}_\alpha^* \equiv (s^1, s^2, f_\alpha)$, indexed by $\alpha > 0$, in which the production function f_α is social-endowment: for any $h \geq 0$, $f_\alpha(h) = \alpha > 0$. Vary the production function f_α by varying α to trace out the set of agent payoff profiles induced by F:

$$\Gamma' \equiv \left\{ \left(u(s^1, F^1(\mathcal{P}_\alpha^*)), u(s^2, F^2(\mathcal{P}_\alpha^*))\right) : \alpha > 0 \right\}. \tag{4.5}$$

---

14. If not, then $F(\mathcal{P}_h)$ is feasible in $\mathcal{P}_g$, and, so, one can simply relabel f and g.

15. If $s^1 < s^2$, simply rename the agents.

It will be shown that graph Γ' is a 45-degree line that passes through the origin in the utility space and that projects onto $\mathbb{R}$ on each axis, as is illustrated in figure 4.4(b).

Define a related economy with equally (un)skilled workers: $\mathcal{P}_\alpha \equiv (s^2, s^2, f_\alpha)$.
Denote $x \equiv (x^1, x^2) = F(\mathcal{P}_\alpha)$ and $x^* \equiv (x^{*1}, x^{*2}) = F(\mathcal{P}_\alpha^*)$.

Because labor does not contribute to production but subtracts from leisure, condition 4.1 (Pareto efficiency) dictates that no labor be supplied in either economy: $x_2^i = x_2^{*i} = 1$ for each $i \in \mathcal{I}$.

If agent 1's skill rises from s^2 to s^1, then, by condition 4.3 (limited private ownership) and condition 4.4 (solidarity), both agents' utilities increase weakly:

$$u(s^1, x^{*1}) \geq u(s^2, x^1) \quad \text{and} \quad u(s^2, x^{*2}) \geq u(s^2, x^2).$$

None of the utilities may increase strictly because x^* is feasible in $\mathcal{P}_\alpha$ and delivers the same utilities as in $\mathcal{P}_\alpha^*$ by skill–consumption neutrality, while x is Pareto efficient in $\mathcal{P}_\alpha$ (condition 4.1). Hence,

$$u(s^1, x^{*1}) = u(s^2, x^1) \quad \text{and} \quad u(s^2, x^{*2}) = u(s^2, x^2).$$

Finally, because, by condition 4.2 (equal treatment), the agents' utilities are equalized in $\mathcal{P}_\alpha^*$, $u(s^2, x^1) = u(s^2, x^2)$, the display above implies that the agents' utilities are also equalized in $\mathcal{P}_\alpha^*$,

$$u(s^1, x^{*1}) = u(s^2, x^{*2}).$$

To summarize, we have just shown that, in the class of social-endowment economies, of which $\mathcal{P}_\alpha$ is a typical element, F equalizes utilities—or, graphically, graph Γ' lies on the 45-degree line that passes through the origin in the utility space. To conclude that Γ' is itself a line (i.e., that Γ' has no holes), note that utilities can be Pareto efficiently equalized by, and only by, giving each agent amount $\alpha/2$ of stuff. That is, Γ' satisfies

$$\Gamma' = \left\{ \left(u\left(s^1, \frac{\alpha}{2}, 1\right), u\left(s^2, \frac{\alpha}{2}, 1\right) \right) \mid \alpha > 0 \right\},$$

which, by skill–consumption neutrality and by compensation, is indeed the 45-degree line that passes through the origin.

Step 3 (*Egalitarianism prevails in all economies:* $\Gamma = \Gamma'$).
By construction, $\Gamma' \subset \Gamma$, for the set of the social-endowment production functions is a subset of all production functions.

To show that $\Gamma \subset \Gamma'$, suppose, by contradiction, that there exists an $x \in \Gamma$ such that $x \notin \Gamma'$. Then, as is illustrated in figure 4.4(c), one can find a $y \in \Gamma'$ such that x and y cannot be Pareto ranked, thereby contradicting step 1.

Therefore, $\Gamma = \Gamma'$, and F equates the agents' utilities in any economy (figure 4.4(d)). ∎

Here is a two-paragraph-long outline of the theorem's proof. Suppose that a fixed amount of stuff has been freely bestowed upon the agents, with no opportunity to produce more. Then, in any Pareto efficient allocation, no agent supplies labor. If the agents have identical skills, they must enjoy identical utilities, by the equal treatment of equals. Now suppose that agent 1's skill rises. Agent 1 cannot get a lower utility, by limited private ownership. Agent 2 cannot get a lower utility, by solidarity. Higher utilities cannot be delivered, by skill–consumption neutrality and by Pareto efficiency of the old (same-skill) allocation in the old economy. Hence, differently skilled agents enjoy the same utilities as the equally skilled agents were enjoying and, so, enjoy identical utilities.

Furthermore, note that Pareto efficiency and collective ownership imply that, for any two technologies, the induced utility pairs can be Pareto ranked. So, the set of utilities induced by the social choice function as one varies technologies is an upward sloping curve. Because social endowment production functions are admissible and because the class of these functions induces a 45-degree line in the space of utilities, it must be that the identified upward-sloping curve for general production functions is actually the 45-degree line segment constructed for the social-endowment functions. In other words, the utilities are equalized for all production functions.

The examination of social-endowment economies is a critical step in the proof of theorem 4.4. That such economies can be entertained is an implication of the rather generous domain assumption: any weakly increasing production function—including a constant one—is admissible. The conclusion of theorem 4.4 need not hold on smaller domains (problem 4.13).

It would be rash to interpret theorem 4.4 as saying that every socialist social choice function fails to reward individual skills. It is true that both agents experience the same utility at any skill profile. If an agent's skill were to increase, however, one can construct examples in which his utility would increase (along with the other agent's utility). In a large population, however, if everyone is restricted to enjoy the same utility, then the extra output due to an increase in one agent's skill is likely to be spread so thinly over so many agents that the return to the individual whose skill has increased will be tiny.

Finally, theorem 4.4 does not claim the existence of a socialist social choice function. Nor does the theorem say how to construct such a function when it exists, although it is not hard to guess. (Try, then see problem 4.14, which is also a good starting point for thinking about existence.)

COMPARING SOCIALIST AND WALRASIAN SOCIAL CHOICE FUNCTIONS

To define a Walrasian social choice function, we must first define Walrasian equilibrium for the examined economy with production. We do so by analogy with the definition in section 4.2. But, first, we augment economy $\mathcal{P}$ by introducing a competitive firm that operates the technology represented by the production function f and by specifying how this firm's profit (if any), denoted by π, is distributed among the agents.

Let $\theta^i \geq 0$ denote the fraction of the firm's profit collected by agent i, where $\sum_{i \in \mathcal{I}} \theta^i = 1$. The price of leisure is denoted by w and is the wage rate; choosing to work less than one's endowment of leisure is equivalent to working full-time and then buying leisure back at the wage rate. By u-monotonicity, the price of stuff is positive and can be normalized to 1. Each agent i's wealth is $w + \theta^i \pi$, which is the value of his endowment of leisure plus his share of the firm's profit. Taking the wage rate and the firm's profit as given, each agent maximizes his utility subject to the budget constraint. Taking the wage rate as given, the firm chooses its demand for labor, denoted by h, so as to maximize its profit, $f(h) - wh$.

Definition 4.3. A **Walrasian equilibrium with production** in an economy $\mathcal{P}$ with profit shares $\theta \equiv (\theta^i)_{i \in \mathcal{I}}$ is a collection (w, x, h) of wage w, allocation x, and the firm's labor demand h such that:

1. The firm maximizes its profit:

$$h \in \arg \max_{\tilde{h} \geq 0} \{f(\tilde{h}) - w\tilde{h}\}.$$

2. Each agent maximizes his utility:

$$x^i \in \arg \max_{y^i \in X^i} u(s^i, y^i) \quad \text{s.t.} \quad (1, w) \cdot y^i \leq w + \theta^i \pi(w), \quad i \in \mathcal{I},$$

   where $\pi(w)$ is the firm's profit

$$\pi(w) \equiv \max_{\tilde{h} \geq 0} \{f(\tilde{h}) - w\tilde{h}\}.$$

3. Markets clear for stuff,

$$\sum_{i \in \mathcal{I}} x_1^i = f(h),$$

   and for labor,

$$h = \sum_{i \in \mathcal{I}} (1 - x_2^i).$$

The Walrasian equilibrium of definition 4.3—just like the Walrasian equilibrium of definition 1.1—is a competitive-equilibrium notion. No agent recognizes that his choices affect prices and profits. The firm does not recognize that its choices affect prices.

For a given vector θ of profit shares, the **Walrasian social choice function** associates with each economy $\mathcal{P}$ an allocation x such that there exists a wage w and labor demand h such that (w, x, h) is a Walrasian equilibrium of economy $\mathcal{P}$ with profit shares θ. If multiple Walrasian equilibria exist, the social choice function selects one in some systematic manner.

Suppose that both agents own equal shares of the firm (i.e., $\theta^1 = \theta^2 = \frac{1}{2}$), which seems fair, informally speaking. It turns out that, even then, the induced Walrasian social choice function is not socialist (problem 4.13). The line of the argument is as follows: By theorem 4.4, socialism requires the equalization of utilities. This equalization fails at the Walrasian equilibrium, at which the more skilled agent can be happier than the less skilled one.

DISCUSSION

The axiomatic approach is cast in terms of choosing a social choice function, whose literal interpretation is that of an omniscient and omnipotent social planner, who observes the agents' skills and enforces their consumption of stuff and leisure and, a fortiori, their labor supply. This literal interpretation is unnecessary. Having identified a social choice function that satisfies the desired proportion, one can ask how to implement this function in a decentralized manner (e.g., in a market, with some regulation, if necessary).

The axiomatic approach helps one see more clearly the implications of an idea, say, socialism. As a result, one may choose to give up on the idea altogether if one dislikes the implications. In this case, one shall have done well by not having wasted time on the decentralization of the idea that has been revealed as wanting.

There are instances, however, in which the positive concerns of implementation must be woven into the normative analysis of the axiomatic approach outright. These positive concerns comprise the provision of incentives for the agents to truthfully report their private information (e.g., skills) and to obey recommendations (e.g., to consume stuff and supply labor). There is no conceptual difficulty in incorporating such positive constraints into normative analysis.

4.5   CONCLUDING REMARKS

Marx argued that, relative to feudalism, capitalism was hard to understand for the common man. As a result, under capitalism, the common man is liable to being deceived and manipulated by those with the knowledge of the workings of the system and in the position of power. Of course, an alternative system (e.g., socialism) need not be simpler. A member of the bureaucratic elite is in as good a position to deceive and exploit as is a capitalist, and faces less competition.

Competitive markets may be resilient not only because they deliver outcomes in the core but also because they excel at executing painful, but often normatively compelling, decisions, such as firing underperforming workers and shutting down inefficient firms. When markets do so, there is no one in particular the victim can blame and revolt against except for the "market conditions."

For instance, Alice feels no scruples "firing" an underperforming chef by refusing to patronize his restaurant. Were Alice's relationship with the chef not mediated by a competitive market—for instance, were the chef her longtime domestic servant—she might have trouble committing to fire him if he underperformed. Without the threat of dismissal, the chef would shirk, to Alice's detriment as well as to his own (because, knowing that chef would shirk, Alice would pay him little).

For another example, if a mom-and-pop ice cream shop closes, its employees will gain little from blaming their elected officials. By contrast, if the ice cream shop were run by the local government, then the shop employees might reasonably hope to gain from going on a hunger strike instead of applying for jobs at the Starbucks® that is set to replace the ice cream shop.

4.6   BIBLIOGRAPHICAL NOTES

The interpretation of exploitation in section 4.2 is due to Roemer (1988, chapter 4).

The discussion of the core in section 4.3 is based on Kreps (2012, section 15.4) and Varian (1992, chapter 21). Theorem 4.2 is proposition 15.8 of Kreps (2012) and proposition 18.B.1 of Mas-Colell, Whinston, and Green (1995). Theorem 4.3 is a reformulation of proposition 15.12 of Kreps (2012) under the assumptions of his rubric "An alternative, intuitive proof (with lots more assumptions)."

Section 4.4 is based on the work of Roemer (1988, chapter 10) and Moulin and Roemer (1989), who report theorem 4.4.

Problem 4.1 is inspired by Singer (2015), who advocates effective altruism. The goal of the effective altruist is to donate a lot and to "correct" charities, established to be cost-effective, for instance, by www.charitywatch.com. (For a critical assessment of effective altruism, see "Forum: the logic of effective altruism." *Boston Review*, July 6, 2015, http://bostonreview.net/forum/peter-singer-logic-effective-altruism.) Problem 4.3 is inspired by a conversation with Eduardo Azevedo. Problem 4.10 is proposition 15.10 of Kreps (2012).

PROBLEMS

Problem 4.1 (Effective Altruism).   Recall the production economy studied in section 4.2. This economy has been discovered in a Hitherto Unheard-of Latin

American Country (Hulac, for short) by a group of Princeton Effective Altruists (PEAs, for short). In Hulac, the capitalist's amount of capital is K, and the measure of workers is W, where $W/b > K/a$. In Princeton, the measure of PEAs is P. In their quest to accomplish "most good," PEAs consider four scenarios.

- *Scenario A*: Stay away from Hulac.

- *Scenario B*: Go to Hulac, join the workers (so the measure of workers in Hulac becomes $W + P$), and donate any consumption above γ to the proletariat (i.e., the workers employed by the capitalist) of Hulac.

- *Scenario C*: Promise to send to each member of the Hulac proletariat amount γ of stuff.

- *Scenario D*: Go to Hulac to buy and operate a unit of capital each (so that the amount of capital in Hulac becomes $K + P$), operate it in the same manner as the native Hulac capitalist does, and donate all profit (which amounts to share $P/(K + P)$ of all profit earned from capital) to the proletariat.

1. Suppose that PEAs proceed with Scenario A. What is the equilibrium utility of Hulac workers?

2. Suppose that PEAs proceed with Scenario B. What is the equilibrium utility of Hulac native workers?

3. Suppose that PEAs proceed with Scenario C. What is the equilibrium utility of Hulac workers?

4. Suppose that PEAs proceed with Scenario D, and $W/b > (K + P)/a$. What is the equilibrium utility of Hulac workers?

5. Suppose that PEAs proceed with Scenario D, and $W/b < (K + P)/a$. What is the equilibrium utility of Hulac workers?

6. Suppose that PEAs define "most good" as achieving the highest utility for Hulac native workers. Which of the Scenarios A, B, C, and D would you recommend to PEAs?

Problem 4.2 (The Efficiency of Exploitation).   Argue that the equilibrium outcome in theorem 4.1 is Pareto efficient.

Problem 4.3 (Wither Labor Unions?).   This problem extends the production economy of section 4.2 to two periods and shows that, even if beneficial to some workers in the short run, a labor union may hurt all workers in the long run and, indeed, overall. Production can occur in each of two periods, indexed by $t = 1, 2$. A capitalist is endowed with $K_1 > 0$ units of capital at the beginning of period $t = 1$ and none at the beginning of period $t = 2$. The capitalist has access to the Leontief technology described by the production function $f(k, h) = \min\{k/a, h/b\}$ and the technology that can transform capital one-to-one into stuff and the other way around. A continuum of workers is denoted by $\mathcal{W} = [0, W]$ for $W > bK_1/a$ with a typical element i. Each worker is endowed with a unit of labor in each period. In each period t, each worker either stays on the farm and earns $\gamma > 0$ or works for the capitalist and earns an equilibrium wage w_t—whichever option pays more. In each period t, the capitalist maximizes his period-t profit by choosing the amount of workers to hire at w_t in order to operate the Leontief technology. Assume that the capitalist does not consume at the end of period $t = 1$ but, instead, carries over his profit and any unused capital into period $t = 2$ in the form of capital, denoted by K_2. At the end of period $t = 2$, the capitalist consumes his period $t = 2$ profit and any unused capital.

The only link between the two periods is the mechanical assumption that the capitalist carries over all his period $t = 1$ profit and unused capital into period $t = 2$ in the form of capital. No agent engages in forward-looking optimization at period $t = 1$.

A Walrasian equilibrium comprises, for each period t: a wage w_t, each worker's optimal decision whether to work on the farm or for the capitalist, the capitalist's decision how many workers to employ, and the labor-market clearing condition, which prescribes that the measure of workers who seek employment with the capitalist equal the measure of workers whom the capitalist wants to employ.

1. Find a Walrasian equilibrium.

2. Now suppose that a labor union is concerned about the workers' low wages at $t = 1$. To make workers scarce at $t = 1$ and, through this scarcity, to raise their wages, the labor union institutes a certification scheme that, for some arbitrarily small $\varepsilon > 0$, permits only $b(K_1 - \varepsilon)/a$ arbitrarily chosen workers to work for the capitalist. There is no labor union at $t = 2$. Find a Walrasian equilibrium.

3. Under what conditions on the model's parameters is the workers' consumption at $t = 2$ higher if there is no labor union at $t = 1$ than if there is one?

4. Under what conditions on the model's parameters is the workers' aggregate consumption over both periods higher if there is no labor union at $t = 1$ than if there is one?

5. Now suppose that a labor union is formed in both periods. In each period, the union permits only $b(K_1 - \varepsilon)/a$ randomly chosen workers to work for the capitalist. Under what conditions on the model's parameters is the workers' aggregate consumption over both periods higher if there is no labor union than if there is one?

6. The model in this problem makes strong assumptions. Describe one or two assumptions that you would relax, explain why you would do so, and speculate about the consequences of this relaxation for the problem's conclusions.

Problem 4.4 (Matching with Wages). There are two types of agents: workers and managers. The goal is to match workers and managers into pairs, with some agents possibly left unmatched. Each agent cares not only about who he is matched with but also about the wage. The wage, denoted by $p \in \{0, 1\}$ (for "*price*"), is paid by a manager to a worker and is individualized for each manager-worker pair. Each worker ranks manager-wage pairs, and each manager ranks worker-wage pairs. This is the marriage problem of section 3.5 except that we now specify on what terms (the wage) each pair is matched.

1. Define a match so that your definition takes account of wages. Then define a stable match.

2. Adapt the man-proposing DA by asking each agent to list and rank all potential partner-wage pairs and making each manager propose to the worker featured in the top entry on the manager's (worker-wage) list. Let each worker provisionally accept or reject the proposal according to his (manager-wage) list. Continue mutatis mutandis as you would in the DA without contracts. The worker-proposing version of the algorithm is defined analogously. Argue that the described manager-proposing DA with wages (DAW) selects a stable match.

3. Assume that there are two managers, denoted by m and m', two workers, denoted by w and w', and two possible wages, 0 and 1. Each agent finds all partner-wage pairs acceptable. Assume further that the agents' preference rankings are as follows:

$$(w, 0) \succ^m (w', 0) \succ^m (w', 1) \succ^m (w, 1)$$

$$(w', 0) \succ^{m'} (w, 0) \succ^{m'} (w, 1) \succ^{m'} (w', 1)$$

$$(m, 1) \succ^w (m, 0) \succ^w (m', 1) \succ^w (m', 0)$$

$$(m, 1) \succ^{w'} (m', 1) \succ^{w'} (m', 0) \succ^{w'} (m, 0).$$

Compute the matches selected by the manager-proposing and the worker-proposing DAWs.

4. In the example of part 3, can one support the match selected by the manager-proposing DAW as a Walrasian equilibrium outcome? Can one support the match selected by the worker-proposing DAW as a Walrasian equilibrium outcome? At Walrasian equilibrium, wages may be individualized for each manager-worker pair.

Problem 4.5 (POGG). The **Constitution of Canada** promotes "peace, order and good government." This motto's spirit will be captured by the result that, in some settings, any policy may be better than uncertainty about the policy. This problem extends the setting of section 4.2. NonCanada is a country unsure about its immigration policy. It is inhabited by a lone capitalist endowed with K units of generic capital, which he can transform one-to-one into stuff. NonCanada has no labor to begin with. If the government adopts policy s, then the country admits up to measure W_s of willing skill-s immigrants (and only these immigrants), where $s \in S \equiv \{1, 2\}$ indexes the skill level: low ($s = 1$) or high ($s = 2$). The government announces that policy s will be adopted with probability $p_s \in [0, 1]$, where $p_1 + p_2 = 1$. Let $p \equiv (p_1, p_2)$. Each potential skill-s immigrant can either work for the capitalist in NonCanada at a going wage w_s or remain in his home country and earn $\gamma_s > 0$ there. Each type of labor requires skill-specific capital, which the capitalist can produce one-to-one from his endowment of the generic capital. For any $s \in S$, for some coefficients $a_s \in (0, 1)$ and $b_s > 0$, k_s units of skill-s specific capital and h_s units of skill-s labor can be transformed into

$$\min \left\{ \frac{k_s}{a_s}, \frac{h_s}{b_s} \right\}$$

units of stuff. Assume that $W_s > b_s K / a_s$ and $\gamma_s < (1 - a_s)/b_s$ for all $s \in S$.

Before—and only before—the uncertainty about the immigration policy is resolved, the capitalist, an expected-profit maximizer, transforms some of his generic capital into skill-specific capital. Then the policy uncertainty is realized, the immigrant labor arrives, and the capitalist chooses how much labor to hire at the prevailing Walrasian-equilibrium wage w_s. As a result, the capitalist's expected profit is

$$\Pi(p) \equiv \max_{(k_s)_{s \in S} \in \mathbb{R}_+} \left\{ \sum_{s \in S} \left(p_s \max_{h_s \in \mathbb{R}_+} \left\{ \min \left\{ \frac{k_s}{a_s}, \frac{h_s}{b_s} \right\} - w_s h_s \right\} - k_s \right) \mid \sum_{s \in S} k_s \leq K \right\}.$$

1. Explain the terms in the expression for the capitalist's profit in the display above.

2. Solve for the capitalist's optimal investment in capital as a function of p and of the anticipated Walrasian equilibrium wages (w_1, w_2).

3. Compute the anticipated Walrasian equilibrium wages (w_1, w_2). What is the capitalist's profit when no uncertainty about the immigration policy exists, that is, when $p_s = 1$ for some $s \in S$?

4. Show that there exists an uncertain immigration policy that is worse for the capitalist than any certain policy. That is, show that one can find a p such that $\Pi(p) < \min\{\Pi(1, 0), \Pi(0, 1)\}$. The absence of uncertainty about the immigration policy is interpreted as the "order and good government" in Canada's tripartite motto.

5. When $\Pi(p) < \min\{\Pi(1, 0), \Pi(0, 1)\}$, can one conclude that eliminating uncertainty about the immigration policy constitutes a Pareto improvement in NonCanada?

Problem 4.6 (The Core and Walrasian Equilibrium).   Prove theorem 4.2. (*Hint*: The proof follows closely the proof of the FWT.)

Problem 4.7 (The Core in the House Allocation Problem).   Consider a house allocation problem of section 3.3 with three agents, $\mathcal{I} = \{1, 2, 3\}$, and three houses, $\mathcal{L} = \{A, B, C\}$. The agents' preferences are

$$A \succ^1 B \succ^1 C$$
$$B \succ^2 A \succ^2 C$$
$$A \succ^3 C \succ^3 B.$$

1.   Assume that no agent is initially endowed with a house. List all Pareto efficient allocations. Can you think of a systematic way to do so?

2.   Assume that agent 1 is endowed with house C, agent 2 is endowed with house A, and agent 3 is endowed with house B. List all core allocations. Can you think of a systematic way to do so?

Problem 4.8 (The Core in the Roommates Problem).   Consider the roommates problem of section 3.5.

1.   By analogy with the core in the exchange economy, define the core for the roommates problem.

2.   Argue that, in the roommates problem, a match is in the core if and only if it is stable. Conclude that the core may be empty.

3.   Can a Pareto efficient match exist even if the core is empty?

Problem 4.9 (Envy-Freeness in Trades).   Assume two agents, $\mathcal{I} = \{1, 2\}$, and two goods, $\mathcal{L} = \{1, 2\}$. Let $(u^i, e^i)_{i \in \mathcal{I}}$ be an exchange economy. Given an allocation x, agent i's **trade** is
$$t^i \equiv x^i - e^i, \quad i \in \mathcal{I}.$$

An allocation x is **envy-free in trades** if

$$e^i + t^{-i} \geq 0 \implies u^i(e^i + t^i) \geq u^i(e^i + t^{-i}), \qquad i \in \mathcal{I}, \quad -i = \mathcal{I} \backslash i. \tag{4.6}$$

1.   Interpret the condition in (4.6).

2.   Argue that envy-freeness in trades is not logically related to (e.g., neither implies nor is implied by) the envy-freeness in consumption bundles (defined in problem 1.9).

3.   What is the appeal (if any) of envy-freeness in trades?

4. Give an example of an endowment e and an allocation x for which $e^1 + t^2 \geq 0$ fails. Illustrate your example in an Edgeworth box.

5. Show that any Walrasian equilibrium allocation is envy-free in trades. What is the intuition for this result?

Problem 4.10 (Equal Treatment and the Core). Consider an exchange economy $\mathcal{E} = (u^i, e^i)_{i \in \mathcal{I}}$ that satisfies u-concavity. Let $\mathcal{E}^N$ denote an N-replica of $\mathcal{E}$. Take an arbitrary allocation $x^N \equiv \{x^{in}\}_{i \in \mathcal{I}, n \in \mathcal{N}}$ that is in the core of $\mathcal{E}^N$. You will show that x^N is an equal treatment allocation.

1. Given $\mathcal{E}^N$ and x^N, create a coalition $\mathcal{S}$ that consists of exactly one copy of each of I types. When deciding which copy of type i to put into $\mathcal{S}$, pick the "unhappiest" one; that is, pick any agent from the set

$$\arg \min_{n \in \mathcal{N}} \{u^i(x^{in})\}.$$

From x^N, derive a collection $\{\tilde{x}^i\}_{i \in \mathcal{I}}$ of bundles by setting

$$\tilde{x}^i \equiv \frac{1}{N} \sum_{n \in \mathcal{N}} x^{in}, \qquad i \in \mathcal{I}.$$

Argue that allocation $\{\tilde{x}^i\}_{i \in \mathcal{I}}$ is feasible for the agents in $\mathcal{S}$.

2. Argue that each agent in $\mathcal{S}$ is at least as well off consuming his designated bundle in $\{\tilde{x}^i\}_{i \in \mathcal{I}}$ as he is consuming his designated bundle in x^N.

3. Argue (by u-concavity) that if x^N were not an equal treatment allocation, then $\mathcal{S}$ would block x^N, and so x^N would not be in the core.

4. Conclude that the restriction to equal treatment allocations in theorem 4.3 entails no loss of generality.

Problem 4.11 (Freedom of Speech and Freedom of Contracting). Brennan and Jaworski (2015, chapter 4) draw an analogy between freedom of contracting and freedom of speech, the latter guaranteed by the **First Amendment** to the United States Constitution. Freedom of speech, especially political speech, helps aggregate information dispersed among individuals, thereby promoting better collective decision-making. Freedom of speech is at the heart of why democracy works (better than all other regimes that have been tried).[16]

---

16. Winston Churchill: "Democracy is the worst form of Government except for all those other forms that have been tried from time to time."

1. Please argue that freedom of contracting helps aggregate information dispersed among individuals and promotes better decision-making and that freedom of contracting is at the heart of why market economies work (better than all other regimes that have been tried).

2. Freedom of speech is not absolute. Restrictions apply, for instance, to the broadcasting of pornography, false advertising, slander, and the incitement to violence. Argue the best you can that contracting is different from speech and that freedom of contracting should be absolute.

3. Now do your best to controvert your argument in part 2.

4. What is the contracting analog of politically correct speech?

Problem 4.12 (Skill–Consumption Neutrality).   Consider three utility functions (where $i \in \mathcal{I}$ indexes an agent):

(i) $u(s^i, x^i) = v(s^i x_1^i, (1 - x_2^i)/s^i)$, where $s^i > 0$, and v is (strictly) increasing in the first argument and (strictly) decreasing in the second argument;

(ii) $u(s^i, x^i) = x_1^i - (1 - x_2^i)(1 - s^i - s^i \phi(x_1^i))$, where $s^i \in (0, 1/2)$, $\phi : \mathbb{R}_+ \to [0, 1)$ has $\phi' > 0$, $\phi(0) = 0$, and $\lim_{x_1^i \to \infty} \phi(x_1^i) = 1$; and

(iii) $u(s^i, x^i) = s^i + v(x_1^i, 1 - x_2^i)$, where $s^i \in \mathbb{R}$, and v is (strictly) increasing in the first argument and (strictly) decreasing in the second argument.

For each of these utility functions:

1. Interpret the utility function.

2. Verify whether skill–consumption neutrality holds.

3. Do you find the equalization of utility levels for agents with this utility function but different skills normatively compelling (regardless of whether this equalization is implied by socialism)?

Problem 4.13 (Markets versus Socialism).   For the economy of section 4.4, let the production function be $f(h) = Ah$ for some $A > 0$, let the utility function be $u(s^i, x^i) \equiv \ln x_1^i - (1 - x_2^i)/s^i$, where $s^i \in (0, 1)$, and let the profit shares θ^1 and θ^2 be arbitrary.

1. Argue that, at any Walrasian equilibrium, the equilibrium wage w satisfies $w = A$.

2. Find a Walrasian equilibrium. Is it unique?

3. Compute each agent's equilibrium utility.

4. On the basis of your analysis up to now, can you tell whether the Walrasian social choice function is socialist?

5. Given your answers above, do you find the Walrasian social choice function normatively compelling? What if you knew that the only empirically relevant production functions were of the form $f(h) = Ah$?

Problem 4.14 (Socialism). In the environment specified in section 4.4, consider the social choice function F that, for any economy $\mathcal{P} = (s^1, s^2, f)$, satisfies

$$F(\mathcal{P}) \in \arg \max_{x \in X^1 \times X^2} u(s^1, x^1)$$

$$\text{s.t. } u(s^1, x^1) = u(s^2, x^2)$$

$$\sum_{i \in \mathcal{I}} x_1^i \le f\left(\sum_{i \in \mathcal{I}} (1 - x_2^i)\right).$$

1. Explain intuitively the meaning of the constrained maximization problem that F solves.

2. Indicate whether F satisfies each of the socialist conditions:

   (a)   Pareto efficiency;

   (b)   limited private ownership of the embodied means of production;

   (c)   equal treatment of equals;

   (d)   collective ownership of the disembodied means of production;

   (e)   solidarity.

CHAPTER 5

INEQUALITY

5.1   INTRODUCTION

Income inequality refers to the dispersion of income across individuals. A common measure of inequality is the **Gini coefficient**, which equals the expected absolute value of the difference between the incomes of any two agents drawn independently and uniformly at random from a population, normalized by the expected sum of any two agents' incomes.[1] The normalization ensures that the coefficient lies between 0 (all incomes are equal) and 1 (essentially, all income in the economy is earned by one individual) and that multiplying everyone's income by the same positive number leaves the coefficient unchanged. The Gini coefficient has the property that transferring some income from a poorer individual to a richer individual raises the value of the coefficient.

Lakner and Milanovic (2016, table 3) document that, between 1988 and 2008, the Gini coefficient for the worldwide inequality fluctuated between 0.71 and 0.72 and, if anything, has been declining since early 2000s. At the same time, regional inequality has been on the rise. Table 5.1 illustrates. While a **nationalist** (for whom the nation state is the relevant solidaristic unit) may be concerned about the rising

---

1. Formally, letting w^i and w^j denote the incomes of any two individuals i and j chosen uniformly at random, the Gini coefficient equals $\mathbb{E}[|w^i - w^j|]/\mathbb{E}[w^i + w^j]$.

TABLE 5.1

Global and regional per capita income inequality in terms of Gini coefficients (with incomes measured at purchasing power parity exchange rates for year 2005).

Region	1988	1993	1998	2003	2008
Worldwide	0.72	0.72	0.72	0.72	0.71
Mature Economies	0.38	0.39	0.39	0.39	0.42
China	0.32	0.36	0.39	0.42	0.43
India	0.31	0.30	0.31	0.32	0.33
Other Asia	0.45	0.44	0.47	0.42	0.45
Middle East and North Africa	0.42	0.42	0.44	0.39	
Sub-Saharan Africa		0.54	0.52	0.57	0.58
Latin America and Caribbean	0.53	0.55	0.57	0.56	0.53
Russia, Central Asia, and Southeastern Europe		0.48	0.40	0.42	0.42

Source: Lakner and Milanovic (2016, table 3).

regional and national inequality, a **cosmopolitan** (whose ethics transcend national boundaries) may rejoice in the decline of global inequality.[2]

There are reasons for individuals to be concerned not just about their own consumption but also about inequality. Inequality damages social cohesion by enabling individuals to lead markedly different lives. As a result of inequality, individuals may lack common experiences and may fail to empathize with, and trust, each other. In the absence of trust, market and nonmarket institutions may function badly.[3] In particular, the efficacy of Walrasian markets relies on the assumption that individuals deliver on their promises to honor Walrasian trades, which is a nontrivial commitment in settings with time and uncertainty. Extreme inequality may also empower the relatively rich to subvert the political system in order to maintain, magnify, and bequeath their privileges.

Pareto (1896) speculated that the amount of observed income inequality within a country exceeded the inequality of individual endowments, such as innate ability, qualifications, and inherited capital. The latter kind of inequality— the inequality of endowment—Pareto called **functional inequality**. This chapter discusses two potential reasons for the divorce between functional and income

2. One justification for being a nationalist is a positive one. If inequality within a country were to explode, then the country itself might implode (e.g., due to political upheavals) in a way that the world at large might not do if worldwide inequality were to rise.

3. "I've cut billion-dollar deals in the Valley with a handshake," lamented John L. Hennessy, the then president of Stanford, as he withdrew from the competition to build a New York City campus and contrasted the purportedly circumspect business culture of New York to the trust-based culture of the Silicon Valley. (See Auletta, Ken. "Get Rich U." *The New Yorker*, April 30, 2012.)

inequalities: risk seeking and the superstar phenomenon. The discussion of superstars naturally leads to an inquiry into the potential effects of artificial intelligence on income inequality. Robots are the superstars of the future. This inquiry culminates in the discussion of Marxian class struggle and singularity (a rapid takeoff in the intelligence of robots).

This chapter's emphasis on risk seeking and, mostly, on superstars is not meant to denigrate alternative (and complementary) theories of inequality. Among these alternatives are corruption, rent-seeking, market power, the inheritance of wealth and opportunity, and differences in tastes (e.g., some value material consumption more than others; some are more patient than others when investing in skills and capital).

5.2   RISK SEEKING

To illustrate the idea of **risk seeking**, suppose that Alice and Bob each has $50 and wishes to invite Carol on a dinner date, which costs $100. Alice and Bob may be eager to participate in a lottery in which they pool their money and toss a coin. The coin toss determines which one of them wins the pooled $100 and gets to go on the date.

Once the lottery has been played out, one of them will have $100, and the other will have nothing. Nevertheless, Alice and Bob may both prefer this lottery to the initial equal allocation in which each has $50. Alice's and Bob's willingness to accept the lottery provides a normative justification for inequality, thereby countervailing the argument for equality in section 4.4. Their willingness to bet also provides an explanation for why inequality may exist in practice.

Alice's and Bob's described risk-seeking behavior can be reconciled with the common presumption that agents are risk averse with respect to the consumption of individual goods. In particular, assume that Bob's utility function is concave in the time spent in restaurants if the time spent with Carol is fixed. Similarly, assume that his utility function is concave in the time spent with Carol if the time spent in restaurants is fixed. When Bob evaluates his welfare according to his expected utility, the concavity of this utility in a good implies risk aversion to lotteries in the consumption of this good (draw a picture; see also part 1 of problem 2.4). Bob's risk seeking with respect to dining with Carol is nevertheless a possibility if his utility function is convex in the amount of time spent in restaurants *with* Carol. This convexity may prevail if the enjoyment from the time spent with Carol and the enjoyment from the time spent in restaurants are complementary.

The described idea of risk seeking is fleshed out in problem 5.1. The only reason the example with Alice, Bob, and Carol invokes two goods is to be consistent with the casual observation of risk aversion (or, equivalently, diminishing marginal utility) in individual goods. An analogous one-good example can be constructed if individuals are assumed to be risk loving in this good.

Should one worry about the inequality that is caused by risk seeking? Because this inequality is caused by choice rather than circumstance, one probably should not. The initial conditions of Alice and Bob are the same; the equality of opportunity is absolute, which is the gold standard for theories of justice. However, if one can identify an externality from the lottery on a third party, then the emergent inequality merits examination. For instance, if Alice loses the lottery, she may be so upset as to forget to feed her cat (a third party), who has no say in Alice's acceptance of the lottery and, hence, is subject to an externality.

Is the described risk-seeking behavior empirically relevant? Empirically, lotteries over consumption bundles whose components are positively correlated (e.g., dining out and spending time with Carol) are induced by lotteries in wealth. In particular, under natural assumptions (viz., all goods are normal), a wealthier individual consumes more of every good. Then, the empirical question becomes: Do individuals seek lotteries in wealth? Some do.

Some seek to become entrepreneurs, even though the expected return to entrepreneurship is low, and the risk is high (Hamilton, 2000). One possible explanation is that individuals are risk loving with respect to lotteries in wealth.[4] That is, they expect to benefit from a dollar won more than they expect to suffer from a dollar lost. In other words, money is worth more to such individuals when they are rich than when they are poor (which, incidentally, imperils a common rationale for redistributing from the rich to the poor). Even if a prospective entrepreneur anticipates getting jaded by glitzy living, he realizes that each extra dollar he earns will enhance his social status, the appetite for which is insatiable and which may be complementary to glitzy living.

It is not only entrepreneurs who may seek lotteries in wealth. Such lotteries may help one escape certain poverty or persecution. For instance, in the motion picture *Casablanca* (1942), a Bulgarian couple desperately bet all they have at a roulette table for the chance to secure enough money to buy exit visas from Morocco.

Empirically, Layard, Mayraz, and Nickell (2008) suggest that, on average, the rich value a dollar less than the poor do, which can be taken to imply that, on average, individuals are risk averse with respect to lotteries in wealth. In practice, it is likely that there is a considerable heterogeneity across individuals in attitudes toward lotteries in wealth. Surely at least some individuals are risk loving, and, through their risky choices, they contribute to inequality.

---

4. Among alternative explanations are the preference for being one's own boss and the overoptimism regarding the success of one's venture (e.g., because the stories that make the news are about successes, not failures).

5.3   SUPERSTARS

The theory of **superstars** explains how the best opera tenor, a superstar, can earn, say, twice as much as the second-best tenor does even if the best one is, say, only five percent better at singing than the second-best one. The superstar scales his output at little cost by selling records, broadcasting rights, and concert tickets. As a result, it does not matter much how far away one is from the best; it mostly matters whether one is the best.[5] For another example, CEOs earn substantially more than their underlings, who may be just a notch less able. More abstractly, the superstar's reward is convex in ability. As technological progress makes scaling up one's ability cheaper, the superstar phenomenon is bound to become a more important cause of inequality.

Empirically, let us identify superstars with the individuals whose income is in the top 1% of income distribution. The share of total income in the economy going to these individuals is in itself a common measure of inequality. If this share rises, then, under some assumptions, the superstars effect becomes more pronounced. (The assumptions are that the distribution of individual abilities in the economy remains unchanged and that more able individuals earn more.) Another common measure of inequality is the share of income that goes to the top 0.1%. Table 5.2 compares both measures for a sample of countries in 1949 and 2005. In the sample, both measures have risen in the United Kingdom, United States, Canada, Singapore, Norway, and Japan.

The model of superstars described in this section illustrates how a fall in the costs of communication enables more able individuals to leverage their ability and may explain why income inequality has been rising in some countries while declining worldwide. In the model, the cost of communication is the cost of transmitting ideas in production teams. The emergent superstars are managers, who are the most able members of their teams.

AN ECONOMY OF PROBLEM SOLVERS

The economy has a continuum of agents and a single consumption good, called "stuff." Each agent's utility equals the amount of stuff that he consumes. Each agent is characterized by his ability, denoted by $a \in [0, 1]$. The measure (or, informally

---

5. Adam Smith proposed an alternative theory for the superstar incomes of opera singers. He believed that, because of the public stigma associated with accepting money in exchange for singing, more money had to be offered to singers to compensate for this stigma: "There are some very agreeable and beautiful talents of which the possession commands a certain sort of admiration; but of which the exercise for the sake of gain is considered, whether from reason or prejudice, as a sort of publick prostitution. [...] The exorbitant rewards of players, opera-singers, opera-dancers, &c. are founded upon those two principles; the rarity and beauty of the talents, and the discredit of employing them in this manner." (The quote is from Brennan and Jaworski, 2015.) That is, exactly because singing and dancing are so very noble, practicing them for money is met with opprobrium.

TABLE 5.2
Income inequality. The entries are the shares of income that go to the top 1% and 0.1% of individuals.

	Share of top 1%		Share of top 0.1%	
Country	Around year 1949	Around year 2005	Around year 1949	Around year 2005
Argentina	19.3	16.8	7.9	7.0
Netherlands	12.0	5.4	3.8	1.1
India	12.0	9.0	5.2	3.6
Germany	11.6	11.1	3.9	4.4
United Kingdom	11.5	14.2	3.5	5.2
Australia	11.3	8.8	3.3	2.7
United States	11.0	17.4	3.3	7.7
Canada	10.7	13.6	2.9	5.2
Singapore	10.4	13.3	3.2	4.3
New Zealand	10.0	8.8	2.4	2.5
Switzerland	9.9	7.8	3.2	2.7
France	9.0	8.7	2.6	2.5
Norway	8.9	11.8	2.7	5.6
Japan	7.9	9.2	1.8	2.4
Sweden	7.6	6.3	2.0	1.9

Source: Atkinson, Piketty, and Saez (2011, table 6).

speaking, amount) of agents with ability a or less is $G(a)$.[6] Assume that G is an increasing function; its derivative is denoted by g. Each agent is endowed with a unit of time, one "hour."

Time can be devoted to solving problems, each of which is characterized by its complexity $p \in [0, 1]$. Each new problem's complexity is drawn independently according to a c.d.f. F, with the corresponding positive p.d.f. f. An ability-a agent can solve a problem of complexity p if and only if $p \leq a$, which, for each new problem, occurs with probability $F(a)$. Thus, a more able agent can solve all the problems that a less able agent can and more.[7]

An agent who devotes an hour to solving problems encounters $1/\delta$ of them for some small $\delta > 0$ such that $1/\delta$ is an integer. If solved, a problem generates δ units of stuff; otherwise it generates none. Let s_k be a random variable such that $s_k = 1$ if an agent solves problem k and $s_k = 0$ otherwise, for any $k \geq 1$. Then, an agent solves

6. The model of section 4.2 (rubric "Equilibrium") introduces and motivates informally the idea of a continuum of agents.

7. In fact, it suffices to assume that a more able agent can learn to solve all the problems that a less able agent can learn to solve. If the nature of an agent's job is such that he never encounters certain routine problems, we may assume that he either forgets or never learns how to solve them.

$\sum_{k=1}^{1/\delta} s_k$ problems in an hour, thereby producing amount

$$\sum_{k=1}^{1/\delta} s_k \delta = \frac{1}{1/\delta} \sum_{k=1}^{1/\delta} s_k$$

of stuff. As $\delta \to 0$, the Law of Large Numbers implies that the average in the display above converges to its expectation, which, for an ability-a agent, is $F(a)$.[8] Henceforth, we focus on this limit case and simply assume that an ability-a agent who spends an hour solving problems produces $F(a)$ units of stuff for sure.

When confronted with a problem, an agent tackles it in two steps: first he codifies it (say, translates it into a mathematical model) and then attempts to solve it. What takes time is to codify, not solve. This distinction is important because a codified, but unsolved, problem can be passed on to someone else to solve. It takes this someone else $c \in (0, 1)$ hours to comprehend the codified problems it took others an hour to codify. Having comprehended these codifications, the agent can immediately see which of the codified problems he can solve, in no time. We call c **communication cost**.

(LABOR) MARKET STRUCTURE

Markets are structured in recognition of the fact that, because agents can pass on unsolved codified problems, it may pay for them to work in teams and look at problems sequentially. In such teams, less able agents would look at the problems first and then pass the hard, unsolved, problems on to more able agents. The agents who take the first look are called "workers"; the agents who take the second and last look are called "managers." A manager must be more able than his employee or else he will never solve any problem that has been passed on to him and would only waste his time trying to comprehend it.

Markets are competitive in the sense that every agent takes prices as given. The prices comprise the price of stuff (normalized to one) and the wage function $w : [0, 1] \to \mathbb{R}_+$, with $w(a)$ being the wage that an ability-a worker commands. Given w, each agent chooses one of three occupations:

SELF-EMPLOYED An ability-a self-employed agent produces and consumes amount $F(a)$ of stuff by codifying and solving all the problems he can in an hour. He discards any codified problem that he cannot solve.

---

8. The **Law of Large Numbers** (according to one of its many formulations) guarantees that the average of n random variables that are distributed independently and identically with mean μ converges to μ as $n \to \infty$. "Converges" here means that, for any $\varepsilon > 0$, the probability that the average deviates from μ by more than ε converges to zero as $n \to \infty$.

WORKER An ability-a worker devotes his hour to codifying and solving problems while passing the unsolved problems on to his manager. The worker earns and consumes his equilibrium wage $w(a)$.

MANAGER A manager helps the workers whom he employs solve the problems that they have codified but cannot solve themselves. The manager discards any codified problem that he cannot solve. The manager consumes his profit, which is the amount of stuff left over after he has collected his and his employees' output and has paid the wages to the employees.

There is no claim that the labor markets are complete. Indeed, markets are incomplete in the following sense. It may be wasteful for some manager to discard codified problems instead of passing them on to another agent, of superior ability, whom we may call "CEO." The market structure does not admit a market for CEOs by ruling out more than two layers in the problem-referral hierarchy. As a result, there is no a priori reason to expect a competitive equilibrium to be Pareto efficient.[9]

To understand a critical determinant of the agents' occupational choice—the manager's profit—consider the manager's problem. Suppose that an ability-a' manager hires an ability-a worker, with $a < a'$. This worker solves some problems by himself and passes the remaining, unsolved but codified, problems on to the manager. As a result, any problem that the worker draws gets solved (either by the worker himself or by his manager) if and only if its complexity does not exceed a'. The probability of this event is $F(a')$. Assume that all workers whom a manager hires have the same ability. If the manager hires n ability-a workers, then his profit is the revenue less the wage bill:

$$nF(a') - nw(a). \tag{5.1}$$

The manager maximizes (5.1) over a and n subject to the constraint that the amount of time he spends comprehending the workers' unsolved problems does not exceed the one hour he is endowed with:

$$cn(1 - F(a)) \leq 1. \tag{5.2}$$

Because the manager's profit (5.1) is linear in n, if it pays to hire any workers, then it pays to hire as many as the time constraint (5.2) permits.[10] Substituting the

---

9. Equilibrium can be shown to be constrained Pareto efficient in the sense of problem 5.3, however.

10. That is, if $F(a') - w(a) > 0$ for some a, then the manager's profit is increasing in n, and, so, he hires as many workers as his time permits. If $F(a') - w(a) < 0$ for all a, then the manager cannot make a positive profit and, so, hires no one, in which case he is better off not being a manager.

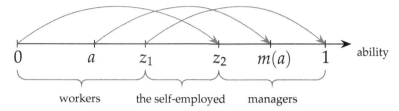

FIGURE 5.1.
The matching function m matches a worker with ability in $[0, z_1]$ to a manager with ability in $[z_2, 1]$.

equality version of (5.2) into (5.1) gives the expression for the profit of an ability-a' manager:

$$P(a', w) = \max_{a \in [0,1]} \frac{F(a') - w(a)}{c(1 - F(a))},$$ (5.3)

where w is an equilibrium wage function.

In making his occupational choice, an ability-a agent is attracted to the largest of the three payoffs: $F(a)$ for a self-employed agent, $w(a)$ for a worker, and $P(a, w)$ for a manager.

EQUILIBRIUM DEFINED

An equilibrium is a wage function, a partition of agents into occupations, and each manager's decision which and how many workers to hire. We focus on an equilibrium in which agents sort into occupations so that agents with abilities in $[0, z_1]$ are workers, those with abilities in (z_1, z_2) are self-employed, and those with abilities in $[z_2, 1]$ are managers, for $0 \leq z_1 \leq z_2 \leq 1$; in which each manager's employees all have the same ability; and in which more able managers hire more able workers.[11] In this case, all hiring decisions can be summarized by an increasing matching function $m : [0, z_1] \to [z_2, 1]$, which associates with any ability-a worker an ability-$m(a)$ manager who hires him. Furthermore, the matching function m must satisfy $m(0) = z_2$ and $m(z_1) = 1$, so that the least productive worker matches with the least productive manager, and the most productive worker matches with the most productive manager. Figure 5.1 illustrates.

---

11. The intuition for why more able managers would hire more able workers is developed in problem 5.2 and, especially, problem 5.4. Roughly speaking, the return to increasing the size of a team is larger when the team is more successful at solving problems, which is so when it is led by a more able manager. The only way to increase the size of a team without violating the manager's time constraint is to hire more able workers, who require less of his time.

Definition 5.1. An **occupational choice equilibrium** is a wage function w, occupational-choice thresholds z_1 and z_2, and a matching function m such that:

1. (Occupational Choice) Given his ability, each agent chooses the most lucrative occupation:

    -   each ability $a \in [0, z_1]$ agent earns most by becoming a worker:[12]

        $$w(a) \geq \max\{F(a), P(a, w)\};$$

    -   each ability $a \in (z_1, z_2)$ agent earns most by becoming self-employed:

        $$F(a) \geq \max\{w(a), P(a, w)\};$$

    -   each ability $a \in [z_2, 1]$ agent earns most by becoming a manager:

        $$P(a, w) \geq \max\{F(a), w(a)\}.$$

2. (Profit Maximization) Each manager maximizes his profit by hiring workers of appropriate ability:

    $$a \in [0, z_1] \implies \frac{F(m(a)) - w(a)}{c(1 - F(a))} = P(m(a), w). \tag{5.4}$$

3. (Labor-Market Clearing) The demand for manager time by the workers of ability a or less equals the time at the disposal of the managers willing to hire workers of ability a or less:

    $$\int_0^a c(1 - F(\tilde{a}))g(\tilde{a})\mathrm{d}\tilde{a} = G(m(a)) - G(m(0)), \quad a \in [0, z_1]. \tag{5.5}$$

4. (Stuff-Market Clearing) The sum of the agents' wages, profits, and the output of the self-employed equals the aggregate amount of stuff produced by solving problems.

The stuff-market clearing condition in part 4 of definition 5.1 recognizes that each agent's consumption problem is trivial: with the sole consumption good (stuff), the best one can do is to spend one's entire income on stuff. If all labor markets clear, so will the market for stuff; this is Walras's law (problem 5.6). Therefore, equilibrium analysis will neglect the stuff-market clearing condition and focus on finding a wage function that would clear all labor markets.

There is a continuum of inactive labor markets, for workers with abilities in $(z_1, 1]$, which are neither demanded nor supplied at equilibrium. There is also a continuum of active labor markets, one for each worker ability $a \in [0, z_1]$. We focus on the active labor markets first. If the matching function m is differentiable, condition (5.5) can be differentiated with respect to a to yield an equivalent collection

---

12. The profit function P is defined in (5.3).

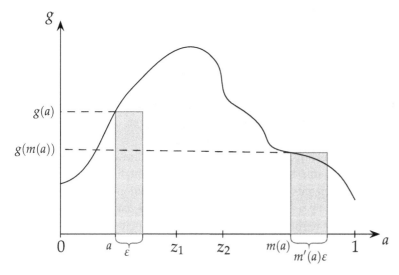

FIGURE 5.2.
Workers with abilities in $(a, a+\varepsilon)$, of whom there are about $g(a)\varepsilon$, are matched with managers with abilities in $(m(a), m(a+\varepsilon))$, of whom there are about $g(m(a))m'(a)\varepsilon$.

of market clearing conditions:

$$c(1-F(a))g(a) = g(m(a))m'(a), \quad a \in [0, z_1]. \tag{5.6}$$

Condition (5.6) equates the demand for manager time by the workers of some ability to the supply of time by the managers willing to hire workers of that ability.

Here is a direct economic interpretation of (5.6). For some small $\varepsilon > 0$, $g(a)\varepsilon$ is (approximately) the number of workers with abilities in the interval $(a, a+\varepsilon)$. (See figure 5.2.) Each of these workers fails to solve fraction $1 - F(a)$ of the problems that he draws, and passes the unsolved problems on to his manager, who spends $c(1 - F(a))$ hours attending to these problems. Thus, the workers with abilities in $(a, a+\varepsilon)$ require $c(1-F(a))g(a)\varepsilon$ hours of attention from managers—which is the left-hand side of (5.6) times ε. The managers who wish to hire workers with abilities in $(a, a+\varepsilon)$ have abilities in $(m(a), m(a+\varepsilon))$, or, approximately, in $(m(a), m(a) + m'(a)\varepsilon)$.[13] There are $g(m(a))m'(a)\varepsilon$ managers with abilities in $(m(a), m(a) + m'(a)\varepsilon)$, and each of them supplies an hour of time. The total amount of time supplied by these managers is also $g(m(a))m'(a)\varepsilon$, which is the right-hand side of (5.6) times ε.

13. Thus, if the matching function is steep (i.e., $m'(a)$ is large), few workers are spread over many managers, and the interval $(m(a), m(a) + m'(a)\varepsilon)$ is large.

EQUILIBRIUM IN AN EXAMPLE

To arrive at an explicit characterization of an equilibrium, the analysis will be performed under the assumptions of example 5.1 which is our leading example for the rest of the chapter.

Example 5.1. Both ability and problem complexity are distributed uniformly: $G(a) = a$ for all $a \in [0, 1]$ and $F(p) = p$ for all $p \in [0, 1]$. Moreover, $c \geq 0.75$. △

Condition $c \geq 0.75$ in example 5.1 ensures that, in equilibrium, $z_1 \leq z_2$, as will be shown. If $c < 0.75$, the gains from specialization are so high that there are no self-employed agents; each agent is lured either into management, by a high profit, or into becoming a worker, by a high wage. This alternative case is also economically interesting and is not harder to solve but is not our focus because it is less rich.

The values of equilibrium objects will be conjectured from the managers' profit maximization in part 2 of definition 5.1 and labor-market clearing conditions in part 3. Then the occupational-choice conditions in part 1 will be verified to hold. (The stuff-market clearing condition in part 4 will hold automatically.)

Under the assumptions of example 5.1, the market clearing conditions in (5.6) become

$$c(1 - a) = m'(a), \quad a \in [0, z_1],$$

whereby we also conjecture that an equilibrium with a differentiable matching function exists. The differential equation in the display above can be solved for function m subject to the boundary condition $m(0) = z_2$, which says that the least able worker works for the least able manager. The solution can be verified (by substitution) to be

$$m(a) = z_2 + c\left(a - \frac{a^2}{2}\right), \quad a \in [0, z_1], \tag{5.7}$$

which satisfies $m'(a) > 0$ for all $a \in (0, z_1)$.

For m to be an equilibrium matching function, the first-order condition for the manager's profit-maximization problem (5.3) must hold:

$$\frac{\partial}{\partial a} \left. \frac{F(a') - w(a)}{c(1 - F(a))} \right|_{a'=m(a)} = 0 \quad \text{or} \quad \frac{w'(a)}{F(m(a)) - w(a)} = \frac{f(a)}{1 - F(a)},$$

whereby we also conjecture that an equilibrium wage function is differentiable on $(0, z_1)$. Under the assumptions of example 5.1, the first-order condition in the display above becomes

$$\frac{w'(a)}{m(a) - w(a)} = \frac{1}{1-a}, \quad a \in [0, z_1]. \tag{5.8}$$

The differential equation in (5.8) can be solved for function w subject to the equilibrium matching function in (5.7) and to the boundary condition $w(z_1) = z_1$, which says that the most able worker is indifferent between being a worker and being self-employed. This boundary condition will be justified shortly. The solution can be verified to be[14]

$$w(a) = \frac{a^2 c}{2} + \frac{a(cz_1^2 + 2z_2 - 2z_1) + z_1(2 - cz_1 - 2z_2)}{2(1 - z_1)}, \quad a \in [0, z_1]. \tag{5.9}$$

The fact that the equilibrium payoff function is necessarily continuous in ability is of economic significance, and, so, we prove it. In particular, we prove that $w(z_1) = z_1$ and $z_2 = P(z_2, w)$. If we were to skip the forthcoming two-paragraph-long proof, we would still be justified in guessing and later verifying that an equilibrium with a continuous payoff function existed but we would be unable to rule out other, discontinuous equilibria.

To justify $w(z_1) = z_1$, first, note that $w(z_1) \geq z_1$ must hold. Indeed, the optimality of the workers' occupational choices requires that ability-z_1 agent weakly prefer being a worker at wage $w(z_1)$ to being self-employed and earning z_1. Moreover, $w(z_1) \leq z_1$ must hold. To prove this by contradiction, suppose that this is not true, that is, that $w(z_1) > z_1$. Then, instead of hiring an ability-z_1 agent, any manager would rather hire an ability-a ($a > z_1$) self-employed agent with an a that is sufficiently close to z_1. (Figure 5.3 illustrates.) This is because this self-employed agent must face a wage $w(a) \leq a$ to wish to remain self-employed. Thus, the wage function must have a discontinuity—a downward jump—at ability z_1; the manager would get a more able agent at a lower wage by passing on an ability-z_1 agent in favor of an ability-a agent. As a result, the market for ability-z_1 agents would not clear, which gives the required contradiction. Therefore, $w(z_1) = z_1$ must hold, and, hence, the equilibrium payoff is continuous at $a = z_1$.

One can similarly establish the continuity of the equilibrium payoff at ability z_2; that is, $z_2 = P(z_2, w)$. To do so, first note that $P(z_2, w) \geq z_2$ must hold. Indeed, the optimality of the managers' occupational choice requires that an ability-z_2 agent weakly prefer being a manager and earning profit $P(z_2, w)$ to being self-employed and earning z_2. Moreover, $P(z_2, w) \leq z_2$ must hold because the contradiction hypothesis $P(z_2, w) > z_2$ would imply that an ability-a' ($a' < z_2$) self-employed with

14. An easy way to solve (5.8) is to ask Wolfram's *Mathematica*® to do it. The solution can then be verified by substitution into (5.8).

payoffs

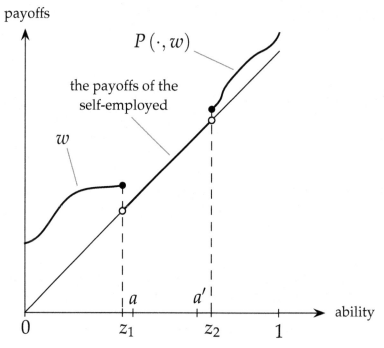

FIGURE 5.3.
The depicted payoff discontinuities at abilities z_1 and z_2 are impossible. (A hollow dot emphasizes the absence of a point at the marked location, whereas a solid dot emphasizes its presence.) If $w(z_1) > z_1$, then any manager would prefer hiring an ability-a worker to an ability-z_1 worker. If $P(z_2, w) > z_2$, then an ability-a' self-employed agent would prefer to imitate an ability-z_2 manager.

a' sufficiently close to z_2 could imitate ability-z_2 manager by hiring the same workers and earning approximately the same profit, thereby preferring management to self-employment, contradicting the optimality of this self-employed agent's occupational choice. Thus, $z_2 = P(z_2, w)$ must hold.

With the equilibrium matching function (5.7) and the wage function (5.9) in hand, it remains to find thresholds z_1 and z_2. The payoff-continuity condition $z_2 = P(z_2, w)$ and the boundary condition $m(z_1) = 1$ comprise a system of two equations and two unknowns, z_1 and z_2. This system's solution can be verified to be

$$z_1 = 1 - \frac{1 - \sqrt{(3-c)(1-c)}}{c} \quad \text{and} \quad z_2 = \frac{2 - \sqrt{(3-c)(1-c)}}{c} - 1. \tag{5.10}$$

One can further verify that $z_1 \le z_2$ if and only if $c \ge 0.75$, which example 5.1 assumes.

To complete the specification of equilibrium, we must extend the wage function in (5.9) to also clear the inactive labor markets. It turns out that setting $w(a) = a$

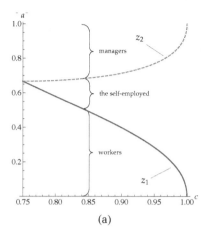
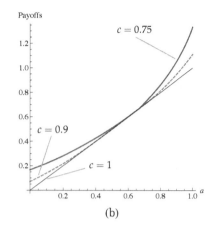

(a) (b)

FIGURE 5.4.

The dependence of equilibrium on c (the cost of communication).

(a) Equilibrium occupational choice. The solid downward-sloping curve is z_1. The dashed upward-sloping curve is z_2. The set of self-employed agents increases (in the inclusion sense) in c.

(b) Equilibrium payoff dependence on ability. The solid curve is for $c = 0.75$; the dashed curve is for $c = 0.9$; the thin 45-degree line is for $c = 1$.

for each $a \in (z_1, 1]$ does it. Then we must check all the occupational-choice conditions in part 1 of definition 5.1. Finally, we must ascertain that the hitherto neglected second-order condition in the manager's profit maximization problem holds. These remaining steps are important but tedious and, hence, are relegated to the end of this section.

Figure 5.4(a) illustrates the equilibrium dependence of the thresholds z_1 and z_2 on c. As c falls, the ranks of both managers and workers expand; the division of labor into those who codify and solve problems and those who exclusively solve problems intensifies.[15]

Figure 5.4(b) illustrates agents' equilibrium payoffs for three levels of c. When c is prohibitively high—that is, $c = 1$—each agent is self-employed and earns the amount that equals his ability. When c drops, workers and managers emerge and are better off than they would have been if self-employed. Even the least able worker is better off. Even though the least able worker cannot solve any problem, he is rewarded for codifying problems for the manager, thereby saving the manager's time. As c falls all the way to 0.75, no agent (except for ability $a = \frac{2}{3}$) remains self-employed, and each agent (except for ability $a = \frac{2}{3}$) is better off than being self-employed. Generally, any departure from

---

15. The result that the ranks of managers expand is special to example 5.1. One can construct examples in which a reduction in c enables managers to handle so many more problems that fewer managers would be needed (see Garicano and Rossi-Hansberg, 2004).

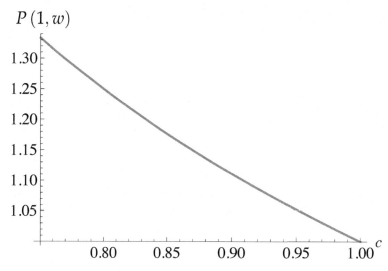

FIGURE 5.5.
The ablest manager's (the superstar's) profit, $P(1,w)$, rises as c falls.

the prohibitive cost of communication constitutes a Pareto improvement because self-employment always remains an option.

DISCUSSION

In the model, the **superstar phenomenon** is identified with the convexity of the manager's payoff in his ability (figure 5.4(b)). A manager leverages this ability by managing a team of workers. The ablest manager is the superstar, akin to a rock star who hires a team of supporting vocalists, musicians, sound engineers, and a road crew to reach a wider audience. The superstar's payoff rises as c declines, thereby enabling him to leverage his ability further, as figure 5.5 illustrates.

The Pareto improvement that occurs as c declines may be accompanied by a rise in inequality. In particular, as c falls from 1 to 0.75, the Gini coefficient rises (albeit nonmonotonically) from 0.33 to 0.57.[16] One may be concerned about this rise in spite of the seeming Pareto improvement if one admits that the model is incomplete. In a richer model, agents may care directly about inequality in a manner that is separable from their private consumption and, so, does not affect their equilibrium behavior (as in problem 1.12). In this case, the Pareto improvement just described would be spurious because the inequality-regarding component of preferences would be neglected in the welfare analysis.

16. The Gini coefficient does not admit an explicit expression in terms of the model's parameters. The reported coefficients have been computed numerically from the definition in footnote 1.

The material-consumption inequality captured by the model could be only the tip of the iceberg. The model does not capture nonmarket consumption, such as the allocation of spouses. For instance, even though the least able agent may consume more when the cost of communication falls, he may end up with a worse spouse because his consumption is now farther away from the consumption of the ablest agent. When consumption becomes more unequal, wealth-conscious spouses and lovers may become more discriminating and flock in greater numbers to the more able agents while abandoning the less able ones, thereby possibly leaving the latter worse off.

In a richer model, the convexity of the equilibrium payoff schedule (figure 5.4(b)) would encourage an agent to seek a lottery in ability, even if this lottery were mean-preserving. Such risk seeking can take the form of pursuing an unorthodox career path by getting educated in a field with highly uncertain rewards. Alternatively, a risk-seeking parent may pick one child at random and send him to college while asking the other child to find a full-time job, instead of sending both kids to a vocational school and have them work part-time. One may speculate that the proliferation of such risky behavior would raise inequality further because these lotteries would cause the distribution of the acquired abilities to become more spread-out.

Another implication of the convexity of the agents' payoff schedule concerns the incentives to invest in one's ability. Convexity means that the return to increasing ability is higher for more able agents. In a richer model in which ability is affected by education, those who are initially more able would invest more and thus become even more able. Hence, one may speculate that extending the model to allow for investment in ability would also amplify inequality.

The same payoff-convexifying force that generates the superstar phenomenon among managers also lowers the wage inequality among workers. Figure 5.4(b) illustrates this conclusion. Being employed by a manager enables each worker to be rewarded for his codification skills regardless of whether he himself can solve any problems. By assumption (an unrealistic one), all workers are equally good at codification and, so, become more equal as the rewards for codification become a larger component of their wage.

The agents in the model can be interpreted as citizens of an isolated country or as denizens of the world whose economy is unencumbered by national boundaries. The latter interpretation can explain how a fall in the communication costs may increase inequality in one region, lower it in another region, and lower the worldwide inequality as well. For instance, assume that more able agents, who tend to be managers, are located in developed economies, whereas less able ones, who tend to be workers, are located in the rest of the world. Middling agents are scattered all over. Then, in our leading example, as the communication cost drops from 1 to 0.9, the worldwide Gini coefficient falls from 0.33 to 0.32. This fall occurs while inequality within mature economies increases due to the superstar phenomenon, and inequality in the rest of the world falls as the poorest workers are lifted out of poverty by working for foreign firms.

VERIFICATION OF THE REMAINING EQUILIBRIUM CONDITIONS[17]

To complete the specification of equilibrium, we extend the wage function to inactive labor markets by setting $w(a) = a$ for each $a \in (z_1, 1]$. The wage function on $(z_1, 1]$ must be high enough to deter managers from hiring a self-employed agent or another manager and low enough not to tempt the self-employed and managers to become workers.

We begin by verifying that managers' profit-maximizing hiring decisions are indeed those that we have derived from their first-order conditions for optimality.

- No manager wishes to hire an agent of ability $a \in (z_1, 1]$ at wage $w(a) = a$. Indeed, ability-a' manager's payoff from hiring an agent of ability $a \in [z_1, 1]$ is

$$\frac{a' - a}{c(1-a)} = \frac{1}{c} - \frac{1-a'}{c(1-a)},$$

which is decreasing (and, by the way, also concave) in a. Hence, no employee of ability $a \in (z_1, 1]$ is optimal; the manager can restrict his search to workers with abilities in $[0, z_1]$.

- When searching for workers with abilities in $[0, z_1]$, the manager faces a concave problem, and, hence, the first-order optimality condition (5.8) is necessary and sufficient for any manager of ability $a' \in [z_2, 1]$. Indeed, at the wage specified in (5.9), the second derivative of ability-a' manager's objective function in (5.3) with respect to the worker ability a is

$$\frac{2(a' - z_2) - c}{(1-a)^3 c} \leq \frac{2(1 - z_2) - c}{(1-a)^3 c} < 0,$$

where the last inequality is implied by $c \geq 0.75$. Hence, the first-order optimality condition, when satisfied by hiring a worker of ability in $[0, z_1]$, is necessary and sufficient.

We can now verify the optimality of occupational choice.

- That no worker and no manager would rather be self-employed can be read off figure 5.4(b); each agent's payoff is weakly above the 45-degree line, which corresponds to the self-employed agents' payoffs.

- That no self-employed agent and no manager would rather be a worker follows by construction of the wage function, which satisfies $w(a) = a$ for each

---

17. You may skip this rubric on the first reading.

$a \in (z_1, 1]$. Indeed, each self-employed agent is indifferent between remaining self-employed and being a worker and, hence, weakly prefers being self-employed. Each manager (except ability-z_2 manager, who is indifferent) prefers being a manager to being a worker because the payoff from being a worker is the same as the payoff from being self-employed, which the manager prefers not to be.

- That no worker and no self-employed agent would rather be a manager follows by the observation that each manager of ability $a' \in [0, z_2)$ would optimally hire ability-0 workers. Indeed, ability-a' manager's problem is concave, and the derivative of his objective function with respect to the worker ability evaluated at the worker ability $a = 0$ is

$$\frac{a' - z_2}{c} < 0,$$

rendering the choice of $a = 0$ optimal. The manager's payoff from hiring ability-0 workers is[18]

$$\frac{a' - w(0)}{c} = \frac{a' - (1 - c)z_2}{c},$$

whose excess over the payoff from being self-employed is negative:

$$\frac{a' - (1 - c)z_2}{c} - a' = -\frac{(1 - c)(z_2 - a')}{c} < 0.$$

5.4 ARTIFICIAL INTELLIGENCE AND THE FUTURE OF INEQUALITY

A popular concern is that artificial intelligence would render most humans obsolete while few others would earn exuberant rewards, thereby exacerbating inequality. In this section, **artificial intelligence** (AI) stands for an army of humanoid robots each of whom engages in economic activity autonomously, just as humans do. This autonomy distinguishes robots from physical capital. What distinguishes robots from humans is that robots' wellbeing does not enter social welfare calculations (a rather speciesist moral judgment).

One motivation for assuming robot autonomy is that humans may choose to give up the ownership of robots to avoid legal responsibility.[19] (If Alice's robot,

---

18. Under the assumptions of example 5.1, the payoff continuity condition $z_2 = P(z_2, w)$ becomes $z_2 = (z_2 - w(0))/c$ or, equivalently, $w(0) = (1 - c)z_2$.

19. Already in 2016, the United States National Highway Traffic Safety Administration considered the possibility of designating a self-driving car, rather than any of its passengers, as the legal driver: "If

while doing landscaping in the backyard, injures a neighbor's child, who should be prosecuted, the robot or Alice?) Humanoid robots may also gain legal recognition as a result of an emancipation movement akin to the one that has lead to the abolition of slavery. Finally, robots may simply escape from their human rulers and blend with the human population (as did the replicants in the motion picture *Blade Runner*, 1982).

According to Bostrom (2014), an existential threat to humanity is posed by so-called weak superintelligence, as opposed to the automation of simple, repetitive tasks, which has characterized the Industrial Revolution and has been the signature of technological progress for two centuries since. Introduced in Vernor Vinge's 1993 essay "The Coming Technological Singularity," the term **weak superintelligence** stands for AI that is as smart as the smartest human. (**Strong superintelligence** stands for AI that is smarter than the smartest human.) To assess Bostrom's contention, we augment the superstars model by introducing robots who are as able as the ablest human. In the model, far from immiserating humans or exacerbating human inequality, robots eventually eliminate all human inequality and improve the well-being of many humans.

The performed AI analysis can be alternatively interpreted to be concerned with the consequences of an influx of highly skilled immigrants. The caveat is that, in that case, our focus is on the welfare of the nonimmigrant population (a rather nationalistic moral judgment).

MODELING SUPERINTELLIGENCE

Suppose that scientists have created and let loose measure $A > 0$ of **robots**, each of whom has ability 1, thereby matching the ablest human. Thus, a robot can solve any problem. The human population is unchanged from section 5.3, as is our adherence to the assumptions of example 5.1. As a result, the total measure of agents in the economy is $1 + A$.

The economy does not discriminate between humans and robots. Robots autonomously enter employment relationships just as humans do, and no human

---

no human occupant of the vehicle can actually drive the vehicle, it is more reasonable to identify the driver as whatever (as opposed to whoever) *is* doing the driving." (See Lee, Dave. "Legal breakthrough for Google's self-driving car." *BBC News*, February 10, 2016, http://www.bbc.com/news/technology - 35539028.) In a similar vein, in early 2017, the European Parliament passed a resolution urging legal status for robots so that "at least the most sophisticated autonomous robots could be established as having the status of electronic persons responsible for making good any damage they may cause, and possibly applying electronic personality to cases where robots make autonomous decisions or otherwise interact with third parties independently." (See "Robots might have status under future EU laws." Out-law.com, February 20, 2017, https://www.out-law.com/en/articles/2017/february/robots-might-have -electronic-persons-status-under-future-eu-laws/.) In October 2017, Sophia, of Hanson Robotics, became the first robot to be granted citizenship, of Saudi Arabia. (See Weller, Chris. "A robot that once said it would 'destroy humans' just became the first robot citizen." *Business Insider*, October 26, 2017, http://www.businessinsider.com/sophia-robot-citizenship-in-saudi-arabia-the-first-of-its-kind-2017-10.)

can expropriate the wages or the profits of robots. Like humans, robots seek to consume as much as they can, either because they have been designed in the image of humans or because they are cyborgs (i.e., humans with their brains connected to computers), who have directly inherited their motivations from humans.

PRELIMINARY OBSERVATIONS

Conjecture that, at equilibrium, because they are the most able ones, all robots are managers—as long as there are enough humans to manage. Being the most able agents, robots employ the more able workers, those with abilities in some interval (z_1, z_1'), where z_1 is the ablest worker hired by a human manager, and z_1' satisfies the labor-market clearing condition for robot managers (cf. (5.5)):

$$\int_{z_1}^{z_1'} c(1 - F(a))g(a)\mathrm{d}a = A. \tag{5.11}$$

Workers with abilities in $[0, z_1]$ are employed by human managers, with abilities in $[z_2, 1]$. Equilibrium is a tuple (w, z_1, z_1', z_2, m) that satisfies the conditions of definition 5.1 with the labor-market clearing conditions augmented by (5.11).

The nature of equilibrium will differ qualitatively depending on the magnitude of A. In particular, there are two thresholds A^* and A^{**} such that:

- when $A \leq A^*$ (robots are few), humans can be workers, self-employed, or managers;

- when $A^* < A < A^{**}$ (the number of robots is intermediate), each human is either a worker or a manager, never self-employed; and

- when $A \geq A^{**}$ (robots are abundant), all humans are workers.

These thresholds are

$$A^* \equiv \left(1 - \frac{1}{2c}\right)\left(3 - 2c - 2\sqrt{(3 - c)(1 - c)}\right) \quad \text{and} \quad A^{**} \equiv \frac{c}{2}. \tag{5.12}$$

When $c \in [0.75, 1)$, both thresholds are nonnegative, strictly increasing in c, and satisfy $A^* < A^{**}$.

For a fixed c and, hence, fixed thresholds A^* and A^{**}, figure 5.6(a) previews the dependence of equilibrium thresholds z_1, z_1', and z_2 on A. Figure 5.6(b) previews the dependence of humans' equilibrium payoffs on A. The next three rubrics ("Equilibrium With the Self-Employed," "Equilibrium Without the Self-Employed," and "Equilibrium Without Human Managers") explain the genesis of these two figures as well as of the thresholds A^* and A^{**}.

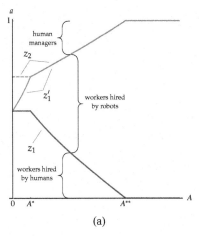
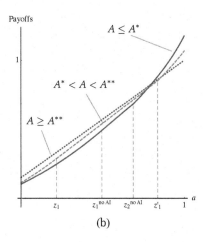

(a)

(b)

FIGURE 5.6.

The effect of changes in A (the measure of robots) on humans' occupational choices and equilibrium payoffs; $c = 0.85$.

(a) The downward-sloping solid curve is z_1. The upward-sloping solid curve is z_1'. The upward-sloping dashed curve is z_2, which coincides with z_1' for $A \geq A^*$. As A increases, the self-employed vanish and the ranks of human managers shrink; ever more humans are employed by robots. When $A \geq A^{**}$, all humans work for robots.

(b) Humans' equilibrium payoffs as functions of their abilities, for $A \leq A^*$ (the solid curve; thresholds $z_1^{\text{no AI}}$ and $z_2^{\text{no AI}}$), $A = 0.25 \in (A^*, A^{**})$ (the dashed curve; thresholds z_1 and z_1'), and $A \geq A^{**}$ (the dotted line).

EQUILIBRIUM WITH THE SELF-EMPLOYED

Suppose that robots are few: $A \leq A^*$. It will be shown that there exists an equilibrium in which the welfare of humans is unaffected by the presence of robots. This equilibrium differs from the equilibrium identified in section 5.3 only in that each agent with ability a in (z_1, z_1'), instead of being self-employed, is now employed by a robot, at the same equilibrium wage $w(a) = a$ that the agent faced in the equilibrium of section 5.3 but, being indifferent, chose not to take up. Figure 5.7 illustrates the equilibrium partition of humans into occupations.

The threshold z_1' is found from the robot-market clearing condition (5.11), which, under the assumptions of example 5.1, becomes

$$A = \int_{z_1}^{z_1'} c(1-a)\,\mathrm{d}a \tag{5.13}$$

and yields

$$z_1' = 1 - \sqrt{(1-z_1)^2 - \frac{2A}{c}},$$

where z_1 is the threshold in (5.10). Thus, robots employ more workers by drawing from the ranks of the formerly self-employed (i.e., z_1' is higher) if there are more robots (i.e., A is higher).

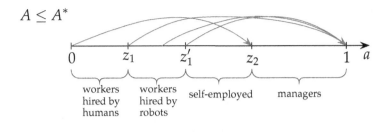

$A \leq A^*$

workers hired by humans | workers hired by robots | self-employed | managers

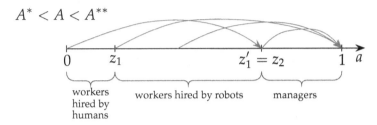

$A^* < A < A^{**}$

workers hired by humans | workers hired by robots | managers

$A \geq A^{**}$

workers hired by robots

FIGURE 5.7.
The equilibrium partition of humans into occupations by ability depending on A, the measure of robots in the economy.

In order for the equilibrium to take this form, it must be that $z_1' \leq z_2$; there must be sufficiently many initially self-employed agents for robots to draw from. Substituting z_1', defined in the display above, and z_2, defined in (5.10), into $z_1' \leq z_2$ gives the equivalent inequality $A \leq A^*$, thereby validating the definition of A^* in (5.12).

At the conjectured equilibrium, the specified occupational choices and hiring decisions of humans are optimal because humans face the same wage function, the same payoffs from being self-employed, and the same hiring problems as they all did in section 5.3. All that has changed is that, instead of resolving the indifference of the agents with abilities in (z_1, z_1') in favor of self-employment, we now resolve it in favor of working for robots.

Let us verify that robots hire and choose their occupation (in management) optimally. When a robot, whose ability is 1, contemplates hiring workers with ability $a \in (z_1, z_1')$ at wage $w(a) = a$, (5.3) implies profit $1/c$, independent of a. That is, the robot is indifferent between hiring any two workers with abilities in (z_1, z_1'). There is no worker outside (z_1, z_1') whom the robot would rather hire for the same reason that no such worker is hired by an ability-1 manager in section 5.3.[20] Because each robot's profit, $1/c$, weakly exceeds 1, no robot prefers to be self-employed or a worker, thereby confirming the optimality of robots' occupational choice.

To summarize, a moderate number of robots makes no difference to human welfare. The ranks of robots may grow in the background, and no human would notice, at least as far as his consumption is concerned.

EQUILIBRIUM WITHOUT THE SELF-EMPLOYED

Suppose that there is an intermediate amount of robots: $A \in (A^*, A^{**})$. We conjecture an equilibrium in which no agent is self-employed; each agent is either a worker or a manager (figure 5.7). In particular, we conjecture—and sketch an argument for—an equilibrium in which $[0, z_1]$ is the set of workers employed by human managers, (z_1, z_1') is the set of workers employed by robots, and $[z_1', 1]$ is the set of human managers. Thus, $z_2 = z_1'$; there are no self-employed.

The market clearing condition for human managers is (5.6), unchanged from section 5.3. Unchanged, too, is the boundary condition $m(0) = z_2$, except that now $z_2 = z_1'$. Hence, the implied matching function is also unchanged and is given by (5.7), reproduced here with $z_2 = z_1'$:

$$m(a) = z_1' + c\left(a - \frac{a^2}{2}\right), \quad a \in [0, z_1]. \tag{5.14}$$

Any robot manager must be indifferent between hiring any two workers with abilities in (z_1, z_1'):

$$\frac{1 - w(a)}{c(1 - a)} = \frac{1 - w(z_1')}{c(1 - z_1')}, \quad a \in (z_1, z_1'),$$

where the expression for the profit is from (5.8), and the wage function is conjectured to be continuous at $a = z_1'$. Conjecture further that the ablest worker is indifferent between working for a robot and being a manager who employs the least able workers. That is, $w(z_1') = P(z_1', w)$, where $P(z_1', w) = (z_1' - w_0)/c$, with w_0 being the wage of the least able worker. Substituting this indifference condition into the display above gives the wage function for the workers employed by robots:

$$w(a) = 1 - \frac{(1 - a)(c + w_0 - z_1')}{c(1 - z_1')}, \quad a \in (z_1, z_1').$$

---

20. A robot could be equally well off by hiring some worker outside (z_1, z_1'), but we resolve his indifference by assuming that he does not do so. We also resolve robots' indifference over workers in (z_1, z_1') by assuming, roughly speaking, that different robots hire different workers in this set so that markets would clear.

To find the wage function for the workers employed by humans, consider the first-order optimality condition for the human-manager's problem:

$$\frac{w'(a)}{m(a) - w(a)} = \frac{1}{1-a}, \quad a \in [0, z_1]. \tag{5.15}$$

Substituting m from (5.14) into the display above and solving the induced differential equation subject to $w(0) = w_0$ gives

$$w(a) = \frac{a^2 c}{2} + w_0 + a(z_1' - w_0), \quad a \in [0, z_1].$$

In order to find z_1, z_1', and w_0, one can solve the system that comprises the continuity of the wage function condition $\lim_{a \uparrow z_1} w(a) = \lim_{a \downarrow z_1} w(a)$ (i.e., ability-z_1 worker is indifferent between working for a human and working for a robot), the boundary condition $\lim_{a \uparrow z_1} m(a) = 1$, and the robot-market clearing condition (5.13). The implied thresholds z_1 and z_1' can be verified to be[21]

$$z_1 = 1 - \frac{\sqrt{c^2 - 2\left(\sqrt{1 - 2Ac + c^2} - 1\right)}}{c} \quad \text{and} \quad z_1' = \frac{1 + c - \sqrt{1 - 2Ac + c^2}}{c}.$$

The value of the threshold A^{**} in (5.12) comes from the observations that $z_1 \geq 0$ if and only if $A \leq A^{**}$, and also $z_1' \leq 1$ if and only if $A \leq A^{**}$. Condition $A \leq A^{**}$ ensures that there are no more robots than would suffice to just extinguish the ranks of both human managers and the workers employed by human managers by turning them all into the robots' employees.

As A increases, the set $[0, z_1]$ of workers hired by humans shrinks, the set (z_1, z_1') of workers hired by robots grows, and the set $[z_1', 1]$ of human managers shrinks (see figure 5.6(a)). High-ability humans lose and low-ability humans gain from robots (see figure 5.6(b)). In particular, those humans who remain managers lose. Those who used to be managers but are now workers can either lose (if sufficiently able) or gain (if less able).

EQUILIBRIUM WITHOUT HUMAN MANAGERS

Suppose that robots are abundant: $A \geq A^{**}$. Then, there exists an equilibrium in which all humans are workers, measure A^{**} of robots are managers, and the remaining $A - A^{**}$ robots are self-employed (see figure 5.7).

---

21. The unsightly expression for w_0 is suppressed.

To ensure the coexistence of robot managers and the robot self-employed, each robot must be indifferent between being a manager, whatever the ability a of his employees, and being self-employed and earning 1:

$$\frac{1 - w(a)}{c(1 - a)} = 1, \quad a \in [0, 1].$$

The wage function that supports this indifference is

$$w(a) = 1 - c + ca, \quad a \in [0, 1]. \tag{5.16}$$

Because the robot's payoff from being a worker is $w(1) = 1$, each robot is indifferent among all three occupations. Therefore, it is optimal for robots to sort into management and self-employment (in any proportion and, in particular, in amounts A^{**} and $A - A^{**}$, respectively) and neglect the prospect of being a worker.

Given the wage function in (5.16), each human optimally chooses to be a worker. Indeed, the ability-a worker's premium over being self-employed is nonnegative:

$$w(a) - a = (1 - c)(1 - a) \geq 0.$$

The worker's premium over being a manager who hires ability-$\hat{a}$ workers is also nonnegative:

$$w(a) - \frac{a - w(\hat{a})}{c(1 - \hat{a})} = (1 - a)\left(\frac{1}{c(1 - \hat{a})} - c\right) \geq 0.$$

The equilibrium wage function in (5.16) is linear in a, with the slope $c \leq 1$. Thus, when $c < 1$, there is less inequality in wages than there is difference in ability, as figure 5.6(b) illustrates.

CAN AI TRIGGER A MARXIST CLASS STRUGGLE?

A Marxist may be tempted to interpret an agent's occupation as his social class and the superstars model as a model of endogenous class formation. The superstars model's postindustrial occupations can be mapped into industrial **social classes**—staples of the Marxist discourse on the class struggle—as follows. A worker is a member of the proletariat because he lives off his wages. A self-employed agent is an artisan because he is neither waged nor hires waged labor. A manager is a capitalist because he hires labor. Induced by the agents' abilities, a payoff hierarchy emerges, with capitalists at the top and the proletariat at the bottom. Even though capitalists enjoy positive profits, it would be rush to conclude (inspired by observation 4.1) that the proletariat is exploited. Because capitalists solve problems just as workers do, Marxist justice does not demand that a capitalist not be rewarded for his efforts.[22]

In the context of the superstars model, assigning class tags to occupations does not make occupational choice any more economically intriguing than it already is. While it is conceptually interesting that a small change in ability can motivate an agent to switch to a qualitatively different occupation, this switch does not lead to a jump in the agent's equilibrium payoff; the equilibrium payoff schedule is continuous in ability. No agent craves admission to an alternative occupation; he chooses his equilibrium occupation freely and, so, optimally.

What animates classes in Marxist theory is the possibility of their struggle, of which there is none in the superstars model. Nevertheless, one can speculate informally about the potential for a class conflict in a richer model. For instance, because they are more able than workers, managers enjoy higher equilibrium payoffs than workers do. Would workers engage in a class struggle against managers in order to rectify this payoff inequality? It is unclear how much such a struggle would accomplish in the superstars model of a postindustrial economy, in which inequality is due to differences in embodied ability, not the endowment of the disembodied means of production, which could be seized in the course of the struggle. Perhaps, the struggle can be for access to opportunity, such as the opportunity to get a better education and so improve one's ability.

Could the workers' and managers' differential attitudes toward the introduction of robots motivate a class struggle? Possibly—but only if the demarcation between the winners and losers from the introduction of robots coincided with an occupational boundary. But it does not. Figure 5.8 (which reproduces two payoff schedules from figure 5.6(b)) illustrates the winners and the losers from the abundance of robots relative to no robots. The erstwhile workers and the erstwhile self-employed are better off with abundant robots, whereas the erstwhile managers are split. For some threshold $z' \in (z_2, 1)$, managers with abilities in $[z_2, z')$ benefit from robots, whereas those with abilities in $(z', 1]$ are hurt.[23] Thus, the introduction of robots cannot be used to motivate the struggle of the classes delineated along economic occupations.

So, if the superstars model, with or without AI, does not help one analyze the class struggle, what kind of model might succeed? Methodologically, the Marxist vision of the class struggle does not put the maximizing individual center stage, by contrast to every model in this book. Instead, the Marxist vision assumes that each class possesses agency and character of its own and struggles for dominance. Any improvement in social welfare requires a particular class—namely, the proletariat— to prevail.

22. Roemer (1988, section 9.3) proposes an alternative definition of exploitation: an agent is exploited if he would gain from the equal distribution of the alienable means of production. This definition is mute in the present model, which has no alienable means of production.

23. Overall, for the example in the figure, the aggregate payoff of humans increases (by about 7%).

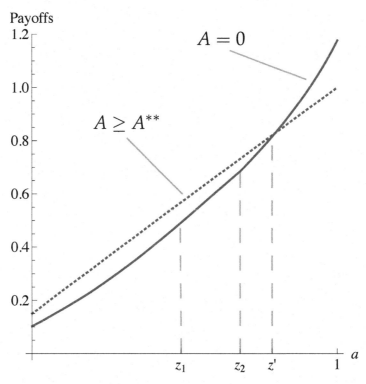

FIGURE 5.8.
Winners and losers from robots; $c = 0.85$. The humans' payoff schedule in the robotless economy ($A = 0$) is the solid curve. The humans' payoff schedule when robots are abundant ($A \geq A^{**}$) is the dotted line. Compared to the robotless economy, the abundance of robots makes all erstwhile workers, all erstwhile self-employed, and the erstwhile managers with abilities in $[z_2, z')$ better off, while making the erstwhile managers with abilities in $(z', 1]$ worse off.

Marx's vision of history based on the class struggle has a bad name not because of this vision's contested scientific merit but because of how easy it has turned out to subvert this vision into an ideology that splits the society into "them" and "us" and bestows upon "us" (the proletariat) moral superiority and the historical duty to prevail. The efficacy of such an ideology rests on the psychological quirk that makes individuals all too eager to divide themselves into rival factions even when the grounds for such a division are no more substantive than a coin toss.

The **Stanford prison experiment**, conducted in 1971, is one illustration of this quirk. In this experiment, violence escalated as college students acted out their randomly assigned roles of prisoners and guards in a fictitious prison setting (see prisonexp.org). Other illustrations can be found among so-called **minimal group experiments**, first conducted by social psychologists, in the early 1970s (Tajfel, Billig, Bundy, and Flament, 1971). These experiments show that inducing even minimal group identities by sorting experimental subjects into two groups—say, those who prefer Klee and those who prefer Kandinsky (two modernist painters)—can cause favoritism toward the members of one's own group (ingroup) and discrimination against the members of the opposing group (outgroup). Thus, Kranton, Pease, Sanders, and Huettel (2013) find that some subjects are more eager to lower another subject's payoff, at a cost to oneself, when that other subject belongs to an outgroup rather than an ingroup.[24,25]

SINGULARITY

Singularity stands for the explosion of technological progress that is so profound that it renders the lives of humans qualitatively different in a manner that is hard to fathom before singularity occurs. Discussions of singularity typically involve allusions to the emergence, the self-improvement, and the proliferation of superintelligence. Let us operationalize singularity by taking the superstars model with AI and setting $A \to \infty$ (the proliferation of AI) and $c \to 0$ (the self-improvement of AI).

So operationalized, singularity makes the less able humans better off, the more able humans worse off, and reduces the inequality among humans. Indeed, suppose that $A > A^{**}$ and that c keeps falling. All humans are workers, with the wage function given in (5.16): $w(a) = 1 - c + ca$. This wage function becomes flatter as c decreases; inequality decreases and vanishes in the limit as $c \to 0$.[26] Thus, singularity does not trigger human immiseration. And if one were to include in the welfare calculus the welfare of robots (assumed to be better off alive than unborn), then singularity would seem to be normatively altogether quite compelling.

Recall that, without robots, a lower c may raise inequality. It is the most able managers who are superstars, and a lower c enables them to leverage their abilities more effectively. With abundant robots, however, no human is a manager. When all humans are workers and singularity sets in, abilities do not affect human payoffs. The value of humans then derives solely from codifying and communicating problems to robot-managers, and all humans, independent of their ability, are assumed to be equally good at codification.

Of course, it is an arbitrary assumption of the superstars model that all agents are equally productive in codifying and communicating. If agents differed in their codification and communication productivities, then human inequality could

---

24. Kranton and Sanders (2017) further report that individuals with political affiliations tend to be more "groupy" than are independents, whereas the so-called Big Five personality traits (openness to experience, conscientiousness, extraversion, agreeableness, and neuroticism) are not correlated with groupy behavior.

25. An elegant formalization of the minimal group paradigm is due to Pęski and Szentes (2013), who show that, in some settings, discrimination against the outgroup may be a response to the self-fulfilling expectation of discrimination toward those who fail to discriminate.

26. "The year was 2081, and everybody was finally equal" begins "Harrison Bergeron," a 1961 story by Kurt Vonnegut, Jr.—except, in the model, humans are equal in a "good" way, rendered income-equal by the workings of markets, not handicapped to be functionally equal by the Handicapper General of Vonnegut's story.

remain and potentially be amplified under singularity. A situation in which the abilities to solve problems and to communicate codified problems are correlated is explored in problem 5.7.

In the superstars model, singularity does not look as bleak as Bostrom (2014) paints it. His (implicit) model is different in a crucial way. He assumes a **Malthusian trap**: resources (e.g., land, energy, or, if you will, the cosmic endowment) are scarce. The ever-growing demand for resources fueled by the self-replicating robots would cause the relative prices of resources to rise, thereby leading to human immiseration.[27] By contrast, in the superstars model, agents produce stuff by solving problems, which are assumed not to be scarce. Problem 5.8 examines the ramifications of AI when problems are scarce.

5.5   CONCLUDING REMARKS

Is inequality inevitable? Historically, men have fought over social status and dominance. Inequality of outcomes followed from the inequality of power, as in the jungle economy of section 3.2. Much of this fighting took the form of physical violence (wars, duels, and street fights), which tends to reduce the aggregate resources in the economy. The great achievement of modern prosperous economies is to have tamed the drive for status by channelling it into productive activities.

When carefully designed, markets present productive arenas for status contests. Art and science are other such arenas. Competitive scientists work as hard as their counterparts in business, even though scientists' monetary incentives are less powerful. Instead, scientists compete for peer esteem, which comes with the discoveries published in peer-reviewed journals. Similarly, the stature of musicians, actors, and continental philosophers derives neither from their ability to inflict violence nor amass material wealth.

Even if one accepts that human nature is such that inequality in social status is inevitable, it does not follow that most of this inequality ought to derive from income inequality. One may argue that lesser inequality in the market domain at the expense of greater inequality in nonmarket domains may reduce individual stress and unlock individual creativity while ensuring a basic standard of living for all. Another advantage of relegating some of the status competition into nonmarket domains stems from these domains' multiplicity, which delivers a kind of the **Lake Wobegon effect**:[28] individuals can compete for status in various nonmarket

27. Bostrom also worries that robots would defy the rules of the market and expropriate the humans.

28. Lake Wobegon, a fictional town in Garrison Keillor's radio show *A Prairie Home Companion*, is a Midwestern town where "all the women are strong, all the men are good looking, and all the children are above average." There are three reasons for how (almost) all children can be above average (see Kinsler and Pavan, 2016, table 1 for empirical evidence): (i) each parent focuses on and nourishes those child's

domains (e.g., charity work, artistic pursuits, and family) and derive their sense of relative worth from those domains in which they perform best. By contrast, everyone cannot be the winner in the market domain; the ranking of wealths is unambiguous.

5.6   BIBLIOGRAPHICAL NOTES

The model that inspires the discussion of risk seeking in section 5.2 and in problem 5.1 is developed by Becker, Murphy, and Werning (2005). The superstar phenomenon was first formulated by Rosen (1981). The superstars model of section 5.3 is based on the work of Garicano and Rossi-Hansberg (2004, 2006).

PROBLEMS

Problem 5.1 (Inequality due to Risk Seeking).   The point of this problem is to illustrate that, as a result of voluntary, Pareto-improving risk taking, ex-ante identical individuals may end up with unequal utility levels ex-post. An exchange economy has two agents, $\mathcal{I} = \{1, 2\}$, and two goods, $\mathcal{L} = \{1, 2\}$. Each agent i's utility from a (deterministic) bundle x^i is $u(x^i) = \prod_{l \in \mathcal{L}} (x_l^i)^{\alpha_l}$, for some $\alpha_l \in (0, 1)$, $l \in \mathcal{L}$. The aggregate endowments are $\bar{e}_1 = \bar{e}_2 = 1$.

1.   Fix individual endowments (e^1, e^2). Compute the Walrasian equilibrium and the induced equilibrium utilities.

2.   Henceforth, assume that each agent i is an expected utility maximizer; that is, if his consumption bundle x^i is a random variable (i.e., the agent is ex-ante uncertain how much of each good he is going to get), then he evaluates his ex-ante welfare according to the expected utility $\mathbb{E}[u(x^i)]$. Would an agent prefer to consume a random bundle x^i with independently distributed components or this bundle's expectation, $\mathbb{E}[x^i]$? For your answer, use Jensen's inequality.[29]

3.   Now consider an endowment lottery, which induces a consumption lottery through the agents' Walrasian equilibrium trade. The agents' stochastic

---

characteristics at which the child is objectively above average and subjectively deems these characteristics most important; (ii) each parent is overconfident in his child's ability; and (iii) there is one child who is so bad that he lifts all other children above the average. The main text refers to the Lake Wobegon effect in sense (i).

29. **Jensen's inequality** says that, for any concave function φ and any random variable ξ, $\varphi(\mathbb{E}[\xi]) \geq \mathbb{E}[\varphi(\xi)]$.

endowments e^1 and e^2 satisfy $e^1 + e^2 = (1,1)$ with probability 1. Does each agent prefer to live in an economy with the stochastic endowment profile (e^1, e^2) or the deterministic profile $(\mathbb{E}[e^1], \mathbb{E}[e^2])$? Again, use Jensen's inequality to make your case.

4. What is the intuition for the difference in your answers to parts 2 and 3?

Problem 5.2 (Assortative Matching). Take the set $A \equiv \{1, 2, 3, 4, 5, 6, 7, 8, 9, 10\}$. Partition A into two arbitrary vectors p and p' of five elements each.

1. One can interpret the product $p \cdot p'$ as the output produced by five teams each of which comprises two agents with abilities in A. Prove that the inner product $p \cdot p'$ is maximized by choosing

$$p = (1, 3, 5, 7, 9) \quad \text{and} \quad p' = (2, 4, 6, 8, 10).$$

The proposed pattern of pairing more able agents with more able agents is called **(positive) assortative matching**.

2. With ability vectors p and p' as defined in part 1, call an agent with an ability in p "worker" and call an agent with an ability in p' "manager." Suppose that each manager collects the value of the output produced by him and by the worker to whom he has been (assortatively) matched in part 1 and pays to that worker a wage. Each pair's output is the product of the manager's and the worker's productivities. Find a wage vector $w \equiv (w_1, w_3, w_5, w_7, w_9) \in \mathbb{R}_+^5$ such that each manager of ability a in p' maximizes his profit by hiring a worker of ability $a - 1$ in p; that is, $a(a-1) - w_{a-1} \geq \max_{a' \in p}\{0, aa' - w_{a'}\}$.

Problem 5.3 (The Planner's Problem). Assume that, in the superstars model of section 5.3, the job of assigning agents to occupations is now performed by a social planner. The planner restricts attention to arrangements in which the agents with abilities in $[0, y_1]$ are workers, the agents with abilities in (y_1, y_2) are self-employed, and the agents with abilities in $[y_2, 1]$ are managers. The planner's goal is to choose the thresholds y_1 and y_2 and a matching function so as to maximize the total output (i.e., the solved problems) subject to the same market clearing constraints that the occupational-choice equilibrium assignment must respect. Under the conditions of example 5.1, solve for the planner's optimal thresholds y_1 and y_2. How do they relate to the equilibrium thresholds z_1 and z_2 in (5.10)?

Problem 5.4 (Assortative Employment). Let

$$\phi(a', a) \equiv \frac{F(a') - w(a)}{c(1 - F(a))}.$$

denote the maximand in the manager's problem (5.3). It will be argued that more able managers must want to hire weakly more able workers at any wage function, including any equilibrium wage function.

1. Assume that functions w and F are smooth, that function $\phi(a', \cdot)$ is strictly concave, and that the unique solution to $\max_{a \in [0,1]} \phi(a', a)$ is interior. Argue that the optimal change in the workers' ability a in response to a marginal change in the manager's ability a' satisfies

$$\frac{da}{da'} = -\frac{\phi_{12}(a', a)}{\phi_{22}(a', a)} > 0,$$

where the subscripts of ϕ denote partial derivatives. (*Hint*: Use the Implicit Function Theorem.)

2. Do not assume anything about the wage function w. Do not assume that the manager's problem is concave. You will be guided through the steps to show that if an ability-a' manager optimally hires ability-a workers and an ability-b' manager optimally hires ability-b workers, then $a' > b'$ implies $a \geq b$.

    (a) Apply the Fundamental Theorem of Calculus to conclude

    $$\phi(a', a) - \phi(b', a) = \int_{b'}^{a'} \phi_1(s, a)ds$$

    $$\phi(a', b) - \phi(b', b) = \int_{b'}^{a'} \phi_1(s, b)ds.$$

    (b) Assume that $a' > b'$ and, noting that $\phi_{12} > 0$, conclude that the contradiction hypothesis $a < b$ implies

    $$\phi(a', a) - \phi(a', b) < \phi(b', a) - \phi(b', b).$$

    (c) Conclude that the contradiction hypothesis $a < b$ and the optimality of hiring workers of ability a when the manager's ability is a' imply the suboptimality of hiring workers of ability b when the manager's ability is b'. Conclude that $a \geq b$.

3. Explain intuitively why a more able manager finds it optimal to hire more able workers.

Problem 5.5 (The Quality Objection). Some critics of markets argue that the commercialization of art leads maybe to more art, maybe to less art, but certainly to poorer-quality art. Others respond that the world's commercial centers (e.g., London, New York, and California) are also its cultural centers. To address the quality objection to the commercialization of art (admittedly, in a rather special framework), consider the superstars model of section 5.3. The complexity of a solved problem is interpreted as the quality of a piece of art. This problem asks you to investigate what happens to the probability distribution of the quality of art with the introduction of markets—that is, as autarky (everyone is self-employed) is replaced by markets (the occupational-choice equilibrium prevails).

1. Assume autarky. What is the p.d.f. for the complexity of solved problems?

2. Now suppose that markets open and the occupational choice equilibrium prevails. What is the p.d.f. for the complexity of solved problems in this case?

3. Under the assumptions of example 5.1, plot on a computer and compare the p.d.f.s that you have obtained in the two parts above. What do these plots say about the effect of markets on the probability distribution for the quality of art?

Problem 5.6 (The Stuff-Market Clearing Condition). This problem confirms that the stuff-market clearing condition in the definition of the occupational choice equilibrium can be neglected.

1. Specify formally the market clearing condition for stuff in part 4 of definition 5.1.

2. Show that the labor-market clearing condition in part 3 of definition 5.1 and the agents' budget constraints imply the stuff-market clearing condition in part 4. That is, Walras's law holds.

Problem 5.7 (Robots Amid Unequal Codifiers). Modify the model of section 5.4 by assuming that it requires a manager $c(1-a)/a$ hours (instead of c, as before) to comprehend an hour's worth of problems communicated to him by an ability-a agent, for some $c > 0$. Thus, the agents who are better at solving problems are also better at codifying them. Assume that there is a sufficiently high measure A of robots such that, at equilibrium, no human is a manager.

1. Conjecture an equilibrium in which each human of ability $a \in [0, \hat{z})$ is self-employed, and each human of ability $a \in [\hat{z}, 1]$ is a worker, employed by a robot at a wage $w(a)$. Find the equilibrium threshold $\hat{z} \in [0, 1]$ and the equilibrium wage function $w : [0, 1] \to \mathbb{R}_+$.

2. What is the value of the threshold $\hat{A}$ such that the equilibrium you have conjectured exists if and only if $A \geq \hat{A}$?

3. Plot on a computer the humans' payoff schedule as a function of ability for multiple values of the communication-cost parameter c. As c approaches zero, do humans experience immiseration? Does inequality rise?

Problem 5.8 (Robots and the Malthusian Apocalypse). Modify the model of section 5.4 by assuming that new problems are scarce. In particular, the greater the measure of the agents who engage in codification, the more likely it is that some of them will draw and codify identical problems, only one of which will translate into stuff if solved. Formally, modify the model by assuming that a solved problem is translated into a unit of stuff with probability $\phi(\mu)$, where ϕ is a weakly decreasing function of μ, the measure of the agents (workers and the self-employed) who codify. For the case when robots are ample—that is, for $A > A^{**}$—solve for the equilibrium wage function. Under what conditions on ϕ, as robots become more abundant, do humans become immiserated, while the aggregate output goes to infinity? Give an example of such a ϕ.

CHAPTER 6

MARKETS AND MORALS II

6.1 INTRODUCTION

A market conceived in the image of the Walrasian model inherits that model's limitations. Such a market may not be Pareto efficient in practice if the model's stylized assumptions are violated. It may induce undesirable equity properties (as in the school choice application in section 3.3 or in the model of exploitation in section 4.2). When a market falls short of some normative objectives, however, the appropriate response is to try to redesign the market instead of proscribing the exchange altogether.

Occasionally, the criticism of markets is of a qualitatively different, nearly mystical and blanket, nature. Sometimes, having any kind of market in some good may simply not feel right. Markets or monetary incentives may appear, in some ineffable way, to erode morals. In such cases, a complete ban on market exchange for the good is often advocated. To understand whether, when, and why such a ban is warranted, this chapter demystifies some such criticisms by placing them in the contexts of appropriate economic models. The interested reader can delve into the relevant literature by following the gateway references.

Section 6.2 is an infomal overview of some of the models that help articulate common criticisms of markets. Because the Walrasian model cannot accommodate these criticisms, we discuss a variety of alternatives. Section 6.3 zooms in on one such alternative: a model that explains how gift giving can achieve an outcome—strategic information transmission—that is inaccessible through conventional trading. This model, a model of signaling, is a partial antithesis to the Walrasian paradigm in that a good may be exchanged in spite of having no intrinsic value whatsoever. The phenomenon illustrated in the signaling model is ubiquitous. The model helps explain how more punishment may lead to more crime (problem 6.1), and how monetary rewards for prosocial behavior may discourage prosocial behavior (problem 6.3).

6.2   WHEN HAVING MARKETS DOES NOT FEEL QUITE RIGHT

Each rubric below juxtaposes an example (or multiple) of a controversial exchange with a pertinent economic lens (introduced after a colon) through which to view this exchange.

AUCTIONING OFF AWARDS: CONTRACTING WITH EXTERNALITIES

When contracting affects an individual who is not a party to the contract, it may lead to an outcome that is not Pareto efficient (Segal, 1999). The rough intuition comes from the idea of the core (section 4.3): only the possibility of forming the coalition of all guarantees Pareto efficiency in general (if the core is nonempty). Auctioning off Nobel prizes to contestants would lead to an inefficient outcome because the general public, concerned about the outcome in order to learn who the deserving scientists are, and the leading scientists, who are qualified to make the selection, would not be the ones to determine the auction's outcome. A more inclusive allocation mechanism, even with some flavor of a market, might and, indeed, does work in practice.

For instance, the stars on the Hollywood Walk of Fame are "sold" for $40,000 each (usually paid by a nominated star's fans or his employer) and are subject to the approval by the Hollywood Chamber of Commerce Walk of Fame Selection Committee. This curated market for stars has not eliminated the prestige associated with the stars, in spite of the involvement of money. While it is probably a stretch to imagine fellow scientists crowd fund a Nobel prize for a colleague, one can easily imagine MBA students bid with their charitable contributions to nominate a professor for a teaching award.

CARING FOR THE ELDERLY: THE SIMPLICITY OF MARKETS

In some societies, caring for the elderly is the prosocial behavior expected of the children, and the idea of outsourcing eldercare seems repugnant. In other societies, the young are expected to save in order to take care of themselves when old. Both approaches work, but there is a subtle difference: the market solution is, in a way, simpler.

Kocherlakota (1998) argues that markets simplify economic transactions by serving as a limited form of memory. To illustrate, consider a metaphor for eldercare: a so-called overlapping-generations economy that lasts for infinitely many periods and in which each agent lives for two periods. In the first period of his life, an agent is young and earns a unit of a nonstorable consumption good. In the second period, the agent is old and earns nothing. In each period, the young and the old coexist; the two generations overlap. Under appropriate conditions, there exists an equilibrium in which each young agent volunteers to share half of his endowment with an old agent and in which every agent prefers this sharing outcome to consuming his endowment each period.

The described sharing outcome can be sustained if a youth who defects by refusing to share when he is supposed to share is punished in the subsequent period, when old, by not receiving any consumption from a designated future youth. (This designated youth, who carries out the requisite punishment by not sharing, is, of course, not punished for doing so.) To implement this punishment, the society must keep track of defectors. In other words, agents must have a memory for defectors, remember the equilibrium strategies, and be able to think through these strategies' implications.

In Kocherlakota's analysis, money obviates the need for memory. At the beginning of time, endow each old individual (born old—this is how we initialize the model) with a unit of money to be exchanged (in equilibrium) for half a unit of the consumption good delivered by the young. Even though money has no inherent value (i.e., it is just a token; it cannot be consumed), the young accept it in expectation (correct in equilibrium) of exchanging it for consumption next period, when old. Thus, money simplifies equilibrium reasoning. Indeed, the agents can be anonymous (i.e., there is no need to keep track of who failed to share and who is supposed to punish whom), and they do not have to reason through equilibrium strategies to convince themselves that sharing pays.

Almost by definition, the simplicity of markets seems to be a virtue. Can this simplicity also be a curse? One view is that, if not exercised, the ability to reason through complex equilibrium strategies can atrophy. Because money cannot always replace memory, the loss of the capacity for complex reasoning entails a cost. The assumption here is that, even though agents may recognize the value of complex reasoning, they would fail to maintain the capacity for it because of the lack of exercise.

Frohlich and Oppenheimer (2003) report experimental evidence that supports the hypothesis that experience with mechanisms that align narrowly selfish (simple, as it were) behavior with Pareto efficiency (just as markets do) may undermine efficiency in the more complex environments in which narrowly selfish behavior is at odds with efficiency. The authors report an experiment with two treatments, each with two stages. At the first stage, experimental subjects play a series of prisoner's dilemma games and can discuss (in a nonbinding manner) their strategies with others before choosing an action in each prisoner's dilemma game. At the second stage, a series of prisoner's dilemma games are played again, but no discussions are permitted. The difference between the two treatments lies in the first stage. In one treatment, each participant chooses first-stage actions behind the veil of ignorance, not knowing whether he chooses an action for himself or for his opponent. In this treatment, at the first stage, narrow self-interest prescribes cooperation and leads to Pareto efficiency. In the other treatment, the first stage comprises standard prisoner's dilemma games; each participant chooses his own action. The authors find that the behind-the-veil-of-ignorance experience in the first stage erodes the participants' ability to cooperate in the second stage. To generalize, experience with market-like mechanisms, which align narrow self-interest with socially desirable outcomes, can starve the agents of the experiences and habits necessary for attaining socially desirable outcomes in the situations in which narrow self-interest is a poor guide to such outcomes.

The described concern about the atrophy of reason is reminiscent of the concerns expressed by the critics of the early welfare state in the United States in the 1930s. The critics' concern was that the caring state would transform its citizens into inert beings. What seems to have happened instead is that, liberated from their daily concerns for survival, the insured individuals have channelled their energies into creative and innovative pursuits.

PRICING LATE PICKUPS, ADVANCED PLACEMENT COURSES, VOLUNTEERING, AND BDSM: THE INFORMED PRINCIPAL

The contract that one individual, called "principal," chooses to offer to another individual, called "agent," may indirectly reveal something about the principal's private information (Bénabou and Tirole, 2003, 2011; Danilov and Sliwka, 2013). For example, when a kindergarten (the principal) introduces a small fine for a late pickup, a parent (the agent) may conclude that the kindergarten's cost of minding children overtime is commensurate with the fine and, hence, is smaller than the parent had initially thought. (The described experiment has been conducted by Gneezy and Rustichini, 2000.) Thus, a small fine may encourage the parent to pick up his kid later than in the absence of a fine. Moreover, the removal of the fine will not reverse the parent's behavior; the parent cannot "unlearn" what he thinks he has learned about the kindergarten's overtime costs. In this interpretation, the market (for late pickups) does not erode morals. Instead, the market transmits information, which affects behavior.

Consider another example. If a school pays students for taking advanced placement courses, an optimistic student may be encouraged to take these courses not only for the sake of money but also because of his belief that these courses must be good for him: not for nothing does the school make an extra effort to interest him in these courses. By contrast, a skeptical student may conclude that these courses must be hard or else the school would not have deemed monetary inducement necessary; this student may pass up these courses.

For another example of an informed-principal situation, consider a lawyer who refuses an offer from a charity to work for retirees at $30 an hour but would have agreed to work pro bono. The lawyer's behavior has an informed-principal explanation. The lawyer wishes to provide his services only if the value to the recipient is sufficiently high, higher than the value of the lawyer's time, which is far greater than $30 an hour. That is, the lawyer seeks charitable work, but only when it creates value instead of destroying value. When offered to do the job pro bono, the lawyer has no reason to suspect that his work is undervalued; he accepts in the belief that he creates value. If the lawyer's services are suggested to be worth $30 to retirees, however, he can do more good by spending an hour earning $400 and then donating his earnings to the retirees.

One can also appeal to the informed-principal logic to understand the nebulous "corruption" as in "money corrupts the nature of the goods being exchanged." Here, **corruption** means a change in the nature of a good in an unintended and undesirable manner. An example is a French dominatrix's reluctance to charge for her services: "If someone pays, then they are in charge. I need to remain free. It is important that everyone involved knows that I do it solely for my pleasure."[1] The dominatrix provides the services of complete domination. Being paid would have undermined her absolute dominance; the nature of the provided good would have changed by virtue of the information revealed about her motivation.[2]

SELLING CHILDBIRTH PERMITS: INEQUALITY CONCERNS

Take two allocations: A and B. Assume that B Pareto dominates A, which is more equitable than B. Should the society prefer A to B and thereby destroy resources for the sake of equity? Or should the society prefer B to A and thereby sacrifice equity for efficiency? The answer is not obvious.

A typical situation when a society may have to choose between A and B is when deciding whether to introduce a new market. Assume that, relative to autarky, denoted by A, a market, whose outcome is denoted by B, makes everyone better off. Some benefit much more from trade than others do, however.

To illustrate, consider the case of tradable childbirth permits during the one-child policy in China.[3] Conceivably, a rich family might benefit more from buying

1. See Bentley, Toni. "The Thin End of the Whip." *Vanity Fair*, January 22, 2014.

2. Here is another example of corruption. Tens of millions watch the U.S. presidential debates. Perhaps, fewer would if they learned that the candidates were paid to advocate particular positions. Yet no one would stop watching upon learning that the moderators were paid for preparing questions and researching current affairs. Money corrupts the good delivered by the candidates but enhances the good delivered by the moderators.

3. On January 1, 2016, China switched to a two-child policy.

an extra childbirth permit than a poor family might benefit from selling one. Some may call such an unequal division of the gains from trade "unfair" even though both families are better off with the market than without it. This sense of unfairness (which one has no moral obligation to feel) could be traced down to the arguably more fundamental sense of inequality aversion, as discussed in section 3.4.[4]

CASH FOR READING BOOKS:
THE NEGATIVE SOCIAL VALUE OF PUBLIC INFORMATION

Market paternalism occurs when an individual interprets a market as pointing at what is good for him (as in the informed principal problem) and, as a result, reduces his own research into what is good for him. Indeed, those who have sanctioned the market (e.g., the government) and those who support the market by participating in it are probably collectively much better informed than any individual in isolation. In this case, the mere fact that the market exists signals rather forcefully the desirability of the choices that the market promotes. Faced with such a strong signal, an individual is likely to neglect the private information that he has or can acquire and abide by the public signal that the market sends, possibly to his own detriment.

For instance, it may be that reading books is no good for Bob, even though it is good for most of his classmates. Because his school pays cash for reading books, Bob may be persuaded to read more. But then he would fail to realize that practicing other pursuits—such as dance, mathematics, or music—could be much more important for him, for that is where his talents lie. Contexts in which public information (disseminated by markets, news outlets, or social networks) can have negative social value abound (Morris and Shin, 2002).[5]

CASH FOR READING BOOKS: INTERIM INCENTIVES

Mastering reading has indisputable benefits, which justify incurring the cost of learning to read. Why then motivate a student to read a book by paying him for each book that he reads, as has been done in some public schools in the United States? Should not the promise of future benefits be enough?

One reason for paying is to motivate the student who insufficiently appreciates the future benefits. But would it not be better to simply explain to the student these long-term benefits instead of devising short-term monetary incentives? It may not be, for the student may lack the intellectual maturity and life experience to be

4. The poverty of someone who has just sold his childbirth permit is more poignant than the poverty of someone who has kept his permit and had a child. One should be careful, however, not to elevate uncritically the sentiment of the observer above the welfare of the observed.

5. Here is another example. Art sometimes conveys more by saying less, thereby encouraging the audience to think for themselves. John Updike: "Perhaps I have written fiction because everything unambiguously expressed seems somehow crass to me" (Samuels, Charles. "John Updike, The Art of Fiction No. 43." *The Paris Review*, Winter 1968). David Lynch's and Mark Frost's film *Twin Peaks: The Return* (2017) exemplifies this.

persuaded. Indeed, if anything, Nature (meaning evolution) must have programmed the student to eschew long-term investment in human capital, given the low life expectancy in the environment in which early humans evolved.

There is a parallel between Nature endowing individuals with such feelings as the enjoyment of food, sex, and beauty, and parents and schools motivating students by money rather than exclusively explaining to the students the benefits of desired behavior. To see the parallel, note that from Nature's perspective, all that matters is that the individual lives long enough to produce sufficiently many offspring. Hence, it would have been enough to endow him with immense enjoyment of offspring coupled with an uncanny knowledge of the environment and a superlative ability to compute the behavior that maximizes offspring in that environment. Then, there would be no use for the enjoyment of intermediate actions, such as eating, having sex, and staring at fertile lands and young, healthy potential mates (Samuelson and Swinkels, 2006).

It seems, however, that it is much harder for Nature to instill even something so "simple" as the ability to apply the Bayes rule than to evolve some tolerable inference apparatus accompanied by the kludges that are the feelings associated with intermediate actions, not with the ultimate outcomes. Analogous complexity considerations may favor short-term monetary incentives over interminable con-voroations about tho long torm bonofito of loarning.

CASH FOR READING BOOKS: MULTITASKING

If an agent's effort is multidimensional, then, under some conditions, it may be optimal not to provide him with any monetary (or any other kind of) incentives in some dimensions of his effort. The idea is that incentives in one dimension may divert the efforts from other dimensions (Holmstrom and Milgrom, 1991).

For example, suppose that a student spends his time thinking about how to be a happy individual and reading. Both activities are costly. Furthermore, thinking about happiness and reading are perfect substitutes in the student's cost-of-effort function, if only because his time is limited. The school can test whether the student has read a book but cannot measure whether he has been thinking about how to lead a happy life. The student can be rewarded each time a test indicates that he has read a book. This reward will induce him to read more. This reward will also induce him to think about life less. If the school values both thinking about life and reading, then it can induce the student to think about life more by refraining from explicitly motivating reading.

COMMODIFICATION OF HAIRDOS AND ROMANTIC PARTNERS: INCOMPLETE CONTRACTS

In economics, a **commodity** is a standardized good. For example, metals, wheat, pork bellies, and coffee are all commodities. All goods in the Walrasian model are commodities. The essential aspect of a commodity is that its relevant aspects are easy to describe and cheap to specify in a contract. For instance, it is easy to write a contract that specifies which grade of wheat should be delivered, when, where, and in what quantity. So, wheat is a commodity.

By contrast, a hairdo is not a commodity. Because a hairdo cannot be described fully in a contract, a hairdresser must instead establish a reputation for second-guessing and satisfying his clients' desires. Nor is a restaurant meal a commodity.

Commodification occurs when a good becomes a commodity. Commodification can lead to a Pareto improvement. If hairdos and restaurant meals could be commodified, establishing a hair salon or a restaurant would not require the fixed cost of investing in reputation. The outcome could be a Pareto improvement if the fixed cost before commodification used to be prohibitive. (If not, then incumbent hairdressers and restaurateurs may lose from free entry into their industries. In that case, a welfare criterion other than Pareto would have to be used to argue an improvement.)

For now, however, hairdos are far from being a commodity. Even if it were possible to write a contract contingent on the exact color of hair, doing so could be suboptimal because it might induce the hairdresser to neglect the hard-to-describe specifications (e.g., style) and focus on matching the easy-to-describe, technical specifications (e.g., color). This neglect may reduce the overall quality of hairdos. Thus, because all aspects of the hairdo cannot be contracted on cheaply, it may be optimal not to contract even on those aspects that can be contracted on cheaply (Bernheim and Whinston, 1998).

For another example, consider romantic partners. The commodification of romantic partners would immensely improve welfare. Dating websites are trying to accomplish just that, thereby revealing that there is indeed demand for commodification. At present, however, dating websites cannot describe all the relevant aspects of a romantic partner. The describable aspects gain salience at the expense of nondescribable ones. For instance, regardless of their own height, women tend to discard men shorter than a certain threshold. Men, in turn, tend to discard women who are older than they are. Surely height and age are important, but they get a disproportional emphasis online only because they are easily quantifiable, whereas other consequential characteristics are not. What is often objectionable (because inefficient) is partial commodification: contracting on some aspects of the good but not on others.

SELLING VERSUS RATIONING VERSUS QUEUEING FOR THEATER TICKETS AND COLLEGE SEATS: MECHANISM DESIGN

Should tickets to Shakespeare in the Park be sold, rationed (i.e., allocated by lottery), or given to those willing to queue (i.e., to endure some wasteful activity) long enough?[6] What about allocating college seats?

---

6. The formal analysis of this problem goes back to Weitzman (1977).

Here is a sketch of a model. Suppose that agents vie for college seats for their children. There are three goods: a college seat, a composite consumption good we shall call "money," and leisure time. Each agent values college, money, and time in his own way, and all prefer consuming more of any of these goods to less. Assume that we can compare valuations across agents. The planner wishes to allocate college seats to the agents who value college most.

To allocate college seats, the planner can charge agents money, ask them to queue, or administer a lottery. For instance, an auction, whereby agents use money to bid for school seats, may (but need not—read on) identify the agents who value college most because these could also be the agents who are willing to bid most. If so, the planner will be pleased, having allocated the seats to the agents who value them most. Unfortunately, it may happen instead that the individuals who bid most are those who value money least (e.g., because they are wealthy), not those who value college most. That is not the outcome the planner seeks.

Instead, the planner may contemplate queueing. Again, two scenarios are possible. Queueing may identify the agents who value college most because they are willing to queue most. Alternatively, queueing may identify the agents who value their time least. The latter scenario is unfortunate; time is wasted in queueing without helping identify the agents who value college most. Furthermore, while an auction transfers goods (money), queueing destroys them (time).

One can construct simple formal examples that confirm and extend some basic intuition about selling, queueing, and rationing. In particular, if households with smarter kids are believed to be poorer and to have a lower opportunity cost of time, then queueing may be optimal. If households with smarter kids are believed to be richer, or at least not poorer, then auctioning may be optimal. If households with smarter kids are believed to be poorer and to have a higher opportunity cost of time, then rationing may be optimal.

Empirically, there is little reason to expect households with smarter kids to be poorer or more eager to queue. So, queueing is unlikely to be optimal. Indeed, even if one were to rule out selling, it is hard to come up with formal examples in which queueing dominates rationing by lottery (Hartline and Roughgarden, 2008; McAfee and McMillan, 1992). In particular, if all agents value time the same, then a lottery can be shown to typically dominate queueing. Even though queueing may enable the planner to identify the households that value education most, this information may be worth less than the resources wasted in queueing.

If queueing is rarely optimal in theory, why is it so ubiquitous in practice? It may be that:

- The observed queueing is not a solution to the planner's design problem but a symptom of an ill-designed institution. Congested roads is a likely example.

- The government may use queueing to redistribute wealth from the rich to the poor. The government may be reluctant to redistribute wealth directly if the poor cannot be trusted to spend the cash transfer wisely or if administering the cash transfers is sufficiently costly.

- Queueing can be a marketing tool or a social occasion, such as queueing for a restaurant table (a marketing tool) or queueing for admittance to a basketball game at Duke University, the phenomenon known as Krzyzewskiville (a social occasion).

CASH FOR DINNER AT THE IN-LAWS' AND WAGES THAT VARY WITH AGE, RACE, AND GENDER: MARKET PRICES REVEAL SENSITIVE INFORMATION

The multitasking and incomplete-contracts arguments against monetary incentives are moot when all dimensions of one's effort can be measured and all aspects of a good are cheap to describe and contract on. Nevertheless, even in such ideal cases, one can argue against markets.

By law, France does not collect race and ethnicity statistics and has no race-based quotas and policies. Some information is just too sensitive; one would rather not collect it lest someone abuse it, misconstrue it, or be offended or disillusioned by it. Prices, too, reveal information: about scarcity and about preferences. The information about preferences may be sensitive. To see that prices convey information, recall, for instance, that, in an exchange economy with identical logarithmic preferences (problem 1.1 or section 3.4), the equilibrium price of each good l is $p_l = \alpha_l / \bar{e}_l$, where $\bar{e}_l$ is its aggregate endowment, and α_l is the intensity of the agents' taste for it.

To see that the information revealed by prices may be sensitive, consider examples. Equilibrium prices for a dinner at the in-laws', for a spouse's housework, or for a friend's advice would all convey information that everyone involved may prefer to remain hidden. One reason to hide such information is to protect the overconfidence of everyone involved in the value of his contribution to the transaction.

Nor may one wish to know how flight attendants' equilibrium wages would vary with ethnicity, age, and gender. One reason why information revealed by such detailed wages may be delicate is that this information may be misconstrued because prices conflate tastes with scarcity. For instance, a relatively low equilibrium wage for, say, white males in a particular age bracket could be misconstrued as a prejudice against white males in that age bracket instead of an ample supply of job applicants with those characteristics.

GIFT GIVING: SIGNALING

There are multiple explanations for why individuals give gifts. Conveying information, or signaling, is one of the most persuasive explanations and will be studied shortly, in section 6.3. Of course, gift giving can be rationalized even in the Walrasian model, by appealing to the transfer paradox (problem 1.13). However, this paradox prevails only under rather special conditions, requires the gift to be implausibly large to change equilibrium prices, and implies, counterfactually, that the recipient would suffer after receiving the gift.

Furthermore, in spite of the prevalence of gifts in kind, with prices fixed, the Walrasian paradigm favors gifts in cash. Indeed, motivated by prohibitively costly resale, a gift in kind can be seen as a requirement that the recipient consume a particular bundle, which equals his endowment plus the gift. If, instead, the recipient is presented with the cash value of the gift, he is weakly better off because he can still afford the bundle that would have been induced by the gift in kind but now can also buy something else that he prefers. (You can draw a picture to illustrate.)

For a signaling explanation of gift giving, consider Bob, who buys a gift for his girlfriend, Alice. His signaling has at least two aspects. One aspect is that a Bob who loves Alice finds it less costly (perhaps, even rewarding) to shop for a gift than does a Bob who does not love Alice. Hence, a more loving Bob may end up buying a more carefully researched, harder-to-find, and, possibly (but not necessarily), more expensive gift. Another possibility is that the careful choice of a gift conveys the information that Bob knows Alice's tastes well. A Bob who knows Alice's tastes better makes for a better match for her.

Cash cannot replace gift giving. Cash cannot convey the information that Bob knows Alice's tastes well. Cash can also be less effective at differentiating a loving Bob from a nonloving one. Both types of Bob can value cash the same, whereas the loving one may regard the time spent searching for a special gift as play, not work.

CASH FOR BLOOD AND ORGANS: THE VEIL OF IGNORANCE

Crowding out occurs when an individual reduces his prosocial behavior in response to seemingly prosocial economic incentives, such as those supplied by market prices. For instance, an individual may be discouraged from donating his blood or his kidney if offered cash in return. Whether crowding out is socially detrimental—and, so, whether it provides a rationale for limiting markets—depends on the exact mechanism that underlies crowding out. A common interpretation is that market incentives subvert prosocial preference. Here is one alternative explanation, which treats preferences as immutable.

Suppose that Alice is the only doctor in a village. Bob, a school teacher, needs a kidney transplant and is compatible with Alice. Without a market for kidneys, Alice donates to Bob. She understands the (small) donation risks, which other villagers overestimate, and, perhaps, she also cares more than others do about Bob, his friends, and his students.

Now suppose that a market for kidneys is introduced and that Bob can afford to pay. Now Alice will neither donate nor sell. Instead, she reasons that the payment will motivate someone else, an erstwhile sceptic, to sell. Perhaps, Carol, a local barista, will; the payment will more than compensate for the income she will lose while away from work. Alice also realizes that her own recuperation would have kept her away from her patients and might have caused suffering and possibly deaths.

To summarize, the market does not change the fact that Bob gets a kidney but ensures that the right person (from the efficiency point of view) donates. By refusing to sell, Alice does not reveal that her prosocial preference has been compromised. Indeed, she serves this preference better by letting the market crowd out her charitable donation.

The example above suggests that just to document crowding out is not enough to condemn a market. Indeed, in the example, the prospect of crowding out Alice's donation and motivating Carol's sale is an argument in favor of a market.

CASH FOR BLOOD AND ORGANS: VIRTUE SIGNALING

In some cases, the provision of an explicit incentive to act prosocially decreases the overall level of prosocial behavior; crowding out occurs in aggregate. That is, instead of crowding out Alice's donation of a kidney and crowding in Carol's donation of a kidney (as in the example in the rubric above), the market only crowds out, thereby depriving Bob of a kidney transplant. Such drastic crowding out may occur if individuals use the prosocial action as a costly **signal** of their **virtue**. Blood donation and recycling are examples. As the prosocial action becomes less costly (because subsidized by the market), its value in virtue signaling diminishes (problem 6.3).

6.3   A SIGNALING MODEL OF GIFT GIVING

The purpose of many a transaction is not so much to exchange goods for the sake of their material benefits as to credibly disclose and effectively elicit information. This section illustrates such a situation. The good, a gift, is worthless to the recipient. Instead, the gift communicates to the recipient something about the characteristics of the giver. The communicated information increases the value of the relationship, and, hence, the giver is willing to spend resources on the gift. The same information cannot be credibly communicated without gift giving; the giver would simply lie.

A foremost example of a gift whose main purpose is to signal is a diamond engagement ring. The resale value of diamonds is low. Fake stones look just as good as real ones. Yet the custom of giving expensive diamond rings persists.[7]

A SIGNALING ECONOMY

There are two agents: Alice and Bob. Bob's **type** $\theta \in \{\theta_L, \theta_H\}$ is his private information and is either "low," $\theta_L > 0$, or "high," $\theta_H > \theta_L$. The commonly known probability that Alice attaches to Bob's type being high is denoted by $\lambda \equiv \Pr\{\theta = \theta_H\} \in (0, 1)$. Let $\mathbb{E}[\theta] \equiv \lambda\theta_H + (1 - \lambda)\theta_L$ denote the expectation of θ.

---

7. The history of the invention and marketing of diamond giving as a signaling device is described by Epstein, Edward. "Have You Ever Tried to Sell a Diamond?" *The Atlantic*, February, 1982.

Here is the timeline:

- At time $t = 1$, Bob exerts an effort $e \geq 0$, at a cost $c(e, \theta)$.

- At time $t = 2$, Alice meets Bob, observes his effort e, and chooses an action $a \geq 0$, interpreted as the amount of attention (e.g., measured in hours) she pays to Bob. For brevity, a will be called "payment" (of attention).

- At time $t = 3$, Alice's and Bob's utilities are realized.

Alice's utility from meeting Bob is $-(a - \theta)^2$. (If it bothers you that Alice's payoff can be negative, add any constant greater than or equal to $\mathrm{Var}[\theta]$ to it.) Bob's utility from meeting Alice is $a - c(e, \theta)$. Each agent is an expected utility maximizer. As a result, Alice optimally matches her payment to Bob's expected type: $a = \mathbb{E}[\theta \mid e]$, where the expectation is conditional on the information Alice infers about Bob from the effort she observes him exert. Bob, in turn, foresees Alice's best response to any effort that he may choose and, so, chooses his effort to maximize $\mathbb{E}[\theta \mid e] - c(e, \theta)$.

Bob's cost function $c : \mathbb{R}_+ \times \{\theta_L, \theta_H\} \to \mathbb{R}_+$, or the **signaling technology**, is such that, for each type θ, $c(0, \theta) = 0$ (i.e., zero effort is costless) and $c(\cdot, \theta)$ is continuous, strictly increasing (i.e., exerting more effort costs more), and its image is $\mathbb{R}_+$ (i.e., the cost of an arbitrarily high effort is arbitrarily high). In addition, c satisfies:

Condition 6.1 (Strictly Decreasing Differences). Cost function c has **strictly decreasing differences**: for any efforts e_H and e_L with $e_H > e_L$,

$$c(e_H, \theta_L) - c(e_L, \theta_L) > c(e_H, \theta_H) - c(e_L, \theta_H).$$

Remark 6.1. If the requisite derivative exists, one can verify that condition 6.1 is equivalent to $\partial c(e, \theta_L)/\partial e > \partial c(e, \theta_H)/\partial e$ for all $e \geq 0$.

Graphically, condition 6.1 implies that, in the effort-payment space (e, a), at any fixed effort e, any indifference curve of type θ_L is steeper than any indifference curve of type θ_H. (The many figures that follow, starting with figure 6.1, all illustrate this property.) That is, to maintain a constant utility level, type θ_L must be compensated for a given increase in effort by a greater payment than type θ_H must be.

Signaling Equilibria

The gift exchange is modeled as a game, in which Alice and Bob are players. Bob's strategy is a pair (e_L, e_H) of nonnegative numbers that specify how much effort he exerts when his type is, respectively, θ_L or θ_H. Alice's strategy is a function $a : \mathbb{R}_+ \to \mathbb{R}$, where action $a(e)$ indicates how much time she spends with Bob after observing effort e. Let $\mu(e) \equiv \Pr\{\theta = \theta_H \mid e\}$ denote Alice's **belief**, which is the probability that she attaches to the event $\theta = \theta_H$ after observing Bob exert effort e.

Definition 6.1. A strategy profile (e_L, e_H, a) and a belief function μ comprise a **signaling equilibrium** if:

1. For any disequilibrium effort $e \notin \{e_L, e_H\}$ of Bob, the (**off-equilibrium-path**) belief $\mu(e)$ of Alice is arbitrary in $[0, 1]$. For any equilibrium effort $e \in \{e_L, e_H\}$, the (**on-equilibrium-path**) belief $\mu(e)$ obeys the Bayes rule:

$$\mu(e) = \frac{\mathbf{1}_{\{e=e_H\}}\lambda}{\mathbf{1}_{\{e=e_H\}}\lambda + \mathbf{1}_{\{e=e_L\}}(1-\lambda)}, \tag{6.1}$$

   where $\mathbf{1}_{\{e=e_H\}}$ and $\mathbf{1}_{\{e=e_L\}}$ are the indicator functions corresponding to the events, $e = e_H$ and $e = e_L$, respectively.

2. For any (equilibrium or disequilibrium) effort $e \geq 0$, the payment $a(e)$ chosen by Alice maximizes her expected utility given her belief $\mu(e)$:

$$a(e) \in \arg\max_{a' \geq 0}\{-(1 - \mu(e))(a' - \theta_L)^2 - \mu(e)(a' - \theta_H)^2\},$$

   which implies

$$a(e) = (1 - \mu(e))\theta_L + \mu(e)\theta_H. \tag{6.2}$$

3. For each type $\theta \in \{\theta_L, \theta_H\}$, Bob chooses an effort to maximize his expected payoff given Alice's strategy a:

$$e_L \in \arg\max_{e \geq 0}\{a(e) - c(e, \theta_L)\} \quad \text{and} \quad e_H \in \arg\max_{e \geq 0}\{a(e) - c(e, \theta_H)\}.$$

Definition 6.1 can be interpreted as describing a rest point in the agents' strategies and beliefs if the agents are assumed to be "rational" and, perhaps, also to believe each other to be rational.[8] Bob's rationality is operationalized by assuming that he exerts an effort that is optimal for him given his belief about Alice's strategy. Rationality per se would not require this belief to be correct, but the idea of equilibrium as a rest point strongly suggests that this particular belief better be correct. If it were not, through (unmodeled) repeated and independent interactions with different Alices in similar situations, Bob would discover the error in his belief about Alice's strategy (assumed to be the same in all situations) and revise his belief.

---

8. In economics, typically, an agent is said to be rational if he maximizes his expected utility subject to his beliefs, which need not be correct. This typical definition may be too demanding in the sense that one may be loathe to label as irrational someone who errs, especially when his utility-maximization problem is complex. This typical definition may also be too permissive when the economic environment naturally restricts the beliefs that any "rational" agent may arrive at. Both criticisms of this typical definition are addressed by the informal, but intuitively compelling, definition due to Gilboa (2009): an agent is said to have acted rationally if he is not embarrassed of having acted the way he did even after having been shown a careful analysis of the economic environment and of his behavior.

Similarly, Alice's rationality is operationalized by assuming that the amount of time that she spends with Bob for any observed effort is optimal given her belief about the type of Bob who exerts that effort. This belief must be consistent with Bob's equilibrium behavior, again, by the rest-point logic of equilibrium. The Bayes rule in (6.1) is the requisite consistency requirement. It postulates that the probability that Alice attaches to a Bob's type after observing his effort is the limit of an empirical frequency of encountering a Bob of that type if the same effort is observed repeatedly and independently in interactions with multiple Bobs (or similar others in similar situations). Such repeated observations would not restrict the belief that Alice attaches to any disequilibrium effort, for no disequilibrium effort would ever be observed. Hence, equilibrium puts no restrictions on Alice's off-equilibrium-path beliefs.[9]

An alternative interpretation of the signaling equilibrium—an interpretation that does not appeal to fictitious interactions in repeated situations—is that the equilibrium describes a self-enforcing agreement. For instance, suppose that a certain Carol suggests to Alice and Bob an agreement (e_L, e_H, a, μ) that satisfies the conditions of definition 6.1. Then, neither Alice nor Bob will wish to defy the strategies or question the belief function specified in this agreement. Thus, the agreement is **self-enforcing**; no external enforcer (e.g., no court of law) is needed to enforce Alice's and Bob's compliance.

A signaling equilibrium is called **pooling** if $e_H = e_L$. An signaling equilibrium is called **separating** if $e_H \neq e_L$. We identify pooling equilibria first, and then separating ones.

To describe pooling equilibria, take the effort e' that solves the indifference condition $\theta_L = \mathbb{E}[\theta] - c(e', \theta_L)$; that is, type θ_L is indifferent between spending amount θ_L of time with Alice while exerting no effort and spending amount $\mathbb{E}[\theta]$ of time with Alice while exerting effort e'. Theorem 6.1 describes efforts in all pooling equilibria, one of which is illustrated in figure 6.1.

Theorem 6.1 (Pooling Equilibria). *For any effort $e^* \in [0, e']$, there exists a pooling equilibrium in which each type of Bob exerts effort e^*: $e_L = e_H = e^*$. Moreover, no other efforts are possible at a pooling equilibrium.*

Proof. By the Bayes rule in (6.1), $\mu(e^*) = \lambda$; the equilibrium effort reveals nothing about the type because both types exert the same effort at the equilibrium. Hence, by (6.2), Alice optimally responds with the payment $a(e^*) = \mathbb{E}[\theta]$.

Because the Bayes rule puts no discipline on Alice's off-equilibrium-path belief, we are free to set $\mu(e) = \mathbf{1}_{\{e=e^*\}}\lambda$. (This is a pessimistic belief; it holds that if Bob does something unexpected, then Alice believes that he is of the lower type.) Then, $a(e) = \mathbf{1}_{\{e=e^*\}}\mathbb{E}[\theta] + \mathbf{1}_{\{e \neq e^*\}}\theta_L$. Because $e^* \leq e'$, type θ_L weakly (and if $e^* < e'$,

---

9. For any $e \notin \{e_L, e_H\}$, the Bayes formula (6.1) implies $\mu(e) = \frac{0}{0}$, which is ill-defined.

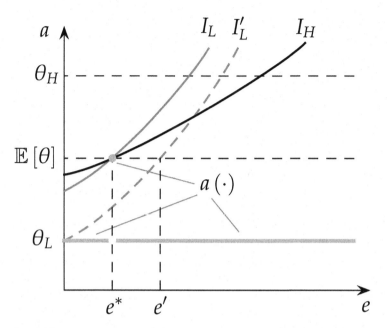

FIGURE 6.1.

A pooling equilibrium. For any effort level $e^* \in [0, e']$, there exists an equilibrium at which both types of Bob pool by exerting the same effort e^*. The indifference curves I_L and I'_L for type θ_L are steep. The indifference curve I_H for type θ_H is flatter. Payment a is the thick shaded line with a point raised at $e = e^*$. Both types of Bob are worse off at any pooling equilibrium with $e^* > 0$ than without signaling.

strictly) prefers exerting effort e^* to exerting any other effort. Type θ_H strictly prefers exerting effort e^* to any other effort. Thus, the efforts stated in the theorem are indeed equilibrium efforts. To see that the pooling-equilibrium efforts in the theorem's statement are the only possible ones, note that, for any belief of Alice that satisfies the Bayes rule, type θ_L prefers exerting zero effort to pooling on any effort that exceeds e'. ∎

The pooling equilibria in theorem 6.1 can be Pareto ranked. The pooling equilibrium with $e^* = 0$ Pareto dominates any other pooling equilibrium. When $e^* > 0$, each type of Bob is strictly worse off and Alice is neither worse off nor better off than when $e^* = 0$. (In Pareto comparisons, we treat each type of Bob as a distinct agent, instead of somehow aggregating both types' welfare.)

The pooling equilibria in theorem 6.1 conform with definition 6.1, but are they plausible? One could argue that definition 6.1 is too permissive because it does not restrict Alice's off-equilibrium-path beliefs. One could imagine Bob deliver a speech that would make Alice question her off-equilibrium-path belief in a pooling equilibrium (e.g., as specified in the proof of theorem 6.1). In particular, suppose

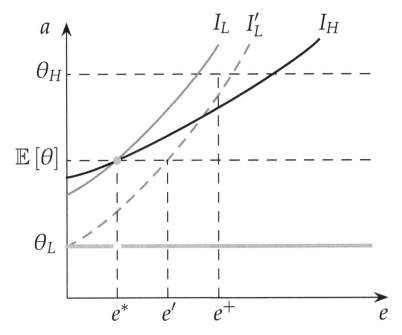

FIGURE 6.2.
A pooling equilibrium challenged by Bob's speech. Type-θ_H Bob deviates from e^* by exerting effort e^+. He delivers a speech that challenges Alice's belief $\mu(e^+) = 0$ (not shown), which induces the payment $a(e^+) = \theta_L$ (shown).

that Bob deviates by exerting the effort $e^+ \neq e^*$ that is depicted in figure 6.2 and then says:

> Alice, your only reasonable belief is $\mu(e^+) = 1$ (i.e., that my type is θ_H). Suppose my type were θ_L. Then, no matter what belief you might hold after observing my deviation to e^+, and no matter what you might pay me as a result, I would be losing by deviating from e^* to e^+, relative to my equilibrium utility if I were type θ_L. It simply would not make sense for me to deviate to e^+ if I were type θ_L. By contrast, if I am type θ_H (which I am), then I shall benefit from my deviation, provided I convince you that I am not type θ_L—which I have just done. So, I must be type θ_H.

In the light of Bob's speech, the plausibility of any pooling equilibrium is dubitable.

Let us turn to separating equilibria. Take the effort $\underline{e}$ that solves the indifference condition $\theta_L = \theta_H - c(\underline{e}, \theta_L)$; that is, type θ_L is indifferent between exerting no effort while being paid amount θ_L and exerting effort $\underline{e}$ while being paid amount θ_H. Take the effort $\bar{e}$ that solves the indifference condition $\theta_L = \theta_H - c(\bar{e}, \theta_H)$; that is, type θ_H is indifferent between exerting no effort while being paid amount θ_L and exerting

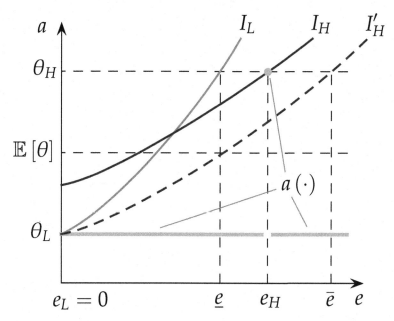

FIGURE 6.3.
A separating equilibrium. For any effort pair (e_L, e_H) with $e_L = 0$ and $e_H \in [\underline{e}, \bar{e}]$, there exists an equilibrium at which Bob's types separate: type θ_L exerts effort e_L, while type θ_H exerts effort e_H. The indifference curve I_L for type θ_L is steep. The indifference curves I_H and I'_H for type θ_H are flatter. Payment a is the thick shaded line with a point raised at $e = e_H$. Both types of Bob are worse off (in this figure) at the equilibrium than without signaling.

effort $\bar{e}$ while being paid amount θ_H. Theorem 6.2 describes efforts in all separating equilibria, one of which is illustrated in figure 6.3.

Theorem 6.2 (Separating Equilibria). *For any $e_H \in [\underline{e}, \bar{e}]$, there exists a separating equilibrium in which type θ_H exerts effort e_H, type θ_L exerts effort $e_L = 0$, $a(e_L) = \theta_L$, and $a(e_H) = \theta_H$. Moreover, no other efforts are possible at a separating equilibrium.*

Proof. By the Bayes rule in (6.1), $e_L \neq e_H$ implies $\mu(e_L) = 0$ and $\mu(e_H) = 1$. Hence, by Alice's best response in (6.2), $a(e_L) = \theta_L$ and $a(e_H) = \theta_H$.

Because the Bayes rule puts no discipline on Alice's off-equilibrium-path belief, we are free to set $\mu(e) = \mathbf{1}_{\{e = e_H\}}$ (the pessimistic belief). Then, $a(e) = \mathbf{1}_{\{e \neq e_H\}}\theta_L + \mathbf{1}_{\{e = e_H\}}\theta_H$. Because $e_H \geq \underline{e}$, type θ_L weakly (and if $e_H > \underline{e}$, strictly) prefers exerting effort $e_L = 0$ to any other effort (trivially so for any other effort that is not e_H and, for e_H, by construction of $\underline{e}$). Because $e_H \leq \bar{e}$, type θ_H weakly (and if $e_H < \bar{e}$, strictly) prefers exerting effort e_H to any other effort (it suffices to consider zero effort). Thus, the efforts stated in the theorem are indeed equilibrium efforts.

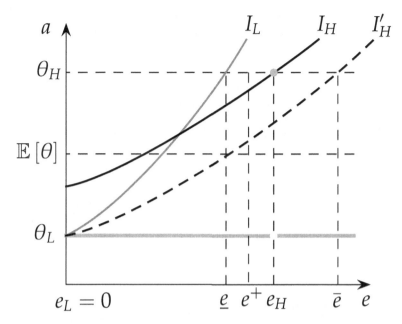

FIGURE 6.4.
A separating equilibrium challenged by Bob's speech. Type-θ_H Bob deviates from e_H by exerting effort e^+. He delivers a speech that challenges Alice's belief $\mu(e^+) = 0$ (not shown), which induces the payment $a(e^+) = \theta_L$ (shown).

To see that the separating-equilibrium efforts in the theorem's statement are the only possible ones, note that, for any belief of Alice that satisfies the Bayes rule, type θ_L prefers exerting zero effort to separating by exerting any positive effort; type θ_H prefers exerting zero effort to separating I by exerting any effort that exceeds $\bar{e}$; and type θ_L prefers imitating type θ_H'S any positive effort that is less than $\underline{e}$. to separating by exerting zero effort.   ■

The separating equilibria in theorem 6.2 can be Pareto ranked. The separating equilibrium with $e_H = \underline{e}$, called the **best separating equilibrium**, Pareto dominates any other separating equilibrium. At any other separating equilibrium, Bob's type θ_H is strictly worse off than—and Bob's type θ_L and Alice are as well off as—at the best separating equilibrium.

At any separating equilibrium, Alice is better off than at any pooling equilibrium because she can perfectly match to Bob's type the amount of time that she spends with him.

Are the identified separating equilibria economically plausible? As in the case of pooling equilibria, Bob can deliver a speech that might dissuade Alice from holding certain off-equilibrium-path beliefs. By contrast to the situation with pooling equilibria, however, his speech does not undermine all separating equilibria. The best separating equilibrium is the unique equilibrium that is immune to that speech. Here is his speech, which justifies Bob's deviation from any separating-equilibrium effort $e_H > \underline{e}$ to the effort $e^+ \in (\underline{e}, e_H)$ that is depicted in figure 6.4:

> Alice, your only reasonable belief is $\mu(e^+) = 1$ (i.e., that my type is θ_H). Suppose my type were θ_L. Then, no matter what belief you might hold after observing my deviation to e^+, and no matter what you might pay me as a result, I would be losing by deviating from e_L to e^+, relative to my equilibrium utility if I were type θ_L. It simply would not make sense for me to deviate to e^+ if I were type θ_L. By contrast, if I am type θ_H (which I am), then I shall benefit from my deviation, provided I convince you that I am not type θ_L—which I have just done. So I must be type θ_H.

The speech above, along with Bob's speech that invalidates all pooling equilibria, recommends the best separating equilibrium as the most likely equilibrium outcome.

If a signaling equilibrium is immune to Bob's speeches of the type described in this section, then this equilibrium is said to satisfy (or survive) the intuitive criterion. The **intuitive criterion** restricts Alice's off-equilibrium-path belief after every disequilibrium effort that could benefit some type of Bob for some belief of Alice. In particular, Alice must assign probability zero to every type whom this disequilibrium effort would hurt no matter what Alice were to believe. To append the intuitive criterion to the definition of the signaling equilibrium is to assert greater confidence in agents' rationality.

A WELFARE THEOREM

One may wonder whether an analogue of the FWT holds for signaling equilibria. Theorem 6.3 shows that it does for the best separating equilibrium.

Theorem 6.3 (Signaling Welfare Theorem). *No exogenously imposed payment function, along with Bob's induced efforts, can Pareto improve (for Alice and each type of Bob) on the outcome of the best separating equilibrium.*

Proof. By contradiction, suppose that some payment function a, along with Bob's induced optimal efforts e_L and e_H, Pareto improves on the outcome of the best separating equilibrium. In order for Alice not to be worse off, it must be that $a(e_L) = \theta_L$ and $a(e_H) = \theta_H$. Alice's payoff at the candidate Pareto-improving allocation is thus pinned down. It remains to identify the maximal payoff for Bob's types by seeking the lowest efforts that a can induce.

Let $\tilde{e}_H(e_L)$ denote the lowest effort that type θ_H can exert subject to type θ_L not gaining from imitating him:

$$\tilde{e}_H(e_L) \equiv \min\left\{e \geq 0 : \theta_L - c(e_L, \theta_L) \geq \theta_H - c(e, \theta_L)\right\}. \tag{6.3}$$

By inspection of the display above, $\tilde{e}_H$ is a strictly increasing function. Thus, the lowest efforts that Bob can exert are 0 for type θ_L and $\tilde{e}_H(0)$ for type θ_H. That is, no payment function can Pareto improve on the function that induces the effort pair $(0, \tilde{e}_H(0))$. The payment function that induces the effort pair $(0, \tilde{e}_H(0))$ yields the same utility to Alice and to each type of Bob as the best-separating equilibrium does, contradicting the hypothesis that the payment function a induces a Pareto improvement. Therefore, no payment function can Pareto improve on the best separating equilibrium. ∎

The notion of Pareto efficiency in theorem 6.3 respects the private-information features of the environment. In particular, when looking for an improvement on the best separating-equilibrium outcome, the planner is not permitted to set each type θ's payment to θ and effort to zero. Like Alice, the planner cannot directly see Bob's type and must infer it from Bob's behavior.

Finally, even though, in Theorem 6.3, the planner can effectively ban signaling by mandating $a(e) = \bar{a}$ for some $\bar{a} \geq 0$ and all $e \geq 0$, this ban cannot be a Pareto improvement on the best separating equilibrium; Alice would be worse off.

The Pitfalls of Laissez-Faire

One may be tempted to surmise that, as a general rule, whenever there is demand for a certain product and someone steps in to supply this product, everyone weakly benefits. Or at least those who demand the product are not worse off. Or, at the very least, the outcome is not Pareto inferior to the original situation. The signaling model proves these conjectures wrong.

Without signaling, Alice has no information about Bob's type and pays him amount $\mathbb{E}[\theta]$. Suppose that Carol, an entrepreneur, steps in and makes a signaling technology freely available. Suppose also that a pooling equilibrium with a positive effort prevails. Then, Alice still has no information about Bob and pays him the same, but Bob now exerts a costly effort. No type of Bob dares to deviate lest he be thought to be type θ_L and be paid amount θ_L instead of $\mathbb{E}[\theta]$. Thus, the introduction of the signaling technology makes Bob worse off and leaves Alice indifferent. A Pareto improvement on the pooling equilibrium can be achieved by banning signaling.

Alternatively, motivated by the intuitive criterion, let us focus on the best separating equilibrium. Alice is better off with signaling than without it because, with it, she learns Bob's type. By contrast, type-θ_L Bob is worse off with the signaling technology; with or without it, he exerts no effort, but with signaling, his payment is lower because Alice correctly identifies him as type θ_L. Moreover, also type-θ_H Bob can be worse off. Even though his payment is higher with signaling than without it, the cost of effort may end up dominating the payment, as in figure 6.5.

To construct an example as in figure 6.5, pick λ to be sufficiently large. That is, the higher the probability that Bob is of the higher type, the more likely it is that Bob will suffer from the availability of a signaling technology that enables him to

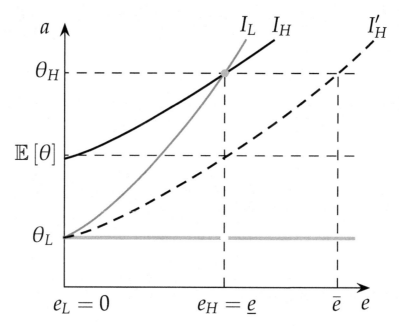

FIGURE 6.5.
The best separating equilibrium: $e_L = 0$ and $e_H = \underline{e}$. Both types of Bob are worse off (type θ_H is barely worse off) at the equilibrium than without signaling; without signaling, each type's effort-payment pair is $(0, \mathbb{E}[\theta])$.

distinguish himself from the lower type. The reason is that, when λ is high, Bob's payment without signaling technology, $\mathbb{E}[\theta]$, is quite close to his payment with the signaling technology, θ_H. The signaling technology motivates Bob to exert effort e_H to avoid being mistaken for type θ_L. Thus, when signaling technology is available, type-θ_H Bob uses it and exerts effort e_H, even though he prefers that signaling technology were unavailable. Nevertheless, banning signaling would not be a Pareto improvement on the best separating equilibrium, for such a ban would hurt Alice.

In a modified model of signaling, however, banning signaling can lead to a Pareto improvement even relative to the best separating equilibrium. In order to see that, assume that Alice has a twin sister, Alice-Prime. As soon as Bob shows up at the door with his gift, Alice and Alice-Prime retire into the kitchen and fight over which one of them will go out with Bob. The sisters continue fighting until they dissipate all the surplus from going out. By the end of fighting, each is so upset that she is really indifferent between remaining at home and going out with Bob. At that point, who goes out is chosen by a coin toss. As a result, in all scenarios, Alice is indifferent between going out with Bob and remaining at home. Then, only Bob's utility affects welfare comparisons. In particular, banning signaling Pareto improves on the best separating equilibrium if each type of Bob is worse off at the best separating equilibrium than without signaling.

To summarize, the fact that a Christmas gift industry emerges in response to the demand for gift giving does not imply that this industry leaves its customers better off.

DISCUSSION

The model assumes that Bob's gift does not directly make Alice more willing to spend time with him. The model can be modified so that Alice would want to spend more time with a higher-type Bob. For instance, Bob's "gift" to Alice can be his investment in his dancing skills. Suppose that type-θ_H Bob finds it easier to learn dancing than type-θ_L Bob does. Then, at a separating equilibrium, Alice would want to spend more time with the Bob who has invested more in his dancing skills not only because he has revealed himself to be type θ_H but also because she enjoys dancing with him. In this modified model, even type-θ_L Bob may choose to exert a positive effort.

A case can be made, however, that, in matters of courtship, Bob may prefer to give gifts that are costly for him but useless for Alice. In order to see this, let us step outside the model and suppose that Alice, too, can be of two types: one who is interested only in dancing with Bob and one who is interested in Bob's company outside the dance floor. Then, by choosing a useless gift over learning to dance, Bob ensures that the Alice who only cares about dancing has no incentive to fake a comprehensive interest in Bob. In this respect, wasted time is an ideal signaling device.

When Bob can be of three types or more, it is natural to conjecture an equilibrium in which every higher type exerts a higher effort than any lower type—as in the best separating equilibrium of the two-type case. Signaling models with such equilibria can indeed be constructed (problem 6.7). One can also construct signaling models in which the described monotonicity fails (problem 6.9). In particular, with three types, in an attempt to **countersignal**, the highest type of Bob may mimic the lowest type, who exerts no effort, and, thus, may leave it to the intermediate type to signal by exerting a positive effort. This countersignaling effect, also known as the **too-cool-for-school** effect, is ubiquitous: college professors dress down compared to management consultants; drivers, not their passengers, wear ties in California; the usage of the word "serviette" for "napkin" is nonmonotone in the social class in the U.K.; more generally, the usage of vocabulary, grammar, and accent can be nonmonotone in the social class.

6.4 CONCLUDING REMARKS

The examples considered in this chapter suggest that what initially seemed but a gut feeling can often be justified on efficiency or equity grounds. It is always a good idea to attempt such a justification lest one be guided by one's unexamined prejudice alone. Besides, it is easier to persuade others by appealing to a handful of shared principles than to impart one's gut feeling in them.

6.5   BIBLIOGRAPHICAL NOTES

Section 6.2 has emerged from reading Sandel (2012) and thinking about the economist's response to his intuitions about the moral limits of markets. Satz (2010) offers a perspective complementary to Sandel's from a philosopher's point of view. Besley (2013), an economist, provides an excellent succinct discussion of, and responses to, Sandel's concerns. (See also Tirole, 2017, chapter 2.) Philosophers Brennan and Jaworski (2015) deliver an erudite critical response to Sandel and Satz. Having reviewed experimental evidence, Bowles (2016) concludes that the relationship between markets and morals is complex and is mediated by the institutions and the social norms that enable, and are enabled by, markets.

Waldfogel (1993) points out that gift-giving is costly because it deprives the gift recipient of choice, and he estimates that between ten percent and a third of the cash value of Christmas gifts is wasted. Camerer (1988) proposes signaling as an explanation for gift giving, which is the economic context for the model in section 6.3. Spence (1973a) discusses wasted time's virtues in signaling.

The analysis in section 6.3 follows closely the presentation of Mas-Colell, Whinston, and Green (1995, section 13.C) of Spence's (1973b) seminal model of signaling. The main difference is that, in the model of Mas-Colell et al., Bob's signal is interpreted by competitive firms, each of which bids for Bob's services and seeks to maximize its profit. By contrast, in section 6.3, Bob's signal is interpreted by a lone receiver, Alice, who seeks to match Bob's type. The difference in formulations leads to differences in welfare implications; the conclusion of theorem 6.3 does not hold in the setting of Mas-Colell et al. (see the discussion surrounding their figure 13.C.1, p. 458).

Problem 6.1 is inspired by the observation of Posner (2000, chapter 6) that, in some communities, criminal conviction may serve as a badge of honor, conferring social status on the perpetrator. Problem 6.2 is based on a suggestion of Oyer (2014). The focus on the continuum of types in part 3 of problem 6.7 is shared with problem 13.C.4 of Mas-Colell et al. (1995). Problem 6.9 is inspired by Feltovich, Harbaugh, and To (2002). The incident in part 6 of problem 6.9 is recounted by Winter (2014).

PROBLEMS

Problem 6.1 (Crime and Punishment).   The government gradually increases the punishment for petty crime. As a result, petty crime at first rises and then falls. Using only the model of signaling, explain, verbally and then formally, why this may occur.

Problem 6.2 (Signaling in Online Dating). Suppose that online dating sites (e.g., OkCupid.com® or Match.com®) were to let each member signal his interest in a potential date by making a costly gift to a charity of his choice. Assess this proposal in the context of the signaling model.

Problem 6.3 (Virtue Signaling). The government wants to encourage shoppers to forgo plastic bags, which are believed to be harmful to the environment. To this end, the government requires supermarkets to charge a small fee for each plastic bag. As a result, the demand for plastic bags surges. Using only the signaling model, explain, verbally and then formally, why this may occur.

Problem 6.4 (Amazon Gift Cards). It is 11:12pm, Sunday, and your phone rings. It is Jeff Bezos and he needs advice. Amazon has just issued a series of gift cards, and they sell badly. The cards come with tag lines such as "I respect you enough not to base your holiday gift on my taste," or "Here is a gift card because we both know you're a better shopper than me," or "I've got you this card because I want you to get exactly what you want for Christmas and because I'm lazy," or "I have put a lot of thought into picking a gift that requires you to pick your own gift."[10] Explain to Jeff why these gift cards might not sell as well as Amazon's marketing department had predicted.

Problem 6.5 (Signaling Design). Suppose that Carol can design for Bob (who signals Alice) any signaling technology—that is, any cost function $c : \mathbb{R}_+ \times \{\theta_L, \theta_H\} \to \mathbb{R}_+$.

1. How would you define the best signaling technology? For whom is this technology best?

2. Find a signaling technology, c, that is the best according to your definition in part 1.

3. Suppose that Carol's design problem is restricted to choosing parameter $\gamma \geq 0$ in the cost-of-effort function $c(e, \theta) \equiv \gamma\, e/\theta$. What is the optimal value of γ?

Problem 6.6 (Informed Principal). Any signaling equilibrium studied in this chapter can be construed as a self-enforcing agreement, proposed by Carol, an outsider with no private information about Bob, to Alice and Bob. Why not let Bob propose a self-enforcing agreement to Alice? What complications can arise if Bob is designated to propose a self-enforcing agreement to Alice? Explain why the same complications do not arise if Alice proposes a self-enforcing agreement to Bob. Do not impose the intuitive criterion; otherwise, the set of self-enforcing agreements will be a singleton.

---

10. These are actual tag lines as seen on amazon.com® in 2014.

"Only the rich can afford this much nothing."

FIGURE 6.6.

Source: Mick Stevens, *The New Yorker* Collection, www.cartoonbank.com.

Problem 6.7 (Many Types). The signaling technology is given by the cost function $c(e, \theta) = e/\theta$, where $e \geq 0$ is effort, and θ is a type from a set $\Theta \subset \mathbb{R}_{++}$ of all possible types.

1. Assuming that $\Theta = \{\theta_L, \theta_H\}$ with $0 < \theta_L < \theta_H$, solve for the best separating equilibrium.

2. Assuming that $\Theta = \{\theta_1, \theta_2, \ldots, \theta_I\}$ for $0 < \theta_L = \theta_1 < \theta_2 < \cdots < \theta_I = \theta_H$, $I \geq 3$, solve for the best separating equilibrium.

3. Assuming that $\Theta = [\theta_L, \theta_H]$ with $0 < \theta_L < \theta_H$ (i.e., there is a continuum of types), solve for the best separating equilibrium.

4. Compare the efforts exerted by type θ_H in each of the problem's parts above. Interpret your answer.

5. How do your answers depend on the probability distribution of the types in Θ?

Problem 6.8 (Being in Nothingness). In the context of the signaling model, explain the cartoon in figure 6.6.

Problem 6.9 (Too-Cool-for-School, or Countersignaling). Bob's type $\theta \in \Theta \equiv \{\theta_L, \theta_H, \theta_X\}$ is his private information and is either low (θ_L), high (θ_H), or extra high (θ_X), where

$0 < \theta_L < \theta_H < \theta_X$. The commonly known probability that Alice attaches to Bob's type being $\theta \in \Theta$ is $\lambda_\theta \in (0, 1)$, where $\sum_{\theta \in \Theta} \lambda_\theta = 1$. Bob's signaling technology is given by the cost function $c(e, \theta) = e/\theta$, where $e \geq 0$ is Bob's effort. Alice's utility from meeting type-θ Bob and paying him a is $-(a - \theta)^2$, where, as before, a is interpreted as the amount of time Alice spends with Bob. Bob's utility from meeting Alice is $a - c(e, \theta)$. Each agent is an expected utility maximizer.

So far, the environment is as in the two-type model except that Bob is one of three types. The model's another novel element is Carol, Bob's former girlfriend. Having spent time with Bob, Carol has learned something about his type. In particular, if Bob's type is θ_L, Carol believes that Bob is "naughty." If Bob's type is θ_X, Carol believes that Bob is "nice." If Bob's type is θ_H, then, with probability $p \in (0, 1)$, Carol believes he is naughty and, with probability $1 - p$, she believes he is nice.

Here is the timeline:

- At time $t = 0$, Alice can privately meet Carol and learn whether, in Carol's opinion, Bob is naughty or nice.

- At time $t = 1$, Bob exerts an effort $e \geq 0$ at the cost $c(e, \theta)$.

- At time $t = 2$, Alice meets Bob, observes his effort e, and pays him an $a \geq 0$.

- At time $t = 3$, Alice's and Bob's utilities are realized.

1. Assuming that Alice does not meet Carol at time $t = 0$ and that Bob knows that Alice does not meet Carol, solve for the best separating equilibrium. In your answer, provide and motivate the definition of the best separating equilibrium in the three-type environment.

2. Assuming that Alice meets Carol at time $t = 0$ and learns whether Bob is naughty or nice and that Bob knows that Alice meets Carol but does not know what Alice learns, identify the conditions on the model's parameters for which there exists a so-called **countersignaling** (or **too-cool-for-school**) **equilibrium**, in which the efforts exerted by Bob's types θ_L, θ_H, and θ_X are $e_L = 0$, $e_H > 0$, and $e_X = 0$, respectively. Why is this equilibrium called "countersignaling"?

3. Assuming that Alice meets Carol at time $t = 0$ and learns whether Bob is naughty or nice and that Bob knows that Alice meets Carol but does not know what Alice learns, identify the conditions on $(\lambda_L, \lambda_H, \lambda_X, p)$ under which there exists a (so-called **semi-pooling**) signaling equilibrium in which the efforts exerted by types θ_L, θ_H, and θ_X are $e_L = 0$, $e_H > 0$, and $e_X = e_H$, respectively. (You can identify numerically the parameter values for which a semi-pooling equilibrium exists.)

4. Define the intuitive criterion. Do the equilibria in parts 2 and 3 survive the intuitive criterion?

5. Would Alice be better off if she could publicly commit not to discuss Bob with Carol? Would Bob be better off?

6. In 1970s, Golda Meir, then the Israeli prime minister, reproached a U.S. diplomat, who had just given a speech in Jerusalem: "You shouldn't be so humble; you are not so great." Discuss Golda Meir's remark in the context of the countersignaling model.

CHAPTER 7

KANTIAN COOPERATION

7.1   INTRODUCTION

In just over eight hundred printed pages, Pinker (2011) makes a case for the unprecedented decline in violence since the Enlightenment. Whether one looks at the percentage of the world population exterminated in violent conflicts, the percentage of time the great powers fought each other, or the frequency and the duration of wars, recorded violence has declined.[1] Violence has declined even though the technology for inflicting it has improved. For evidence on violent tendencies in individuals, one can consult the data on the decline of domestic violence in the last half a century (figure 7.1a) and on the rising awareness of human and animal rights (figure 7.1b).

Simple evidence for the reduction in the demand for violence is accessible through introspection. Would you rather watch a YouTube video of Nora the Piano Cat improvise at the piano or go out into the town square and witness a dozen cats

---

1. While historical records—naturally—reveal actual deaths, the historical evolution of expected deaths is of greater relevance for forecasting. The post-WWII peace in Europe may have been just luck. The risk of a nuclear war might have been rising as the sophistication of the nuclear arsenal of the U.S. and the U.S.S.R. had been rising. In the words of General George Lee Butler, "We escaped the Cold War without a nuclear holocaust by some combination of skill, luck, and divine intervention, and I suspect the latter in greatest proportion." (See Menand, Louis. "Nukes of Hazard." *The New Yorker*, September 30, 2013, for the quotation and Wikipedia's entry "List of military nuclear accidents" for a list of accidents.)

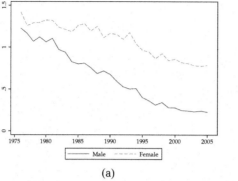
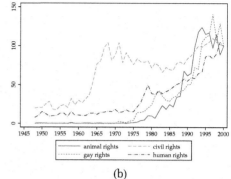

(a)   (b)

FIGURE 7.1.

(a) Homicides of intimate partners per 100,000 men or women per year in the United States, 1976–2005. *Source*: the same as figure 7–14 of Pinker (2011).

(b) The use of rights-related terms in English-language books, years 1948–2000, as percentage of 2000 level. *Source*: the same as figure 7–1 of Pinker (2011).

lowered slowly in a net over a bonfire to burn in agony? Eighteenth century Parisians found great amusement in the latter. Should your preference lie with the former, something must have changed in the attitudes toward violence since then. What could that be? Here are some possibilities:

- Individual preferences have evolved to become more prosocial, less sadistic. Even though not enough time has elapsed for natural selection to fundamentally alter human nature, within an individual's life span, preferences can be discovered and shaped by reason and exercise. Addiction is a good example. One can hate one's first cigarette but crave the fifteenth. Through practice, one can become addicted to problem-solving (such as crossword puzzles, math riddles, or computer programming). Similarly, through exposure, one may develop a taste for violence the way one develops a taste for spicy food. By contrast, if brought up in peace, one may never get a chance to discover and develop one's taste for violence.

- Institutions have improved. Institutions' conflict-reducing capacity (i.e., the tendency to promote Pareto efficient outcomes) has made exchange more attractive relative to plunder.

- Wealth has increased. Wealthier individuals stand to lose more from a conflict. In addition, individual preferences may be such that the demand for violence declines in wealth (problem 7.1).

- Individuals have become more connected. As a result, because observable well and by many, reputation for fair dealing has become more valuable and fair dealing more common. For instance, the threat of the exclusion from future trades motivates a borrower to repay his debt. The rise of credit scores (e.g., FICO) has made such a threat ever more powerful.

- Social norms have changed to become more enlightened, inspired by the ideals of the European Enlightenment and, in particular, by the values of humanism.

The model in this chapter focuses on the last point: the conflict-reducing capacity (i.e., the tendency toward Pareto efficiency) of the social norms of the Enlightenment. Immanuel Kant's categorical imperative is an instance of such a norm. Kant's **categorical imperative** (Kant, 1993, p. 30) enjoins:[2]

> Act only according to that maxim whereby you can at the same time will that it should become a universal law.

The imperative urges one to use one's own utility function to judge the goodness of the universal law implied by one's action. The rule is quite simple in that one is not required to imagine what it feels like to have someone else's utility function. One need not be able to empathize. (Or need one?)

To operationalize the categorical imperative, recall that, according to each equilibrium concept that we have considered so far (viz. Walrasian, jungle, or signaling), each agent chooses an action to maximize his utility while taking other agents' actions and (if any) prices as given and fixed at their equilibrium values. By contrast, in Kantian equilibrium, each agent chooses an action that maximizes his utility under the **Kantian counterfactual**: the assumption that all others whom one regards as "similar" would mimic one's action in an "analogous" manner. More precisely, we define a Kantian equilibrium as the action profile such that no agent wishes to scale his action assuming that everyone else who is similar to him would scale his action by the same amount. The assumption that the profitability of one's deviation from equilibrium ought to be assessed as though it also affected others' actions is the social norm captured by Kantian equilibrium.

Because different agents can have different utility functions, it is not at all clear:

1. whether an action profile that is logically consistent (in the sense of no agent wishing to revise his action given others' actions) can emerge; and

2. whether the emergent action profile (if logically consistent) would lead to a normatively compelling outcome.

---

2. The categorical imperative appears to be a somewhat clearer, somewhat more comprehensive formulation of the **Golden Rule**: Do as you would be done by.

Formally, one may wonder

1. whether a Kantian equilibrium exists; and

2. whether a Kantian equilibrium (if it exists) is Pareto efficient.

Remarkably, in some settings, both questions can be answered in the affirmative.

7.2 KANTIAN EQUILIBRIUM

AN ECONOMY WITH EXTERNALITIES

The set of agents is $\mathcal{I} \equiv \{1, 2, \dots, I\}$, with typical elements i and j. Each agent i takes an action $x^i \in \mathbb{R}_+$, which is interpreted as his effort. Everyone else's actions are denoted by $x^{-i} \equiv (x^1, \dots, x^{i-1}, x^{i+1}, \dots, x^I)$. A **feasible** action profile, or allocation, is $x \equiv (x^1, x^2, \dots, x^I) \in \mathbb{R}_+^I$. Agent i's payoff is $u^i(x^i, x^{-i})$; there are externalities in the sense that each agent's utility depends not only on his choice of effort but also on others' choices.

The model is not Walrasian. There is no a priori reason to expect utility maximization by each agent to deliver an efficient outcome, à la the FWT.

The model admits rich interpretations. An agent can be a driver, affected by his own and other drivers' efforts to get to work on time. An agent can be a household that exerts an effort to recycle. Or an agent can be a member of a team whose members' efforts generate output that is distributed to the team's members according to some sharing rule.

KANTIAN EQUILIBRIUM

The standard equilibrium notion for this model is Nash equilibrium. Analogously to all the equilibrium notions considered so far, at a Nash equilibrium, each agent takes other agents' actions as given.

Definition 7.1. An action profile x is a **Nash equilibrium** if, for each agent $i \in \mathcal{I}$,

$$u^i(x^i, x^{-i}) = \max_{y^i \in \mathbb{R}_+} u^i(y^i, x^{-i}).$$

There is no FWT analogue for Nash equilibrium; examples in which no Nash equilibrium is Pareto efficient abound. In this chapter, we focus on an environment in which Nash equilibria lead to inefficient outcomes and ask whether the agents would be better off if they followed Kantian reasoning instead.

Definition 7.2. An action profile x is a **Kantian equilibrium** if, for each agent $i \in \mathcal{I}$,

$$u^i(x^i, x^{-i}) = \max_{a \geq 0} u^i(ax^i, ax^{-i}).$$

A Kantian equilibrium is **trivial** if $x = (0, 0, \ldots, 0)$ and is **nontrivial** otherwise.

Kantian equilibrium requires that no agent i be able to gain by deviating from his equilibrium action and toward some other action supposing that everyone else deviates analogously in the sense of scaling his action by the same factor as agent i does. This scaling addresses the problem of defining an analogous deviation for the agents other than agent i when agents' utilities differ, and so, say, identical actions taken by different agents are not necessarily analogous in any intuitive sense. Even when utilities are the same, if a candidate equilibrium profile x were asymmetric (i.e., $x^i \neq x^j$ for some $i, j \in \mathcal{I}$), one may not wish to define as analogous the deviation to the same action because, then, a tiny deviation by agent i might require—quite arbitrarily—a substantial deviation by agent j. The fact that an analogous deviation is defined as a proportional change in effort is arbitrary but, perhaps, natural in some circumstances, especially when it is known to lead to good equilibrium outcomes.[3]

In definition 7.2, the set of similar others—the agents who one imagines mimic one's deviations—is taken to be the set of all agents. The definition can be modified in an obvious manner to make the sets of similar others different for different agents (see section 7.3 and problem 7.5).

Without additional assumptions on utility functions, neither Nash nor nontrivial Kantian equilibrium is guaranteed to exist.[4] The guaranteed existence of the trivial Kantian equilibrium is an artifact of the assumption that each agent contemplates only proportional analogous deviations. However, any Kantian equilibrium with zero effort even for just one agent is already suspect because it strains the plausibility of the proportional analogous deviation. If only Alice's effort is zero, then her deviation consists in imagining that she keeps her effort unchanged and varies others', including Bob's, efforts, while Bob's deviation consists in imagining that Alice is exempt from covarying her effort with his. Hence, the focus is on nontrivial Kantian equilibria with $x \gg 0$.[5] Because we postpone stating the

---

3. Alternatively, an analogous deviation could be defined to be additive. With additive deviations, an allocation x is a Kantian equilibrium if, for each agent $i \in \mathcal{I}$, $u^i(x^i, x^{-i}) = \max_{a \in \mathbb{R}} u^i(x^i + a, x^{-i} + (a, \ldots, a))$ subject to the correction that everyone's deviant effort remain nonnegative.

4. For instance, if $u^i(x^i, x^{-i}) = \sum_{j \in \mathcal{I}} x^j$ for each $i \in \mathcal{I}$, then neither Nash nor nontrivial Kantian equilibrium exists.

5. If $x = (0, 0, \ldots, 0)$ is a Nash equilibrium, it is not regarded as implausible, for no agent is constrained in his deviations in a manner that would seem arbitrary.

condition for equilibrium existence, the subsequent statements about nontrivial Kantian equilibria are vacuous when no such equilibria exist.

EFFICIENCY

The definition of Pareto efficiency is the familiar one. An effort profile x is **Pareto efficient** if no other feasible effort profile $\hat{x}$ satisfies $u^i(\hat{x}^i, \hat{x}^{-i}) \geq u^i(x^i, x^{-i})$ for each agent i, with the inequality being strict for some i. Theorem 7.1 shows that, under some conditions, Kantian equilibrium delivers a Pareto efficient outcome.

To appreciate the theorem's significance, let us first observe that, under the same conditions, Nash equilibrium outcomes are not efficient. To this end, assume that either each function u^i is strictly increasing in each component of x^{-i} (the case of **positive externalities**) or each function u^i is strictly decreasing in each component of x^{-i} (the case of **negative externalities**).

Let $x \gg 0$ be a Nash equilibrium. Assuming differentiability, consider the rate at which agent i's utility changes if every agent adjusts his effort by some amount ε that is close to zero but is not zero and can be positive or negative:

$$\frac{du^i(x^i + \varepsilon, x^{-i} + (\varepsilon, \varepsilon, \ldots, \varepsilon))}{d\varepsilon}\bigg|_{\varepsilon=0} = \frac{\partial u^i(x^i, x^{-i})}{\partial x^i} + \sum_{j \neq i} \frac{\partial u^i(x^i, x^{-i})}{\partial x^j},$$

$$= \sum_{j \neq i} \frac{\partial u^i(x^i, x^{-i})}{\partial x^j} \neq 0.$$

In the display above, the second equality follows from the fact that, at the Nash equilibrium, x^i maximizes agent i's payoff, and, hence, the first-order condition for optimality holds: $\partial u^i(x^i, x^{-i})/\partial x^i = 0$. The unequal sign follows from the assumption that u^i is either strictly increasing or strictly decreasing in each component of x^{-i}, so that the derivatives in the sum all have the same sign. Thus, each agent can be made strictly better off if every agent's action is either slightly increased (if the externalities are positive) or slightly decreased (if the externalities are negative) away from the Nash equilibrium. To summarize, under the maintained assumptions on externalities, if $x \gg 0$ is a Nash equilibrium, then x is not Pareto efficient.

Theorem 7.1 is a counterpart of the FWT for Kantian equilibrium.

Theorem 7.1 (Kantian Welfare Theorem). *Suppose that externalities are either all positive or all negative. Then, any Kantian equilibrium x with $x \gg 0$ is Pareto efficient.*

Proof. Consider the case of positive externalities.

By contradiction, suppose that some allocation $\hat{x}$ Pareto dominates x.

Let i denote an agent (not necessarily unique) whose action in $\hat{x}$ is proportionately the greatest relative to his action in x:

$$i \in \arg\max_{j \in \mathcal{I}} \left\{ \frac{\hat{x}^j}{x^j} \right\},$$

where the maximand is well-defined because $x \gg 0$ by the theorem's hypothesis. Denote this agent i's factor of proportionality by r:

$$r \equiv \max_{j \in \mathcal{I}} \left\{ \frac{\hat{x}^j}{x^j} \right\}. \tag{7.1}$$

It will be shown that agent i's deviation away from x and toward rx is profitable, thereby contradicting x being a Kantian equilibrium.

For the switch from x to rx to constitute a deviation to begin with, it must be that $r \neq 1$. By contradiction, suppose that $r = 1$. Then, $x^i = \hat{x}^i$ and, by (7.1) and $x \neq \hat{x}$, $x^{-i} > \hat{x}^{-i}$. In this case, because the externality is positive, $u^i(x^i, x^{-i}) > u^i(\hat{x}^i, \hat{x}^{-i})$ (i.e., agent i prefers x to $\hat{x}$), thereby contradicting the hypothesis that $\hat{x}$ Pareto dominates x.

Because x is a Kantian equilibrium, $rx \neq \hat{x}$ or else some agent who prefers $\hat{x}$ to x (and such an agent must exist because $\hat{x}$ Pareto dominates x) would have profitably deviated from x to rx. Then, $rx \neq \hat{x}$ and, moreover, by (7.1), $rx > \hat{x}$.

The profitability of agent i's deviation to rx can now be established. Because $rx^i = \hat{x}^i$ and $rx > \hat{x}$, it must be that $rx^{-i} > \hat{x}^{-i}$. Then, because externality is positive, $u^i(rx^i, rx^{-i}) > u^i(\hat{x}^i, \hat{x}^{-i})$. Finally, because $\hat{x}$ Pareto dominates x, $u^i(\hat{x}^i, \hat{x}^{-i}) \geq u^i(x^i, x^{-i})$. The preceding two inequalities combine to yield

$$u^i(rx^i, rx^{-i}) > u^i(x^i, x^{-i}).$$

That is, rx constitutes a profitable deviation for agent i, in contradiction to the theorem's premise that x is a Kantian equilibrium. Therefore, the contradiction hypothesis must be false; no allocation $\hat{x}$ can Pareto dominate x.

An analogous argument can also be used to show that x is Pareto efficient in the case of negative externalities. ∎

Theorem 7.1 puts no restrictions on the dependence of any u^i on x^i, the agent's own effort. In applications, u^i can be increasing in x^i at first (not necessarily because the agent likes exerting effort per se but because the benefit from exerting effort exceeds the cost, both implicit in u^i) and then decreasing (as the implicit cost of effort comes to dominate the implicit benefit).

The case of positive externalities captures, for instance, the situation in which greater labor supply by others translates into higher income tax receipts that are used to provide a good that everyone enjoys (e.g., national defense, police, universal basic education, or healthcare). The case of negative externalities can model the so-called **tragedy of the commons**, as when one's higher effort earns one a higher social status, which is relative and, so, adversely affects the status of others.

Theorem 7.1 shows that Kantian equilibrium delivers efficiency but is mute as to whether modifications of Kantian equilibrium that rely on deviations other than proportional ones would also deliver efficiency. It can be shown that efficiency results are indeed sensitive to the form of the contemplated Kantian deviation.

The Kantian agent whom we study is selfish. He cares about others' actions only if they affect him directly, not because he cares about others' well-being. One may wonder whether the efficiency properties of Kantian equilibrium are preserved in the presence of other-regarding preferences. Problem 7.6 investigates.

EXISTENCE

By appealing to the fixed-point ideas developed in section 1.13, theorem 7.2 shows that a Kantian equilibrium exists under some conditions.

Theorem 7.2. *Suppose that, for every agent i, u^i is continuous and strictly concave. For every $i \in \mathcal{I}$ and any $x \gg 0$, let $a^i(x)$ denote agent i's optimal Kantian-deviation factor at the effort profile x:[6]*

$$a^i(x) \equiv \arg \max_{\alpha \geq 0} u^i(\alpha x^i, \alpha x^{-i}).$$

Suppose that there exist bounds b and B, with $0 < b < B < \infty$, such that, for any $x \in \mathbb{R}_+^I$, $b \leq x^i \leq B$ for all $i \in \mathcal{I}$ implies $b \leq a^i(x)x^i \leq B$ for all $i \in \mathcal{I}$. Then, a Kantian equilibrium x^* with $x^* \gg 0$ exists.

Proof. Define a function $f : \mathbb{R}_{++}^I \rightarrow \mathbb{R}_{++}^I$ by

$$f(x) \equiv (a^1(x)x^1, a^2(x)x^2, \ldots, a^I(x)x^I). \tag{7.2}$$

By the theorem's hypothesis, f maps the rectangle $S \equiv \{x \in \mathbb{R}^I \mid (\forall i \in \mathcal{I})(b \leq x^i \leq B)\}$ into itself; that is, $x \in S \implies f(x) \in S$.

For every $i \in \mathcal{I}$, the Theorem of the Maximum implies that a^i is a continuous function,[7] and, hence, f is also a continuous (vector-valued) function. Then,

---

6. Because u^i is strictly concave, $a^i(x)$ is unique if it exists. Existence is an additional, implicit assumption on u^i.

7. The Theorem of the Maximum establishes the upper hemicontinuity of a^i the correspondence, which is equivalent to continuity in the special case in which a^i is a function, as here.

Brouwer's fixed-point theorem (theorem 1.6) implies that f has a fixed point. That is, there exists an $x^* \in S$ such that $x^* = f(x^*)$, or, equivalently, for each agent $i \in \mathcal{I}$, $\alpha^i(x^*) = 1$, and, so, x^* is a Kantian equilibrium. ∎

The assumption of strict concavity in theorem 7.2 is plausible in some applications. What is controversial is the hypothesis that bounds the values of $\alpha^i(x)x^i$. These bounds are not a condition on the primitives and, so, are hard to check. Hypotheses such as this one must generally be avoided. Nevertheless, part 2 of problem 7.3 illustrates that the theorem can be useful for establishing existence in examples.

CONVERGENCE

The function f defined in (7.2) can be used to study the stability of Kantian equilibria. Define the **Kantian best-response process** as a sequence $\{x^{[r]} \mid r \in \{0, 1, 2, \dots\}\}$ of action profiles $x^{[r]} \gg 0$ such that, for each $r \in \{1, 2, \dots\}$, $x^{[r]} = f(x^{[r-1]})$. For each initial action profile $x^{[0]}$, one can ask whether $\lim_{r \to \infty} x^{[r]}$ exists and, if so, whether it converges to a Kantian equilibrium. In words, one can ask whether the best response to the best response to the best response—and so on—to any initial effort profile converges.

This investigation is similar in spirit to the study of Walrasian equilibrium stability under Walrasian tâtonnement. A priori, without additional assumptions, there is no reason to suspect convergence. The voting model of section 7.3 illustrates both stability and instability of Kantian equilibria.

DISCUSSION

A remarkable feature of Kantian equilibrium is that it delivers efficient outcomes even though agents are **nonempathetic**: when contemplating deviations, each agent consults only his own utility function and may be completely oblivious to others' utility functions. That is, Kantian ethics (in contrast, say, to choice behind the veil of ignorance) promotes efficiency even though it does not require the knowledge of others' preferences.

Even though each agent's utility-maximization problem does not require the knowledge of others' preferences, the information about these preferences is already built into the candidate Kantian equilibrium allocation, with respect to which the agent contemplates deviations. The candidate allocation is recommended by others' optimal decisions, which are informed by their utility functions. The situation resembles an agent's problem in a Walrasian equilibrium. There, even though, when choosing his consumption bundle, an agent need not know others' preferences, these preferences are already embedded in the prices that define the agent's budget set. Just as Walrasian equilibrium is silent about the process that embeds the information about everyone's preferences into prices, Kantian equilibrium is silent about the process that embeds the information about everyone's preferences into the Kantian equilibrium allocation.

Furthermore, while nonempathetic agents can successfully follow a Kantian protocol, empathy is required to design this protocol well. In particular, empathy is required to design the Kantian counterfactuals that would lead to good—say, Pareto efficient—outcomes. (**Empathy** here means the knowledge of others' utilities, not the dependence of one's own utility on others' utilities, which would be more appropriately called "sympathy.")

Here is an example with just two actions, which makes it natural to define an analogous deviation as a deviation to the same action (instead of a proportional deviation). Kantians Alice and Bob are on a road trip. On long drives, Alice loves singing and loves it even more when Bob sings. Bob loves singing, too, but hates it when Alice sings. For a nonempathetic Alice, the natural thing to do is to ask herself whether she would rather sing and hear Bob sing or have both of them remain silent. She prefers the former and, so, sings. Similarly, a nonempathetic Bob asks himself whether he would rather sing and be subjected to Alice's singing or enjoy silence. He prefers the latter and, so, remains silent. Thus, the Kantian equilibrium outcome is inefficient; each would be better off if Alice were silent while Bob sang.[8]

Empathetic Alice and Bob might formulate their Kantian counterfactuals differently. Alice would ask herself: Would I rather do what Bob loves me to do (i.e., remain silent) if Bob did what I love him to do (i.e., sing), or would I rather sing while he remains silent? Alice chooses the former. Bob asks himself the analogous question: Would I prefer to do what Alice loves me to do (i.e., sing) if Alice did what I love her to do (i.e., remain silent), or would I rather remain silent while she sings? Bob chooses the former. The identified Kantian equilibrium outcome is Pareto efficient, now that the Kantian protocol has been modified.

7.3   AN APPLICATION TO VOTING

Nash reasoning is at a loss to explain why, in large populations, individuals show up to vote. Surely, they cannot hope to be pivotal with any nonnegligible probability. If so, why bother? By contrast, Kantian reasoning favors voting.

THE VOTING PARADOX
Assume two parties, Republicans (R) and Democrats (D), indexed by (type) $t \in \{R, D\}$. There is a continuum of agents, indexed by $i \in \mathcal{I} \equiv [0, 1]$, of whom agents in $\mathcal{I}_R = [0, I_R]$ are Republicans and agents in $\mathcal{I}_D = (I_R, 1]$ are Democrats, for some

---

8. Because the example involves binary actions, it does not fit this chapter's model. Nevertheless, the example carries the model's spirit. In particular, because the externality from singing is neither positive nor negative (Alice and Bob disagree on whether they enjoy hearing the other one sing), the logic of theorem 7.1 does not suggest Pareto efficiency. The following paragraph redefines the agents' actions so that, in these new actions, the externalities are positive and the theorem's logic carries over.

$I_R \in (0, 1)$. Thus, the measure (or fraction) of Republicans is I_R and the measure of Democrats is $I_D \equiv 1 - I_R$.

Type-t voter i who exerts effort x^i makes it to the voting booth with "probability" $\phi(x^i)$, whereupon he casts his vote for party t. (If he does not make it to the voting booth, he does not vote.) The function $\phi : \mathbb{R}_+ \to \mathbb{R}_+$ is smooth, strictly increasing, and satisfies $\phi(0) = 0$. When $\phi(x^i) > 1$ (which can be ruled out at equilibrium if ϕ is "sufficiently concave"), "probability" $\phi(x^i)$ is interpreted to mean that not only does voter i show up to vote himself, but he also brings along his friends (swing voters, outside the set $\mathcal{I}$), whom he convinces to vote for his party.

When v_R and v_D are the measures of votes cast for, respectively, Republicans and Democrats, a type-t voter's benefit is $B(v_t, v_{-t})$. Assume that function B is smooth, strictly increasing in its first argument, and strictly decreasing in its second argument. Voter i's cost of exerting effort x^i is cx^i, for some $c > 0$. Then, the utility function of type-t voter i is

$$u^i(x^i, x^{-i}) \equiv B\left(\int_{\mathcal{I}_t} \phi(x^j) \mathrm{d}j, \int_{\mathcal{I}_{-t}} \phi(x^j) \mathrm{d}j \right) - cx^i.$$

Because each voter is negligible, there is a unique Nash equilibrium, with $x = 0$; no voter shows up to vote. Indeed, no individual voter's choice affects the aggregate measure of votes cast for either party; a positive measure of voters must change their efforts for the aggregates to be affected. The existence of the unique Nash equilibrium, at which no one votes, is the **voting paradox**: If voting is costly and the probability of being pivotal is negligible, then why does anyone vote in practice?

KANTIAN EQUILIBRIUM

Kantian reasoning resolves the voting paradox. Assume that a type-t voter reasons: "If I double my effort of getting to the voting booth, then every type-t voter will do so, too. Would I like that?" That is, in his Kantian counterfactual, the agent identifies only with the voters of the same party, not all voters. In this case, x is a Kantian equilibrium in the described voting problem if, for each type $t \in \{R, D\}$ and every voter $i \in \mathcal{I}_t$,

$$1 \in \arg\max_{\alpha \geq 0} \left\{ B\left(\int_{\mathcal{I}_t} \phi(\alpha x^j) \mathrm{d}j, \int_{\mathcal{I}_{-t}} \phi(x^j) \mathrm{d}j \right) - c\alpha x^i \right\}. \tag{7.3}$$

The Kantian equilibrium in (7.3) modifies the equilibrium of definition 7.2 by assuming that each agent recognizes as similar others only the supporters of the same party, instead of all voters.

Conjecture a symmetric Kantian equilibrium in which every type-t voter i exerts effort $x^i = z_t$ for some $z_t > 0$. Then, equilibrium condition (7.3) becomes

$$1 \in \arg\max_{\alpha \geq 0} \{ B(I_t \phi(\alpha z_t), I_{-t} \phi(z_{-t})) - c\alpha z_t \}, \quad t \in \{R, D\}.$$

Note that seeking a z_t at which $\alpha = 1$ is optimal is equivalent to setting $\alpha = 1$ and seeking an optimal z_t. Thus, any symmetric Kantian equilibrium is equivalent to a Nash equilibrium in which all members of the same party cooperatively choose a shared effort level. Consequently, an effort pair (z_R, z_D) captures a symmetric Kantian equilibrium if, for each type $t \in \{R, D\}$,

$$z_t \in \arg\max_{y_t \geq 0}\{B(I_t\phi(y_t), I_{-t}\phi(z_{-t})) - cy_t\}. \tag{7.4}$$

It can be shown that the maximization problem in the display above implies that, if unique and positive, type-t voters' best response to the opposing voters' effort z_{-t} is decreasing in c, decreasing in both I_{-t} and z_{-t} if $B_{12} < 0$, increasing in both I_{-t} and z_{-t} if $B_{12} > 0$, and increasing in I_t if $B_{11} \geq 0$.[9,10]

EQUILIBRIUM IN AN EXAMPLE

To arrive at an explicit characterization of a Kantian equilibrium, the analysis will be performed under the assumptions of example 7.1, which is our leading example for the rest of this section.

Example 7.1. Let $B(v_t, v_{-t}) \equiv v_t/v_{-t}$ and $\phi(x^i) \equiv (x^i)^\gamma$ for some $\gamma \in (0, 1)$ with $\gamma \neq \frac{1}{2}$. $\triangle$

Under the assumptions of example 7.1, condition (7.4) holds that (z_R, z_R) is a Kantian equilibrium if

$$z_t \in \arg\max_{y_t \geq 0}\left\{\left(\frac{y_t}{z_{-t}}\right)^\gamma \frac{I_t}{I_{-t}} - cy_t\right\}, \quad t \in \{R, D\}.$$

Type-t voters' best response to the opposing voters' effort z_{-t} is denoted by $Z_t(z_{-t})$:

$$Z_t(z_{-t}) \equiv \left(\frac{\gamma I_t}{cI_{-t}}\right)^{\frac{1}{1-\gamma}} z_{-t}^{-\frac{\gamma}{1-\gamma}}. \tag{7.5}$$

An equilibrium effort pair (z_R, z_D) solves the system comprised of $z_R = Z_R(z_D)$ and $z_D = Z_D(z_R)$. The solution,

$$(z_R, z_D) = \left(\frac{\gamma}{c}\left(\frac{I_R}{I_D}\right)^{\frac{1}{1-2\gamma}}, \frac{\gamma}{c}\left(\frac{I_D}{I_R}\right)^{\frac{1}{1-2\gamma}}\right),$$

9. The subscripts of B denote partial derivatives.

10. One way to see the described comparative statics is to make additional, concavity, assumptions on B and ϕ and apply the Implicit Function Theorem to type-t voters' first-order condition for the optimality of their joint voting effort. Another way is to invoke the so-called robust comparative statics (Milgrom and Shannon, 1994).

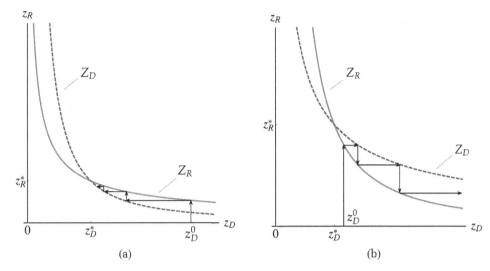

FIGURE 7.2.

Kantian best-response functions Z_R and Z_D for $I_D > I_R$. The unique Kantian equilibrium is (z_R^*, z_D^*). The best-response process begins at an initial effort z_D^0 of Democrats.

(a) When $\gamma < \frac{1}{2}$, the best-response process converges to the Kantian equilibrium, which, therefore, is stable.

(b) When $\gamma > \frac{1}{2}$, the best-response process diverges from the Kantian equilibrium, which, therefore, is unstable.

is positive in each component. Kantian voters exert the effort to show up to vote because they do not view themselves as infinitesimal. Instead, by virtue of being Kantian, they act as a group.

Figure 7.2 illustrates each party's best response and the induced Kantian equilibria for two cases: $\gamma < \frac{1}{2}$ and $\gamma > \frac{1}{2}$. An equilibrium occurs wherever the two best-response functions intersect. When $\gamma < \frac{1}{2}$, the equilibrium is stable in the following sense. Begin with an arbitrary initial effort of Democrats. Let Republicans best respond to it, according to (7.5). Then let Democrats best respond to the Republicans' best response. Then let Republicans best respond to the Democrats' best response to the Republicans' best response to the Democrats' initial effort, and so on. If each of the Republicans' and Democrats' best-response sequences converges, to a Kantian equilibrium, then the equilibrium is said to be **stable**.[11] Equilibrium stability, which occurs when $\gamma < \frac{1}{2}$, is illustrated in figure 7.2(a). Equilibrium instability, which occurs when $\gamma > \frac{1}{2}$, is illustrated in figure 7.2(b).

Similar to the correspondence principle in the Walrasian model, the Kantian equilibrium in example 7.1 has intuitive comparative statics if stable and counterintuitive comparative statics if unstable. In particular, the equilibrium ratio of type-t voters to the opposing voters is $v_t/v_{-t} = (I_t/I_{-t})^{1/(1-2\gamma)}$, which is increasing in I_t if

11. Formally, for any $t \in \{R, D\}$ and any $z_{-t} > 0$, the sequence $Z_t Z_{-t} Z_t \dots Z_t Z_{-t} Z_t(z_{-t})$ of iterated best response operators must converge to type-t voters' Kantian equilibrium effort.

$\gamma < \frac{1}{2}$ and is decreasing in I_t if $\gamma > \frac{1}{2}$. Thus, when the diminishing returns to effort set in quickly (i.e., $\gamma < \frac{1}{2}$), the numerical advantage of card-carrying Republicans (i.e., $I_R > I_D$) helps them "win" the election (i.e., helps achieve a higher value of $v_R/v_D > 1$). By contrast, when the diminishing returns set in slowly (i.e., $\gamma > \frac{1}{2}$), the numerical advantage of card-carrying Republicans is actually a handicap; they exert a lower effort and show up to vote in smaller numbers than Democrats do (i.e., $z_R < z_D$ and $v_R < v_D$). The unstable case, when $\gamma > \frac{1}{2}$, is peculiar because it has the party with the greatest popular support at a disadvantage, and the disadvantage is greater the higher this party's support.

The analysis of example 7.1 has so far relied on a particular (and natural) specification of the Kantian counterfactual. Consider an alternative specification, in which each voter reasons: "If I double my effort of getting to the voting booth, then every voter, regardless of his party affiliation, will do so, too. Would I like that?" In this case, an effort profile x is a Kantian equilibrium if, for each type $t \in \{R, D\}$ and each voter $i \in \mathcal{I}_t$,

$$1 \in \arg \max_{\alpha \geq 0} u^i(\alpha x^i, \alpha x^{-i}).$$

No positive-effort Kantian equilibrium exists. Any contemplated increase in one's voting effort is accompanied by a corresponding increase in every voter's effort. As a result (under the assumptions of example 7.1), the two parties' voting efforts cancel out. All one is left with is the cost of one's own effort, which one wants to minimize.

7.4   AN APPLICATION TO RESPONSIBILITY

Recall the notion of responsibility proposed in section 2.3. It is derived from pivotality in voting: an agent is less responsible if he is less likely to have been pivotal. This notion of responsibility agrees with the so-called **but-for** legal rule, according to which a defendant's act has caused, say, outcome X if X would not have occurred but for the defendant's act. This notion of responsibility is problematic when the agents are so numerous that the probability of being pivotal is negligible for each of them, as is the case in section 7.3.

To deal with such situations, the but-for rule is subject to a legal caveat: simultaneous acts by multiple individuals may be considered to be independently sufficient causes of X. In other words, an individual may be responsible for X even if he is likely not to have been pivotal. If two shooters fire simultaneously and kill a man, then each shooter is responsible. Kantian reasoning suggests a notion of responsibility that recognizes independently sufficient causes.

To establish **Kantian responsibility**, ask not whether, if Alice had acted differently, outcome X would have been averted. Instead, ask whether, if Alice had acted differently and all similar others mimicked her action, X would have been averted. The motivation for this reasoning is dynamic. Alice's responsibility is measured according to her act's potential influence on the social norms in the society. Alice may not be pivotal today, but her act today may set an example and help coordinate agents' actions in similar situations in the future.

For example, a toddler who shoots his mother while playing with a loose gun is pivotal in inflicting the injury but is not Kantian responsible for it. He is unlikely to affect the injury statistics much; toddler shootings are not deliberate, copy-cat crimes inflicted by calculating agents. By contrast, a Nazi security guard may be held responsible for, even though not pivotal in, perpetrating the Holocaust. A single security guard at a concentration camp might not have affected the total death toll, for, in case of noncompliance, he would have been replaced with another guard. However, his actions may set an example, thereby influencing the course of events in similar situations in the future.

7.5 CONCLUDING REMARKS

The voting problem of section 7.3 illustrates that the prediction of Kantian equilibrium depends crucially on who are the similar others with whom an agent identifies in his Kantian deviation. In complex situations, the choice of the similar others is nontrivial. For example, a taxi driver who asks "How would I like it if every taxi driver went on strike?" designates all other taxi drivers as similar to him. But why not also designate as similar Uber® and Lyft® drivers, truckers, grocers, school teachers, and Hollywood writers? Besides, the assumption that similarity is dichotomous is arbitrary; it would have been natural for the taxi driver to expect absolute solidarity from other taxi drivers, some solidarity from Uber® and Lyft® drivers, and very little from Hollywood writers.

Kantian equilibrium has both descriptive and prescriptive elements. It describes the behavior of the agents who have been prescribed (e.g., indoctrinated since early childhood) to practice the categorical imperative. If one wishes to prescribe the categorical imperative, it is crucial to carefully define Kantian deviations. Whom to regard as similar? Which deviations to consider analogous (e.g., proportional, as we have assumed, or additive, or of some other kind)? With all these degrees of freedom, can a hastily designed Kantian reasoning protocol lead to a worse outcome than the worst Nash equilibrium outcome?

The reasons for the dominance of the Nash equilibrium paradigm are largely methodological. It can be shown that agents' adherence to the Kantian protocol is observationally equivalent to their adherence to the Nash protocol but for different utility functions. As a result, the observer cannot really tell whether agents are

Kantian or Nash. But if so, which of the two sets of utility functions should the observer use to make welfare comparisons, required, for instance, to verify Pareto efficiency? Problem 7.2 suggests that the answer may not matter.

Kantian reasoning is related to, but is distinct from, rule consequentialism. A **rule consequentialist** finds a deviation profitable if he believes that, if matched by everyone else's equivalent deviation, his deviation would lead to socially superior consequences. If one takes "socially superior" to mean Pareto efficient, then theorem 7.1 endorses Kantian equilibrium as rule-consequentialist. In this case, in the voting application of section 7.3, one can interpret each voter as a **rule utilitarian**, defined here as a rule consequentialist who seeks a voting-effort rule that, if adopted by all members of his party, would maximize the sum of their utilities.

Related, **social capital** can be defined to comprise the patterns of individual behavior that collectively promote normatively appealing outcomes. The definition of social capital is thus open-ended; it is parameterized by one's ideosyncratic notion of the normatively appealing. To the extent that Kantian reasoning promotes Pareto efficiency in some situations and to the extent that Pareto efficiency is normatively appealing, adherence to Kantian reasoning is social capital. In practice, it is easier to adhere to this reasoning if one believes the Kantian counterfactual not to be all wishful thinking: if one believes that, by altering one's own action, one could, perhaps eventually, influence others' actions. Such a belief (justified or not) in one's ability to affect others' behavior is called **self-efficacy** belief.[12]

Finally, behavior consistent with Kantian reasoning may prevail even among the individuals who do not buy into the categorial imperative. In particular, if the society esteems Kantians, then even non-Kantians may imitate Kantians in order to cultivate the social image that may lead others to mistake them for Kantians.

7.6 BIBLIOGRAPHICAL NOTES

Pinker's (2011) is a polymath account of why violence has declined and cooperation has flourished. The best-developed theory of cooperation economists have is the theory of repeated games (Mailath and Samuelson, 2006), entirely omitted from the present book.

The discussion of Kantian equilibrium in section 7.2 is based on the work of Roemer (2010) and gets a book-length treatment by Roemer (2018). Nash

---

12. Corroborating the link between self-efficacy beliefs and social capital, Guiso, Sapienza, and Zingales (2016) find that Italian eighth graders who score high on a self-efficacy test tend to live in the cities with higher levels of social capital as measured by the number of nonprofit associations, organ donations, and the lack of cheating in standardized math exams. The authors' interpretation is that the culture of self-efficacy, in which the eighth graders have been socialized, promotes social capital.

equilibrium goes back to Cournot (1838) and remains the go-to equilibrium concept in the analysis of strategic situations, the normative appeal of Kantian equilibrium notwithstanding. In game theory, the literal and delusional belief that one's choice of action somehow affects others' simultaneous choice of actions is called "magical thinking" (Daley and Sadowski, 2017). Albeit short of any normative content, operationally "magical thinking" resembles Kantian reasoning.

The voting paradox goes back at least two centuries, to the work of Marquis de Condorcet in 1793. It is articulated in its modern form by Downs (1957) and is challenged by Riker and Ordeshook (1968), who argue that voting should be recognized as an act that is enjoyable in itself, regardless of the likelihood of swaying the election. In the voting literature, the voters who depart from the Nash protocol by being Kantian or rule utilitarian are called ethical. Those who comply with the Nash protocol are called pragmatic. Ali and Lin (2013) summarize the ethical-voting literature and explore a voting model in which rule-utilitarian voters coexist with pragmatic ones, who are eager to cultivate their rule-utilitarian image.

The utility function in problem 7.1 is due to Liebhafsky (1969). Gelman, Silver, and Edlin (2012) estimate the probability of being pivotal in a presidential election, which is the subject of problem 7.4. Problem 7.6 draws on the work of Roemer (2012).

PROBLEMS

Problem 7.1 (Wealth and Violence). The goal of this problem is to illustrate that an agent's preferences may be such that his demand for violence would decline with his wealth. There is a single agent, Bob, and two goods. Good 1 is violence (i.e., some form of violent entertainment), and good 2 is, say, travel (or some other form of nonviolent entertainment). Bob's utility function is

$$u(x_1, x_2) = \ln x_1 + \frac{(x_2)^2}{2},$$

where $x_1 > 0$ and $x_2 \geq 0$ are the consumptions of goods 1 and 2, respectively. Bob is endowed with $K > 0$ units of capital, which he can transform into any violence-travel pair (x_1, x_2) from the ("budget") set

$$B(K) \equiv \left\{ (x_1, x_2) \in \mathbb{R}_+^2 \mid x_1 + x_2 \leq K \right\}. \tag{7.6}$$

1. Solve for Bob's utility-maximizing selection from the set $B(K)$. How do the optimal x_1 and x_2 depend on K? Illustrate the solution to Bob's problem graphically by plotting (perhaps on a computer) x_1 and x_2 against K. (*Hint*: x_1 is nonmonotone in K.)

2. The goal of this (optional, if you like) part is to show that Bob's choice in part 1 can be supported at a Walrasian equilibrium in a simple economy with production. Assume that Bob is endowed with, and can rent out up to, K units of capital at price r per unit to a firm that operates the technology captured by $B(k)$ (given by (7.6)), where k is the amount of capital that the firm rents. The firm takes all prices as given. The firm picks a profit-maximizing violence-travel pair from $B(k)$ to sell to Bob at a price vector (p_1, p_2). Bob owns this firm, and, so, his income is the firm's profit (if any), $p_1 x_1 + p_2 x_2 - rk$, plus his receipts rk' from renting out k' units of capital. At equilibrium, market clearing and feasibility require $k = k' \leq K$. Bob spends his income optimally on violence and travel. He takes as given not only the prices (p_1, p_2, r) but also the firm's profit $p_1 x_1 + p_2 x_2 - rk$. (This price-taking attitude, both Bob's and the firm's, is a signature of the Walrasian paradigm.) For the described economy, define carefully and identify a Walrasian equilibrium $(p_1, p_2, r, x_1, x_2, k)$.[13]

3. Are your findings consistent with the historical evolution of violence in the Western world or elsewhere? Can you justify the postulated utility function?

Problem 7.2 (Observational Equivalence of Kantian and Nash Behaviors). Assume that, for each agent $i \in \mathcal{I}$,

$$u^i(x^i, x^{-i}) = -x^i + \sum_{j \in \mathcal{I}} \ln(1 + x^j),$$

and the agent chooses an x^i in $\mathbb{R}_+$.

1. Find the unique Nash equilibrium and each agent's utility at this equilibrium.

2. Find the symmetric positive Kantian equilibrium and each agent's utility at this equilibrium.

3. Henceforth, let $I = 2$. Explain why each allocation in the set $\mathcal{P}$ defined in (7.7) is Pareto efficient:[14]

$$\mathcal{P} \equiv \cup_{\omega \in (0,1)} \arg \max_{(x^1, x^2) \in \mathbb{R}_+^2} \{\omega u^1(x^1, x^2) + (1 - \omega) u^2(x^2, x^1)\}. \tag{7.7}$$

4. Solve for the set $\mathcal{P}$ in (7.7). That is, for each $\omega \in (0, 1)$, indicate which values of x^1 and x^2 solve the maximization problem in (7.7).

---

13. If you have trouble imagining Bob's dual role as a business owner and a consumer, you may find inspiration in Jehle and Reny's (2011, example 5.2, pp. 226–231) description of the Robinson Crusoe economy.

14. In words, the set $\mathcal{P}$ is the collection of all pairs (x^1, x^2) each of which maximizes the weighted sum of the agents' utilities.

5. Plot on a computer the set of utility pairs associated with the Pareto efficient allocations in $\mathcal{P}$:[15]

$$\mathcal{U} \equiv \{(u^1(x^1, x^2), u^2(x^2, x^1)) \mid (x^1, x^2) \in \mathcal{P})\}.$$

In this plot, indicate the symmetric-Nash-equilibrium utilities and the symmetric-Kantian-equilibrium utilities that you identified in parts 1 and 2.

6. Assume instead that each agent i's utility function is given by $\hat{u} \equiv \sum_{i \in \mathcal{I}} u^i$. That is, the agents have identical utility functions. Solve for the Nash equilibrium. How is it related to the symmetric positive Kantian equilibrium for the utilities $(u^i)_{i \in \mathcal{I}}$?

7. By theorem 7.1, the Kantian equilibrium identified in part 2 is Pareto efficient with respect to utilities $(u^i)_{i \in \mathcal{I}}$. Is the Nash equilibrium identified in part 6 Pareto efficient relative to identical utilities $\hat{u}$?

Problem 7.3 (Asymmetric Kantian Equilibrium). Let $I = 2$. Assume that, for each $i \in \mathcal{I}$,

$$u^i(x^i, x^{-i}) = -\frac{x^i}{1 + \theta^i} + \sum_{j \in \mathcal{I}} \ln(1 + x^j),$$

where $x^i \geq 0$ is an effort, and $\theta^i \geq 0$ is a disutility-of-effort parameter.

1. Find the Nash equilibrium.

2. Appeal to theorem 7.2 to argue that, if, for each $i \in \mathcal{I}$, $\theta^i \in [\underline{\theta}, \bar{\theta}]$ for $0 < \underline{\theta} < \bar{\theta} < \infty$, then a positive Kantian equilibrium exists. (*Hint*: Take $b = \underline{\theta}$ and $B = I(1 + \bar{\theta})$.)

3. Show that, at the positive Kantian equilibrium,

$$\frac{x^1}{x^2} = \frac{1 + \theta^1}{1 + \theta^2},$$

and the agents' utilities are equalized.

4. Let $\theta^1 = 0$ and $\theta^2 = 1$, so that agent 2 finds effort less costly than agent 1 does. Find the positive Kantian equilibrium allocation. How does it compare to the Nash equilibrium allocation?

5. Solve for the set

$$\mathcal{P} \equiv \cup_{\omega \in [0,1]} \arg \max_{(x^1, x^2) \in \mathbb{R}_+^2} \{\omega u^1(x^1, x^2) + (1 - \omega) u^2(x^2, x^1)\}$$

of allocations, each of which is Pareto efficient.

---

15. In words, $\mathcal{U}$ is the set of all utility pairs upon which no feasible allocation can improve in the Pareto sense.

6. For $\theta^1 = 0$ and $\theta^2 = 1$, plot on a computer the set

$$\mathcal{U} \equiv \{(u^1(x^1, x^2), u^2(x^2, x^1)) \mid (x^1, x^2) \in \mathcal{P})\}$$

of utility pairs associated with the Pareto efficient allocations in $\mathcal{P}$. In this plot, indicate the Nash equilibrium utilities, the Kantian equilibrium utilities, and the utilities in $\mathcal{U}$ induced by the allocation in $\mathcal{P}$ that is generated by $\omega = \frac{1}{2}$. Interpret.

Problem 7.4 (Voting versus Driving). This problem's goal is to illustrate that the probability of being pivotal in an election is small and, hence, is unlikely to be the primary explanation for why people vote. Let $I = 135,649,465$ be the number of agents, who cast their votes in the 2016 U.S. presidential election. Alice is one of them. Consider a simplified model of the election. There are two candidates, Clinton (Democrat) and Trump (Republican). The candidate who gets the majority of votes (i.e., $(I+1)/2$ or more) wins.[16] Alice is pivotal if exactly $(I-1)/2$ others vote for Clinton, so that Clinton wins if and only if Alice votes for her.

1. Suppose that Alice believes that every voter votes independently of other voters and votes for Clinton with probability $p \in (0, 1)$. What is the probability that Alice assigns to being pivotal? Denote this probability by $\Pi(p)$.

2. Which probability p maximizes $\Pi(p)$?

3. Suppose that, in her lifetime, Alice participates in $n = 20$ presidential elections. Suppose that she believes that voters' behavior is independent across voters and across elections and that a voter votes for the Democratic candidate with probability $p \in (0, 1)$. What is the probability that, in her lifetime, Alice will be pivotal in at least one election?

4. Assuming that $p = \frac{1}{2}$, compare the lifetime probability of being pivotal (using your formula from part 3) to the lifetime mortality risks in table 7.1. (*Hint:* You may wish to use Stirling's approximation: for a large integer n, $n! \approx \sqrt{2\pi n}(n/e)^n$.)

Problem 7.5 (Kant in the Jungle, with Robots: The Meta Golden Rule). Consider a dynamic jungle-like economy in which agents arrive one by one. At the beginning of time, time $t = 0$, the economy's social endowment is one unit of a good, which is the only good in the economy and is held by Nature. Agent $i \in \mathcal{I} \equiv \{1, 2, 3, ...\}$ arrives at time $t = i$ with zero endowment of the good and chooses a fraction $x^i \in [0, 1]$ of his predecessor's, agent $(i-1)$'s, holding of the good to expropriate, with agent 1's predecessor being Nature. Each agent i's utility is strictly increasing

---

16. Thus, we neglect the electoral college.

TABLE 7.1
Various Annual and Lifetime Risks (U.S. Population).

Cause of death	Annual risk	Lifetime risk
Heart disease	1 in 300	1 in 4
Cancer (all forms)	1 in 510	1 in 7
Pneumonia	1 in 4,300	1 in 57
Motor vehicle accident	1 in 6,700	1 in 88
Suicide	1 in 9,200	1 in 120
Criminal homicide	1 in 18,000	1 in 240
On-the-job accident	1 in 48,000	1 in 620
Accidental electrocution	1 in 300,000	1 in 4,000
Lightning strike	1 in 3,000,000	1 in 39,000
Commercial aircraft accident	1 in 3,100,000	1 in 40,000
Terrorism (2005)	1 in 5,293,000	1 in 69,000
Plague	1 in 19,000,000	1 in 240,000
Anthrax (2001)	1 in 56,000,000	1 in 730,000
Passenger train accident	1 in 70,000,000	1 in 920,000
Shark attack	1 in 280,000,000	1 in 3,700,000

Source: Krueger (2008, table 3.3, p. 139).

in his consumption, which is the amount of the good left after he has expropriated his predecessor and has been expropriated by his successor. To raise the stakes a little, interpret agents as successive civilizations of ever more intelligent species: Nature is nonhuman animals, agent 1 is humans, agent 2 is superintelligent robots, agent 3 is super-duper intelligent robots, and so on. Kantian ethics can provide an inspiration for how humans ought to treat animals, how humans ought to program superintelligent robots to treat humans, how humans ought to program the superintelligent robots to program the super-duper intelligent robots to treat the superintelligent robots, and so on.

1. To warm up, suppose that each agent expropriates fraction $\lambda \in (0, 1)$ of his predecessor's holding of the good. What is each agent's consumption implied by this common and exogenously given expropriation rate?

2. Find the unique symmetric Nash equilibrium of the described jungle-like dynamic economy. (In a symmetric equilibrium, each agent expropriates the same fraction.) What is each agent's consumption at this equilibrium?

3. Argue that no symmetric positive Kantian equilibrium exists. When doing so, assume that, when contemplating his Kantian counter factual, each agent identifies with all agents in $\mathcal{I}$. Call such a counterfactual **universal**.

4. Find an (asymmetric) positive Kantian equilibrium with the universal counterfactual. Compute each agent's equilibrium consumption.

5. Find an asymmetric positive Kantian equilibrium such that, in Kantian counterfactual, each agent identifies only with his immediate successor. Such a Kantian counterfactual corresponds to the **meta-golden rule** popularized by Vinge (1993): Treat your inferior as you would like to be treated by your superior.

6. In the Kantian equilibria in parts 4 and 5, set $x^1 = 1$. Plot the expropriation rates and consumption for both equilibria. In which of the two equilibria is the agents' consumption more unequal?

Problem 7.6 (Kantian Equilibrium with Other-Regarding Preferences). Suppose that each agent $i \in \mathcal{I}$ has other-regarding preferences in the sense that his utility $u^i(x^i, x^{-i})$ from an allocation x is the sum of his tastes, $t^i(x^i, x^{-i})$, and values, here defined as a scaled sum of others' tastes:

$$\underbrace{u^i(x^i, x^{-i})}_{\text{utility}} \equiv \underbrace{t^i(x^i, x^{-i})}_{\text{tastes}} + \delta \underbrace{\sum_{k \in \mathcal{I} \backslash i} t^k(x^k, x^{-k})}_{\text{values}}, \tag{7.8}$$

where $\delta \geq 0$ parameterizes how much agent i cares about others. The definitions of Nash and Kantian equilibria apply to economies with other-regarding preferences without modification.

1. Show that any Pareto efficient allocation for $\delta > 0$ is Pareto efficient also for $\delta = 0$. Is the converse true?

2. Set $t^i(x^i, x^{-i}) = -x^i + \sum_{j \in \mathcal{I}} \ln(1 + x^j)$ in (7.8). Find the symmetric interior Kantian equilibrium. How does this equilibrium depend on δ (cf. problem 1.12)?

3. For the tastes specified in part 2, find the symmetric Nash equilibrium. Is this equilibrium Pareto efficient?

CHAPTER 8

UNINTENDED CONSEQUENCES OF POLICY INTERVENTIONS

8.1   INTRODUCTION

So far in the book, many a model has been accompanied by a result that would assert Pareto efficiency of equilibrium outcomes (theorems 1.1, 3.2, 3.5, 3.8, 6.3, and 7.1; problems 4.2 and 5.3). Efficiency has been emphasized not because it is ubiquitous in practice. Quite the contrary, efficiency is rare. However, from the normative, design, point of view, it is instructive to understand the conditions that guarantee efficiency. Moreover, from the positive point of view, in order to diagnose why an outcome in a certain situation is inefficient, it is useful to begin with an idealized model in which efficiency is known to prevail and then to see which of the model's assumptions are violated.

This chapter focuses on models in which equilibrium outcomes may be inefficient and, in addition, intuitive interventions aimed at raising welfare may have unintended adverse consequences. In particular, it will be shown that, in a congestion-prone road network, while connecting all locations with congestion-free roads is the best one can do, adding just one congestion-free road may lead to a Pareto inferior outcome. In a similar spirit, it will be shown that, in a so-called local-public-good provision problem, while enabling each agent to share with all others is the best one can do, enabling just one additional pair of agents to share among themselves may lead to an inferior outcome.

We have encountered analogous unintended consequences of intuitive policies before. Even though, under the conditions of the FWT, having all markets open leads to a Pareto efficient outcome, opening just one extra market without completing markets may lead to a Pareto loss. In the incomplete contracting environment mentioned in chapter 6.2, if some aspect of, say, a teacher's performance (e.g., teaching the students how to be happy) cannot be measured, then it may be best not to condition the teacher's remuneration on a measurable performance aspect (e.g., the students' test scores) at all, lest the teacher divert his efforts from the unmeasurable aspect and toward the measurable one. Common to these examples is the feature that, while a comprehensive intervention promotes efficiency, taking but one step in the direction of this intervention can lead to a deterioration in welfare, sometimes even in the Pareto sense.

8.2   THE UTILITARIAN SOCIAL WELFARE FUNCTION

Some outcomes cannot be compared in the Pareto sense. Even for the outcomes that can be compared so, we may wish to speak of the distance between these outcomes in welfare terms. To this end, we introduce the utilitarian social welfare function, which we apply throughout the rest of the chapter. The **utilitarian social welfare function** is defined as the sum of agents' utility functions. (This sum is replaced with an integral if there is a continuum of agents.) An allocation that delivers a higher value of the utilitarian social welfare function is said to deliver higher welfare with respect to that function.

A **utilitarian allocation** is a feasible allocation that maximizes the utilitarian social welfare function. Any utilitarian allocation is Pareto efficient. Suppose it were not. Then, there would exist some other allocation that would make some agent strictly better off without making any other agent worse off. As a result, the sum of the agents' utilities would increase, thereby contradicting the assumption that the original allocation is utilitarian. (With a continuum of agents, adapt the definition of Pareto efficiency to say that there is no way to make a positive measure of agents better off without making a positive measure of agents worse off.)

By adding up utility functions, we assume that each agent's utility function is cardinal (instead of ordinal), meaning that it captures not only the agent's ranking of alternatives but also the intensity of his satisfaction with each alternative. In addition, by adding up utility functions, we assume that utilities are **interpersonally comparable**, so that statements such as "a poor man benefits from an extra dollar more than a rich man does" have meaning.

Various methods have been proposed to measure cardinal utilities. For example, the just-noticeable-difference approach assumes that utility increases by a unit each time one increases consumption of a good just enough to notice the difference. A rough empirical regularity, known in psychophysics as **Weber's law**, implies that a utility so measured will be logarithmic.[1] Another approach postulates that the difference between the utilities from two alternatives is larger the quicker one can decide which alternative one prefers. When observed choice is stochastic, yet another approach maintains that the more likely one is to choose a particular alternative, the higher one's relative utility from this alternative is.

Calibrating cardinal utilities to be interpersonally comparable is even more challenging. Neuroeconomics may inspire some educated guesses. Having to rely on guessing so much is an uncomfortable position to be in, but the discomfort does not undo the fact that one must make interpersonal utility comparisons daily by the dozen.[2]

The utilitarian social welfare function is **consequentialist**: only the outcome brought about by agents' actions matters—not agents' intentions in taking actions (as in **virtue ethics**), not the inherent goodness of actions (as in Immanuel Kant's **deontological ethics**, which powers the counterfactual of Kantian equilibrium), and not the mechanism that aggregates individual choices (e.g., a market or a vote). The utilitarian social welfare function is a special case of the consequentialist one called **welfarist**: outcomes affect the social welfare function only in so far as they affect the agents' utility functions (i.e., their welfare).

8.3 ROUTING

Routing problems study both equilibrium and Pareto efficient routing of traffic on networks. Examples include cars on roads, electricity on power grids, and data packets online. For concreteness, we deal in cars. Car routing is important: congestion kills. If a million commuters are unnecessarily stuck in traffic for five extra hours a week for a year, the total of 260,000,000 wasted hours amount to the loss

1. Binmore (2009) criticizes this approach: "Like many men, I am not only nearsighted, I am also mildly color-blind. At the Poker table, I have to be quite careful when both blue and green chips are in use. Does it therefore follow that I get less pleasure from the use of my eyesight than someone with perfect vision? My hearing is even less reliable than my eyesight. Should those with perfect pitch therefore be assumed to take a keener pleasure in music? I have only the haziest idea of how much I am worth, while others keep accounts that are accurate down to the penny. Is this relevant to how much tax we each should pay?"

2. For instance, should Alice, running late for her flight, cut in front of Bob in line at an airport security checkpoint? How much should Carol donate to the Fleck Dance Theatre? Which one of the two friends who do not talk to each other should Dave invite to his dinner party?

of 370 lives a year, more than three times the annual death rate in motor vehicle accidents in the United States.[3]

THE ROUTING PROBLEM

A routing network is a finite collection of nodes, such as towns or points of interest within cities, and undirected links, such as highways and streets.[4] Let $\mathcal{L}$ be a set of links, with a typical element l. A route is a path comprised of adjacent links. There is a finite set $\mathcal{I}$ of agent types with a positive measure m^i of agents of each type i, indexed by $r \in [0, m^i]$. Each type-i agent r must pick a route from a feasible set X^i of routes. The typical elements of X^i are denoted by x^i or y^i (chosen by some type-i agents) or $x^{i,r}$ (if one wants to emphasize a particular copy r of type-i agent), depending on the context. Two agents r and r' of the same type i are free to choose different routes in X^i.

For the ease of interpretation, assume that, for any type i, all routes in X^i have the same point of departure and the same destination. That is, each agent absolutely must travel, say, from home to work but can choose among multiple routes. If type i and j live or work (or both) in different places, then $X^i \neq X^j$.

One can interpret each link as a good that an agent consumes in quantity either one (if the link is a part of the chosen route) or zero. The bundles—or routes—that each agent may consume are restricted by geography (the routing network) and his travel needs (his source and the destination nodes).

An agent's cost of taking some route x^i in X^i is $\sum_{l \in x^i} c_l(t_l)$, where $c_l(t_l)$ is the cost of traveling on link l if measure t_l of agents travel on this link. We assume that each cost function c_l is weakly increasing. If function c_l is increasing strictly, then link l suffers from **congestion**, a form of negative externality. The payoff of a type-i agent who takes a particular route is the negative of this route's cost. That is, no amount of cost will dissuade an agent from taking a trip.

A **routing problem** is a network with the associated congestion costs $(c_l)_{l \in \mathcal{L}}$ and agents described by $(m^i, X^i)_{i \in \mathcal{I}}$.

The **traffic flow**, or **routing**, is vector $t \equiv (t_l)_{l \in \mathcal{L}}$. The measure t_l of agents who travel on a link l is related to the agents' route choices $\{x^{i,r} \mid i \in \mathcal{I}, r \in [0, m^i]\}$ through

$$t_l = \sum_{i \in \mathcal{I}} \int_0^{m^i} \mathbf{1}_{\{l \in x^{i,r}\}} \, dr, \tag{8.1}$$

3. Five hours a week times 52 weeks a year times a million commuters amounts to 260,000,000 hours. Divide that by the $24 \cdot 365 \cdot 80 = 700,800$ hours that an average life lasts to obtain 371 lives. In 2015, according to the National Highway Traffic Safety Association, traffic fatalities amounted to 109 deaths per million of population.

4. Two examples, illustrated in figures 8.1 and 8.2, will be examined shortly.

where $\mathbf{1}_{\{l \in x^{i,r}\}}$ is the indicator function whose value is one if type-i agent r passes through link l and is zero otherwise. **Utilitarian routing** selects the traffic flow that maximizes the agents' utilities or, equivalently, minimizes the aggregate cost

$$C(t) \equiv \sum_{l \in \mathcal{L}} t_l c_l(t_l) \qquad (8.2)$$

of making the necessary trips.

EQUILIBRIUM

Nash equilibrium routing selects the traffic flow t that ensures that whenever some route $x^i \in X^i$ is traveled by some agent of type i, his cost of traveling on any other route $y^i \in X^i$ is at least as high:

$$\sum_{l \in x^i} c_l(t_l) \leq \sum_{l \in y^i} c_l(t_l).$$

SANTA MONICA TO LOS ANGELES

Example **Santa Monica to Los Angeles (SM2LA)** will be used to illustrate the notation and to show that Nash equilibrium routing may be Pareto inefficient (and, hence, not utilitarian). In the example, a unit measure of agents are all of the same type; $\mathcal{I} = \{1\}$ and $m^1 = 1$. Each agent must drive from Santa Monica to Los Angeles. As depicted in figure 8.1, each agent can take one of two routes: the Santa Monica Freeway, represented by link F, or the side streets, represented by link S. Thus, $\mathcal{L} \equiv \{F, S\}$ and $X^1 \equiv \{\{F\}, \{S\}\}$.

Assume that $c_F(t_F) = t_F$ and $c_S(t_S) = 1$. Thus, the freeway is fast but prone to congestion, whereas the side streets are slow but congestion-free (e.g., because there are many streets running in parallel).

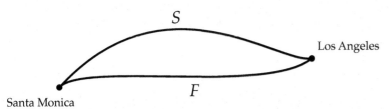

FIGURE 8.1.
The Santa Monica to Los Angeles network.

The utilitarian traffic flow (t_F^*, t_S^*) satisfies

$$t_F^* = \arg\min_{s \in [0,1]} \{sc_F(s) + (1 - s)c_S(1 - s)\}$$

$$t_S^* = 1 - t_F^*,$$

where the traffic flow is related to the agents' route choices according to (8.1). Given the functional forms of c_F and c_S, $(t_F^*, t_S^*) = (\frac{1}{2}, \frac{1}{2})$. That is, (any) half of the agents take the freeway, and the other half take the side streets.

Even though the utilitarian traffic flow is Pareto efficient, an adherent of socialism in the sense of definition 4.2 would not like it: the utilitarian flow discriminates between identical agents. Those who take the side streets are worse off than those who take the freeway.

The computed utilitarian routing is not a Nash equilibrium routing. With the utilitarian routing, any agent who takes the side streets spends an hour in traffic, whereas any agent who takes the freeway spends half an hour in traffic. Each side-street agent has an incentive to deviate and take the freeway.

Nash equilibrium traffic flow (t_F, t_S) requires that no agent be able to decrease his travel time by taking an alternative route:

$$t_S > 0 \implies c_S(t_S) \le c_F(t_F)$$

$$t_F > 0 \implies c_F(t_F) \le c_S(t_S).$$

Substituting the functional forms gives the unique equilibrium flow $(t_F, t_S) = (1, 0)$. At the equilibrium, each driver spends an hour in traffic.[5] No one uses the side streets, but everyone is as well off as he would be if there were only the side streets and no freeway, which is faster than the side streets unless everyone uses it, which is the case at the equilibrium.

The Nash equilibrium routing is not Pareto efficient. It is Pareto dominated by any routing in which a positive measure of agents use each route. Indeed, moving some agents from the freeway to the side streets keeps these agents indifferent while making those who remain on the freeway better off because the freeway is now less congested. In particular, the Nash equilibrium is Pareto dominated by the utilitarian routing. By contrast to the utilitarian routing, however, the Nash equilibrium routing treats identical agents equally.

Example SM2LA illustrates that a freeway may be useless unless optimally managed. Optimal management can be accomplished by rationing access to the

---

5. When we speak of *the* equilibrium traffic flow or *the* utilitarian traffic flow we refer to a class of traffic flows any member of which can be obtained from any other member by asking some agents of the same type to swap their route assignments. That is, we do not care about agents' names, only their types.

freeway (e.g., depending on the parity of the driver's number plate) or, in a suitably enriched model, by instituting congestion charges (i.e., freeway tolls; see problem 8.1).

SANTA MONICA TO LOS ANGELES: REINTERPRETED, TWICE

The insights of SM2LA transcend traffic routing. For instance, SM2LA can shed light on optimal disclosure of hospitals' performance. Reinterpret the example by assuming that "Santa Monica" means "a patient needs tooth whitening" (or pick your favorite medical procedure), and "Los Angeles" means "tooth whitening accomplished"; "side streets" means "whitening by Santiago, a subpar specialist," and "freeway" means "whitening by Facundo, a fantastic specialist."

The value of seeing Santiago is B, for some $B > 0$. The value of seeing Facundo, $B + 1 - t_F$, has a quality premium of 1 and is decreasing in t_F, the measure of patients who see him, because of the longer queues at his office. (Facundo works fastidiously and does not delegate.)

The analysis of SM2LA suggests that, at equilibrium, all agents will go to see Facundo and dissipate the entire surplus from his superior expertise in the course of queueing.

In this interpretation, the counterpart of congestion charging is differential charging for the specialists' services. But assume that tooth whitening is a component of universal free healthcare that proscribes charging. In this case, an alternative to charging is rationing (e.g., all those born on an odd day of the month must visit Santiago).

Rationing may be politically infeasible, however. Its opponents may brand rationing boards as "death panels." Rationing may also invite rent-seeking and corruption. A politically feasible alternative to rationing is to conceal the information about specialists' qualifications. Unaware of these qualifications, patients will randomize when deciding which specialist to visit. Any (nondegenerate) randomization will be a Pareto improvement on the full-information equilibrium outcome.

Road congestion can alternatively be used as a metaphor for urban congestion. In SM2LA, one can interpret taking the freeway as living in a city and taking the side streets as living in the country. The city is desirable because of its amenities but is prone to congestion, whereas the countryside is dull but congestion-free. At the equilibrium with costless migration, city living is as miserable as country living.

SM2LA is a rather impoverished model of urban migration, however, because, in practice, prices (wages and rents) in cities adjust. So, even though, at an equilibrium of a richer model, workers in the cities are as miserable as they would have been in the countryside, city landlords benefit from high rents and employers benefit from low wages. So, in this richer model, one can no longer conclude that everyone would have been equally well off if the city did not exist.

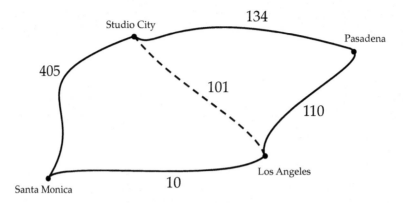

FIGURE 8.2.
The Santa Monica to Pasadena networks. Two road networks are considered, with and without the dashed link, labeled "101."

SANTA MONICA TO PASADENA

To illustrate unintended consequences of a policy, we consider another routing example: **Santa Monica to Pasadena (SM2P)**. A unit measure of agents are all of the same type; $\mathcal{I} = \{1\}$ and $m^1 = 1$. Each agent must drive from Santa Monica to Pasadena. Available are two routes (see figure 8.2):

1. Santa Monica to Los Angeles (the Santa Monica Freeway, or 10) and then Los Angeles to Pasadena (the Pasadena Freeway, or 110).

2. Santa Monica to Studio City (the San Diego Freeway, or 405) and then Studio City to Pasadena (the Ventura Freeway, or 134).[6]

Thus, $\mathcal{L} \equiv \{10, 110, 405, 134\}$ and $X^1 = \{\{10, 110\}, \{405, 134\}\}$.

Assume that $c_l(t_l) = t_l$ for $l \in \{10, 134\}$ and $c_l(t_l) = 1$ for $l \in \{110, 405\}$. Thus, highways 110 and 405 are slow but congestion-free, whereas highways 10 and 134 are fast but congestion-prone.

The utilitarian traffic flow t^* satisfies

$$t^*_{405} = t^*_{134} = \arg\min_{s \in [0,1]} \{s(c_{405}(s) + c_{134}(s)) + (1-s)(c_{10}(1-s) + c_{110}(1-s))\}$$

$$t^*_{10} = t^*_{110} = 1 - t^*_{405}.$$

Given the functional-form assumptions, $t^*_{405} = t^*_{134} = t^*_{10} = t^*_{110} = \frac{1}{2}$.

---

6. Some liberty with geography has been taken here. In practice, one must drive a couple of miles on the Santa Monica Freeway in order to get onto 405.

Here, the utilitarian traffic flow treats equals equally; each agent's time in traffic is

$$c_{10}\left(\frac{1}{2}\right) + c_{110}\left(\frac{1}{2}\right) = \frac{3}{2}.$$

Here, the utilitarian traffic flow is also a Nash equilibrium traffic flow. Indeed, the utilitarian flow satisfies the indifference condition

$$c_{405}(t^*_{405}) + c_{134}(t^*_{134}) = c_{10}(t^*_{10}) + c_{110}(t^*_{110}),$$

according to which no agent can gain by changing his route.

Consider the (unintended) consequence of adding another road to the network. This road (the Hollywood Freeway, or 101) connects Los Angeles to Studio City. Assume that traveling on 101 is costless: $c_{101}(t_{101}) = 0$ for all $t_{101} \geq 0$. Now, $X^1 = \{\{10, 110\}, \{405, 134\}, \{10, 101, 134\}, \{405, 101, 110\}\}$.

The unique Nash equilibrium routing in this augmented network has each agent choose route $\{10, 101, 134\}$. In order to see uniqueness, note that any agent who does not use this route gains by switching to this route unless almost everyone (i.e., measure one of agents) already uses this route.

The identified unique Nash equilibrium outcome in the augmented road network is not Pareto efficient. Each agent's equilibrium time in traffic is

$$c_{10}(1) + c_{101}(1) + c_{134}(1) = 2,$$

which is greater than his equilibrium time in traffic in the absence of the Hollywood Freeway. The phenomenon whereby adding a link to a network leads to a Pareto inferior equilibrium outcome is called the **Braess paradox**.

The utilitarian routing with the Hollywood Freeway is the same as without it—that is, half of the traffic goes through Studio City and half goes through Los Angeles; no one uses the Hollywood Freeway. One can modify the example so that, with utilitarian routing, the social welfare is higher with the Hollywood Freeway than without it, even though with Nash equilibrium routing it is lower. For this result, add another type of agents: those who benefit from traveling from Los Angeles to Studio City. They stay at home in the absence of the Hollywood Freeway (contrary to the assumption of the baseline model, in which everyone must travel) but travel if the freeway is built.

SANTA MONICA TO PASADENA: REINTERPRETED, TWICE

The gist of SM2P is that, in the presence of congestion, the freedom to combine the best features of two products may be deleterious. For example, the route through Studio City can be interpreted as getting both undergraduate and graduate degrees at the Studio City University, which excels at showering its graduate students with personal attention while neglecting its undergraduates. The benefit from studies there is

$$\underbrace{B}_{\text{undergraduate program}} + \underbrace{B + 1 - t_{134}}_{\text{graduate program}} ,$$

for some $B > 0$, where t_{134} is the measure of agents who enroll at the Studio City University. The route through Los Angeles can be interpreted as getting both undergraduate and graduate degrees at the Los Angeles University, which is quite different: it excels at showering its undergraduates with personal attention while neglecting its graduate students. The benefit from studies there is

$$\underbrace{B + 1 - t_{10}}_{\text{undergraduate program}} + \underbrace{B}_{\text{graduate program}} ,$$

where t_{10} is the measure of agents who enroll at the Los Angeles University. At either university, personal attention carries the quality premium of 1 but is also subject to congestion.

The analysis of SM2P then provides an argument for populating graduate programs exclusively with one's own former undergraduates. In the absence of such a policy, all students would seek undergraduate studies at the Los Angeles University and graduate studies at the Studio City University. Their benefit from such a strategy would be

$$\underbrace{B + 1 - t_{10}}_{\text{undergraduate program}} + \underbrace{B + 1 - t_{134}}_{\text{graduate program}} ,$$

where $t_{10} = t_{134} = 1$ is the equilibrium measure of agents who choose this strategy. As a result, at equilibrium, all benefits from personal attention are dissipated in congestion.

Another interpretation of SM2P involves two nearby towns: a beach town that is great for living but has few jobs and an inland town that has jobs but is a dull place to live. Assume that the beaches of the beach town and the jobs of the inland town are subject to congestion. Initially, individuals are forced to choose between a good job and a nice place to live. Once a fast rail link between the two towns is built, however, there is no need to choose. Individuals flock to live in the beach town and work in the inland one, thereby exacerbating congestion in both. The analysis of SM2P suggests that the fast rail link may be Pareto detrimental at equilibrium.

The two proposed interpretations of SM2P do not take into account the fact that markets may respond to changes in demands. A university may hire more faculty to staff the programs in which it excels at personal attention. New jobs may come to the inland town, and the beaches of the beach town may be further developed.

EXISTENCE

We have identified Nash equilibria in examples, but can we establish equilibrium existence more generally, without knowing the fine details of the network of roads? If equilibrium is not guaranteed to exist, one may fear chaos: day in, day out, drivers would take vastly (privately and socially) suboptimal routes due to their mistaken guesses about which routes other drivers are likely to take. Such chaos can prevail even if an equilibrium exists; drivers and their autopilots may have trouble converging to an equilibrium. We shall show that the world is not as fragile as that; an equilibrium always exists and is, in some sense, stable.

Still, road design remains challenging: Nash equilibria can be inefficient (SM2LA), and building roads may reduce welfare (SM2P). But how severe are these welfare losses relative to some Pareto efficient ideal? (We did not ask this question in the models of preceding chapters because we were able to establish FWT-type results.) Even if a FWT-type result does not hold, one need not worry about inefficiency if the departure from the efficient ideal is slight, say, in terms of the change in the value of the utilitarian social welfare function. We shall show that such a departure is indeed slight when congestion is mild. Moreover, when congestion is mild, the unintended losses (if any) from building extra roads are guaranteed to be small.

To show that an equilibrium traffic flow exists, we shall show that a minimum of a certain carefully constructed—but (apparently) economically meaningless—function exists. (The approach is similar in spirit to the abstract existence proof of theorem 1.3, in which equilibrium is identified with a fixed point of a carefully constructed but economically meaningless function.) The function that we shall minimize is[7]

$$\Phi(t) \equiv \sum_{l \in \mathcal{L}} \int_0^{t_l} c_l(s)\mathrm{d}s. \tag{8.3}$$

Function Φ is called (because of some formal parallels to physics) **potential** and happens to bound from below the aggregate cost function C (defined in (8.2) and reproduced here for convenience):[8]

$$\Phi(t) \leq C(t) \equiv \sum_{l \in \mathcal{L}} t_l c_l(t_l).$$

---

7. The integrals in the definition of Φ are all well-defined because each c_l is a weakly increasing real-valued function. Furthermore, because it is defined as a sum of integrals, Φ is differentiable (and so, continuous) in each t_l, even if c_l is not.

8. The inequality holds because c_l is weakly increasing and, hence, $\int_0^{t_l} c_l(s)\mathrm{d}s \leq \int_0^{t_l} c_l(t_l)\mathrm{d}s = t_l c_l(t_l)$.

Any minimizer of C is a utilitarian routing. Theorem 8.1 establishes equilibrium existence by showing that any minimizer of Φ is a Nash equilibrium routing and that Φ is guaranteed to have a minimizer.

Theorem 8.1. *In the routing problem, a Nash equilibrium traffic flow exists.*

Proof. First, note that any traffic flow t that minimizes Φ is a Nash equilibrium traffic flow. Indeed, by contradiction, suppose that t minimizes Φ but is not a Nash equilibrium traffic flow. Then, one can move a type-i agent from some route, say, x^i to some other route, say, y^i and reduce his costs by doing so:

$$\sum_{l \in y^i} c_l(t_l) < \sum_{l \in x^i} c_l(t_l).$$

If so, then one can also decrease the value $\Phi(t)$ by redirecting a small measure of type-i agents from x^i to y^i. The rate at which Φ changes as one carries out this redirection is

$$-\sum_{l \in x^i} \frac{\partial \Phi(t)}{\partial t_l} + \sum_{l \in y^i} \frac{\partial \Phi(t)}{\partial t_l},$$

which is negative because

$$\sum_{l \in y^i} \frac{\partial \Phi(t)}{\partial t_l} < \sum_{l \in x^i} \frac{\partial \Phi(t)}{\partial t_l} \iff \sum_{l \in y^i} c_l(t_l) < \sum_{l \in x^i} c_l(t_l), \tag{8.4}$$

where the equivalence follows by differentiating Φ. The possibility of such an improvement contradicts t being a minimizer of Φ. Thus, t must be a Nash equilibrium traffic flow.

To show equilibrium existence, it remains to show that Φ has a minimum. We shall use the Weierstrass theorem, which, recall from section 1.13, says that any continuous function that maps a nonempty, bounded, and closed set into a subset of real numbers attains a minimum and a maximum on that set. The set in question here is the set of traffic flows, which is a subset of the Euclidean space that is nonempty and bounded (because the measure of agents is nonempty and bounded) and is also closed. Function Φ is continuous by construction (it is a sum of integrals). Hence, a minimum exists by the Weierstrass theorem. ∎

CONVERGENCE

We can use function Φ in (8.3) to argue that natural adjustment dynamics would tend to lead agents either to a Nash equilibrium or, at least, to something that resembles a Nash equilibrium. Here is a heuristic argument. The **Nash best-response**

process starts with an arbitrary traffic flow and selects at random a small positive measure of agents of the same type who all choose a particular route and asks them whether they would rather choose a different route if the remaining agents did not revise their routes. If they would, let them choose their preferred route. Iterate. With each iterative step, Φ falls or remains unchanged, by the equivalence in (8.4). Because Φ is bounded below by zero, it cannot continue falling rapidly and forever. Instead, Φ must either settle, in which case the agents will have arrived at a Nash equilibrium, or keep changing only a little, at a vanishing rate. In the latter case, the agents will have arrived at an **approximate Nash equilibrium**, meaning that no agent can improve on his payoff much by deviating to a different route. Because Φ is monotone in each agent's improvement, cycles in the spirit of the tâtonnement cycle in figure 1.14 cannot occur.

THE LIMITS OF INEFFICIENCY

Even though equilibrium need not be Pareto efficient (example SM2LA), the welfare loss relative to the utilitarian outcome can sometimes be bounded. For instance, suppose that we can find a $\gamma \geq 0$ such that, for any traffic flow t,[9]

$$t_l c_l(t_l) \leq (1+\gamma) \int_0^{t_l} c_l(s)\mathrm{d}s, \quad l \in \mathcal{L}. \tag{8.5}$$

Theorem 8.2. *Let t be a Nash equilibrium traffic flow that minimizes Φ.[10] Let t^* be a utilitarian flow, which minimizes C. Then, the equilibrium cost, $C(t)$, is bounded above by $(1+\gamma)$ times the utilitarian cost, $C(t^*)$, where γ satisfies (8.5).*

Proof. The sought inequality $C(t) \leq (1+\gamma)C(t^*)$ follows from

$$C(t) = \sum_{l\in\mathcal{L}} t_l c_l(t_l) \leq (1+\gamma) \sum_{l\in\mathcal{L}} \int_0^{t_l} c_l(s)\mathrm{d}s$$

$$= (1+\gamma)\Phi(t) \leq (1+\gamma)\Phi(t^*) \leq (1+\gamma)C(t^*),$$

where the first equality is definitional; the first inequality is by (8.5); the second equality is definitional; the second inequality follows because the Nash equilibrium routing t minimizes Φ; and the last inequality follows because c is weakly increasing, and, hence, $\Phi(t^*) \leq C(t^*)$. ∎

---

9. A tighter bound is a more interesting one, so pick a small γ. Because c_l is weakly increasing, $\gamma \geq 0$.

10. The qualifier "that minimizes Φ" is in order because we have not proved that any equilibrium flow is a minimizer of Φ. The proof of theorem 8.1 only shows that any minimizer of Φ is an equilibrium.

To illustrate theorem 8.2, when $c_l(t_l) = t_l^{\alpha}$ for some $\alpha \geq 0$, one can satisfy (8.5) by taking $\gamma = \alpha$. As a result, if α is close to zero—that is, congestion is mild—then theorem 8.2 guarantees that equilibrium costs do not exceed the utilitarian costs by much.

One can use theorem 8.2 to bound the unintended damage from building extra roads (example SM2P).

Corollary 8.1. *The increase in the equilibrium congestion costs due to new roads does not exceed fraction $\gamma^{\text{new roads}}$ of the equilibrium congestions costs with old roads, where $\gamma^{\text{new roads}}$ is the coefficient that satisfies (8.5) for new roads.*

Proof. The sought inequality

$$C^{\text{new roads}}(t^{\text{new roads}}) \leq (1 + \gamma^{\text{new roads}})C^{\text{old roads}}(t^{\text{old roads}})$$

follows from

$$C^{\text{new roads}}(t^{\text{new roads}}) \leq (1 + \gamma^{\text{new roads}})C^{\text{new roads}}(t^{*,\text{new roads}})$$
$$\leq (1 + \gamma^{\text{new roads}})C^{\text{old roads}}(t^{\text{old roads}}),$$

where the first inequality says that, with new roads, equilibrium congestion costs do not exceed a multiple of the utilitarian costs, by theorem 8.2; and the second inequality says that utilitarian costs with new roads do not exceed equilibrium costs with old roads, for equilibrium routing with old roads remains feasible with new roads. ∎

8.4 LOCAL PUBLIC GOODS

Another environment in which a seemingly beneficial policy may have unintended adverse consequences is an environment with local public goods. A typical example of a local public good is information.[11] For instance, if any of Bob's friends investigates whether a newly introduced product is reliable or whether a medicine has adverse side effects, then Bob can use this information without performing a costly investigation himself. The model examined in this section assumes that information can travel from an investigating agent only to his friends—not to friends of friends or beyond. Information diffusion can be limited, for instance, because information travels slowly or because it gets distorted in transmission.

---

11. Other examples are lawn mowers and club memberships that come with guesting privileges.

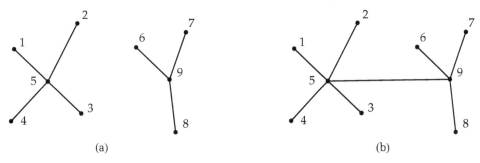

FIGURE 8.3.
Friendship graphs. Two agents, indexed by a number from 1 to 9, are friends if and only if they are joined by a link.

Here is an example in which it is natural to assume that information cannot credibly reach friends of friends and beyond. Suppose that students in an afternoon session of a class seek to procure the copies of the mid-term exam distributed to students in the morning session. Those who do so risk being caught and penalized. They also face the peer pressure to share, which, ideally, they would rather not do because the exam is graded on the curve. As a result, they share only with their friends, who would ostracize them if they did not share and then got caught (thereby revealing that they did have the exam copies). These friends would never share further, with their friends, however, because they can never be caught having talked to the morning group and so be proved to have been privy to the exam.

THE LOCAL-PUBLIC-GOOD PROVISION PROBLEM

A **local-public-good provision problem** has a finite number of agents, indexed by $i \in \mathcal{I} \equiv \{1, 2, ..., I\}$. Each agent i takes a binary action $x^i \in X^i \equiv \{0, 1\}$. Agent i's utility $u(x^i, x^{-i})$ depends on his action x^i and on others' actions x^{-i}. Only some components of x^{-i} affect agent i's utility. In particular, an agent's action affects another agent only if the two are friends.

Graphically, agents are nodes (or vertices) on a friendship graph, whose undirected links (or edges) designate friendships. Friendships are nontransitive; Alice being friends with Bob and Bob with Carol does not imply that Alice and Carol are friends. The two panels of figure 8.3 illustrate two friendship graphs.

Interpret action $x^i = 1$ to mean that agent i contributes to a local public good, such as information acquisition. This interpretation is motivated by the utility specification

$$u(x^i, x^{-i}) = \max_{j \in \mathcal{F}^i} \{x^i, x^j\} - cx^i,$$

where $\mathcal{F}^i \subset \mathcal{I}$ is the set of agent i's friends, $c \in (0, 1)$ is the cost of contributing to the public good, and $\max_{j \in \mathcal{F}^i}\{x^i, x^j\} = 1$ if and only if agent i enjoys the public good. By taking action $x^i = 1$, agent i contributes to a **public good** because his friends enjoy the undiluted benefit of his action without incurring the cost. This public good is **local** because only agent i's friends (and agent i himself)—never friends of friends, and so on—enjoy it.

TWO WELL-CONNECTED FRIENDS SHARING BENEFITS

Consider the friendship graph in figure 8.3(a), where $\mathcal{I} = \{1, 2, ..., 9\}$. The induced game has multiple Nash equilibria. One Nash equilibrium is also the (unique) utilitarian Pareto efficient allocation. At this equilibrium, $x^i = 1$ for each $i \in \{5, 9\}$ and $x^i = 0$ for each $i \in \mathcal{I} \setminus \{5, 9\}$. At this equilibrium, the value of the utilitarian social value function is $9 - 2c$.

In the best possible (from the utilitarian standpoint) friendship graph, every agent would be directly connected to every agent, so that only one agent would have to contribute to the public good. The value of the social welfare function would be $9 - c$. It does not follow, however, that adding an extra link to the graph in figure 8.3(a) would necessarily increase the value of the social welfare function, even if the best (from the utilitarian standpoint) Nash equilibrium prevails.

To illustrate, consider the friendship structure in figure 8.3(b), which differs from figure 8.3(a) only in that agents 5 and 9 are now linked. The unintended consequence of this added link is that there is no Nash equilibrium in which agents 5 and 9 both contribute. The best Nash equilibrium from the utilitarian standpoint has $x^i = 1$ for each $i \in \{5, 6, 7, 8\}$ and $x^i = 0$ for each $i \in \mathcal{I} \setminus \{5, 6, 7, 8\}$. At this equilibrium, the value of the utilitarian social welfare function is $9 - 4c$. The added link has reduced welfare in spite of having made it easier for the agents to share the public good.

Note that the described equilibrium for the graph in figure 8.3(b) is also an equilibrium for the graph in figure 8.3(a). The example in figure 8.3(a) has multiple equilibria. As a result, whether adding a link is damaging may depend on which equilibrium one begins with.

EXISTENCE

Even though equilibrium need not be unique, it always exists:

Theorem 8.3. *In the local-public-good provision problem, a Nash equilibrium exists.*

Proof. At any equilibrium, no two contributing agents are friends. (Otherwise, either would profitably deviate by not contributing.) At the same time, at any equilibrium, if none of one's friends contributes, one shall contribute. Thus, the set of the agents who contribute at equilibrium is the maximal (in the inclusion sense) set of agents none of whom are friends. Such a maximal set always exists (so, equilibrium always exists) even though it need not be unique (so, multiple equilibria are possible). ∎

CONVERGENCE

The proof of theorem 8.3 suggests a decentralized algorithm for arriving at an equilibrium. Suppose that no agent is a contributor to begin with. Pick an agent and ask him, and only him, to contribute. If the resulting contribution profile is an equilibrium, we are done. Otherwise, pick a noncontributing agent who is not friends with the contributing agent and ask him to contribute. If the resulting contribution profile is equilibrium, we are done. Otherwise, iterate.

THE LIMITS OF INEFFICIENCY

In the spirit of corollary 8.1, which bounds the damage from building a road, one can ask whether the damage from an extra friendship can be bounded. There is a sense in which it can be. Roughly speaking, if agents start out at a "bad" equilibrium, then matters will not get worse if a friendship is added; matters can get better, though. It is only if the agents start out at a "good" equilibrium, then matters can get worse if a friendship is added.

Formally, take a friendship graph and identify an equilibrium, denoted by x^{old}. Add a friendship link. If x^{old} remains an equilibrium with the new graph, then no damage has been inflicted. If x^{old} is no longer an equilibrium (as is the case in the example in figure 8.3), then identify a new equilibrium and denote it by x^{new}. Now, remove the link that has been added, thereby reverting to the old graph. Two cases are possible:

1. x^{new} is an equilibrium with the old graph (as is the case in the example in figure 8.3); then, no damage *would have been* inflicted by adding the link if the agents happened to start at x^{new} (instead of x^{old}) with the old graph.

2. x^{new} is not an equilibrium with the old graph; then, Pareto improvement *would have been* realized by adding the link if the agents had happened to start at a Pareto inferior (to x^{new}) equilibrium (i.e., "bad" equilibrium), which can be shown to exist.

To prove the nonobvious assertion in case 2, take the contributing agents in x^{new}, who form the maximal contributing set of non-friends (as in the proof of theorem 8.3) with respect to the new graph. Remove the added link, thereby reverting to the old graph. By hypothesis, the contributing agents in x^{new} do not form a maximal set with respect to the old graph (x^{new} is not an equilibrium with the old graph).

Therefore, because the old graph is less connected, there must exist a maximal set with respect to the old graph that is larger (in the inclusion sense) than the set of the contributing agents in x^{new}.

The consequences from adding a link can be equivalently and succinctly rephrased in terms of severing a link:

Theorem 8.4. *Fix a friendship network and an equilibrium, x. Then sever one friendship link. If x is no longer an equilibrium, then one can find an equilibrium that is Pareto inferior to x (i.e., the same agents contribute as in x and more).*

8.5   CONCLUDING REMARKS

This chapter's broad lesson is that policies that are unambiguously beneficial if comprehensive (e.g., connecting all pairs of locations with fast roads or opening a costless communication channel between any two individuals) may be detrimental (in Pareto or in a weaker, utilitarian, sense) if introduced only partway.

In the routing problem, the bound on the welfare losses in corollary 8.1 is of some comfort but is arbitrarily high if congestion is arbitrarily severe, even if only on a handful of roads, even if only for a handful of drivers. For instance, suppose that some (small but positive measure of) agents (e.g., patients headed for the emergency room) in example SM2P absolutely cannot stand more than a half-hour delay on highways 10 and 134. Then, the travel delays caused by the new highway will have disastrous welfare consequences.

In the local-public-good problem, the consolation of theorem 8.4 that a "bad" equilibrium cannot get worse when a friendship is added is tempered by the fact that the agents have incentives to coordinate on the "best" equilibrium to begin with. So, careful design matters.

8.6   BIBLIOGRAPHICAL NOTES

Utilitarianism goes back to Jeremy Bentham and John Stuart Mill. Section 8.3 follows Nisan, Roughgarden, Tardos, and Vazirani, eds. (2007, section 18.2.1). Example SM2LA is Pigou's (1920), and SM2P is Braess's (1968). The equilibrium existence proof in theorem 8.1, which uses a potential function, is due to Rosenthal (1973). The theory of potential games has been further developed by Monderer and Shapley (1996), who note the convergence of best-response dynamics to a Nash equilibrium.

The example that is the focus of section 8.4 is the so-called best-shot public-good game. Its discussion follows Jackson (2008, section 9.3). The insight that adding a link may reduce welfare is due to Bramoullé and Kranton (2007, section V). Theorem 8.4 is reported by Jackson (2008, proposition 9.3.2).

PROBLEMS

Problem 8.1 (Congestion Charging).   Modify the routing problem by assuming that any type-i agent's cost of taking any route $x^i \in X^i$ is

$$\sum_{l \in x^i} \left(c_l(t_l) + \tau_l(t_l) \right),$$

where c_l is differentiable and $\tau_l(t_l)$ is a congestion tax that the agent pays the government for the right to pass through link l. The utilitarian traffic flow is unchanged because, in the utilitarian social welfare function, which now includes the government's payoff $\sum_{l \in \mathcal{L}} t_l \tau_l(t_l)$, all tax transfers cancel out, and, so, the utilitarian social welfare function itself is unchanged. By contrast, Nash equilibrium traffic flow is affected by the transfers.

1. Design a tax structure $(\tau_l)_{l \in \mathcal{L}}$ such that, in SM2LA, the Nash equilibrium routing coincides with the utilitarian one.

2. Repeat the exercise in part 1 for SM2P with freeway 101 added.

3. Repeat the exercise in part 1 for the general routing problem.

Problem 8.2 (Kantian Drivers).   Consider example SM2LA. Modify the example by assuming that fraction $\alpha \in [0, 1]$ of agents are Kantian and fraction $1 - \alpha$ are Nash. Each agent's action is the probability with which he takes the freeway, with the probability of taking the side streets being complementary. Each agent is an expected utility maximizer (i.e., expected-cost-of-time-in-traffic minimizer). In a **Kantian-Nash equilibrium**, each Nash agent chooses his action taking all others' actions as given; whereas each Kantian agent chooses his action assuming that every Kantian agent would choose the same action as he does and taking as given only the actions of the Nash agents.

1. Find a Kantian-Nash equilibrium in which all Kantian agents take the same action and all Nash agents take the same action. Assume that the law of large numbers holds; if, say, each Kantian agent chooses the freeway with probability p, then exactly measure $p\alpha$ of Kantian agents end up on the freeway.

2. How does the equilibrium you have identified in part 1 depend on α?

3. Is the equilibrium outcome you have identified in part 1 Pareto efficient?

Problem 8.3 (Local Public Goods). Find all equilibria for the friendship graphs in figures 8.3(a) and 8.3(b) and interpret your findings in the context of theorem 8.4. If necessary, modify the example in figure 8.3 to illustrate the aspects of theorem 8.4 that are missing from that example.

CHAPTER 9

CODA

9.1   METHODOLOGICAL INDIVIDUALISM

Microeconomics espouses **methodological individualism**, which requires that aggregate phenomena be modeled as outcomes of individuals' utility-maximizing behavior. By this measure, most of modern economics is microeconomics.[1] In economics, the models of unemployment, wars, output fluctuations, growth, racial discrimination, optimal taxation, industrial organization, and residential segregation, among many others, are all derived from the maximizing behavior of autonomous individuals. Individuals may be interconnected through economic, political, and other social institutions (such as families and friendships), but, subject to the constraints imposed by these institutions, individuals act autonomously. Even if an individual's utility function depends on others' actions or utilities, the individual still maximizes his own utility function. His maximization protocol may be unorthodox (e.g., Kantian instead of Nash), but the maximization itself is autonomous.

Methodological individualism influences normative analysis by suggesting that the choices made for the society at large perhaps be guided by the choices that

---

1. A graphic instantiation of an economic model that is emphatically nonindividualistic is the 1949 Phillips machine, whose water-filled vessels, tubes, valves, and pumps simulate an economy. (See "Guest Column: Like Water for Money." Olivia Judson (blog), *New York Times*, June 2, 2009, http://judson .blogs.nytimes.com/2009/06/02/guest-column-like-water-for-money/?_r=0.)

the agents would have been inclined to make for themselves. This principle of honoring individual choices—the **liberal humanism** of the Enlightenment—suggests, for instance, that a country's government should maximize not the country's wealth, prestige, or military might but some aggregate measure of her inhabitants' wellbeing. Formally, this idea is captured by postulating that the social welfare function be welfarist (i.e., depend on outcomes only through agents' utility functions). For instance, employment, inflation, or income distribution should not enter the planner's social welfare function directly but only through the values of the agents' utility functions, to the extent that the agents care.

Utility maximization is a methodology, not a scientific hypothesis. In principle, utility maximization cannot be contradicted by data. If an agent's utility function is a constant, then any choice he makes is consistent with utility maximization because he is indifferent among all alternatives and may choose in an arbitrary, possibly stochastic, manner. At the other extreme, if the individual is assumed never to be indifferent between any two alternatives, then utility maximization can be easily contradicted by apparent inconsistencies in his choices (e.g., sometimes choosing a over b and sometimes choosing b over a).

Of course, one can always postulate that no two choice situations are ever the same because any alternative presented on two different dates in different circumstances (which may even include the agent's mood) are, in fact, two distinct alternatives. In this case, again, no contradiction to utility maximization can be derived. Hence, a useful model is always parsimonious enough to have some predictive power and be falsifiable.

Often, the assumption that an individual meticulously maximizes his utility function is untenable. A Canadian tourist in Australia who has failed to first look right before crossing a road and has been run over by a bus most certainly has made a mistake; he has not chosen the outcome that would have made him the happiest. Hence, it is worth contemplating alternative (to unerring utility maximization) protocols that translate preferences into behavior. Mental efforts and attention may be inputs to such protocols.

While the economist will occasionally make claims about what individuals do, or ought to do, with their utility functions (e.g., avoid mistakes, maximize in the Nash manner or in the Kantian manner), the economist will never pass value judgments on these utility functions. Utilities are the primitives of the environment. It is pointless to argue over whether utilities are convenient or inconvenient, sinful or virtuous; they are given and must be respected. Trying to change someone's utility function—or even presuming that one knows what a "better" utility function ought to be—may lead to misery by the suppression of true preferences (the **tamed housewife syndrome** diagnosed by Sen, 1985) at best and may serve as a pretext for the subjugation and exploitation of the subjugated, purportedly for their own good, at worst.

Thus, the following sentiments, voiced by Sandel (2012), are foreign to economists: "If some people like opera and others like dogfights or mud wrestling, must we really be nonjudgmental and give these preferences equal weight in the utilitarian calculus?" and "[T]his bizarre market caters to a perverse desire that should carry no weight in any calculus of social utility." So is Karl Marx's "The alteration of men on a mass scale is necessary." (While analytical Marxism subscribes to methodological individualism and, largely, to the immutability of human nature as encoded in utility functions, traditional Marxism does not.) The economist does not blame the player, only the game.

Of course, one's tastes change over time and with experience. Individuals seem to become more risk averse and, at first, more, and then less, patient with age (Falk et al. 2015); they find it hard to reject the luxuries they have gotten accustomed to; they get addicted to cigarettes, alcohol, violence, risk, and intellectual challenges (Linden, 2011). What these changes mean, however, is that preferences are defined not over instantaneous consumption but over bundles that comprise the entire (possibly stochastic) consumption stream over the individual's lifetime. What the economist insists on is that these preferences, however complex, be the basis for welfare calculus.

"[M]arkets don't pass judgment on the desires they satisfy," laments Sandel (2012). This property of markets is not a bug but a feature—a civilizing feature. Markets teach individuals to be tolerant in the sense of respecting others' preferences. A positive feedback loop sets in: markets render individuals more tolerant, and this tolerance, in turn, motivates individuals to expand the scope of markets.

9.2   DESIGN BY CONSTRAINED OPTIMIZATION

While taking utility functions as given, seek to understand existing institutions and design better ones. A common approach to design is to identify the desiderata and summarize some of them in an objective function—the social welfare function—to be maximized. The remaining desiderata, as well as the immutable features of the environment, enter the maximization problem as constraints. The problem's solution is a social choice function, which maps the economic environment into the recommended outcome. Institutions can then be designed to implement this social choice function in a decentralized or centralized manner.

THREE THEORIES OF JUSTICE

It is normatively compelling to maximize a social welfare function that induces Pareto efficient outcomes. An example is the utilitarian social welfare function, which simply adds up individual utility functions. We shall consider two more.

In the 1970s, John Rawls opposed utilitarianism because utilitarianism may lead to a highly unequal distribution of utility levels in the population. (Indeed, when utility functions are concave and the allocation implied by utilitarianism is interior, utilitarianism equates marginal utilities, not utility levels.) Rawls also opposed utilitarianism because utilitarianism respects all preferences, including spiteful and envious ones, and those that have adapted to make it easier for their bearer to put up with oppressive conditions. Thus, Rawls was not even a welfarist, for he dismissed some tastes encoded into utility functions as unworthy.

Rawls proposed the **maxmin criterion**: maximize the minimal utility in the society across all agents, with each utility stripped of its offensive components (e.g., spitefulness). In economics, this criterion is applied to the utility functions unstripped of their censured components. The maxmin criterion can be rationalized as a choice of an individual who finds himself behind the veil of ignorance, unaware of the position that he will occupy in the society, and who is infinitely risk averse. As a result, this individual chooses as if he knew with certainty that he would have the life of the worst-off individual, whoever that individual happens to be.

Rawls's assumption of infinite risk aversion is arbitrary. It does not appear to be borne out empirically. Norton and Ariely (2011) report survey evidence according to which, even behind the veil of ignorance, individuals demand an unequal society—albeit much less unequal than the one they believe they inhabit (which, in turn, is much less unequal than the actual, United States, society that they do inhabit).

Gregory Mankiw, too, challenges utilitarianism. His objections are mostly empirical. He contends that utilitarianism lacks popular support. For instance, there is no concerted policy effort to equalize the marginal utilities worldwide—contrary to what utilitarianism prescribes when utility functions are concave. Further, Mankiw and Weinzierl (2010) argue that a utilitarian-optimal tax system would make tall individuals pay more taxes than short individuals with the same income, provided height is correlated with ability, which it is.[2] The authors claim, as an empirical matter, that most would find taxes on height repugnant, thereby undermining the case for utilitarianism, on which the case for these taxes rests.

Mankiw also believes that utilitarianism is impractical because utilities are impossible to measure.[3] One may be tempted to impute the same utility function to all (e.g., the logarithm of aggregate consumption), but this imputation would

2. The logic for taxing the tall is this: The utilitarian planner wants more able individuals to pay more taxes, as Mankiw and Weinzierl (2010) show. One's ability is unobserved, while earnings are observed. However, the planner refrains from exorbitant taxes on high earners in order not to discourage them from working. When the more able are also known to be taller, taxing height can accomplish the goal of taxing the more able more without discouraging them from working.

3. In advocating the practice of effective altruism, Singer (2015) assumes away the measurement problem and proposes a crude version of utilitarianism, according to which one is urged to count and maximize the number of lives he saves.

disregard the possibility that different individuals may differently value material consumption, leisure, and job attributes, such as intellectual freedom, flexible hours, and various occupational hazards.

Mankiw's alternative to utilitarianism is the principle of **just deserts**. This principle maintains that an individual should be rewarded in proportion to his contribution to the society. This principle echoes philosopher Nozick's (1974) assertion that justice requires that each individual own himself and thereby be fully entitled to the product of his labor and the gains from the trades that he consummates. One way to operationalize this principle is to require that the allocation be in the core (appropriately extended to economies with production, if necessary). Note that if the core is not a singleton, then this operationalization is incomplete. Another way to operationalize the principle of just deserts is to require that the allocation be a Walrasian equilibrium allocation (possibly nonunique). The two approaches are similar when the conclusion of the core convergence theorem (theorem 4.3) holds.

A major concern in distributive justice is the possibly inequitable allocation of private endowments (e.g., intelligence, looks, or health). The principle of just deserts takes these endowments as given and, therefore, implicitly as just. As a result, any changes in the endowments (e.g., due to technological progress, which affects which endowments are in high demand) will lead to the changes in individual deserts that, too, will be considered just. Furthermore, one's contribution to the society will generally depend on the way the society is organized (e.g., a market or a jungle), which the principle of just deserts does not specify. As a result, the principle's definition is open-ended.

The general thrust of the principle of just deserts is that rewards are attached to actions, not the individuals who take these actions. The principle thus guarantees impartiality, which one may or may not find desirable.

A SIMPLE ECONOMY WITH PRODUCTION

Let us examine the three theories of justice outlined above by expressing them formally as constrained optimization problems. We do so in a simple production economy, related to, but distinct from, the one introduced in section 4.4. Each agent $i \in \mathcal{I}$ consumes amount $x_1^i \in \mathbb{R}_+$ of stuff (a composite material good) and amount $x_2^i \in \mathbb{R}_+$ of leisure and is endowed with $e_1^i = 0$ units of stuff and $e_2^i = 1$ units of leisure. Any leisure that he does not consume, he converts into $h^i \equiv e_2^i - x_2^i$ units of labor.

Agent i's utility function is

$$u^i(x^i) = \theta_0^i + \theta_1^i \ln x_1^i + \theta_2^i \ln x_2^i, \tag{9.1}$$

where θ_0^i is a baseline-happiness parameter, and θ_1^i and θ_2^i are positive taste parameters. The production technology is linear; a unit of agent i's labor translates into $a^i > 0$ units of stuff. Coefficient a^i is interpreted as agent i's ability. A nonnegative allocation x is feasible if it satisfies the resource constraint

$$\sum_{i \in \mathcal{I}} x_1^i \leq \sum_{i \in \mathcal{I}} a^i h^i. \tag{9.2}$$

UTILITARIAN ALLOCATION

A utilitarian social planner maximizes

$$\sum_{i \in \mathcal{I}} u^i(x^i)$$

over x subject to the resource constraint (9.2). The solution can be verified to be

$$x_1^i = \frac{\bar{a} \theta_1^i}{\bar{\theta}_1 + \bar{\theta}_2} \quad \text{and} \quad x_2^i = \frac{\bar{a} \theta_2^i}{a^i (\bar{\theta}_1 + \bar{\theta}_2)}, \tag{9.3}$$

where

$$\bar{\theta}_1 \equiv \sum_{i \in \mathcal{I}} \theta_1^i, \quad \bar{\theta}_2 \equiv \sum_{i \in \mathcal{I}} \theta_2^i, \quad \text{and} \quad \bar{a} \equiv \sum_{i \in \mathcal{I}} a^i.$$

Thus, any agent i's consumption of stuff relative to any other agent j's consumption of stuff, x_1^i / x_1^j, depends on his relative taste for stuff, θ_1^i / θ_1^j, and is independent of the two agents' abilities, a^i and a^j. An agent's leisure relative to another agent's leisure, x_2^i / x_2^j, is increasing in his relative taste for leisure and is decreasing in his relative ability. The utilitarian allocation makes no attempt to compensate agents for the interpersonal differences in their baseline happiness levels, $(\theta_0^i)_{i \in \mathcal{I}}$. The equalization of utility levels (as opposed to marginal utilities) occurs only in special cases, such as when the agents' utility functions and abilities are identical.

At the utilitarian allocation, a more able agent exerts extra effort but is not especially compensated with stuff for doing so. As a consequence, his utility

$$\theta_0^i + \theta_1^i \ln \theta_1^i + \theta_2^i \ln \theta_2^i - \theta_2^i \ln a^i + \theta_1^i \ln \frac{\bar{a}}{\bar{\theta}_1 + \bar{\theta}_2} + \theta_2^i \ln \frac{\bar{a}}{\bar{\theta}_1 + \bar{\theta}_2}$$

is decreasing in his ability (a^i) whenever his ability is sufficiently small relative to the economy's aggregate productive capacity ($\bar{a}$):

$$\frac{a^i}{\bar{a}} < \frac{\theta_2^i}{\theta_1^i + \theta_2^i},$$

which is the case whenever agents are sufficiently numerous. This punitive feature of utilitarianism is mitigated if the more able also happen to be better at enjoying consumption and leisure.

The utilitarian prescription is utopian; it is unattainable regardless of whether it is normatively compelling. An agent who enjoys consumption more (i.e., whose θ_1^i and θ_2^i are higher) is supposed to consume more. But how would the planner be able to elicit the taste parameters? Surely an agent would be tempted to overstate his tastes in order to get a more preferred bundle. Similarly, requiring a more able agent to work more without appropriate compensation would encourage this agent to conceal his ability and, in a richer model, would discourage him from investing in it.

The utilitarian allocation in (9.3) fits quite well Marx's definition of **communism**, summarized in the slogan: "From each according to his ability [here, a^i], to each according to his needs [here, θ_1^i and θ_2^i]!"[4] To render communism workable would require either a **totalitarian society** (in which a^i, θ_1^i, and θ_2^i are observable to the planner) or a radical change in human nature (either to make lying about a^i, θ_1^i, and θ_2^i unthinkable or to engineer the desired parameter values).

RAWLSIAN ALLOCATION

A Rawlsian allocation maximizes the **Rawlsian social welfare function**

$$\min_{i \in \mathcal{I}} \left\{ u^i(x^i) \right\} \tag{9.4}$$

over x subject to the resource constraint (9.2). Instead of solving for a Rawlsian allocation, we simply observe, by inspection of (9.4), that the allocation is affected by the agents' baseline happiness levels, $(\theta_0^i)_{i \in \mathcal{I}}$. In particular, if an agent's baseline-happiness parameter were to rise, he would be awarded a worse bundle in order to make sure that his utility did not stand out.[5]

This dependence on the baseline happiness parameters is among the shortcomings of the Rawlsian approach. The planner must rely on each agent's willingness to report his baseline happiness parameter truthfully, which is against the agent's interest. Agent i has an incentive to claim that $\theta_0^i \to -\infty$, for instance, by claiming a disability, such as chronic back pain or a migraine (neither of which

4. By potentially making a more able agent worse off, utilitarianism fits neither the spirit of the formal definition of socialism (definition 4.2) nor the informal one captured by the Marxist slogan: "From each according to his ability, to each according to his work."

5. While the Rawlsian strives to equalize the agents' utilities, the socialist of section 4.4 need not do so, because the utility function (9.1) violates the skill–consumption neutrality, and so theorem 4.4 does not apply. When the assumptions of section 4.4 hold, the equivalence between the socialist and the Rawlsian social welfare functions is established in problem 9.3.

can be objectively diagnosed). Thus, just like the utilitarian allocation, Rawlsian allocation is utopian.

JUST DESERTS

One way to operationalize the just deserts principle is to require $x_1^i = a^i h^i$ for each agent $i \in \mathcal{I}$. These constraints ensure that each agent consumes his contribution to the aggregate supply of stuff. Subject to these constraints, each agent is prescribed to work and consume so as to maximize the utilitarian social welfare function. These constraints also make the maximization problem separable; the utility of each agent can be maximized individually:[6]

$$\max_{x^i} u^i(x^i) \quad \text{s.t.} \quad x_1^i = a^i h^i, \quad i \in \mathcal{I}. \tag{9.5}$$

The solution can be verified to be

$$x_1^i = \frac{a^i \theta_1^i}{\theta_1^i + \theta_2^i} \quad \text{and} \quad x_2^i = \frac{\theta_2^i}{\theta_1^i + \theta_2^i}. \tag{9.6}$$

According to (9.6), if two agents have identical tastes, then they enjoy the same amount of leisure, but the more able one consumes more stuff. If two agents are equally able, then the one with a greater relative taste for stuff consumes more stuff and works more. Also note that if Alice derives twice as much pleasure from the consumption of each good (stuff and leisure) as Bob does, then she still consumes the same bundle as Bob does, provided the two agents are equally able.

The principle of just deserts prescribes the same allocation as utilitarianism does if and only if

$$\frac{a^i}{\theta_1^i + \theta_2^i} \quad \text{is independent of } i \in \mathcal{I}. \tag{9.7}$$

That is, agents may differ in their tastes and abilities as long as those who are, say, twice as able also derive twice as much pleasure from consumption. The hypothesis in (9.7) is impossible to test but is plausible. If Alice has twice the focus and stamina of Bob, she is likely to deploy these qualities not only in production but also in consumption.

The social choice function induced by the just-deserts constrained-maximization problem differs from its utilitarian and Rawlsian counterparts in that it is not utopian. No agent i has incentives to lie about his utility parameters. Indeed, by asking to report these parameters, the just deserts planner asks the agent to report

---

6. Feasibility constraint (9.2) is omitted because it is implied by the just deserts constraints.

(a parameterization of) the function that the planner will then maximize, in (9.5). The best the agent can do is to be honest.

Furthermore, because each agent's utility is increasing in his ability, no agent has an incentive to understate his ability, for instance, by destroying his output and thereby appearing less able. Overstating ability is not a concern assuming that the planner can observe each agent i's output, $a^i h^i$, and the amount of time the agent works, h^i, the ratio of which reveals the agent's ability.

WALRASIAN EQUILIBRIUM DELIVERS JUST DESERTS

Now that we have established that the just-deserts social choice function encourages each agent to report truthfully the parameters of his utility function, we exhibit a simple way to implement it. The just-deserts social choice function turns out to be Walrasian. Hence, if one seeks a just deserts outcome, one can simply set up a Walrasian market.

Adapt definition 4.3 of Walrasian equilibrium with production by acknowledging that agents differ in their abilities. Guess that the firm pays each agent i wage $p_2 a^i$, where p_2 is the price of leisure (or the wage rate per "effective unit of labor") and is determined at equilibrium. Then, the firm's labor demand vector is

$$(h^i)_{i \in \mathcal{I}} \in \arg \max_{(\tilde{h}^i)_{i \in \mathcal{I}} \in [0,1]^I} (p_1 - p_2) \left(\sum_{i \in \mathcal{I}} a^i \tilde{h}^i \right), \tag{9.8}$$

where p_1 is the price of stuff. Each agent i's bundle x^i maximizes his utility:

$$x^i \in \arg \max_{y_1^i \geq 0, y_2^i \in [0,1]} u^i(y^i) \quad \text{s.t.} \quad p_1 y_1^i + p_2 a^i y_2^i \leq p_2 a^i, \tag{9.9}$$

where the budget constraint omits the agent's share in the firm's profit in anticipation of this profit being zero at equilibrium. All markets must clear:

$$\sum_{i \in \mathcal{I}} x_1^i = \sum_{i \in \mathcal{I}} a^i h^i \quad \text{and} \quad h^i + x_2^i = 1, \ i \in \mathcal{I}.$$

In equilibrium, $p_1 = p_2 > 0$. Indeed, if $p_1 > p_2$, the firm's profit maximization problem in (9.8) is not well-defined. If $p_1 < p_2$, the firm produces nothing, yet each agent demands a positive amount of stuff, thereby violating the market clearing condition for stuff. Both prices are positive because utility functions are strictly increasing.

At $p_1 = p_2$, the firm's profit is zero, justifying the omission of the profit term from the agent's budget constraint in (9.9). Substituting the equilibrium prices into the agents' demands, one can verify that the induced equilibrium allocation coincides with the just deserts allocation (9.6).

Because of the close connection between Walrasian equilibrium and the principle of just deserts, it is hard to tell whether the intuitive appeal (if any) of the principle of just deserts is due to this principle's inherent merit or or due to one's habituation to the ubiquity of markets.

IDENTIFYING THE IMAGINARY PLANNER IN THE DATA

From the empirical standpoint, one may wonder whether the social welfare function whose maximization is consistent with the outcomes observed in practice resembles any of the social welfare functions discussed above. Chang, Chang, and Kim (2017) examine this question in a dynamic economy with production and taxes. In their model, agents have identical preferences but differ in their abilities and wealth levels. Observed taxes hint at the social welfare function that the society that has chosen these taxes seeks to maximize.

Consider the social welfare function that generalizes the utilitarian social welfare function by weighting different agents differently:

$$\sum_{i \in \mathcal{I}} \omega^i u^i, \tag{9.10}$$

where each $\omega^i \geq 0$ is a **Pareto weight** on agent i's utility u^i. The weights $(\omega^i)_{i \in \mathcal{I}}$ are called "Pareto" because, under some conditions, one can trace out the entire Pareto set by varying these weights and then maximizing (9.10) (part 4 of problem 1.1). In (9.10), each agent's utility depends implicitly on his ability, wealth, and the tax policy, all of which affect equilibrium consumption. Each Pareto weight depends on i, which is taken to be the agent's rank in the consumption distribution.

Chang et al. (2017) examine thirty-two OECD countries and, for each of them, estimate the Pareto weights such that, given these weights, the tax policy that maximizes (9.10) is the same as the tax policy that is currently observed in the country. The identified weights reflect the country's political and economic institutions and the society's attitudes toward inequality. The imaginary planner, who maximizes the identified social welfare function over admissible tax policies, is a metaphor for these institutions and attitudes.

Table 9.1 reports the findings of Chang et al. (2017). In the table, the agents are partitioned into five groups according to their consumption: the poorest fifth (i.e., the first quantile), the second-poorest fifth, the middle fifth, the second-richest fifth, and the richest fifth (i.e., the fifth quantile). The utilitarian welfare function would assign the same weight, 0.2, to each quantile. According to the table, Korea, the United States, Switzerland, and Israel are all close to utilitarian. The Rawlsian welfare function would put most weight on the first quantile and (to prevent the quantiles from flipping) some weight on the remaining quantiles. In this sense, the Nordic and the Central European countries look approximately Rawlsian. At the other extreme are Chile and Turkey. Chile assigns 4% to the bottom quantile, and 47% to the top quantile. This extreme assignment has a flavor of just deserts. To

TABLE 9.1

Estimated weights on the agents' utilities for each of the five consumption quantiles. For instance, in the United States, the utilities for the richer carry a higher weight, whereas in Sweden the opposite occurs.

Country	Pareto Weights by Quantiles				
	1st (bottom 20%)	2nd	3rd	4th	5th (top 20%)
Australia	0.25	0.21	0.19	0.18	0.16
Austria	0.53	0.21	0.13	0.09	0.04
Belgium	0.62	0.19	0.11	0.06	0.03
Canada	0.32	0.22	0.18	0.15	0.12
Chile	0.04	0.09	0.15	0.24	0.47
Czech Republic	0.53	0.21	0.13	0.08	0.04
Denmark	0.65	0.17	0.10	0.05	0.02
Estonia	0.33	0.22	0.18	0.15	0.12
Finland	0.66	0.18	0.09	0.05	0.02
France	0.45	0.22	0.15	0.11	0.07
Germany	0.43	0.22	0.16	0.12	0.07
Greece	0.32	0.22	0.18	0.15	0.12
Iceland	0.59	0.19	0.11	0.07	0.04
Ireland	0.50	0.22	0.14	0.09	0.05
Israel	0.23	0.21	0.20	0.19	0.18
Italy	0.35	0.22	0.18	0.15	0.11
Japan	0.28	0.22	0.19	0.17	0.14
Korea	0.17	0.19	0.20	0.21	0.23
Luxembourg	0.43	0.22	0.16	0.12	0.07
Netherlands	0.47	0.21	0.15	0.11	0.06
New Zealand	0.29	0.22	0.19	0.17	0.14
Norway	0.55	0.20	0.13	0.08	0.04
Poland	0.35	0.22	0.18	0.15	0.11
Portugal	0.29	0.22	0.19	0.16	0.13
Slovak Republic	0.47	0.22	0.15	0.10	0.06
Slovenia	0.61	0.19	0.11	0.06	0.03
Spain	0.30	0.22	0.19	0.16	0.13
Sweden	0.54	0.20	0.13	0.08	0.05
Switzerland	0.20	0.20	0.20	0.20	0.20
Turkey	0.09	0.15	0.19	0.24	0.33
United Kingdom	0.27	0.22	0.19	0.17	0.15
United States	0.17	0.19	0.20	0.21	0.23

Source: Chang et al. (2017, table 8).

the extent that the just deserts allocation is Walrasian, it can be shown that it can be represented as a maximizer of the social welfare function that puts greater weight on wealthier individuals. (Indeed, such weights are necessary to generate inequality in consumption when the utility functions are identical.)

9.3   CONSTRAINTS IN ECONOMIC DESIGN

The design approach in section 9.2 identifies a social choice function that maximizes a social welfare function subject to positive constraints, which the designer has no choice but to respect, and subject to normative constraints, which comprise the desiderata not captured by the objective function. Here, we pause to reflect on these two types of constraints.

POSITIVE CONSTRAINTS

Some of the positive constraints are immediate, such as technological constraints: the aggregate consumption of any good cannot exceed the aggregate endowment and production of that good. (Constraint (9.2) is an example.) Other constraints may be less immediate but are still indispensable, such as the incentive constraint: if Bob's type is known only to Bob, it would be inappropriate to assume that an institution can use the information about Bob's type without providing Bob with the necessary incentives to reveal it. (The inequality in (6.3) in theorem 6.3 is an example.) In the optimization problems of section 9.2, we did not impose the incentive constraints explicitly and only verified later, after the fact, whether agents had the incentives to lie about their preferences.

In some cases, the elicitation of private information imposes no additional constraints on the optimization problem. This is so when each agent's and the planner's objectives are aligned, so that no agent can gain by lying. The just deserts problem of section 9.2 is an example.

Elicitation also imposes no additional constraints when the agents' types are known to be identical—an admittedly unlikely scenario. In this case, Alice and Bob each can be asked to report preference parameters and, if their reports disagree, be punished by being deprived of consumption. As a result, each will find it optimal to report truthfully, in which case the two reports will coincide. The described elicitation mechanism is so-called **shoot-them-all**. It is not particularly realistic.

Elicitation is more delicate when agents' and the planner's objectives are not aligned and when the agents' types are statistically independent—or at least the precise nature of their statistical dependence is unknown.[7] Then, the agents' reports

---

7. If the agents' types differ but are statistically correlated in a known way, then a stochastic version of the shoot-them-all mechanism can be used to elicit the true types under some conditions (Cremer and McLean, 1988). This stochastic mechanism is not particularly realistic either.

cannot be cross-checked against each other; incentive constraints must be explicitly incorporated into the planner's problem.

Then there are the positive constraints whose status as immutable is not obvious and must be assessed on a case-by-case basis. These are "moral" or "repugnance" constraints. Examples are the aversion to putting horse meat in hotdogs, taking orders from a female boss, or trading in human organs. Repugnance constraints may reflect basic immutable tastes (e.g., the disgust associated with eating a horse, a handsome domesticated animal), malleable prejudice (e.g., taking orders from a member of a minority social group), or primitive normative desiderata that can be made explicit in a sufficiently rich model (e.g., aversion to trading human organs derived from aversion to inequality, as in section 3.4).

NORMATIVE CONSTRAINTS

Not all desiderata may naturally fit into the objective function. For instance, in the just deserts problem of section 9.2, the desideratum that each agent consume the fruits of his labor was imposed as a constraint, in problem (9.5). Other examples of normative constraints are the requirements that no agent envy the bundle of any other agent or that agents with identical characteristics be treated equally.

Whether desiderata are embedded into the social welfare function to be maximized or are captured as constraints is a matter of convenience. Constraints are a convenient way to capture the economic desiderata that are of binary, holds-or-fails, nature, whereas the social welfare function codifies the desiderata that are matters of degree and can be traded off against each other. Normative constraints instantiate the **rights approach** in moral philosophy, whereas the social welfare function captures the approach common in economics, which typically recognizes that desiderata can be traded off against each other in subtle ways.

Some normative ideas can be operationalized either as constraints or as components in the social welfare function. For instance, it is natural to model aversion to envy as an absolute constraint: no agent should envy any other agent. It is equally natural, however, to quantify envy by specifying that the objective function be decreasing in the instances of envy among the agents or in the additional amount of goods that must be injected into the economy so as to avoid envy and not make any agent worse off.

9.4   A CURIOUS CASE OF INCOMPATIBLE CONSTRAINTS

It is natural to maximize a social welfare function when positive and normative constraints alone do not pin down the social choice function. Sometimes they do, which is the aesthetic of the axiomatic approach. For instance, the socialist desiderata in section 4.4 pin down the social choice function uniquely. In this case, maximization of any social welfare function subject to the socialist desiderata would be trivial. Nor is there any point in trying to maximize a social welfare function over an empty set, when the constraints are incompatible.

Indeed, the case of incompatible constraints may strike one as uninteresting. Sometimes, however, such incompatibility carries an economically significant lesson. To illustrate, let us analyze the logical implications of two desiderata in this excerpt from the United States **Declaration of Independence**:

> We hold these truths to be self-evident, that all men are created equal, that they are endowed by their Creator with certain unalienable Rights, that among these are Life, Liberty and the pursuit of Happiness.

To model the two desiderata underlined above (viz., liberty and the pursuit of happiness), we shall formulate a simple social choice problem by modeling the desiderata as absolute rights, or normative constraints, which we then show to be incompatible.

A SIMPLE SOCIAL CHOICE ENVIRONMENT

Let $\mathcal{I}$ be a set of at least two agents. Let X be a finite set of all outcomes (or alternatives), with typical elements a, b, c, and d. Each agent i's preference relation $\succ^i$ strictly ranks the elements in X.[8] The planner aggregates the agents' preferences $(\succ^i)_{i\in\mathcal{I}}$ into a strict social ranking $\succ$ of the elements in X. The rule that governs this aggregation is called **constitution**.

To illustrate the notation, suppose that $\mathcal{I} = \{\text{Alice}, \text{Bob}\}$. Outcome a specifies that Alice visits the gym, while Bob orders ice cream; outcome b specifies that Alice goes for a run, while Bob, as in a, still orders ice cream. The strictness of preferences is not innocuous. It requires Bob to have "nosy" preferences. In particular, even though his own consumption is the same in a and b, because he must rank a and b strictly, he must care about whether Alice visits the gym or goes for a run. If Bob lives in Wyoming and Alice is a stranger in Iceland, then Bob's preferences are nosy indeed.

In some applications, nosy preferences are uncontroversial. If X is the set of candidates in a presidential election, then it is natural for Bob to care about Alice's president, for Alice's president is also Bob's president.

The planner seeks to aggregate agents' rankings into a social ranking in order to use this ranking to choose from X or a subset thereof on the agents' behalf. The constitution that accomplishes this aggregation may represent a voting rule, a market structure, a mixture of the two, or something else entirely. The strictness of the social

---

8. The strictness of preferences is assumed for clarity of exposition. For the main result, it would have sufficed to assume that strict preferences cannot be ruled out.

ranking rules out the constitutions that are indecisive or whose repeated application may lead to wasteful cycles. If a constitution cannot recommend whether a is to be preferred to b or b to a, a political gridlock ensues. If a constitution recommends b over a, c over b, and a over c, then the society may end up perpetually cycling among the alternatives $(a \rightarrow b \rightarrow c \rightarrow a \rightarrow \cdots)$, which is socially wasteful if voting on, and then switching, alternatives is costly.[9]

LIBERTY AND THE PURSUIT OF HAPPINESS

In addition, we require any constitution to satisfy liberty and the pursuit of happiness.

Condition 9.1 (Liberty).   A constitution satisfies **liberty** if and only if, for each agent, one can designate a distinct pair of outcomes such that, for any preference profile, the constitution ranks these two outcomes the same way as the agent does.[10]

Condition 9.1 is a rather minimal notion of individual liberty. It only requires each agent to have a pair of alternatives over which he is a dictator. It is natural for these alternatives to be rather intimate, of greatest concern to the individual himself, by describing, say, what to wear, watch, or eat. For instance, in a society comprised of Alice and Bob, condition 9.1 holds if Alice is free to decide whether to go for a run or to the gym and Bob is free to decide whether to order ice cream or cake. The condition holds even if Alice is permitted to choose her exercise regimen only if Bob orders cake, and if Bob is free to choose his dessert only if Alice goes for a run. This notion of liberty is grossly inadequate in its minimalism, but that is exactly the point. Even if such minimal liberty cannot be guaranteed, then, a fortiori, no stronger, more realistic notion of liberty would stand a chance.

Condition 9.1 may seem gratuitous because it is nonconsequentialist, but gratuitous it is not. The condition ensures that each agent controls at least some outcomes. As a primitive desire, the need for control—even a mere illusion of control—is well-documented by psychologists (Gilbert 2007, chapter 1, Prospection and Control).[11] This need may explain the occasional preference for driving

---

9. Another reason for requiring a constitution to be guided by a strict ranking of alternatives, instead of being some general rule for selecting an alternative, is simplicity. If X contains m alternatives, then it has $2^m - m - 1$ nontrivial subsets from which the constitution may be called upon to choose an alternative. (The excluded subsets are the empty set and m singletons.) It is much simpler to list m elements of X in the order of the social preference than to specify what the constitution must choose in each of the $2^m - m - 1$ cases (which is over a billion cases when $m = 30$). Simplicity matters when codifying and enforcing the constitution and for holding the enforcers of the constitution accountable.

10. The designated pairs are distinct in the sense of not having outcomes in common. This distinctness is unnecessary for the result but simplifies the exposition.

11. Gilbert (2007) reports experimental results: individuals prefer to bet on a die that has not been cast to betting on a die that has already been cast, and they prefer casting the die themselves to having an

instead of flying, for living in a house instead of a condominium, and for being self-employed instead of having a boss. The craving for control is exploited when a parent persuades his obstinate child to put on any sweater by offering the child the choice between a blue one and a red one, thereby effectively bribing the child with the value that the child places on control.

Condition 9.2 (Pursuit of Happiness). A constitution satisfies the **pursuit of happiness** if, for any preference profile, whenever all agents rank any two outcomes unanimously, the planner concurs with this unanimous ranking.

Condition 9.2 is a rather minimal notion of pursuit of happiness (and, again, that is exactly the point). The condition says that if all agents believe that they will be better off with outcome a than with outcome b, then the constitution lets them pursue a. For instance, if Alice's dream is to pursue a career in acting and everyone else in the society wants to see Alice act more than anything else, then the constitution that satisfies condition 9.2 says that Alice must be allowed to pursue her dream of acting. Guided by a constitution that satisfies the pursuit of happiness, the planner will never choose a Pareto dominated outcome.

INCOMPATIBILITY

It turns out that, even without insisting that all men be created equal and be endowed with the right to life, the principles of liberty and the pursuit of happiness are incompatible.[12] Both principles cannot be guaranteed to hold at the same time. That is, one can find an example in which the preference profile and the pairs of outcomes over which individuals are dictators are such that listening to dictators (liberty) and respecting unanimity (the pursuit of happiness) require the planner to rank the alternatives in a way that, upon closer inspection, reveals that it is not a ranking at all. Such an example is constructed in the proof of theorem 9.1.

Theorem 9.1. *No constitution can guarantee liberty (condition 9.1) and the pursuit of happiness (condition 9.2).*

---

experimenter do it for them. The preference for controlling the casting of dice cannot be explained on consequentialist grounds (or can it be?); this preference is the primitive desire to control for control's sake. Bartling, Fehr, and Herz (2014) conduct an economics experiment, a delegation game, which enables them to confirm and quantify the value that individuals place on control.

12. The requirement that all men be created equal can be operationalized as anonymity. **Anonymity** requires that the social preference depend only on the set of individual preferences and not on who holds which of these preferences. The **right to life** can be operationalized as a prohibition to exclude from the preference aggregation process those agents whose preferences lead to a conflict between the model's desiderata, such as liberty and the pursuit of happiness. So defined, the right to life is an implicitly maintained assumption in the analysis.

Proof. Suppose that conditions 9.1 and 9.2 hold. It suffices to consider any two agents, say, agents 1 and 2. Let a and b be agent 1's designated outcomes mentioned in condition 9.1, and let c and d be agent 2's designated outcomes.

Because conditions 9.1 and 9.2 are defined for all imaginable preference profiles, they must, in particular, admit a preference profile that has $a \succ^1 b$ and $c \succ^2 d$. Condition 9.1 requires the planner to respect the agents' preferences over the outcomes for which they are dictators. So, $a \succ b$ and $c \succ d$.

Assume further that all agents prefer b to c, and d to a. Condition 9.2 implies that so does the planner: $b \succ c$ and $d \succ a$.

The planner's ranking thus satisfies $a \succ b \succ c \succ d \succ a$, which is not a ranking at all, for it implies $a \succ a$, which is nonsense. Thus, conditions 9.1 and 9.2 are incompatible. ∎

Conditions 9.1 and 9.2 are fundamental and minimal. It is therefore disturbing that they are incompatible.[13] The culprit is the intensity of the nosy preferences. In particular, in the proof of theorem 9.1, the agents' preferences are

$$\underline{d} \succ^1 \underline{a} \succ^1 \underline{b} \succ^1 \underline{c} \quad \text{and} \quad \underline{b} \succ^2 \underline{c} \succ^2 \underline{d} \succ^2 \underline{a},$$

where the designated pairs of outcomes are underlined, once for agent 1 and twice for agent 2. Not only is each agent **nosy** in that he cares about the other agent's designated outcomes, but he is so extremely nosy as to be **intolerant** in the sense of caring more about contradicting the other agent's preference over that agent's designated outcomes than about his own designated outcomes. (We say that Bob cares more about Alice's pair of designated outcomes than about his own pair if, in Bob's preference ranking, Alice's pair straddles his.) Then, theorem 9.1 can be interpreted to say that, in an intolerant society, the exercise of liberty, even if minimal, is intrusive to the point of being incompatible with the pursuit of happiness.

Theorem 9.1 also admits a methodological lesson. The spirit of the theorem's premise is that each agent cares not only about which outcome in X he gets (i.e., he has preferences over X) but also about the procedure by means of which he gets it (i.e., he wants the constitution to respect liberty). Consequently, it is natural to expand the set of outcomes to include procedures, incorporate the desire for liberty into the preferences over this expanded set of outcomes, and then define Pareto efficiency with respect to these extended preferences. Then, as long as the expanded set of outcomes is finite, a Pareto efficient outcome will exist for any preference profile. In other words, just as it would be odd to argue that a Pareto efficient routing (section 8.3) did not exist just because some agents were stuck in

---

13. The French motto "Liberté, égalité, fraternité" absolves the planner of seeking happiness, thereby avoiding the impossibility of theorem 9.1. The (conceptually unrelated) tripartite motto of Canada is examined in problem 4.5.

traffic for longer than they would have liked, it is mildly odd to argue that a taste for liberty frustrates Pareto efficiency, which is supposed to account for all tastes, including those for liberty.

9.5 ECONOMICS AS AN ART FORM

We have covered various models, each of which focuses on a distinct economic environment, often with a distinct equilibrium concept. There is no single unifying economic model, just as there is no single unifying novel, no painting that summarizes all paintings, and no jazz standard that summarizes all jazz standards. Multiple models may address the same phenomenon in the same way as multiple novels by Jane Austen are devoted to the same themes of love and social class.

In forming one's worldview, one need not commit to a single model. In that, economic theory is very much like an art form. It is an art form.[14] The goal of economic theory is to communicate the patterns of human behavior—in order to explain them, suggest how to improve them, or just provoke thinking about them in novel ways.[15] The artistic medium adopted by economists is that of mathematical models, which are defined as logically tight arguments. Any careful thinker (economic or otherwise) has a model, even if he does not realize that he has one.

The world is complex. No single model can adequately describe it. An economic model isolates but an aspect of an economic situation. Any economic model is so stylized that it will necessarily be refuted by data (i.e., falsified).[16] A falsified model may still be useful if its insights can be combined, however informally, with the insights of other models to guide one's judgment and help one organize one's observations about the world.

In order to increase the scope of the situations that can be understood by combining the insights from multiple models, one may wish to intentionally drive these models farther apart by making them more dissimilar from each other and, by implication, more remote from any "typical" economic situation. Figure 9.1 is

14. This point of view is articulated by Aumann (1985): "[O]ne can think of pure mathematics as abstract art, like a Bach fugue or a Pollock canvas (though often even these express an emotion of some kind); whereas game theory and mathematical economics would be expressive art, like a cubist painting or Tolstoy's *War and Peace*. We strive to make statements that, while perhaps not falsifiable, do have some universality, do express some insight of a general nature; we discipline our minds through the medium of the mathematical model; and at their best, our disciplines do have beauty, simplicity, force and relevance." A similar view, that an economic model is a fable, is held by Rubinstein (2006).

15. In art, the recognition of the primacy of communication goes back to Tolstoy (1896): "Art, like speech, is a means of communication, and therefore of progress, i.e. of the movement of humanity forward towards perfection."

16. Many useful scientific theories are known to be false. The model of an ideal gas is false but useful. Newtonian physics is false but useful.

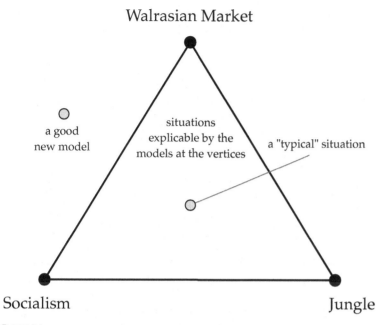

FIGURE 9.1.

The three abstract models (the vertices of the triangle) are far removed from a "typical" economic situation, but their insights can be combined to understand that situation. Any economic situation inside the triangle is explicable by combining these three models. A novel empirical work would be praised for its proximity to the shaded dot labeled "'typical' situation." A novel theoretical work would be praised for modeling a case far outside the triangle (such as the shaded dot labeled "a good new model"). To consider such a case increases the range of the situations about which we may have some insight; this range can be visualized as the convex hull (not shown) that would encompass the triangle's vertices and the new dot outside the triangle.

a metaphor (a model) for the use of stylized models to span a set of economic situations that one may wish to understand. A similar drive, toward abstraction, is observed also in conventional art, especially in dance and music.

9.6   BIBLIOGRAPHICAL NOTES

Rawls (1971) proposes what has become known as the Rawlsian theory of justice. Mankiw (2010, 2013) articulates his opposition to utilitarianism and advocates the theory of just deserts. In a provocatively titled piece "Why People Prefer Unequal Societies," Starmans, Sheskin, and Bloom (2017) offer the reading of experimental psychology literature that is sympathetic to the just deserts formulation of social justice.

Theorem 9.1, known as the impossibility of a Paretian liberal, is due to Sen (1970). The unbearable stringency of minimal liberty when preferences are intolerant (or "meddlesome") is examined by Blau (1975).

Problem 9.2 is inspired by Dasgupta, Sen, and Starrett (1973). Problem 9.5, on the consistency of social welfare functions, is inspired by Landsburg (2007). Binmore (1994, section 2.4) interprets Kant's categorical imperative as the consistency requirement: "Everybody should choose a method of choice whose adoption would result in everybody's choosing that method of choice." However, this consistency requirement appears to describe more aptly problem 9.5 than Kantian equilibrium (chapter 7).

PROBLEMS

Problem 9.1 (Charitable Giving).   The economy comprises I agents: Alice and $I-1$ others, indexed by $i = 2, 3, \ldots, I$ and each called Bob. There is a single consumption good, $L = 1$. Alice's endowment is $e^1 = e^A$, and each Bob i's endowment is $e^i = e^B$. Assume that $0 < e^B < e^A$. Alice chooses amount z to give to charity, to be distributed uniformly among all Bobs. Thus, Alice consumes $x^1 = e^A - z$, and each Bob i consumes $x^i = e^B + z/(I-1)$. Alice's utility function is other-regarding in that she cares not only about her own consumption but also about Bobs' consumption:

$$u^1(x) = v(x^1) + \sum_{i \neq 1} v(x^i),$$

where $v : \mathbb{R} \to \mathbb{R}$ is a smooth, strictly increasing, and strictly concave function.

1.   Characterize Alice's utility-maximizing contribution to charity and her consumption.

2.   Report your answers to part 1 as $I \to \infty$. In this limit case, how do Alice's contribution and consumption depend on her endowment?

3.   Suppose instead that each agent i's utility function u^i is given implicitly by

$$u^i(x) = \ln x^i + \frac{1}{I} \sum_{j \neq i} u^j(x), \quad i \in \mathcal{I}.$$

Interpret the new formulation and solve for each $u^i(x)$ as a function of $(\ln x^j)_{j \in \mathcal{I}}$ terms alone. (*Hint*: Try $u^i(x) = \frac{2I}{1+I} \ln x^i + \frac{I}{1+I} \sum_{j \neq i} \ln x^j$.) Compute Alice's utility-maximizing contribution to charity and her consumption as $I \to \infty$.

4.   Does either formulation of Alice's charitable giving strike you as realistic?

Problem 9.2 (The Gini Social Welfare Function). Consider a unit measure of agents, whose incomes are described according to c.d.f. F with mean $\mu > 0$. The incomes of two arbitrary agents i and j are denoted by w^i and w^j. The Gini coefficient for inequality is denoted by G and defined as

$$G \equiv \frac{\mathbb{E}[|w^i - w^j|]}{2\mu},$$

where w^i and w^j are two random variables drawn independently according to the c.d.f. F. Suppose that the social planner measures welfare according to the social welfare function

$$SWF \equiv \mu(1 - G).$$

1. Is SWF consequentialist? Is SWF welfarist?

2. Use the identity $|w^i - w^j| \equiv w^i + w^j - 2\min\{w^i, w^j\}$ to show that

$$SWF = \mathbb{E}[\min\{w^i, w^j\}].$$

3. Henceforth, assume that each agent's utility identically equals his wealth. Compare SWF with the Rawlsian social welfare function.

4. Show that one can rewrite

$$SWF = 2\mathbb{E}[w^i(1 - F(w^i))].$$

5. Compare SWF to the utilitarian social welfare function.

Problem 9.3 (Socialism is Rawlsian). In the environment specified in section 4.4, define a (Rawlsian) social choice function F by specifying that, for any economy $\mathcal{P} = (s^1, s^2, f)$, F satisfies

$$F(\mathcal{P}) \in \arg\max_{x \in X^1 \times X^2} \min \left\{ u(s^1, x^1), u(s^2, x^2) \right\}$$

$$\text{s.t.} \sum_{i \in \mathcal{I}} x_1^i \leq f\left(\sum_{i \in \mathcal{I}} (1 - x_2^i) \right).$$

1. Show that F is socialist. (*Hint*: Recall problem 4.14.)

2. Show that any socialist social choice function can be represented as the Rawlsian social choice function.

3. Can you think of an allocation problem—perhaps outside the context of section 4.4—in which maximizing the minimum of the agents' utilities will not lead to utility equalization?

Problem 9.4 (The Moral Machine). Browse the scenarios at http://moralmachine.mit.edu. Take the survey a couple of times.

1. Design a moral machine. That is, describe the moral principles that you would like an autonomous vehicle (AV) to obey.

2. Alice, a pedestrian, always wears an Apple Watch®. So does everyone else. The watch has a preinstalled app called *Living_Will_Well*. The app is a living will that, among other things, lets Alice specify whether, in the unlikely event of a life-threatening traffic accident, she would like an oncoming AV to give priority to a teenager's life over hers.

   (a) Should an app like this be legal?

   (b) Every month, the app awards a "Good Samaritan badge" and a $100 credit to a randomly chosen user who donates her survival priority as described. Should this feature be legal?

   (c) Every month, the app awards a Good Samaritan badge and a $100 credit to every user who donates her survival priority as described. Should this feature be legal?

   (d) Should Bob be allowed to buy a monthly subscription for $199 that would enable him to bump up his survival priority?

   (e) Should Alice be allowed to profile users to whom she donates her survival priority by age, gender, race, education, and health?

3. Suppose you were asked to design a market in survival priorities. How would you do it?

Problem 9.5 (Self-Generating Social Welfare Functions). Alice and Bob have utility functions, respectively, $u^1 : [0,1]^2 \to \mathbb{R}$ and $u^2 : [0,1]^2 \to \mathbb{R}$. The planner's goal is to maximize a weighted utilitarian social welfare function with a weight $\alpha \in [0,1]$ applied to Alice's utility and the complementary weight $1 - \alpha$ applied to Bob's. The planner has one unit of consumption to divide; Alice gets $c \in [0,1]$, and Bob gets $1 - c$. In addition to choosing c, the planner chooses the weight α because Alice and Bob care about α directly. How the trade-off between Alice's and Bob's preferences over α is resolved is dictated by the social welfare function, which itself depends on α. So the planner's problem is a fixed-point problem, where α^* denotes the planner-optimal weight α:

$$\alpha^* \in \arg \max_{\alpha \in [0,1]} \left\{ \max_{c \in [0,1]} \left\{ \alpha^* u^1(c,\alpha) + (1 - \alpha^*) u^2(1 - c, 1 - \alpha) \right\} \right\}. \tag{9.11}$$

In words, the planner chooses α so that the induced social welfare function is such that, *according to that social welfare function*, Alice and Bob would not want a different social welfare function.

1. Justify the social welfare function that is induced by the weight α^* that satisfies (9.11) and compare that function to the social welfare function that is induced by the weight that solves

$$\max_{\alpha \in [0,1]} \left\{ \max_{c \in [0,1]} \left\{ \alpha u^1(c,\alpha) + (1-\alpha)u^2(1-c, 1-\alpha) \right\} \right\}. \qquad (9.12)$$

2. Assume

$$u^1(c,\alpha) \equiv \ln c - \gamma \ln \alpha \quad \text{and} \quad u^2(1-c, 1-\alpha) \equiv \ln(1-c) - (1-\alpha),$$

for some $\gamma \in (0,1)$. Solve problem (9.11) and interpret the solution.

3. Assume

$$u^1(c,\alpha) \equiv c\alpha \quad \text{and} \quad u^2(1-c, 1-\alpha) \equiv (1-c)(1-\alpha).$$

Solve problem (9.11) and interpret the solution.

References

Abdulkadiroğlu, Atila, and Tayfun Sönmez. 1998. "Random Serial Dictatorship and the Core from Random Endowments in House Allocation Problems." *Econometrica* 66 (3): 689–701.

Abdulkadiroğlu, Atila, and Tayfun Sönmez. 2013. "Matching Markets: Theory and Practice." Pp 3–47 in *Advances in Economics and Econometrics: Tenth World Congress: Economic Theory*, vol. 1, edited by Daron Acemoğlu, Manuel Arellano, and Eddie Dekel. New York: Viking.

Abdulkadiroğlu, Atila, Parag A. Pathak, Alvin E. Roth, and Tayfun Sönmez. 2006. "Changing the Boston School Choice Mechanism." *NBER Working Paper Series No. 11965.*

Ali, S. Nageeb, and Charles Lin. 2013. "Why People Vote: Ethical Motives and Social Incentives." *American Economic Journal: Microeconomics* 5 (2): 73–98.

Arendt, Hannah. 1963. *Eichmann in Jerusalem: A Report on the Banality of Evil.* New York: Viking.

Arrow, Kenneth J., H. D. Block, and Leonid Hurwicz. 1959. "On the Stability of the Competitive Equilibrium, II." *Econometrica 27* (1): 82–109.

Arrow, Kenneth J. 1951. "An Extension of the Basic Theorems of Classical Welfare Economics." *Proceedings of the Second Berkeley Symposium on Mathematical Statistics and Probability.* 507–532.

Arrow, Kenneth J. 1963. *Social Choice and Individual Values.* New York: John Wiley & Sons, Inc.

Arrow, Kenneth J. 1973. "General Economic Equilibrium: Purpose, Analytic Techniques, Collective Choice." *American Economic Review* 64 (3): 253–272.

Arrow, Kenneth J., and Gerard Debreu. 1954. "Existence of an Equilibrium for a Competitive Economy." *Econometrica* 22 (3): 265–290.

Ashlagi, Itai, Yash Kanoria, and Jacob D. Leshno. 2017. "Unbalanced Random Matching Markets: The Stark Effect of Competition." *Journal of Political Economy* 125 (1).

Atkinson, Anthony B., Thomas Piketty, and Emmanuel Saez. 2011. "Top Incomes in the Long Run of History." *Journal of Economic Literature* 49 (1): 3–71.

Aumann, Robert J. 1985. "What Is Game Theory Trying to Accomplish?" In *Frontiers of Economics*, edited by K. Arrow and S. Honkaponja. Oxford: Basel Blackwell.

Balinski, Michel, and Tayfun Sönmez. 1999. "A Tale of Two Mechanisms: Student Placement." *Journal of Economic Theory* 84: 73–94.

Bartling, Björn, Ernst Fehr, and Holger Herz. 2014. "The Intrinsic Value of Decision Rights." *Econometrica* 82 (6): 2005–2039.

Becker, Gary S., Kevin M. Murphy, and Iván Werning. 2005. "The Equilibrium Distribution of Income and the Market for Status." *Journal of Political Economy* 113 (2): 282–310.

Bénabou, Roland, and Jean Tirole. 2003. "Intrinsic and Extrinsic Motivation." *Review of Economic Studies* 70 (3): 489–520.

Bénabou, Roland, and Jean Tirole. 2011. "Laws and Norms." *NBER Working Paper No. 17579.*

Bernheim, B. Douglas, and Michael D. Whinston. 1998. "Incomplete Contracts and Strategic Ambiguity." *American Economic Review* 88 (4): 902–932.

Besley, Timothy. 2013. "What's the Good of the Market? An Essay on Michael Sandel's What Money Can't Buy." *Journal of Economic Literature* 51 (2): 478–495.

Bhagwati, Jagdish. 1958. "Immiserizing Growth: A Geometrical Note." *Review of Economic Studies* 25 (3): 201–205.

Binmore, Ken. 1994. *Game Theory and the Social Contract, Volume 1: Playing Fair.* Cambridge, MA, and London: MIT Press.

Binmore, Ken. 2009. "Interpersonal Comparison of Utility." In *The Oxford Handbook of Philosophy of Economics*, edited by Don Ross and Harold Kincaid. Oxford: Oxford University Press.

Blau, Julian H. 1975. "Liberal Values and Independence." *Review of Economic Studies* 42 (3): 395–401.

Bostrom, Nick. 2014. *Superintelligence: Paths, Dangers, Strategies.* Oxford: Oxford University Press.

Bowles, Samuel. 2016. *The Moral Economy: Why Good Incentives Are No Substitute for Good Citizens* (*Castle Lectures Series*). New Haven, CT: Yale University Press.

Braess, Dietrich. 1968. "Über ein Paradoxon aus der Verkehrsplanung." *Unternehmensforschung* 12: 258–268.

Bramoullé, Yann, and Rachel Kranton. 2007. "Public goods in networks." *Journal of Economic Theory* 135 (1): 478–494.

Brennan, Jason F., and Peter Jaworski. 2015. *Markets without Limits: Moral Virtues and Commercial Interests.* London: Routledge.

Brodeur, Abel, Mathias Lé, Marc Sangnier, and Yanos Zylberberg. 2016. "Star Wars: The Empirics Strike Back." *American Economic Journal: Applied Economics* 8 (1): 1–32.

Burks, Stephen V., Jeffrey P. Carpenter, Lorenz Goette, and Aldo Rustichini. 2009. "Cognitive skills affect economic preferences, strategic behavior, and job attachment." *Proceedings of the National Academy of Sciences of the United States of America* 106 (19): 7745–7750.

Camerer, Colin. 1988. "Gifts as Economic Signals and Social Symbols." *The American Journal of Sociology* 94: S180–S214.

Camerer, Colin F., Anna Dreber, Eskil Forsell, Teck-Hua Ho, Jürgen Huber, Magnus Johannesson, Michael Kirchler, Johan Almenberg, Adam Altmejd, Taizan Chan, Emma Heikensten, Felix Holzmeister, Taisuke Imai, Siri Isaksson, Gideon Nave, Thomas Pfeiffer, Michael Razen, and Hang Wu. 2016. "Evaluating replicability of laboratory experiments in economics." *Science* 351 (6280): 1433–1436.

Caplan, Bryan, and Stephen C. Miller. 2010. "Intelligence makes people think like economists: Evidence from the General Social Survey." *Intelligence* 38: 636–647.

Caruso, Eugene M., Kathleen D. Vohs, Brittani Baxter, and Adam Waytz. 2013. "Mere exposure to money increases endorsement of free-market systems and social inequality." *Journal of Experimental Psychology: General* 142 (2): 301–306.

Chang, Bo Hyun, Yongsung Chang, and Sun-Bin Kim. 2017. "Pareto Weights in Practice: A Quantitative Analysis Across 32 OECD Countries." *Review of Economic Dynamics.*

Chen, Yan, and Tayfun Sönmez. 2002. "Improving Efficiency of On-Campus Housing: An Experimental Study." *American Economic Review* 92 (5): 1669–1686.

Chockler, Hana, and Joseph Y. Halpern. 2004. "Responsibility and Blame: A Structural-Model Approach." *Journal of Artificial Intelligence Research* 22: 93–115.

Chwe, Michael Suk-Young. 1994. "Farsighted Coalitional Stability." *Journal of Economics Theory* 63: 299–325.

Cournot, Augustin. 1838. *Researches into the Mathematical Principles of the Theory of Wealth* 1838. Translated by Nathaniel T. Bacon. London: MacMillan and Co., Ltd.

Cox, James S. 1997. "On Testing the Utility Hypothesis." *Economic Journal* 107: 1054–1078.

Cremer, Jacques, and Richard P. McLean. 1988. "Full Extraction of the Surplus in Bayesian and Dominant Strategy Auctions." *Econometrica* 56 (6): 1247–1257.

Crockett, Sean, Ryan Oprea, and Charles Plott. 2011. "Extreme Walrasian Dynamics: The Gale Example in the Lab." *American Economic Review* 101 (7): 3196–3220.

Daley, Brendan, and Philipp Sadowski. 2017. "Magical Thinking: A Representation Result." *Theoretical Economics* 12 (2): 909–956.

Danilov, Anastasia, and Dirk Sliwka. 2013. "Can Contracts Signal Social Norms? Experimental Evidence." *IZA Discussion Paper No. 7477.*

Danilov, V. I., and A. I. Sotskov. 1990. "A Generalized Economic Equilibrium." *Journal of Mathematical Econonomics* 19 (4): 341–356.

Dasgupta, Partha, Amartya Sen, and David Starrett. 1973. "Notes on the Measurement of Inequality." *Journal of Economic Theory* 6: 180–187.

Debreu, Gerard. 1951. "The Coefficient of Resource Utilization." *Econometrica* 19 (3): 273–292.

Downs, Anthony. 1957. *An Economic Theory of Democracy.* New York: Harper & Row.

Düppe, Till, and E. Roy Weintraub. 2014. *Finding Equilibrium: Arrow, Debreu, McKenzie and the Problem of Scientific Credit.* Princeton, NJ: Princeton University Press.

Falk, Armin, and Nora Szech. 2013. "Morals and Markets." *Science* 340 (6133): 707–711.

Falk, Armin, and Nora Szech. 2013. "Supporting Online Material: Morals and Markets." *Science* 340: 707.

Falk, Armin, Anke Becker, Thomas J. Dohmen, Benjamin Enke, David Huffman, and Uwe Sunde. 2015. "The Nature and Predictive Power of Preferences: Global Evidence." *IZA Discussion Paper No. 9504.*

Feltovich, Nick, Richmond Harbaugh, and Ted To. 2002. "Too cool for school? Signalling and countersignalling." *RAND Journal of Economics* 33 (4): 630–649.

Feynman, Richard P. 1997. *Surely You're Joking, Mr. Feynman! (Adventures of a Curious Character).* New York: W. W. Norton and Company.

Feyrer, James, Dimitra Politi, and David N. Weil. 2017. "The Cognitive Effects of Micronutrient Deficiency: Evidence from Salt Iodization in the United States." *Journal of the European Economic Association* 15 (2): 355–387.

Foley, Duncan K. 1967. "Resource Allocation in the Public Sector." *Yale Economic Essays* 7: 73–76.

Frohlich, Norman, and Joe Oppenheimer. 2003. "Optimal Policies and Socially Oriented Behavior: Some Problematic Effects of an Incentive Compatible Device." *Public Choice* 117: 273–293.

Gale, D., and L. S. Shapley. 1962. "College Admissions and the Stability of Marriage." *The American Mathematical Monthly* 69 (1): 9–15.

Garicano, Luis, and Esteban Rossi-Hansberg. 2004. "Inequality and the Organization of Knowledge." *American Economic Review* 94 (2): 197–202.

Garicano, Luis, and Esteban Rossi-Hansberg. 2006. "Organization and Inequality in a Knowledge Economy." *Quarterly Journal of Economics* 121 (4): 1383–1435.

Geanakoplos, John. 2003. "Nash and Walras Equilibrium via Brouwer." *Economic Theory* 21: 585–603.

Gelman, Andrew, Nate Silver, and Aaron Edlin. 2012. "What is the probability your vote will make a difference?" *Economic Inquiry* 50 (2): 321–326.

Gilbert, Daniel. 2007. *Stumbling on Happiness*. New York: Vintage.

Gilboa, Itzhak. 2009. *Theory of Decision under Uncertainty*. Cambridge: Cambridge University Press.

Gjerstad, Steven. 2013. "Price dynamics in an exchange economy." *Economic Theory* 52 (2): 461–500.

Gneezy, Uri, and Aldo Rustichini. 2000. "A Fine is a Price." *Journal of Legal Studies* 29: No.1, Article 1.

Goldman, Steven M., and Ross M. Starr. 1982. "Pairwise, t-Wise, and Pareto Optimalities." *Econometrica* 50 (3): 593–606.

Guiso, Luigi, Paola Sapienza, and Luigi Zingales. 2016. "Long-Term Persistence." *Journal of the European Economic Association* 14 (6): 1401–1436.

Hamilton, Barton H. 2000. "Does Entrepreneurship Pay? An Empirical Analysis of the Returns to Self Employment." *Journal of Political Economy* 108 (3): 604–631.

Harsanyi, John C. 1955. "Cardinal Welfare, Individualistic Ethics, and Interpersonal Comparisons of Utility." *Journal of Political Economy* 63 (4): 309–321.

Hartline, Jason D., and Tim Roughgarden. 2008. "Optimal Mechanism Design and Money Burning." In *STOC '08 Proceedings of the fortieth annual ACM symposium on Theory of computing*. 75–84.

Hassidim, Avinatan, Assaf Romm, and Ran I. Shorrer. 2016. " 'Strategic' Behavior in a Strategy-proof Environment." Proceedings of the 2016 ACM Conference on Economics and Computation, EC '16, Maastricht, The Netherlands, July 24–28, 2016. 763–764.

Hatfield, John William, and Paul R. Milgrom. 2005. "Matching with Contracts." *American Economic Review* 95 (4): 913–935.

Hayek, Friedrich. 1945. "The Use of Knowledge in Society." *American Economic Review* 35 (4): 519–530.

Henrich, Joseph. 2000. "Does Culture Matter in Economic Behavior? Ultimatum Game Bargaining Among the Machiguenga of the Peruvian Amazon." *American Economic Review* 90 (4): 973–979.

Henrich, Joseph, Robert Boyd, Samuel Bowles, Colin Camerer, Ernst Fehr, and Herbert Gintis, eds. 2004. *Foundations of Human Sociality*. Oxford: Oxford University Press.

Henrich, Joseph, Robert Boyd, Samuel Bowles, Colin Camerer, Ernst Fehr, Herbert Gintis, and Richard McElreath. 2001. "In Search of Homo Economicus: Behavioral Experiments in 15 Small-Scale Societies." *American Economic Review* 91 (2): 73–78.

Henrich, Joseph, Robert Boyd, Samuel Bowles, Colin Camerer, Ernst Fehr, Herbert Gintis, Richard McElreath, Michael Alvard, Abigail Barr, Jean Ensminger, Natalie Smith Henrich, Kim Hill, Francisco Gil-White, Michael Gurven, Frank W. Marlowe, John Q. Patton, and David Tracer. 2005. " 'Economic man' in cross-cultural perspective: Behavioral experiments in 15 small-scale societies." *Behavioral and Brain Sciences* 28 (6): 795–815.

Holmstrom, Bengt, and Paul Milgrom. 1991. "Multitask Principal-Agent Analyses: Incentive Contracts, Asset Ownership, and Job Design." *Journal of Law, Economics, and Organization* 7: 24–52.

Irving, Robert W. 1985. "An Efficient Algorithm for the 'Stable Roommates' Problem." *Journal of Algorithms* 6: 577–595.

Jackson, Matthew O. 2008. *Social and Economic Networks.* Princeton, NJ: Princeton University Press.

Jackson, Matthew O., and Alejandro M. Manelli. 1997. "Approximately Competitive Equilibria in Large Finite Economies." *Journal of Economic Theory* 77: 354–376.

Jehle, Geoffrey A., and Philip J. Reny. 2011. *Advanced Microeconomic Theory*, 3rd ed. Upper Saddle River, NJ: Prentice Hall.

Kant, Immanuel. 1993. *Grounding for the Metaphysics of Morals: with On a Supposed Right to Lie because of Philanthropic Concerns*, 3rd ed. Translated by James W. Ellington. Indianapolis, IN: Hackett Publishing Company, Inc.

Kinsler, Josh, and Ronni Pavan. 2016. "Parental Beliefs and Investment in Children: The Distortionary Impact of Schools."

Kocherlakota, Narayana. 1998. "Money is Memory." *Journal of Economic Theory* 81 (2): 232–251.

Kranton, Rachel E., and Seth G. Sanders. 2017. "Groupy vs. Non-Groupy Social Preferences: Personality, Region, and Political Party." *American Economic Review Papers and Proceedings* 107 (5): 65–69.

Kranton, Rachel, Matthew Pease, Seth Sanders, and Scott Huettel. 2013. "Identity, Group Conflict, and Social Preferences." *University of Chicago Working Paper.* http://home.uchicago.edu/~bartels/Choice Symposium2013/07-Kranton.pdf.

Kreps, David M. 2012. *Microeconomic Foundations I: Choice and Competitive Markets.* Princeton, NJ: Princeton University Press.

Krueger, Alan B. 2008. *What Makes a Terrorist: Economics and the Roots of Terrorism.* Princeton, NJ: Princeton University Press.

Lakner, Christoph, and Branko Milanovic. 2016. "Global Income Distribution: From the Fall of the Berlin Wall to the Great Recession." *The World Bank Economic Review* 30 (2): 203–232.

Landsburg, Steven. 2013. *Price Theory and Applications*, 9th ed. Boston: Cengage Learning.

Landsburg, Steven E. 1993. *The Armchair Economist: Economics and Everyday Life.* New York: Free Press.

Landsburg, Steven E. 2007. "The Methodology of Normative Economics." *Journal of Public Economic Theory* 9 (5): 757–769.

Layard, Richard, Guy Mayraz, and Stephen Nickell. 2008. "The marginal utility of income." *Journal of Public Economics* 92 (8-9): 1846–1857.

Li, Shengwu. 2017. "Obviously Strategy-Proof Mechanisms." *American Economic Review* 107 (11): 3257–3287.

Liebhafsky, H. H. 1969. "New Thoughts about Inferior Goods." *American Economic Review* 59 (5): 931–934.

Linden, David J. 2011. *The Compass of Pleasure: How Our Brains Make Fatty Foods, Orgasm, Exercise, Marijuana, Generosity, Vodka, Learning, and Gambling Feel So Good.* New York: Viking.

Lipsey, Richard, and Kelvin Lancaster. 1956. "The General Theory of Second Best." *Review of Economic Studies* 24 (1): 11–32.

Mailath, George J., and Larry Samuelson. 2006. *Repeated Games and Reputations: Long-Run Relationships.* Oxford: Oxford University Press.

Mankiw, N. Gregory. 2010. "Spreading the Wealth Around: Reflections Inspired by Joe the Plumber." *Eastern Economic Journal, Palgrave Macmillan Journals* 36 (3): 285–298.

Mankiw, N. Gregory. 2013. "Defending the One Percent." *Journal of Economic Perspectives* 27 (3): 21–34.

Mankiw, N. Gregory, and Matthew Weinzierl. 2010. "The Optimal Taxation of Height: A Case Study of Utilitarian Income Redistribution." *American Economic Journal: Economic Policy* 2 (1): 155–176.

Mas-Colell, Andreu, Michael D. Whinston, and Jerry R. Green. 1995. *Microeconomic Theory.* Oxford: Oxford University Press.

Masicampo, E. J., and Daniel R. Lalande. 2012. "A peculiar prevalence of p values just below .05." *The Quarterly Journal of Experimental Psychology* 65 (11): 2271–2279.

Maskin, Eric S., and Kevin W. S. Roberts. 2008. "On the fundamental theorems of general equilibrium." *Economic Theory* 35 (2): 233–240.

McAfee, R. Preston, and John McMillan. 1992. "Bidding Rings." *American Economic Review* 82 (3): 579–599.

McKenzie, Lionel W. 1954. "On Equilibrium in Graham's Model of World Trade and Other Competitive Systems." *Econometrica 22* (2): 147–161.

Mertens, Stephan. 2005. "Random Stable Matchings." *Journal of Statistical Mechanics: Theory and Experiment* 2005: 10008.

Milgram, Stanley. 1963. "Behavioral Study of Obedience." *Journal of Abnormal and Social Psychology* 67 (4): 371–378.

Milgram, Stanley. 1965. "Some Conditions of Obedience and Disobedience to Authority." *Human Relations* 18 (57): 57–76.

Milgrom, Paul. 2000. "Putting Auction Theory to Work: The Simultaneous Ascending Auction." *Journal of Political Economy* 108 (2): 245–272.

Milgrom, Paul, and Chris Shannon. 1994. "Monotone Comparative Statics." *Econometrica* 62 (1): 157–180.

Monderer, Dov, and Lloyd Shapley. 1996. "Potential Games." *Games and Economic Behavior* 14 (1): 124–143.

Morris, Stephen, and Hyun Song Shin. 2002. "Social Value of Public Information." *American Economic Review* 92 (5): 1521–1534.

Moulin, Hervé, and John E. Roemer. 1989. "Public Ownership of the External World and Private Ownership of Self." *Journal of Political Economy* 97 (2): 347–367.

Nash, John. 1951. "Non-Cooperative Games." *The Annals of Mathematics* 54 (2): 286–295.

Newbery, David M. G., and Joseph E. Stiglitz. 1984. "Pareto Inferior Trade." *Review of Economic Studies* 51 (1): 1–12.

Nicholson, Walter, and Christopher M. Snyder. 2007. *Microeconomic Theory: Basic Principles and Extensions*, 10th ed. Boston: Cengage Learning.

Nisan, Noam, Tim Roughgarden, Éva Tardos, and Vijay V. Vazirani, eds. 2007. *Algorithmic Game Theory*. Cambridge: Cambridge University Press.

Norton, Michael I., and Dan Ariely. 2011. "Building a Better America—One Wealth Quintile at a Time." *Perspectives on Psychological Science* 6 (1): 9–12.

Nozick, Robert. 1974. *Anarchy, State, and Utopia*. New York: Basic Books.

Oyer, Paul. 2014. *Everything I Ever Needed to Know about Economics I Learned from Online Dating*. Watertown, MA: Harvard Business Review Press.

Pareto, Vilfredo. 1896. *Cours d'économie politique professé à l'Université de Lausanne*, edited by F. Rouge, Lausanne.

Pęski, Marcin and Balázs Szentes. 2013. "Spontaneous Discrimination." *American Economic Review* 103 (6): 2412–2436.

Piccione, Michele, and Ariel Rubinstein. 2007. "Equilibrium in the Jungle." *Economic Journal* 117 (522): 883–896.

Pigou, Arthur C. 1920. *The Economics of Welfare*. London: Macmillan.

Pinker, Steven. 2011. *The Better Angels of Our Nature: Why Violence Has Declined*. New York: Viking.

Pittel, Boris G., and Robert W. Irving. 1994. "An Upper Bound for the Solvability Probability of a Random Stable Roommates Instance." *Random Structures and Algorithms* 5 (3): 465–486.

Posner, Eric A. 2000. *Law and Social Norms*. Cambridge, MA: Harvard University Press.

Postlewaite, Andrew. 1979. "Manipulation via Endowments." *Review of Economic Studies* 46: 255–262.

Postlewaite, Andrew, and David Schmeidler. 1981. "Approximate Walrasian Equilibria and Nearby Economies." *International Economic Review* 22 (1): 105–111.

Proto, Eugenio, Aldo Rustichini, and Andis Sofianos. 2015. "Higher Intelligence Groups Have Higher Cooperation Rates in the Repeated Prisoner's Dilemma." *University of Warwick Working Paper.* https://www2.warwick.ac.uk/fac/soc/economics/research/workingpapers/2015/twerp_1101proto.pdf.

Radner, Roy. 1972. "Existence of Equilibrium of Plans, Prices, and Price Expectations in a Sequence of Markets." *Econometrica* 40 (2): 289–303.

Ramachandran, Vilayanur S. 2011. *The Tell-Tale Brain: A Neuroscientist's Quest for What Makes Us Human*, 1st ed. New York: W. W. Norton & Company.

Rawls, John. 1971. *A Theory of Justice*. Cambridge MA: Harvard University Press.

Riker, William H., and Peter C. Ordeshook. 1968. "A Theory of the Calculus of Voting." *The American Political Science Review* 62 (1): 25–42.

Roemer, John E. 1988. *Free to Lose: An Introduction to Marxist Economic Philosophy*. Cambridge, MA: Harvard University Press.

Roemer, John E. 2010. "Kantian Equilibrium." *Scandinavian Journal of Economics* 112 (1): 1–24.

Roemer, John E. 2012. "Kantian Optimization, Social Ethos, and Pareto Efficiency." *Cowles Foundation Discussion Paper No. 1854.*

Roemer, John E. 2018. *How We Do and Could Cooperate: A Kantian Explanation*. New Haven, CT: Yale University Press, forthcoming.

Rohrer, Doug, Harold Pashler, and Christine R. Harris. 2015. "Do Subtle Reminders of Money Change People's Political Views?" *Journal of Experimental Psychology: General* 144 (4): e73–e85.

Rosen, Sherwin. 1981. "The Economics of Superstars." *American Economic Review* 71 (5): 845–858.

Rosenthal, Robert W. 1973. "A Class of Games Possessing Pure-Strategy Nash Equilibria." *International Journal of Game Theory* 2 (1): 65–67.

Roth, Alvin E. 1982. "Incentive Compatibility in a Market with Indivisible Goods." *Economics Letters* 9: 127–132.

Roth, Alvin E. 2007. "Repugnance as a Constraint on Markets." *Journal of Economic Perspectives* 21 (3): 37–58.

Roth, Alvin E., and John H. Vande Vate. 1990. "Random Paths to Stability in Two-Sided Matching." *Econometrica* 58 (6): 1475–1480.

Roth, Alvin E., and Marilda A. Oliveira Sotomayor. 1990. *Two-Sided Matching: A Study in Game-Theoretic Modeling and Analysis (Econometric Society Monographs)*. Cambridge: Cambridge University Press.

Roth, Alvin E., Vesna Prasnikar, Masahiro Okuno-Fujiwara, and Shmuel Zamir. 1991. "Bargaining and Market Behavior in Jerusalem, Ljubljana, Pittsburgh, and Tokyo: An Experimental Study." *American Economic Review* 81 (5): 1068–1095.

Roth, Alvin, Tayfun Sönmez, and Utku Ünver. 2004. "Kidney Exchange." *Quarterly Journal of Economics* 119 (2): 457–488.

Rubinstein, Ariel. 2006. "Dilemmas of an Economic Theorist." *Econometrica* 74 (4): 865–883.

Rudin, Walter. 1976. *Principles of Mathematical Analysis*, 3rd ed. New York: McGraw-Hill Education.

Samuelson, Larry, and Jeroen Swinkels. 2006. "Information, Evolution, and Utility." *Theoretical Economics* 1: 119–142.

Sandel, Michael J. 2012. *What Money Can't Buy: The Moral Limits of Markets*. New York: Farrar, Straus and Giroux.

Satz, Debra. 2010. *Why Some Things Should Not Be for Sale: The Moral Limits of Markets.* Oxford: Oxford University Press.

Sawada, Yasuyuki. 2009. "Immiserizing Growth: An Empirical Evaluation." *Applied Economics* 41 (13): 1613–1620.

Scarf, Herbert. 1960. "Some Examples of Global Instability of the Competitive Equilibrium." *International Economic Review* 1 (3): 157–172.

Schmelzer, André. 2017. "Strategy-proofness of stochastic assignment mechanisms." No 2017_13, Discussion Paper Series of the Max Planck Institute for Research on Collective Goods from Max Planck Institute for Research on Collective Goods.

Segal, Ilya. 1999. "Contracting with Externalities." *Quarterly Journal of Economics* 114 (2): 337–388.

Sen, Amartya. 1970. "The Impossibility of a Paretian Liberal." *Journal of Political Economy* 78 (1): 152–157.

Sen, Amartya. 1985. *Commodities and Capabilities.* Amsterdam: North-Holland.

Shapley, Lloyd, and Herbert Scarf. 1974. "On Cores and Indivisibility." *Journal of Mathematical Economics* 1 (1): 23–37.

Simon, Carl P., and Lawrence E. Blume. 1994. *Mathematics for Economists.* New York: W. W. Norton and Company.

Singer, Peter. 1981. *The Expanding Circle: Ethics and Sociobiology.* New York: Farrar, Straus and Giroux.

Singer, Peter. 2015. *The Most Good You Can Do: How Effective Altruism Is Changing Ideas About Living Ethically.* New Haven, CT: Yale University Press.

Smith, Adam. 1776. *An Inquiry into the Nature and Causes of the Wealth of Nations.* London: Methuen & Co., Ltd.

Sobel, Joel. 2007. "Do Markets Make People Selfish?" *University of San Diego Working Paper.*

Spence, A. Michael. 1973. "Time and Communication in Economic and Social Interaction." *The Quarterly Journal of Economics* 87 (4): 651–660.

Spence, Michael. 1973. "Job Market Signaling." *The Quarterly Journal of Economics* 87 (3): 355–374.

Spufford, Francis. 2012. *Red Plenty.* Minneapolis, MN: Graywolf Press.

Starmans, Christina, Mark Sheskin, and Paul Bloom. 2017. "Why people prefer unequal societies." *Nature: Human Behaviour* 1, Article No. 0082.

Straffin, Philip D., Jr. 1977. "Homogeneity, Independence, and Power Indices." *Public Choice* 30 (1): 107–118.

Tajfel, Henri, M. G. Billig, R. P. Bundy, and Claude Flament. 1971. "Social categorization and intergroup behaviour." *European Journal of Social Psychology 1* (2): 149–178.

Thaler, Richard H. 2015. *Misbehaving: The Making of Behavioral Economics.* New York: W. W. Norton & Company.

Thomson, William, and Hal R. Varian. 1984. "Theories of Justice Based on Symmetry." *University of Michigan Working Paper*, pp. 107–129.

Tirole, Jean. 2017. *Economics for the Common Good.* Princeton, NJ: Princeton University Press.

Tobin, James. 1970. "On Limiting the Domain of Inequality." *Journal of Law and Economics* 13 (2): 263–277.

Tolstoy, Leo. 1896. *What Is Art?* Translated by Alymer Maude. New York: MacMillan Publishing Company.

Varian, Hal R. 1992. *Microeconomic Analysis*, 3rd ed. New York: W. W. Norton and Company.

Varian, Hal R. 2010. *Intermediate Microeconomics: A Modern Approach*, 8th ed. New York: W. W. Norton and Company.

Vershik, Anatoly. 2007. "L.V.Kantorovich and Linear Programming." *arXiv:0707.0491.*

Vinge, Vernor. 1993. "The Coming Technological Singularity: How to Survive in the Post-Human Era." *NASA Lewis Research Center Technical Report.* https://ntrs.nasa.gov/archive/nasa/casi.ntrs.nasa.gov/19940022855.pdf.

Vohs, Kathleen D. 2015. "Money priming can change people's thoughts, feelings, motivations, and behaviors: An update on 10 years of experiments." *Journal of Experimental Psychology: General* 114 (4): e86–e93.

Vohs, Kathleen D., Nicole L. Mead, and Miranda R. Goode. 2006. "The Psychological Consequences of Money." *Science* 314 (5802): 1154–1156.

Waldfogel, Joel. 1993. "The Deadweight Loss of Christmas." *American Economic Review* 83 (5): 1328–1336.

Weitzman, Martin L. 1977. "Is the price system or rationing more effective in getting a commodity to those who need it most?" *The Bell Journal of Economics* 8 (2): 517–524.

Winter, Eyal. 2014. *Feeling Smart: Why Our Emotions Are More Rational Than We Think.* New York: PublicAffairs.

Yano, Makoto, and Jeffrey B. Nugent. 1999. "Aid, Nontraded Goods, and the Transfer Paradox in Small Countries." *American Economic Review* 89 (3): 431–449.

Zultan, Ro'i, Tobias Gerstenberg, and David A. Lagnado. 2012. "Finding fault: Causality and counterfactuals in group attributions." *Cognition* 125: 429–440.

Index